S0-ACA-285

THE INNOCENT AMBASSADORS

BOOKS BY PHILIP WYLIE

HEAVY LADEN

BABES AND SUCKLINGS

GLADIATOR

THE MURDERER INVISIBLE

FOOTPRINT OF CINDERELLA

THE SAVAGE GENTLEMAN

FINNLEY WREN: HIS NOTIONS AND OPINIONS

AS THEY REVELED

TOO MUCH OF EVERYTHING

AN APRIL AFTERNOON

THE BIG ONES GET AWAY

SALT WATER DAFFY

THE OTHER HORSEMAN

GENERATION OF VIPERS

CORPSES AT INDIAN STONES

FISH AND TIN FISH

NIGHT UNTO NIGHT

AN ESSAY ON MORALS

CRUNCH AND DES: STORIES OF FLORIDA FISHING

OPUS 21

THE DISAPPEARANCE

THREE TO BE READ

DENIZENS OF THE DEEP

TOMORROW!

THE ANSWER

TREASURE CRUISE AND OTHER CRUNCH AND DES STORIES

THE INNOCENT AMBASSADORS

by Philip Wylie and William W. Muir

THE ARMY WAY

THE INNOCENT AMBASSADORS

.....BEING THE ACCOUNT OF A TRIP AROUND THE
WORLD AND A COMPENDIUM OF DATA NOT FOUND IN
STANDARD GUIDEBOOKS.....CERTAIN CANDID
AUTOBIOGRAPHICAL FRAGMENTS AND VARIOUS BIO-
GRAPHICAL NOTES ABOUT THE AUTHOR'S WIFE,
A FINE WOMAN.....A SURVEY OF PLACES, BOTH EXOTIC
AND TROUBLED, UNDERTAKEN IN THESE
TERRIFYING TIMES.....ALONG WITH DIVERSE PSYCHO-
LOGICAL OBSERVATIONS, PHILOSOPHICAL
COMMENTS, HORRID SIGHTS, VIVID INSIGHTS, ASSORTED
ENJOYMENTS, REVELATIONS, PRACTICAL
SUGGESTIONS FOR THE SALVATION OF LIBERTY AND
SUNDRY FLIGHTS OF FANCY (NOT TO MENTION
27,500 MILES OF LITERAL TRAVEL BY AIR).....IN SUM,
A PERFECTLY WONDERFUL BOOK THAT ANYBODY
WOULD BE FASCINATED TO READ.

PHILIP WYLIE

RINEHART & COMPANY, INC.
NEW YORK • TORONTO

PUBLISHED SIMULTANEOUSLY IN CANADA BY
CLARKE, IRWIN & COMPANY, LTD., TORONTO

© 1957 BY PHILIP WYLIE
PRINTED IN THE UNITED STATES OF AMERICA

ALL RIGHTS RESERVED

LIBRARY OF CONGRESS CATALOG CARD NUMBER: 57-6578

G
440
.W98
1957

9104
W983i
cop 2

LIBRARY
FLORIDA STATE UNIVERSITY
TALLAHASSEE, FLORIDA

For reasons but partly indicated here
And with love beyond expression
I dedicate this book to
Frederica Ballard Wylie
My traveling companion
'Round the world
And on the great journey of Life

273366

contents

introduction

In a writer whose principal public is literate youth, one whose favorite sports involve strenuous outdoor activities such as skin-diving, the news that his daughter expects a child produces a dramatic effect. The author wants to see the grandchild at the earliest possible moment; his reaction, in short, is like that of anybody else. But this first grandchild was to be born in Hawaii. And I, who once had relished travel, lived abroad, had finally gone too far. Afterward, and for twenty years, I had so deep a fear of journeying far from home that Bermuda was my limit.

The grandchild, however, outweighed the phobia. With my wife, Frederica Ballard Wylie (who had no hesitation in the matter), I reserved passage by air to Honolulu. A modest plan that was destined to become a flight around the world!

Some days after I nervously committed myself, my wife (whom we call "Ricky") put forward the idea that since we would fly to Hawaii we "might as well" go on to Tokyo and Hong Kong—two places I had not expected to see in this life. The mere idea made me panicky and I hoped she'd forget it. But she and I dined, soon after that, with our close and long-time friends, Helen and Michael Lerner, who have hunted, fished, led scientific expeditions and traveled for its own sake in every quarter of the earth. They not only backed Ricky's wistful suggestion but pointed out, over coffee, that Hong Kong was halfway around the world from Miami, Florida, where we live. Why not, they asked, go there—and just keep going?

I put up a frightened defense:

It would take too much time. It would cost more than we could afford. I would not risk visiting areas that might be taken over by the Reds. And so on. Futile: You could see the Ginza, the Emerald Buddha and the Taj Mahal already shining in Ricky's eyes.

Helen and Mike dismissed every objection I put forward. They said a vacation would be good for both of us. I could not deny that. As an author, they asserted, I should have firsthand knowledge of many peoples and lands I'd never seen. (True.) The trip would provide me with "background" which—in future writing—would more than repay the expense, they said. (Problematical, but at least probable.) They ganged up on me; and the truth is, I began to want to go more than I feared going.

Two deaths occurred in our families—tragedy that made it impossible to plan and to prepare for so extensive a trip. But Mike and Helen once more stepped forward. They designed our itinerary, made flight arrangements, reserved the hotel rooms we would occupy and even supplied, as going-away gifts, luggage of their own design for "on board" use in air travel—lightweight satchels that would hold a change of clothing, a few necessities, and an accordion file for letters. Mike had said, "Helen and I will do everything except pose for your passport pictures and take your inoculations." They did.

We left Miami on the last day of January, 1956. We flew around the globe. We spent a little less than three months—and considerably more than twenty thousand dollars. We were in the air a hundred and three hours. The cost of transportation (first class wherever possible) was about a sixth of the total. Flying is fast and reasonable. But to the time it takes must be added time taken by frequent delays and by long drives to and from airports. With customs examinations and port entry procedures that are necessary, whatever the means of travel, the figure cited above is a bit misleading. We were *air-borne* for about four days; we must have spent six more en route to and from terminals—or hanging around in them waiting. . . .

If vacation means rest, we had no vacation.

We never worked so hard in a comparable period, or saw as many people. We never slept less; never talked more or listened. We were ill; we lost more than twenty pounds, apiece; we came home exhausted—after times when we thought we might not get home.

Nearly all the world we saw was new to us. Nearly all differed from preconceptions I'd formed; books, motion pictures, lectures and TV programs had failed to convey the right clues for me. That was not a surprise. Prior to 1936 (when grim travel experiences set up my travel phobia), I found I did not see anything as most others see it. One of my reasons for writing this book, the minor one of two, is to enter my dissent and assent where it deviates from general opinion.

The other, major reason is more important:

All the world not yet Communist is engaged in a desperate struggle against being made Communist either by evangelism or by every amoral and inhumane method available to convinced, determined agents of one billion people. But the overwhelming majority of Americans cannot at present even understand this ghastly engagement, since not one in a hundred of us can even define "Communism" acceptably!

To think Communism is just a "conspiracy" is to confuse the whole with but one of its means. To think that its most dangerous aspect is "atheism"—or to imagine Communism can be effectively opposed by Christianity—is not to understand it at all. For Communism is, essentially, also a *belief*, a religion which "converts" where it can by persuasion, and if that fails, by an Inquisition brought up to date and used on a world-wide scale. In that very realistic sense Communism is the most successful religion yet evolved, one that controls more devotees, after a mere forty years, than there are human beings who claim to be Christian. Communism, moreover, has but one "protestant" sect, a negligible one.

Communism, acting on the theory of permanent military

stalemate, is proceeding to dismember the world. But American statesmen still appear to assume that war may be risked, even that an "all-out" war can be won, by the "free peoples." The Communists have no intention of committing suicide to achieve our ruin, I am sure. If they seem to threaten holocaust, it will not be calculated risk but calculating bluff. Their target is the intellect of every living person; where people cannot be persuaded, the target becomes the heart, nerves, sanity and the body of each of us. Against such endeavor, no "Eisenhower Doctrine," no guarantee of borders, no economic aid, no such "information" as we now dispense overseas—and not the possession of shattering atomic power—is of any final avail.

So I have here tried to tell what Communism is and what it is doing. For I am sure the fate of America itself hinges on a reversal of the Red world mission *by Americans*—who do not yet know what it is that must be annihilated. The so-called cold war is not what we think it. The striving of great military powers is not involved. In the Red mind, such "power" is now self-effacing . . . obsolete. What the cold war concerns is *human belief*: primarily *your* belief!

Certain friends in Washington heard we'd planned this trip and asked me to do, en route, some chores related to the above. That "assignment" increased my fear; and I kept it from Ricky as long as I could. . . .

You can read this as a travel narrative, for it is that. Some who have seen it in typescript say it reads "like a novel." But this is not fiction: it happened. I have departed from the actual chronology of events, slightly, for convenience. And I have disguised a few individuals for good reason: what certain real men or women said to me was said in confidence; to attribute the words to their actual speaker would violate a trust and, in some cases, bring harm to a forthright citizen of another land.

Mrs. Wylie feels I have too much "fictionalized" a few passages. She was there; and she accepts my need for the "disguises" I've occasionally used. An editor, who said this book was "among other things, a love letter to Ricky," enlightened me about that. Ricky feels I have fictionalized *her*. But there again, my viewpoint is involved; and I hope I have given the reader material for an independent judgment of the modest woman I have as wife.

The rest lies ahead: an astounding trip—a journey that informed and appalled me, even in the areas where I thought myself both better informed and more appalled than most of my fellow Americans. I would not have missed the experience for anything I possess. Yet I cannot say, with many tourists, that its main effect was to make me glad I live in USA.

Its main effect was to make me wonder how much time was left to save USA from a cannibalizing Faith of Fiends. So, when I'm asked if we "had a good time," I answer within myself:

"It depends on you."

THE INNOCENT AMBASSADORS

	DISTANCE (STATUTE MILES)	AIRBORNE TIME
Miami to San Francisco	2,661	10:48
San Francisco to Honolulu	2,400	10:15
Honolulu to Wake	2,301	8:45
Wake to Tokyo	1,987	8:30
Tokyo to Hong Kong	1,789	8:45
Hong Kong to Bangkok	1,065	4:45
Bangkok to Calcutta	1,001	4:35
Calcutta to Benaras	400	3:05
Benaras to New Delhi	385	2:45
New Delhi to Karachi	666	2:40
Karachi to Beirut	1,998	9:10
Beirut to Istanbul	684	2:45
Istanbul to Athens	345	1:40
Athens to Rome	650	2:55
Rome to Nice	305	1:35
Nice to Paris	430	2:05
Paris to Gander	2,547	8:55
Gander to New York City	1,101	5:20
New York City to Miami	1,100	3:30
TOTAL	23,815	102:48 Hours

1
we're off!
or are we?

The pilot was restless. Not the pilot of our Stratocruiser but one whose route crossed Canada. Most pilots are a little overattentive, a little sharp around the eyes when they fly as paying guests and somebody else is in the cockpit.

This man—tall, black-haired, not young but vital for whatever his years might be—had an additional reason for restlessness. Beside him sat his wife. She was a love-shaped woman with hair that glowed like hot-drawn wire, and distressed eyes. Afraid.

Ricky and I had learned that in the San Francisco airport. For the Stratocruiser had made a false pass at starting—taxiing out to the runway, vibrating there interminably and at last moving back to the hardstands. We passengers were disembarked and fed while a disconnected wire was hunted down and resoldered.

At luncheon, the pilot passenger and his wife told us about three young children they'd left with a sister in Montreal and about the arguments they'd had over whether or not to fly to Hawaii together—since an accident could orphan three. The pilot's wife had told us, too, that she did not mind crossing the Rockies in bad weather but was frightened of a long flight over water. Her husband smiled at her but did not pat her hand or tease her about nervousness as most husbands might have done.

The false start, the long delay, aggravated her tenseness.

Now, as the Stratocruiser moved over the Pacific, an hour and more beyond the photogenic coast of California, it was the pilot who rearranged the hand luggage and leafed through magazines. His love-shaped wife had closed her eyes to deal with apprehension in a way that would communicate it to no one else.

Ricky and I were reading. She read *Life* and I read *Time*; when we'd finished, we would exchange. Then we'd read *Newsweek* and *Harper's*. Then the *Atlantic* and the *Scientific American*.

There is not much novelty in flying, for us; there had been some, on this plane. One of the stewardesses was Japanese—though you could not have told it from her speech. And the "Fasten-seat-belts-no-smoking" signs were translated, not into Spanish as on so many planes we'd booked out of Miami, but into Chinese and Japanese. We would disembark in Hawaii, but the plane would go on to Tokyo.

The pilot went restively below, nodding as he corkscrewed out of sight on the circular stairway. Perhaps he had a drink in the luxurious lounge that makes it possible, on this one aircraft, to move about freely. Assuredly, he looked down through the random clouds at the Pacific that rolled beneath: a glinting, blue monotony. Certainly, because he *was* a pilot, he scrutinized and listened to the engines. After a while, he noticed something.

Oil was running down a wing from an inboard engine. Too much oil. (The know-your-plane folders had, of course, pointed out that *some* oil normally dribbles onto the wings from working motors.) But now the pouring oil began to stain the air with trembling smoke. The pilot may have lost a little color. He may even have waited briefly for some reaction from the flight deck.

However, the Canadian soon realized that this particular leak might not register on the gauges until it started a fire. He also knew that such a fire would doubtless be swiftly extinguished. But an engine fire would not be good for the reputation of commercial flying, or for his wife, or for anybody. And he remembered this plane was so constructed that the darkening foxtail of smoke could not be seen by the flight crew: the angle of visibility doesn't permit such vision.

He rang for the stewardess. The Japanese girl appeared quickly. He pointed. She ran up the spiral steps and went through the long fuselage swiftly, without revealing her loss of composure.

A moment later, the inboard engine was shut down. Its feathered propeller slowed to a standstill. Our plane turned about and headed east again, toward the postcard coast of California.

I knew about it only when Ricky said—with no distress, no emotion at all, "Have you noticed we've turned around?"

I looked up from *Time* annoyedly.

She added, "And have you seen that one engine is stopped?"

I hadn't—but I then saw.

My "annoyance" was not owing to the engine difficulty or to the certain, new delay, but to vanity.

I had my first flight in a Navy craft with a Liberty motor and DEP controls in 1921. I commuted to Hollywood in the beginning thirties on Ford's trimotors. Toward the end of the war, for a time, I was in charge of a team of military and civilian writers who collected an official history of the B29's and their men. I had flown every type of training "mission." Before that, I'd supported in writing the Billy Mitchell philosophy of war when most Americans regarded war as a finished folly.

Now, I was annoyed; for I would have bet heavily that no plane on which I rode could stop an engine, feather a prop, and come about, without my instant awareness. Nevertheless it had happened, and Ricky had perceived what a deaf and older *I* had not.

Moments later, the captain's voice came over the loud-speaker. A compressor had developed an oil leak. We were going back to San Francisco. We would be able to make Hawaii on three motors but the conservative policy of the air line demanded we turn around. Gasoline would be dumped—so there would be no smoking.

I've been on bombers when an engine fire occurred and the long, black comettail of smoke streamed out of view behind. So I found this already controlled trouble unalarming: merely one more thing to make two tired people tireder. I talked to Ricky about it briefly—and needlessly: her calm was complete.

Then I looked at other passengers.

The Canadian pilot was patting his wife's hand, now.

Several people were staring fixedly at the motionless propeller. Others were reading life jacket instruction booklets and trying, doubtless, to remember the step-by-step demonstration the stewardesses had given in the first minutes of flight.

These stewardesses speedily appeared with trays of martinis, manhattans and champagne, drinks eagerly accepted. I felt that somebody ought not to take a drink, to demonstrate there was no need for souped-up courage in so trivial an emergency. So I refused, took out of my handbag a cigarette holder made of bone, and began filing its mouthpiece with a new emery board. I had such holders in good supply in my luggage since I constantly wear, chew, bite and grind them to bits, but the mouthpiece is too thick for my taste and I file them to suit.

An elderly man was standing in the aisle chatting with somebody in the seat behind his own. Later, I learned he was a stockbroker from Omaha. He—even more than the cocktail-bearing girls—helped to settle the surge of anxiety felt by the big plane's passengers. For he did not stop his amiable conversation when the engine went out. His expression remained unaltered. One would have thought nothing whatsoever had occurred, an impression, I presently realized, which the broker intended to convey. People looked at him standing conspicuously, gabbing, and finished their drinks. Few asked for another. Most went back to their reading, their sales charts, their business notes, diaries, postcard writing.

By and by, the broker noticed me filing busily on a white cigarette holder. Since the act seemed odd, he came over and asked what I was doing. I told him and he went back to his acquaintance—satisfied. But his inquiry made me aware of the comic fact that I often say or do something which, to others, seems suspiciously offbeat. . . .

There was that day when I was lying in the Red Cross Blood Bank with the needle taped in a vein. A solicitous Gray Lady asked me how I felt and, thinking of the red sap running out of

me, I answered, "Like a maple tree." She hurried away, conceal-
ing her dismay. Moments later, an Army psychiatrist was rushed
to my side! So you will see in the adventures ahead how my
penchant for doing and saying what seems relevant to me but
not to others creates certain dilemmas for all concerned. . . .

The plane mumbled east. Soon the smell of raw gasoline
came thinly into the cabin, making it evident that we had been
ordered not to smoke with good reason. Time passed.

Our landing was perfect. For a second time, we trailed down
the portable stage into the airport. It was becoming very familiar, as if we'd been registered in it for days. There were more
cocktails, more rumors and, ultimately, vague announcements
concerning our next scheduled departure time.

The captain who'd taken us out over the Pacific (and
brought us back) came into the lounge and talked. During the
flight he had already explained every known detail of our trouble.
Now, he told us of a private disappointment. A different crew
would take us up when our plane was again repaired. In the
event that repairs would require the whole night, he said the new
crew would fly us in a different Stratocruiser. But he had counted
on keeping both his schedule and an important date in Singapore. Since he'd used up so many hours that he and his crew
would be replaced, his next flying assignment would land him
in Manila. In consequence, he would miss his Singapore appoint-
ment.

It dashed him. It fascinated me.

I cannot accommodate my mind to that shape of the
world taken for granted by sky-casual young people nowadays.
I cannot manage to feel practicality in making a date in Singapore on a Monday for the following Friday evening, when one
knows a trip to and from America lies between—a trip by way of
Bangkok, Hong Kong, Tokyo, Wake Island and Honolulu.

The world has shrunk—but I have not shrunk enough to
match. Ricky, I believe, felt the same way. For the captain's frustrated date beguiled her, too. "Imagine," she said, "worrying
about standing up somebody in Malaya next Tuesday!" And
she added, "But it's very good psychology."

"Why?"

"Because it reminds all these more-or-less worried people that flights usually do go through on schedule."

The "more-or-less worried" adults consumed scotch and gin; they dozed, wrote more postcards, fraternized and kept mistakenly asking employees of other air lines when our flight would depart. Their restive children weighed themselves, ate Hershey bars and peanuts, wrestled and grew sleepy as night deepened. We should have been far past the point of no return; but we were just sitting there in the chilly California dark.

When, finally, our plane was repaired and ready for another try, we trooped on board. I was glad to see that the wife of the Canadian pilot still accompanied us.

We taxied out for the third time to take-off position. For the third time, the props revolved and soon we felt the fractional G of acceleration. The new captain's voice boomed cheerfully over the loud-speakers.

"Trouble was—a gasket gave out in an oil compressor, folks. Kind of thing that rarely happens. That gasket wasn't even due for inspection for a long while. Nothing serious at all. Don't expect the slightest bit of further trouble—and we're all sorry you are so delayed. The weather ahead all the way is just about ideal. And as beautiful a clear night doesn't happen often in Frisco. Since we're already so far behind schedule, I'm going to give you a treat. San Francisco by night is one of the greatest spectacles in America and you'll never have a better chance to look at it. So I'll take ten minutes more of your time and we'll go sight-seeing over Frisco before we hop to Hawaii. How about it?"

We curved in over the city where Ricky and I had spent a few days of sight-seeing—on the ground.

We looked out and down at the saffron reflection of the sodium lights on the Oakland bridge, the silhouetted fire tower on Telegraph Hill and the lights that bead Golden Gate Bridge. Ten thousand sparks disclosed the city contour and their absence defined the Park, where tree ferns grew that Ricky had wondered why we couldn't raise in Florida. The rectilinear darkness reached the shimmering sea front: Cliff House and now-invisible rocks where sea lions bobbed and honked all day.

Below, too, was the tower light on Berkeley campus and identifiable winding streets where friends of ours had homes. Nearly everybody, I thought, has at least one "old friend" in or around San Francisco. And their city is magnificent; I thought, truly "cosmopolitan." Railroad yards in the distance connected a dazzling counterpane with winking reds and greens to all the continent. An irregular reach of darkness was The Bay and had, from the air, its recognizable map shape. On its invisible bosom, anchored ships from everywhere were individually delineated by their lights and it was rimmed by murky wharves.

I, peering, could make out cable cars bugging up and down steep streets I'd known the names of, for a few days at a time, in 1922—when I first went there—streets I knew again at that moment and have again forgotten. I could imagine smells of coffee, beer, tidewater—and the curious slapping sound of the cables that pulled the firefly cars.

San Francisco has glamour—historical glamour from old Spain, and the forty-niners; it has substance, also, augmented by Nevada where Comstock found the silver mother lode, Mackay mined the top and Sutro tunneled to the bottom. It even has the romance of a spectacular calamity, an earthquake-called-fire that I'd heard of, often, as a child from still-popeyed eyewitnesses. Besides, its dramatic and practical admixture of land and sea, along with its not-so-practical but equally dramatic hills, give the city gaudy distinction.

The passengers were enthralled: our skipper's sight-seeing tour had been a brilliant means to allay irritation and restore confidence.

Soon we could see the peninsula entire. I remembered how, in the early days of the Federal Civil Defense Administration, we had puzzled futilely in Washington over means to evacuate so many people through such a bottleneck, in the event of an air raid. There were, I knew, experts of fifty sorts in Washington (or Battle Creek) still maundering over that plainly unsolvable dilemma and others like it. But by just contemplating the great, golden blur I saw how futile it was to consider fleeing—or even turning such vast city populations to troglodytes. Present weapons made the very ideas absurd.

We went out beyond the Golden Gate where stars shone. The city became a diminishing aura, then a nothing lost behind the unseeable Pacific, a memory in a dark space we alone occupied.

The overhead cabin lights went out. Inadequate reading lights made dim funnels in the cigarette haze; a book was vaguely illumined here, a girl's hair shimmered down the aisle, a stewardess now and then passed by smoothly on the sensible slippers with which she'd replaced high heels.

Ricky and I opened handbags that Mike and Helen Lerner had given us for on-board use. We, too, took off our shoes and put on slippers; we changed our reading matter and strained our eyes awhile, then went below to the pretty salon where we had a highball or two and a sandwich and talked to other passengers. We talked especially to the Canadian pilot's lovely wife. She could not sleep, she said: she kept thinking of all that water below . . . and her children.

Much later, while Ricky and I leaned stiff and stuporous against our slanted seats, the first light showed. Out of an opal immensity came land. We saw the dull glare of the Marine Base at Kaneohe and the vague silhouettes of precipitous mountains. The plane came down. We stood up, collected our possessions and tiredly walked through cool-warm darkness to the dingy glitter of a waiting room.

No bands were playing *Aloha*.

No brown girls kissed us and put leis around our necks.

But, while I stood meaninglessly beside my wife and our hand dunnage, a heavy-set young man stepped forward. "Are you," he asked dubiously, "named Wylie?"

I said I was.

"Are you, by chance, Philip Wylie?"

I thought he had come from the hotel, owing to the concern over my name. I told him I was Philip Wylie.

For quite a while he stared at me. "*The* Philip Wylie?" he finally asked.

Nobody likes to be asked if he is *the* Wilbur K. Billik, or *the* Marilyn Monroe, either. (Furthermore, people who rush up and ask me excitedly if I am *the* Philip Wylie usually take a long look after being so assured, and murmur disappointedly, "*Oh!*" Then they go away.)

However, it was getting on toward four A.M. and we had not slept so I didn't even bother to inform the man that I was "*the* Philip Wylie, if he meant the *meteorologist.*" I just said yes.

He muttered, still skeptically, "The *writer?*"

So much incredulity stirred even my numb nerves. I told him I was the writer and I asked who in hell he was.

It turned out he was a Honolulu businessman who'd heard we were coming and had stayed up, with his wife, all night simply to be certain somebody would greet us and drive us to Waikiki. He was, also, a fisherman of renown and forthwith invited us to go out with him for marlin.

I never did find out what it was about me that so plainly put him off, unfortunately. Maybe, that night, I didn't look strong enough to take a marlin. Maybe I looked too old. Usually, admirers of my books are disappointed with me simply because *I* look like fifty thousand other American males of fifty-odd. That, at least, is what *I* hope. And, though disillusioned, he introduced his attractive wife, helped us with our luggage when it was finally brought, and drove us the many miles to our hotel.

We drove past smart shops and modernistic hotels, palm trees draped with philodendrons, classy liquor stores and a neon-glazed radio station on dim-lit avenues deserted of pedestrians. Late traffic rumbled around us and sometimes turned corners on chattering tires, overaccelerated by alcohol. An all-night drive-in blazed near a lawn where frangipanis and oleanders bloomed in the dark. Night sea showed through trees and hotel profiles. Waikiki, finally reached, was so like home and Miami Beach that Ricky said testily, "We've sure traveled a long way to get—nowhere!"

Our unexpected hosts enjoyed that: they'd seen South Florida. Besides, neither of us felt that we were "nowhere"; Hawaii was already different—for where else do two charming people wait all night in an air terminal just to say to a pair of strangers, "Aloha"?

2
Oahu, Kauai, Wake
and points west or east

All good Americans ought to go to Hawaii before they die. They should go as long before they die as possible—a proposition which holds for most American travelers, everywhere. For the great majority of our long-distance tourists are at least sixty years old, men who have retired from business (more rarely, the professions), accompanied by their wives.

That somber fact was plain even in Hawaii. We wakened after our late arrival on a "cruise day." The hotel teemed with the lei-bearing passengers of a big ship. Hawaiian girls performed hulas out by the swimming pool and handsome beach boys made the music. In the distance, sinewy young men rode surfboards on the languid ground swells of the Pacific. Everywhere—dancing, waiting on tables, walking the palm-shaded streets—were lovely young women, real life samples of the alluring native girls displayed on every Come-to-Hawaii poster. But that athletic manhood and swaying beauty was displayed for America's grizzled gadabouts: aging people who have money and leisure for foreign travel.

Younger Americans do go to Europe in collegiate hordes. But there ought to be a way to transport similar hordes to the Pacific islands, the Orient, Asia and the Near East. It would favorably alter a poor world opinion of our country; and by "young people" I do not mean soldiers.

People sixty years old are usually rigid in their opinions. They have countless biases both obsolete and fixed. Americans with money, moreover, have too often spent their lives in the pursuit of that one possession. They have not had the time (or, at least, they have not *taken* the time) to learn anything, much, excepting (in the case of the men) wheat futures, the structure and assembly of steam shovels, or the techniques of selling and also foisting Buicks. Their wives, as limited, have devoted themselves to Society and Things. Such people are not just uninformed; they do not know information exists. Yet because human beings are believed to become wise with age they mistake a void of imminent senility for omniscience. They also usually believe that quaint American myth which holds pre-eminence in any field—save the intellectual!—as a warrant of competence in all.

There are exceptions. Not every well-to-do American of middle or old age thinks, for instance, that all human beings with a slightly different skin hue are mere natives. Not every one is positive that, in any category of human living and being, the people of other nations are inferior to the people of USA. Not every tourist, having won his fare by cornering putty, assumes he has thereby become an authority on Tropical Medicine, Judo, Jade, and Taoism. But most such persons bask in brassy ignorance and bristle with prejudice. Those who attempt to "mingle" with the "natives" do it as a kind of slumming. And since "there is no fool like an old fool," their condescending concupiscence often leads to activities abroad that would not be deemed bearable even on a gala night, even in a country club, even in Toledo or Sacramento or Dallas.

These people represent one kind of American success. But they do not represent America. They do not represent the knowledge in America, the understanding, the capacity for brotherhood, the willingness to learn, the widespread ability to evaluate truly or the common wish to appreciate correctly. Those are endowments of millions of educated or decently bred Americans who are mostly younger than the tourists and nearly always so much less concerned with money that they are unable to afford travel as mere sport even if they could think of it in such terms. The sad, human truth is that vulgarians and unconsciously hostile people are conspicuous. The same cruise ship undoubtedly imported men and women from America of the opposite sort. But they were already gone—reuniting with friends, getting up a luau with native pals, hiking in the jungle, fishing—and only the Whiskey Sour for Breakfast Set was left to represent Americans.

It was repellent to watch so many pot-bellied men watch the young girls dance and comico-pathetic to see their wives in pretty leis and the exclamatory print dresses of the islands. In nine cases out of ten the women were too old and too prudish to mean what they wore and their husbands were past all doing save drooling. Their sons and daughters should have replaced them in Hawaii, not to slum, but to get to know some interesting fellow citizens.

For Hawaiians are, of course, Americans: inhabitants of a territory. They call the rest of their country "the mainland," not "the States," as non-Americans often do. They are among the handsomest, happiest and pleasantest members of the human species; they are, also, among the most racially mixed.

The full-blooded Hawaiian is rare though Hawaiians are sometimes pure Americans like you and me. That is to say, they are Nordic and white—a mixture of no more than a dozen major bloods in which the Asian and the Negro have become recessive through generations our ancestors spent in the British Isles, Scandinavia, or other parts of Europe. Hawaiians, in short, are as mixed as our own ancestors used to be. The original island people mingled with Chinese and Japanese, with Portuguese and Spaniards, with unknown myriads of sailors from Britain, Sweden and Norway, Holland, France and the United States.

Hawaiians are, also, many thousands of "unmixed" (or not yet mixed) Japanese and Chinese. They include some Negroes —mixed and not.

They have no color line. Segregation in Hawaii would be as impossible to practice as is genuine segregation in the United

States. For not one white person can know how close he or she may be to a Negro or an American Indian, a Chinese or a Jew. To know, a person would have to possess a guaranteed pedigree of parents, grandparents and great-grandparents, back through generations, in a world where it is "a wise child that knows his own father"—a world where only two or three ancestral lines may be traced back any distance by anybody and not one solitary ancestor even in such a pedigree can be guaranteed! It would be a great lesson to people of integrity who yet imagine there is value in what they call racial purity to spend a year or two in Hawaii.

However, I have said "integrity" here. The word assumes the visitor would be merely misinformed and capable, in the presence of new fact, of changing his mind. In the Islands, such a visitor would see every sort of racial "mongrel" and "hybrid" who yet exhibited every sort of intellectual, cultural and physical superiority—just as he would see (if ever he used his mind for seeing) that "thoroughbred" dogs lose by inbreeding and the mutt is usually superior. He could and should have seen that he is a human mutt, himself—a white man only by special hairsplitting superimposed on guesswork; any difference he can find between his white self and others is infinitesimal compared to the similarities and identities.

The wondrously commingled Americans in Hawaii have an ambition to become a State. They say—with complete justice and as our forebears said it—No taxation without representation. The same slogan is current in Alaska for the same reason. Yet certain senators who visited Hawaii have held its population to be politically immature and unready for self-government or participation in national government. Some of those same senators came out of the swamps of Mississippi and the hills of Kentucky, where maturity of any sort is regarded as heretical. And the words the senators used to indict the people of Hawaii are the same words, exactly, that Communists employ to alibi their enslavement of others.

Since our overt prejudice against other races and our partly unconscious prejudice toward other religions may presently cost us Americans our liberty, our self-government and even our existence—and since that peril, so little seen or foreseen in America, is the principal reason for this travelogue—I recommend Hawaii as the best, first place to encounter living refutations of one of those two risky forms of American arrogance and error: *whitemanism.*

To observe the people in the Islands accurately is to see that to imagine the white race unique and superior is nonsense, and to begin to see that, nowadays, the concept is *suicidal* nonsense. In Hawaii, that wisdom will come forcefully to any honest person, and even rather painlessly, since the fantastic religious bigotry that most of us do not know we have is not ubiquitously and grievously aroused. To be sure, Hawaii has Shinto shrines and Buddhist temples. But Baptist, Presbyterian, Methodist and other Protestant churches—along with Mormon temples, Roman Catholic Cathedrals, Synagogues and Reading Rooms of Christian Science—predominate.

The neon signs are in English and if they include Hawaiian words or names their letters, at least, will be decipherable. The same drugstores stuffed with the same glittering products stand on similar corners. If some of the school kids have slanting eyes and black pigtails, they will still order ice cream cones and hamburgers in good Americanese. Indeed, to any of the millions of citizens of USA who are familiar with South Florida, Hawaii will seem like that part of home—with mountains added; and a large proportion of locals will talk and act (but not necessarily look!) exactly like the main street crowds in Miami Beach, Fort Lauderdale, Fort Myers or Palm Beach.

The Islands are among the best examples of natural beauty the planet displays. Precipitous mountains rise above jade valleys, mountains jungle-covered save where eroded knife-edges point into the prevailing winds or stark cliffs glare at the Pacific. Clouds are impaled continually by the highest ridges. All around, the near sea runs in parallel white crests and its distant reaches are tourmaline blue. Coconut palms overhang beige beaches; these rim the inside curves of innumerable coves; and in such secretive places, the water is usually emerald. Headland escarpments of dark volcanic rock pound back breakers in a roaring war whereof the issue is foam. Foam lathers beaches, soapsuds highways and flies in spindrift to the inland fern trees where it is caught like cotton on Christmas spruces.

The islands are never cold, usually warm, never very hot—and it rains a great deal, especially in wintertime. But it does not rain for long, as a rule. An hour's wait will salvage almost any Baptist picnic or Polynesian luau.

Certain islands are actively volcanic, a fact almost too well known since tourists are often frightened by something they should have learned to admire—through casual reading in the press of Des Moines or Schenectady. The volcanoes smoke, mutter and erupt at intervals of some years, burping lava through the green jungles and occasionally down to the sea, which is then set aboil. But such dramatic interruptions of island tranquillity, expectable in kind and degree, seldom menace so much as an evacuated straw-hut village and never turn bevies of *Lurline* passengers into pumice molds like those that mark the end of sundry Pompeians.

Orchids grow wild in Hawaii and the cultivation of orchids is a household hobby as well as an industry. Great stands of sandalwood trees once flourished. They were virtually exterminated to make soap and fans for grandma, as well as medicaments of no great value for grandpa. Hau trees adorn the banks of short, fresh-water rivers and somewhat resemble mangroves. Tremendous monkeypod trees tower in the slanted jungles, shade streets, and provide wood for exquisite carving. Abundant are various members of what were called legumes till recently—a botanical family that furnishes much of the flowering tree splendor of tropical lands: poincianas, jacarandas, cassias, acacias, and many "shower" trees—pink, rose, red, white, yellow, orange. They cover the ground with petals, creating colored carpets beneath Brobdingnagian bouquets.

Some of the island wild flowers were familiar to Ricky and me, as were many of the ornamental trees, shrubs and garden plants. We were, indeed, a disappointment to several of our island hosts for we, too, have *dendrobiums* growing in our trees, *phalaenopsis* blooming on our porch, and not only a *cassia fistula* to shower goldenly on our lawn, but *tabebuia argentea*, besides. The Hawaiian flora gave us an instant sense of familiarity, and other regions even less like home seemed less odd for that reason: wherever we looked along the klongs of Bangkok, for example, we could see trees, vines, shrubs and annuals that flourish in our South Miami yard.

Yet I presume that even in Florida not five residents per hundred could identify a dozen common street trees or as many conventional shrubs or a comparable fraction of the ordinary flowers. Most people are born, and live, and die, in a world half animal and half vegetable. Upon the latter, they ultimately depend for their whole sustenance. Vegetation, furthermore—whether wild or arranged by man—is the cloak of their planet. Yet they do not have time, most of them, to learn even the names of the verdure around them, let alone its nature. They do not care. And by the degree that they do not care, they miss a great part of the meaning of themselves. For they have been given brains. But they used the brains, not to become at home in the world, but to exploit whatever aspect of that world lay handiest. They are therefore parasites and not really a contributing part of Nature; unnatural—wherefore, not truly alive.

Perhaps I should rejoice that five Floridians in a hundred do know their flora. And I'm aware that visitors to Hawaii often do appreciate its flowers—that some are first-rate botanists and that others come by a lifelong interest in the verdant world owing to a visit to the Islands. But my own concern is with the great, insensitive majority, for I am not only vexed by their emptiness but I would like to fill their voids with better pleasures than they know.

In any case, the people of Hawaii dwell on ocean stepping-stones that resemble carefully planted tropical rock gardens and they are more aware than most of the meaning of plants to men. Their lei is no accidental symbol, or set of symbols, since, originally, different flowers were used to convey different meanings. Yet many Americans, who had lived in Hawaii long enough to appreciate flowers more and Buicks less, were amazed that their green canopy was pretty much repeated in a place so commercial and prosaic as Miami. Some were irritated, rather than astonished, to find we raised at home what they grew "out there." I guess they thought their grass was greener just because they'd gone so far away to notice grass.

We had counted, Ricky and I, on two weeks of rest at Waikiki before commencing the strenuous part of our journey—the flight to Japan and thence on around the world. We needed such respite.

There wasn't any to be had in Hawaii—for us.

The principal reason was that here, for the first time, we undertook the grandparental function. Beyond that, we spent a day on Kauai, an evening in Chinatown, an afternoon with a lady who raised orchids, and a few hours with some very worried military men. We didn't even go fishing or swimming. Full-time work, grandparentry!

Our daughter, Karen, had written us long since about settling in Oahu, which is the island site of Honolulu, Pearl Harbor, and Waikiki Beach. She and her husband had bought a small house and a considerable amount of land on its windward side—a term without significance to us until we crossed the insular divide.

How different their lives were! How different are the lives of most such young Americans from the life of my generation!

Karen and "Tap" had met at Cornell and married in a church not far from our house in South Florida. My father performed the ceremony; Ricky gave a reception afterward; I saw them off in a rented limousine; and there all resemblance ended.

Our son-in-law had trained for the Marine Corps Reserve in college. He'd gone to boot camp in summers, finished at Parris Island and received his commission before he had wed Karen. They went, the day after their marriage, to Pensacola and flight training and thence to California from where they'd been almost immediately transferred to Hawaii.

Now, they had a bayside home—and a newborn son.

When Ricky and I came to Oahu, most of Tap's "outfit" had departed for Thailand to fly helicopters in SEATO maneuvers; Tap himself was made C.O. of those who remained at the Kaneohe Base. The long furlough he had anticipated at the time his son was to be born had been canceled. His responsibilities were trebled instead, and his plans for making his house ready for a baby were thus summarily postponed. Karen was making do without many needed auxiliaries of motherhood.

Her plans had not materialized either:

She'd written to Ricky and me with the aplomb of a midwife about the progress of her pregnancy. Her letters had shown a confidence gained from up-to-date textbooks on natural childbirth which was so objective that I felt our daughter was getting ready for motherhood exactly as she had prepared for a final examination in mathematics.

Things had not turned out as she'd expected, precisely, though the main result, her son and our grandson, was in every way splendid. However, Karen was not only alone by day in a rather lonely spot on that jungle-and-mountain coast, but she was obliged to stay in bed for quite a while.

At their age, I was employed in New York. By the time Karen was born, I'd become what Spectorsky has called an "exurbanite"—a person with a home and acreage beyond the true suburbs of Manhattan. We had a nurse for Karen and a "couple" to cook and garden. Karen first saw light through windows in the Harkness Pavilion of Columbia-Presbyterian Medical Center, in New York. Now, Karen had borne a child in a territory of USA five thousand miles from any place she could call home. Her obstetrician was Japanese—and she had no maid. Just a very happy husband who came home at dusk, dog-tired. Because the world has been at war so much lately and because it now stands always so near its brink, hundreds of thousands of young American couples, brought up in comfort like Karen and Tap, have gone far away to bear and rear families somehow—the wives often more alone than Karen, the husbands under orders in the Army, Navy, Air Force or, as in Tap's case, the Marine Corps.

Some, like our two, faced the hardships and novel problems with courage and resourcefulness. A few have come to know alien people and unfamiliar land. Tap and Karen, for example, plan to make their permanent residence on that windward side of Oahu.

But most of the service families I've seen in far lands huddle in protective shoals, seeing only each other and scorning indigenous food, customs, people and languages. Our government spends great sums to send overseas young men who must go to such areas. Then it doubles or triples the sum to send, also, their wives, kids—and also American food in American tin cans or frozen packages, American movies and everything else that will make a little Main Street of some foreign quarter. For most such Americans will not shop in a native market or make friends with a native person—even one who speaks English. When, after their dreadful ordeal, they finally get back to their own Main Street they swear before God they will never go abroad again—never visit the land of a wog or a wop or a kuki. Their opinion of the people and their lands is expressed lifelong in loud anathema—though they actually learned nothing whatever about either, during their foreign tour of duty.

I have said we should send young Americans abroad in great numbers. As Ricky and I found out and this book will show, it is probably the only way to win a life-or-death struggle we did not seek but cannot evade. But the ambassadors we need—American youths who must learn the world and whom the world desperately needs to meet—will have to be screened. Because our average young citizen is unfit to mingle with humanity: unable to outgrow bobby sox sentiments and incapable of being weaned, even by the officers of our armed forces, from the cloying teats of American technology.

Yet we *must* find and export the right people, in sufficient numbers, and not in uniforms. For the war ahead will not involve a total struggle with arms, as I also hope to show; at least, if it does, we need not worry about the fate of any next American generation: there will be none. . . . Rather, it will be—it is —a war for the souls of men.

The Soviets, together with the Red Chinese, have already trained and exported hundreds of thousands of comparable emissaries—young zealots who not only learn the language and adopt the customs of their assigned nations, but who have so effectively corrupted the world which our young people must cleanse and inspire that the task ahead is titanic—if we are to survive. Wop-haters, wog-baiters, young men and women who grow dour or fall into weeping fits after six days of separation from chocolate malteds will not defeat the rugged missionaries of Communist Faith.

From our hotel at Waikiki to the house on Kaneohe Bay was a drive of about thirty miles through spectacular country. The road climbed by cliff-hanging switchbacks over something called Pali Pass—a road only two cars wide, often smothered in foglike cloud, usually glittering with slick moisture and sometimes deluged by one of the brief, beautiful cascades that form in Hawaii's mountains during heavy rain. For an hour or a day, those waterfalls leap hundreds of feet down black cliffs and out over the near-vertical jungle. At its summit, Pali Pass is often swept by winds of full gale force. A car, driven with excruciating care to the crest, may be abruptly blown to a standstill or, more alarming, accelerated toward steep slick hairpin turns and abysses beyond them.

That drive across Oahu, which we made nearly every day, and the return, which we generally made in the dark, was sometimes arduous enough for a day's work. Many Hawaiians think of it as suitable only for annual pilgrimage, which didn't surprise us; what did, was the number of daily commuters.

On the windward side of the island, we had to pitch in and work. Ricky, especially, labored at women's tasks. There was, however, the consummate reward of our grandson, as well as his mother—and his father, come dinnertime. People who have never been grandparents will not comprehend our rapture—and I do not want to get a reputation for fatuity by trying, here, to enlighten them.

Another occupation less exhausting but, in its way, stressful, consisted in refusing as politely as we could numberless invitations. Hospitality is a common human virtue, even though most travelers seem to deem it a rarity which only they somehow encountered and only among peoples they luckily visited. The Hawaiians are among the world's many extremely hospitable people. That businessman who stayed up all night with his wife, just to drive us to our hotel, was but a harbinger of what was to come.

There is superb sports fishing off all the Islands; and I have written a great deal about fishing in various American magazines and in books. But I had not thought of marlin-catching when I'd thought, in past months, of Hawaii. I'd thought of family and grandchild. Yet, every night when Ricky and I parked our rented Ford behind the hotel (sometimes with shaky nerves), we found in our mailbox invitations to fish. Along with them were invitations to see orchid collections (I've also written, some, about orchids). There were social invitations in addition, and requests for newspaper interviews. Ricky or I wrote notes to those pleasant-sounding strangers explaining that our Hawaiian trip was principally for the purpose of baby-seeing and baby-sitting. That did not discourage our would-be hosts. We began to feel anxiety about what must have seemed our constant rudeness. So we accepted a few requests.

We had intended to visit the whole archipelago, using the excellent local air lines. We actually set aside one day for at least one glimpse of more than Oahu. Even that plan was deferred when the local anglers, eager to ask questions about International Game Fish Association rules and regulations, invited me to a lunch. I happen to be on the board of governors. Their questions were searching. I learned new lore about fish, fishing and artificial baits. The lunch was excellent. I made a speech afterward—probably not excellent.

Then I hurried back to the hotel to start, belatedly, the scenic, tricky trip to the windward side.

One other afternoon, we inspected a magnificent orchid collection. And finally we did visit Kauai.

We flew there in the morning. We'd hired a car and a driver to take us on a trip up a navigable river and show us the deep, magnificent "Grand Canyon of the Pacific"—a duplicate in miniature of the famous gorge of the Colorado. We had considered asking the tour bureau for a man who knew something about the native flora of Kauai, which is called the "garden island." But we decided a chauffeur-botanist would not be obtainable.

With some astonishment, as we drove into the green splendor, we found that the driver (half Hawaiian and half Irish) was a University graduate and the son of a nurseryman; he knew the name of every tree, bush, vine and wild flower on Kauai: the English name, the Hawaiian name and the botanical, or Latin name, besides!

Ricky filled a notebook.

Later, we learned our guide was also a Mormon preacher! That embarrassed me. For I am given to profanity, which I use even more often to express enthusiasm than wrath. The excess (if, as I suspect, I swear more than most people) is owing to the fact that I am self-conscious. Thus, if I endeavor to express aloud and publicly such feelings as rise in me—say, on beholding Kauai's many-colored canyon or its flower-fringed seascapes or some tree exploded into bloom—my inner response would sound pretentious. After all, I am a literary man. So I have fallen, long ago, into the habit of not uttering a half-baked approximation of words I would not write down until I'd cut and reconstrued them.

"Darling," I do *not* say to my wife when strangers are standing nearby, "isn't that just about the most incandescent cerise you ever saw? Especially against those chartreuse leaves? And with that background of cobalt water? Schiaparelli ought to see it! Would you call the scheme 'primitive' or, perhaps, 'banal'?"

Such talk turns heads and brings snickers; it sounds affected.

What I do say is, "God-damned gaudy view!"

That startles practically nobody. But I still wonder what the Mormon minister thought. I dislike to offend the Faithful by my speech. And, as a minister's son, I possess an inner censor that can shut off blasphemy securely when I wish. But who'd expect a

Hawaiian-Irishman to be Mormon? Besides, I didn't expect car drivers to be devout. I learned better—later on.

In Kauai, I made an observation about tourists I was to repeat the world around. It does not apply to all tourists but to that great number who might be called "camera tourists. . . ."

Ricky and I had a camera and color film. We'd even once owned and operated fairly elaborate cameras. Their complexity caused us to take along a simple Kodak: we wanted to avoid needless distraction on our journey but it would be pleasant, we thought, to have a snapshot that would show our friends what everybody wants to show: Mr. and Mrs. Wylie on a bench—in the background, the Taj Mahal; Mrs. Wylie on a Lebanese road —camel caravan in the b.g.

An incredible number of tourists, however, appear to travel for the principal purpose of bringing home a photographic record. They are hung about with as much gear as an infantryman: still cameras in leather bags and movie cameras, lenses in cases, light meters, tripods, filters and waterproof sacks full of film. I have even seen a few manifest amateurs with professional motion picture machinery—Bell & Howell apparatus.

On Kauai, a fresh water river makes possible a round trip by boat through hills, rice fields, hau-hung banks and a boulder-strewn jungle. En route, the tourist is taken to a scooped-out cliff from the rim of which hangs a fern tapestry. Maiden hair fern grows upon the walls and ceiling of this natural band-shell which was blasted out by a volcanic spasm; the lava tube that created it can be inspected. A man and woman render the beautiful "Hawaiian Wedding Song" while the tourists listen from the cavern: singing that would give a statue gooseflesh.

A dozen of the people who took that trip with us, spent all their time watching clouds to ascertain when the sun would emerge, peering through light meters, shifting lenses and filters and—infrequently—snapping a picture or running off a few feet of movie film. Their attention was concentrated on their gadgets. The regard they gave to their unique and beautiful environs was not to perceive, appreciate, enjoy or rhapsodize, but merely to appraise camera angles.

The constant photographer at best can bring back unrelated fractions of travel. By his very assiduity, he is removed from the human environment. He has no time to become acquainted even with the people he photographs. He wants a mere picture of them—not any knowledge of who they are, what they think and feel, or how they relate themselves to him. He has to remain immune to relationships and wholes.

It may be that I have a specialized habit of wanting, always, to absorb new surroundings into my brain. It may be, too, that I have a concern with other human beings which differs from the usual interest. It may be I am almost alone in wanting, when I travel, or at any time, billions of clear brain-imprints—aural and visual and those of smell and touch—which do not readily fade and are not subject to damage owing to old film, careless development and the mishaps that befall delicate gear. Maybe I'm just a writer, compounding human and scenic impressions as a banker does interest.

But I believe that is not so. Other tourists, whom I felt were more absorbed than the photographers, had my kind of attention. Ricky has it more intensely than I.

Camera compulsives, I suspect, are motivated by inner forces. They are more eager to collect evidence of travel itself than concerned with the people or places they visit. They also seem to feel, unconsciously, that their training in observation, their capacity to explore other human beings, and their mere memory, are so limited that Kodacolor fragments will furnish a more real record than their own minds ever could.

It is very good for Eastman. But it is also very naive of the lensmen. For a picture "says more than a thousand words" only to those who cannot truly read, think or make friends—and have a paltry imagination, besides. A man of modest understanding, for instance, can feel what a Japanese feels; but I would like to see a photograph taken by an American *in Japanese*.

One night, during the Chinese New Year's Festival, we went to Honolulu's Chinatown. The papers had reported that the celebrants would set off two hundred thousand firecrackers, made in Hong Kong, the largest string every constructed. And I am a fan for firecrackers.

Ricky and I had dinner in a Chinese restaurant. In New York, in a few places, real Chinese food is served. We had a physicist friend who liked it—as we did, too—so we were accustomed to the menu. After a fine if somewhat unidentifiable meal we watched from a window while the Hong Kong masterpiece blew up. It was a singularly satisfying experience. A fire truck hoisted one end on its extension ladder until it was fully raised at a near-vertical angle. Even so, the Honolulu official who ignited the fuse started yards of the thing on the ground. He used a Dunhill briquette—and stepped back swiftly. Then commenced such a roar as would easily have drowned Niagara: every one of the near quarter million firecrackers was good-sized; and at short intervals an enormous "salute" had been included.

The street, a wall-to-wall carpet of Chinese who watched with a kind of enthusiastic solemnity, shuddered as if an earthquake were in progress. Lovely Chinese dancing girls gazed in tranquil joy from their lighted booths. The musicians sat with their odd instruments in their laps and stared meditatively. Ice cream sellers and the vendors of orchid plants also gazed with reverent mirth at the continual, flaring blast. It took nine minutes for the string to explode; all that time, Ricky and I hung out the restaurant window. Afterward, the street beneath was hip-deep in truckloads of shattered red paper. I felt certain that all demons had been frightened from Hawaii for the ensuing year by that apotheosis of all blasts ever set off in innocence.

Ricky and I subsequently walked down a shadowed street of Chinatown, sharing a general smile and coming, soon, to a quiet avenue. The cabalistic shop signs—Cantonese-neon characters—were here replaced by a faint yet luminous gleam of flowers in Chinese lawns. And we could see, through a notch in the monkeypod trees, the moon-polished Pacific.

An island remote from the main reminds one of earth more than a vista of horizoned plain or some stacked-up cordillera of earth's erupted essence. The sea that glitters around such an island bespeaks continents merely by reminding of their farness. The horizon's circularity is a further witness of the globe. And no person of sensibility will have come to his island without learning how latitudes and longitudes draw the geometry of his sphere and without heeding the zones of time that tell of the earth's turning.

It was that sort of evening: the air hyacinthine, the earth a jewel in the purple box of night and each of its seven seas becoming a moon-lustered facet as the whole turned in the fingers of God.

Smiling still over the demon-exorcising and coming to a corner, we saw a young Chinese woman. In the lamplight she read our expressions while we perceived her beauty. She turned her head toward us and knew where we had been. She, too, then smiled. Her dark hair stirred against the neckline of a red silk dress; because she paused, a sculptured thigh showed palely as it opened her slit skirt. Her voice was gentle sincerity:

"I hope you enjoyed us," she said.

Besides our regular drives to the windward side of Oahu, besides our almost daily acts of applied grandparenthood, we made one further visit: an innocent and courteous call that was to begin a change in the nature and mood of our trip. . . .

I have a brother-in-law who is the owner of a prodigious business which he started on the mere metal tip of a shoestring. His enterprise covers most of USA and in administering it he has made "contacts" with many people of many sorts, among whom many are important. Through John's connections, we had an introduction to one of the Admirals at Pearl Harbor and owed him a call, since he had made the arrangements for us at our Waikiki hotel.

We duly dispatched a note to the Admiral and we were invited to tour Pearl Harbor.

This we did, one sunny afternoon. . . .

I don't know what "Pearl Harbor" meant on its "day of infamy" to other Americans.

It meant, to me, a signal something like the light old Paul Revere beheld in the North Church tower in 1775.

Before the Nazis marched, I'd been active in the "Stop Hitler" movement. Before that, I'd visited Nazi Germany. I could not tolerate its genocidal paranoia and its tyranny any more than I could the rape of Nanking or what I have seen in Soviet Russia. Certain Americans like me, long before Pearl Harbor, had been quietly asked by government officials if we would serve in various posts in Washington—providing war came. It is worth noting that they were officials in the "Roosevelt Government" and that the war they anticipated was war with Germany—not Japan. Hence the idea Roosevelt deliberately caused Pearl Harbor to occur seems to me evidence of a kind of insanity.

"Pearl Harbor" meant that Ricky and I at once made ready to leave our house on the Miami Beach bay front for a desk in wintry Washington.

In the real Pearl Harbor that sunny day we cruised on a Navy small boat. Here was not the figure of speech, but the fact. We looked at the rusting iron of battleships taken by treacherous surprise. We gazed landward while the sailor explained over which mountains which flights of Japanese dive bombers, torpedo planes and fighters came, and at what times and intervals. We started seaward to note the path this great battlewagon had taken in attempted escape—and where it failed. We surveyed a stripped-decked vessel that had been furiously bombed in the mistaken notion it was a carrier. And we were shown where the miniature submarines had come into the harbor.

Finally, we boarded that small portion of the *Arizona* which still stands above the tide, trod her buckled plates and followed the long, dim line of her beneath the water that is still coffin for hundreds of American sailors and officers. We read the bronze plaque that an Admiral put on the wreck at his own expense when a stingy Congress would not mark the grisly memorial. And we looked at the American flag that flies in the blue, Hawaiian air above the *Arizona*.

I felt again a tremendous anger. I guess our Navy guide, who saw and survived that morning, felt the same emotion, and more strongly; his face hardened and his throat went dry when he told about it.

Later, we sat in Navy offices on shore and talked, over coffee cups, about that old war and the new cold one. I spoke vehemently—as I have written—concerning military and atomic matters and the Red antagonist whose belief I've so long feared.

The Navy people had been noncommittal about my opinions —but not the men in Washington who'd sent for me before we went on our trip. And as Ricky and I drove back toward our hotel I knew it was time to "confess" about Washington. We'd soon be outside American territory. The afternoon we'd just spent reminded me painfully of the strategies of struggle amongst nations—of physical combat and other, subtler sorts of "war."

I hate to have anything to confess to Ricky; but I began, in the cab, gingerly: "Lot of problems in the Pacific aren't solved. These Navy guys, for instance, are committed by Washington to defend Formosa, if the Chinese Reds attack. We've also said officially, in effect, that we'll use A-bombs if we think they're indicated in any scrap. If Formosa's attacked, A-bombs would probably be the only way to defend the place."

Ricky was looking at me intently. "Why?"

"Defending Formosa by sea power, at the end of a long, long supply line, against land-based air power on the China coast —well—what navy wants to try that?"

"There's a Chinese National Army on Formosa—"

"Sitting ducks. Aging, too." I pressed toward my point: "Some Washington jerks think we could put them ashore to wallop Red China, and *supply* them over the same transpacific routes and defend Formosa, also! How can people think that— when the Red Chinese armies gave *us* so much hell in Korea? Only chance we'd have, if Red China moved against Formosa, would be to flatten their bases on the continental coast with A-bombs. But what if we do that?"

"You mean—what if America uses atomic weapons first, *again?*"

"Yeah." The car was nearing our hotel. I tried to sound casual. "Some of the people I saw in Washington asked me to poll as many Chinese as I could on the Chinese and the Asiatic reaction to that. You see, smashing Red coastal bases wouldn't amount to another Hiroshima—but, still, it would kill a lot of civilians."

"*Who* asked you?" Ricky had begun to perceive: "Your Pentagon pals? Senators? Somebody else in the government? Or the atomic wizards you keep having mutual nervous breakdowns with?"

"I didn't say."

"What *else* did they ask you to do?" She was bitter. "Set up cold war plans for Asia?"

I deserved her sarcasm. "Just—a couple of small things, dear. Take a daybreak hike alone through the Red refugees in Hong Kong——"

"Why?"

"I don't know. They suggested it. Said I'd see why, if I took the walk at dawn." We had reached the Kaiulani Hotel and I didn't finish my reply till we were in our room:

"You mustn't be upset, dear. Some pretty bright men in Washington feel that the military aren't generally aware of the nature of cold war or its danger. Those who are—can't participate the way they want to."

"But you can! The Orient will be saved by brassy authors, not the Brass, I suppose?"

"When military men use ideological tactics, somebody at home—newspaper publishers, congressmen—men who are isolationist, or plain saps—jump on the soldiers. Soldiers are trained to take their lumps from the enemy in a fire fight—not from the home front, over acts they performed to conduct a war that's being fought without weapons. A war America is losing—that will end in a defeat like atomic defeat if we lose much longer!"

She kicked a wastebasket in a rare show of frustrated wrath. "Phil, Phil! You're always taking on some hopeless assignment for somebody in the government! Always running yourself ragged trying to do something you can't do—and maybe nobody can! How many times have you come home a wreck from Washington? Or those damned bomb tests? What did it ever achieve? *Nothing!* And now—you're going to be a cold war expert and undercover observer—in areas where you're utterly ignorant! It would be funny, except——! There goes our lovely trip. 'Vacation'—you said! How *can* you, Phil?"

I flopped on the bed feeling a traitor to my wife and not a good patriot: just a man made foolish by concern for freedom. I said, "If you'd been with me in Washington, Ricky, you'd have agreed. As I did."

When you tell Ricky that something you have done, which she feels is a mistake, would have been done by her under the same circumstances, Ricky will think about it. That may be a rare reaction in women: it's certainly a possible one. For, now, she walked to the balcony of the Princess Kaiulani Hotel and looked at Diamond Head. She lit a cigarette—her hands shaking slightly—and blew smoke, too hard.

"All I have to do is stay aware," I said. "And a couple of other things that won't take three hours apiece. And if you will help me—maybe, together, we can find out more for ourselves. After all, we started out to learn. Maybe we could even think of something. Do some little thing to help those men—in a cold war Americans don't understand—but must win."

If you ask Ricky to help—she almost never refuses, whether it's to collect for the Community Chest or to get a cat out of a tree. And when her eyes go back from gray to the greenish shade composed of blue and gray and amber specks, which people call hazel, she's not angry any more.

"All right," she said, "we'll be Special Agents."

"Nothing like that! Just tourists alerted to be extra observant."

"Sure," she smiled. "I realize. Only—you'll play that role as if you were a master spy. Did you buy any disguises on the way home?"

"Frankly," I said, "nuts! Also, crap! Also——"

"I know," she grinned. And she said the rest of them.

We had made our farewell to the kids. They'd brought the wonderful little baby to the hotel for a night, and we'd had a sitter, and the sitter had called the parents from dinner at Don-the-Beachcomber's. Both went, though only Karen was needed. We'd drunk a bottle of champagne together and put a lei on Karen and another on the baby—since it was Valentine's Day as well as Ted's one-month anniversary. Besides, Ricky and I had missed an as-advertised lei welcome to Hawaii.

Ricky had a pain in her heart about leaving them—as I had. There is nothing, after all, precisely like a first grandchild.

The parting occurred a day and a night before our departure because Tap had to be at the Base early every morning and they lived on that "windward side."

Ours is a very affectionate family. It is a close and confiding family. But most people tend to assume, from our outward behavior, that we are too matter of fact. We don't meet one another at airports—we arrive by ourselves and take cabs to our homes or to hotels. We don't yell or weep on re-encounter, even if we haven't seen each other for a long time. It's seldom any one Wylie cries in front of any other. We don't even write often—though when we do our letters run for pages and contain everything in our minds and our hearts. If there's trouble or sorrow in the family we sustain each other. We are quite practical—and we are not sentimentalists—but we love each other.

So the kids had gone for practical reasons and that part of our journey, which had caused us to begin it, was over—till we go back, or they come to the "mainland."

We had a dinner we expected to be lonely and quite sad. It wasn't.

In the hotel dining room were several Japanese-American waitresses we'd come to know a little, and to like. There was a

Japanese-American headwaitress who was lovely, intelligent and very sweet. And that night, a Hawaiian orchestra played.

We were invested with leis, after all.

When they heard we were leaving on the ten o'clock plane, the "dining room girls" made us promise to send them a card from Tokyo. (We sent it.) And they put around our necks not a lei apiece, but three apiece. Moreover, the exquisite headwaitress kissed us both with all the diners watching, women in the raised-brow belief that so much "aloha" was show-offish—all men envious. The girls also asked us to name our favorite Island songs and the orchestra played every one.

When we left I tipped the musicians. The lovely, lovable headwaitress tried to refuse the tip I pressed on her. We were conspicuous under the tropical decorations at the dining room entrance. But Ricky suddenly and impulsively kissed the Japanese girl. And the girl, whom we'll never forget and maybe even see again, but whose name we do not know, blushed as beige-pink as a vanda, and kissed Ricky back. . . .

In the salon of the Stratocruiser, towards midnight, Ricky and I had a couple of highballs and some sandwiches. By and by the plane's captain joined us and we talked about this and that—the collected anecdotes of flying, of passengers who got drunk and pets that escaped from the baggage compartment, which interest people who ride on planes and men who fly them.

Presently, there came a tremendous hammering. The startled skipper exclaimed, "What's that?" He stared at us as if we were engineers. The pounding overhead was repeated.

He was gone in another second and back in a few minutes. "Generator out," he reported laconically. "Engineer was trying to get the housing off and reset it. No dice. But we've got plenty of spare electrical power."

We went to our berths after that, took sleeping pills and drowsed off in the droning darkness.

Hours and hours later, I woke because something had changed: a rhythm, a sound, some sensory constant. We were coming down; the propeller-pitch had been shifted. I poked my head out to see Ricky's tousled, ebony-silver curls and her sleepy eyes—eyes which, I sometimes tell her, look like large, green olives. We grinned. Soon I jockeyed for a place at the stainless steel washbowls in the crowded men's room.

The plane landed.

We had breakfast on Wake Island in a restaurant rebuilt after a typhoon had blown the atoll bare—a year or two ago. The morning was fair and hot.

In time, the generator was replaced and we and the plane that looks like a winged whale took off for Japan.

A sunless afternoon. The sky was like dirty glass and haze dimmed the Japanese earth as we approached. Even so, I could see steep hills with trees upon them—random, warped pines and leafless hardwoods. The hills, nubbly and eroded, had the precise contour of hills in Japanese prints. I'd believed those drawings exhibited a convention or mannerism peculiar to Japanese artists. Now, suddenly, I saw they'd sketched their land as it was. It surprised me somehow, and somehow brought to mind the childhood idea that the colors on maps indicate the ground colors of the nations they delineate—as if every land except our own were magical. Japan had a Japanese topography, that was certain!

Warning lights came on.

The flaps went down.

The plane bounced in the cold mist. It had been warm in Hawaii the evening before, torrid on Wake Island. Now, it was winter in a smoggy mill city—the weather contaminated and verging on snow.

We raced past a hangar, or what was left of it: a rusted steel frame that sagged like a worn-out wire trash burner. An unplanned war memorial.

Ricky turned, smiled at me.

I knew why.

Twenty years before, in the capital of Poland, my prior love of travel came to an end so terrible that afterward I could not bring myself to voyage farther from America than the Bahamas, which can almost be seen from Miami, or Cuba, or Bermuda. I was afraid of going beyond—with a nightmarish, un-

conquerable fear. The mere thought of a trip even to Paris—
where I'd once lived—would make me sweat and shake just as the
thought of becoming a steeple jack would stickily shatter someone morbidly afraid of height.

Ricky had not traveled outside our continent before we'd
married. So, whenever anyone talked of adventures in Naples,
beauty in Panama, or shopping in London, Ricky grew wistful
and usually volunteered in a quiet voice, "I've never been anywhere." To Ricky, Hawaii had seemed too much like home for
that exotic "somewhere" that she had never seen, smelled, tasted,
listened to and possessed. But now, we had wheels on Japanese
earth: she was, at last, "somewhere," by her own definition.

And the man beside her was not—as yet, anyhow—showing
signs of terror due to his violation of a formidable phobia.
Ricky's smile was to encourage me, if this landing stirred that
sickly dread. I could detect no panic, though I might have sweat
if I'd known how unexpectedly the hideous beginning of my fear
would be recapitulated. But that happened later, and I shall later
explain what frightened me of travel.

Ricky's smile was also for herself: from this moment, she
would not say—softly—"I've never been anywhere."

3
Tokyo

We assembled our hand baggage. We put on the overcoats, mufflers and gloves abruptly returned by the stewardesses.

Like everyone on board, we were a little stunned by the long flight from Hawaii and Wake Island. Planes, even more than transcontinental trains, set one down with a specific disorientation and a particular debility. I cannot say whether those symptoms are occasioned by the motor noise or the peculiar confinement of a plane which obliges one to sit in the space of a big barrel almost continually for the whole of a day or night. They may even come from some unconscious stress owing to travel through a medium for which man is not prepared by evolution.

The very advantage of the plane, that it takes you appalling distances in brief intervals, may cause the aftermath of haunted slight depression. Rape of time and devastation of distance leaves most older people with some such morbid process though the young do not seem to suffer.

The door of the plane opened to let Japanese health authorities enter.

Two men in rather shabby uniforms walked along the aisle and peered at us. We looked at them. Health authorities in foreign lands (and our own land) are forever making such inspections. I suppose, if Ricky had had a red mottling on her face, if I'd been unconscious, if the man next to us had been in convulsions or hemorrhaging, these doctors would notice and take steps. But they certainly cannot and do not observe incipient or unobtrusive contagion.

These, like all, were satisfied with what they did—or didn't—see.

People rose, spilled things from overhead racks, bumped their heads, struck other people with brief cases—and edged into the aisle. The door opened again and they surged toward it.

Ricky and I (as usual) stayed in our seats: we dislike to be shoved.

Then the second, unexpected "phase" of our vacation began:

Before anybody reached the exit, a voice called, "Will Mr. and Mrs. Wylie please get off first?"

We looked at each other in astonishment: nothing explained this sudden priority. But we snatched our "on board" bags and jammed through the palpably irritated people.

It was cold outdoors—about forty degrees.

We reached the landing on the wheeled steps and were yelled at again: "Mr. and Mrs. Wylie?"

I nodded. Ricky turned.

"Hold it!" the same voice commanded.

We stood there. Below, in a scattered group, were a dozen men aiming newspaper cameras. Flash bulbs commenced to wink dazzlingly. It was the sort of thing I'd seen happen to other people. Ricky and I had been photographed by one newspaper man at a time, occasionally two. But never a press corps.

"Okay!" an American voice yelled. "Come on down!"

We came on down. I felt stunned. Ricky winked at me and said, "There's a Japanese edition of *Reader's Digest*, Phil."

"You," I murmured, "go to hell."

Then we were on the ground and the little eyeball-piercing lights were going again. Young Japanese wearing thin business suits were all around us, saying, in accents that would have baffled me even if they hadn't spoken in unison, such things as:

"Your first trip Jopon?"

"Where at what hotel you stay?"

"You write books, yes, how many, what title?"

"You plan article about Japanese people?"

"Write big novel maybe our country?"

I gave a brief résumé of my disappointing lack of interesting purpose and I recited—then, by request, spelled out—the titles of some books I'd written. I heard Ricky tell somebody she hadn't been in Japan long enough to say she *liked* it but that she'd read so much about Japan she *expected* to like it very much.

"We're Florida Crackers," I said to the encircling press, to show I, too, could be obscure if I felt like it. "We're not used to cold weather. We want *in!*" I grabbed Ricky's cashmere coat by a convenient fold and propelled her toward a building that loomed in the late-afternoon distance.

Somebody took my handbag. A hand seized mine.

"George Smith," said a beaming, husky young man. "I'm in public relations here, for the air line. Hi!"

The Tokyo press was still writing in notebooks. I shook hands with George and introduced Ricky. "Did you call out this committee?"

George chuckled. "They look at the passenger lists. I showed 'em one of your books that I like, myself. Impressive number of other books listed in the forematter. 'Great American author arriving,' I said."

"Great American author, my seat-beat backside! And think of the 'impressive number of books' by Erle Stanley Gardner!"

George's bright blue eyes twinkled. "If he comes to Tokyo, he would also be a great American author." Then he took a long look at Ricky. People do—men *and* women. "Tired?"

Ricky smiled. "A little."

"I've got my car outside. Take you to the hotel. Follow me. Do what I gesture. Don't talk at all. If talking's necessary—I'll do it."

We felt grateful to George. We did, that is, till he said to the reporters, "Now, boys. The Wylies are bushed. They'll be at the Imperial. If you want long interviews—call me and I'll arrange it." He turned cheerily to me. "Or will I?"

"My God! What can I contribute to the Tokyo *Telegram and Bugle?*"

He said, "You're a famous man. I arranged it. Contribute fame." And he led Ricky toward the distant, warm-looking indoors.

Queues from our plane were waiting for several things: health card inspection, visa scrutiny, passport stamping, the issue of currency books. George hauled us unwillingly to the head of every line.

A customs inspector, evidently waiting for us, came briskly. At his gestured order, I opened one of the lightweight, ultra-strong "flight" suitcases Ricky and I had bought for the trip. (We had three, of the same gray hue, and a national brand. All of them had required repair and reinforcement after the Miami-Hawaii journey; when we reached Florida again, all were badly worn and mine was held together by hotel stickers. It pays the advertiser to advertise.)

The Japanese customs man looked into my suitcase which I had packed guilefully: a top layer of dirty clothes greeted his probing eye, garments exceedingly dirty owing to the muddy windward side of Oahu. As I had anticipated, the man nodded and immediately stuck on a stamp.

George nodded in solemn concurrence, whereupon my wife displayed the authentic Ricky:

Guidebooks had told us how many cigarettes we'd be allowed to bring into Japan as well as how much liquor, what to do about jewelry, and the intricate rest. We had counted our packages. I now had a permissible quota of Chesterfields. The customs man, stamping and marking with speed, said perfunctorily, "Cigarettes?"

We produced our supply; he started stamping each package in purple ink; and Ricky said, wildly for her, "Oh, lord! I forgot!"

From a different source in our luggage she began to produce cigarettes, pack after pack—until we were well over par. The customs man stopped stamping and gave us a transfixed, slightly hostile stare. Ricky turned toward George. "I only just now re-

membered I had these in the shoe bag! I'll throw them away."
She pushed the impermissible surplus toward the official with a
gesture of jettison.

But when you have brought to any customs something beyond or above or different from whatever the law specifies, you
cannot toss your contraband into a waste bin. I guess the only
way to get rid of it without suffering impost, fine, shame or other
penalty is to take a plane back to America, leave the goods there,
and return. Certain countries do allow people to put articles "in
bond." These may be picked up when one leaves. To the best of
my knowledge, however, such "bonding" requires a warehouse
expert who's also good at math and enjoys tax forms.

Only one person I ever heard of beat the world-wide, asinine
rule which prevents travelers from quietly discarding some trivial
item they did not mean to bring into a country illegally and
would far rather forfeit than suffer over.

A man arrived at Idlewild, New York, bearing a forgotten,
illicit fifth of scotch in his satchel. Our customs people wouldn't
let him bring it in—though he offered to pay duty: he had no
importer's license. They would not, like the present Japanese,
permit him to throw it away. He began to feel that he might
have to go to jail and wait for the Treasury Department to make
a special ruling anent his bottle. But while he and the inspector
continued to glare in deadlock, he suddenly picked up the bottle
and let it drop to the concrete floor. He then had no "illegal"
wares to baffle the law or frustrate himself; and even the customs
man is said to have seemed relieved.

Ricky's suggestion that the official throw away the excess
cigarettes was received like an insult to the old samurai tradition.
She suggested paying duty. The man didn't want duty.

What he wanted, as George swiftly understood, was a means
to get two "important" Americans quickly and politely on their
way without losing official "face."

"This lady," George said urgently, "did not know the Japanese regulations. She made a very bad mistake. Perhaps—if you
told her never to do this again, the next time she visits Japan, she
will have learned her lesson."

The official thereupon scowled fiercely at Ricky. As if he had not heard George, he said censoriously, "Madam. This time we be generous. *Another* time—take care to learn our most strict Japanese laws." He broke into a smile and stamped the extra packages.

Porters began grabbing the now-cleared dunnage.

Pleased by this official, who had performed his duty while yet expediting us, I decided to try my Japanese: a little international quid pro quo. The man spoke good English; I would show him that the Japanese are not the only polite people in the world.

During the tumbling night flight across the Pacific, I'd wakened and decided a cup of coffee might restore my slumber. Coffee does, sometimes. So I put on a bathrobe and went to the galley where I was served by the nisei stewardess. The imminence of Japan caused me to ask her how to say "thank you" in Japanese. Many people consider the first phrase one should learn in a foreign language to be "How much?" and the next, "Too much." I learn "Thank you" first. The stewardess wrote down several syllables which I memorized.

Now I spoke them:

"*Adigato gosae masu!*"

I gave it my best Tokyo accent. The man looked at me as if I had lost my mind.

George yanked us out of the airport. He was bent over as if stricken by gallstones.

"What's the matter?" I asked. "What's so funny? I merely said 'thanks' to that old bird."

"You sure as all hell did say 'thanks!' You said the kind of thanks that Japanese use for a great favor performed by a social superior. Something like, 'I throw myself with craven gratitude at your feet!'"

I could hear Ricky chortling. The car started. "How do you say 'thanks' to a waiter, then?"

"Just"—George avoided a man on a bike, two kids, a load of straw and a curious truck with only three wheels: two in back and one in front—"just—'*adigato*.'"

Literary critics have sometimes called me a writer of "purple" English. Turns out, my Japanese is even more so.

In the web of a dingy afternoon we drove toward Tokyo, George laboring through hectic traffic. The street was cobblestoned, the ride rough. People were walking and pedaling bicycles, people with burdens on their backs and heads; bikes, cars, wagons and many tricycle trucks banged along. We passed through a factory area and another with many shops, into the windows of which Ricky and I peered. Through these purlieus tramped women in bright-colored kimonos dulled by the dull day and men in dark kimonos, people with no hats, people wearing straw "coolie" sort, and others with a huge sombrero that seemed to be woven of raffia. Kids in rags. Men and women in Western dress, in work clothes, in every combination of two worlds' styles. All their clothes looked worn and grimy: these truck drivers, cyclists and the rest were working Japanese. People with black hair and "slanted" eyes.

But the general effect was that of the outskirts of our own cities on a wintry day. Only a portion of the architecture and only an occasional shop selling temple offerings, odd viands, or a rainbow-bright selection of artificial flowers seemed strange to me when I did not take into close account the Oriental cast of most features. Except for one sight in that area, I did not feel it alien; and the exception had a psychological rather than visual strangeness.

We began to pass buildings that looked like private mansions. They were made of brick and of wood. Some were enclosed by woven bamboo fences. Several had small yards and winter-browned formal gardens where, in summer, there would be brooklets and blossoms. Miniature wooden bridges arched over the now-drained watercourses. The grim environs had deposited soot upon those modern-looking houses so that even their gardens, like the people in bright garments, were overlaid with grubbiness made even grubbier by the weather. All around the ornate, incongruent structures stretched slums.

"What are those?" Ricky asked.

"Some of the fanciest geisha houses in Tokyo," George said. . . .

Differing buildings piled up around us after that—stores, dwellings fenced from the street, warehouses and wholesale markets. Trade names and shop signs had been painted, in the manufacturing area; now, their equivalents began to glow with light. We soon saw a shopping street, with department stores, and sidewalks crowded to the curbs by hurrying people. An electric train roared over an elevated track. Neon, argon, sodium, mercury vapor spangled the Tokyo sky with Japanese characters. But even then—though fascinated, bemused—I could not find much sensation of the bizarre.

It doesn't take great differences to create a sense of foreignness for most tourists, I guess. Tropical sun and shade, Spanish architecture and unreadable electric signs make even Havana a land so not USA that nothing Cuban gives most visitors from the United States a sense of identification. But what continually surprises me about foreign cities—Paris, Rostov-om-Don or Tokyo— is the similarity of ways and cityscapes.

That may be an acquired point of view and not, perhaps, innate in anybody. For the first time I saw Manhattan it seemed very alien compared with towns, villages and cities of the Middle West. Quebec, when I first visited it, was as different as imagined Mars. And my initial view of Europe—the harbor front of Le Havre, seen through a porthole—gave me, too, that overpowering shock of otherness. Only gradually did I come to feel identities and parallels more than differences. Unfamiliar features, tongues, signs, shapes of buildings, roof styles, contents of markets and clothes slowly became of minor importance to me. What now impresses is the universality of human ends and means and being.

We might almost have been entering Chicago, Philadelphia or Cleveland.

"I'm not going to take you straight to the hotel," George suddenly said. "There's a spot I want you to see on the way. It's really choice! We'll have a drink there."

I silenced an incipient demurrer because Ricky was nodding with what I thought to be pleasure. It was, again, just Ricky. She wanted, as much as I, to get to a warm, private room where she could unpack, bathe and spend a few hours free of the company even of this single, amenable stranger. But I found out her real wish later, since, in all our years together, I've not learned to discriminate reliably between such actual desires and her warm-hearted manners.

George swung into a great thoroughfare walled by impressive buildings. Some displayed English as well as Japanese signs: offices of air lines, shops catering to foreigners, American shipping corporations. We parked in a place where people thronged amongst honking, zigzagging cars—an alleylike street lined by little shops and restaurants that had a Japanese-tearoom look. Big, gay lanterns glowed above bamboo-framed doors and it was hard to believe this reality was not some byway in a Western city turned Oriental to create a bohemian or arty atmosphere.

We were conducted down the main street and into a restaurant. A Japanese headwaiter, in a dinner jacket, bowed. A hat check girl bowed—and took our wraps. From beyond a sunken room, which was filled with young men and women, came music like that of Russian balalaika. We went up a flight of carpeted stairs and were shown to a table. Alongside it was a metal rail and beyond that—an abyss. Small lamps gleamed on other tables where more young Japanese were drinking tea, or coffee, beer or cocktails.

A waitress came, kimono rustling and obi bobbing. George fumbled in his pockets, drew out a few unfamiliar-shaped bills, and grinned. "I wanted you to see this place. But"—he counted —"it turns out I've only got yen enough for three coffees. Hope you don't mind! Had to take some V.I.P.'s to lunch . . ."

I said, not unnaturally, "Don't worry about that. Order what you like and I'll pick up the tab. We're indebted to you in a dozen ways already."

His answering smile was broad. "You'll pay—with what?"

"I've got a pocketful of travelers' checks!"

"Any yen?"

"Not yet. But——"

"Then—we're having three coffees." He repeated the order to the waitress. "You can't cash a travelers' check in a restaurant. Only in an authorized place." I committed that widely useful lesson to memory. He gestured. "Look!"

Up from the "abyss" at our side came a huge elevator, gaudily decorated but like a freight lift in that it had neither sides nor a top. On it sat an orchestra industriously playing American popular songs. The majority of instruments were mandolins, which explained the balalaika sound effect. The lift stopped when it came level with our floor.

George was delighted. "Did you ever see anything like it in your life? This place has three floors. The band rides up and down—playing for one floor at a time. It's an all-Chinese orchestra and it plays American tunes—in Tokyo!"

I had, indeed, never seen (or heard) anything like it in my life.

The coffee was first rate, guidebooks to the contrary notwithstanding. And George drove us, finally, to Frank Lloyd Wright's earthquake-proof Imperial Hotel.

I'd read a good deal—as who has not?—about that engineering masterpiece: a modern hotel built on foundations sunk in Tokyo's mud, contrived so that during quakes the edifice stands still while its underpinnings slide. Somehow, I'd envisaged the Imperial as a Statlerlike skyscraper. But it is low and as rambling as a boxwood maze and made of brick, ornamented with a volcanic stone heavily—almost monstrously—carved. Smog has darkened the yellowish brick; time and Tokyo's quakes have chipped the sculpture. A contemporary architect (however much Mr. Wright would resent the adjective) would be horrified by the waste space within; but the Imperial is very comfortable; and I was amused that my image of the Imperial as an American product was so inaccurate—that its reality was more strange to me than the strangeness of downtown Tokyo.

Ricky and I unpacked. We bathed—in a rough-tiled tub which left checkerboard imprints on the backside of the long soaker—a tub with piping as complex as the snakes around old Laocoön. I went down to the cashier's office and got some yen for my dollar checks.

That was a relief. I find it not just inconvenient, but psychologically distressing, to be without negotiable funds. Like many a grown-up minister's son, I have a pathological fear of any cash shortage; and like any American tourist, I'd been indignant to find my dollars nonexpendable.

George invited us to dinner that night with his wife and son. We'd expected to eat in ignorant solitude. Now, suddenly, we had friends and would foregather in a "tempura place"—whatever that might mean. . . .

It meant one of those restaurants with a lantern at the door. A pretty, interior "patio" with paving, pebbles and stunted trees. Beyond, rooms with wooden counters and wondrous smells.

The waitresses here also wore kimonos and obis—bustlelike cushions tied on with broad sashes, at which I later heard several American women laugh—American women who were doubtless wearing girdles and possibly "falsies." The young ladies bowed and bowed and smiled, but seemed upset when we entered the patio (which was chilly) sat down on low benches in front of low tables, and ordered sake. That caused a conference. Presently, however, they brought sake—hot, in earthen pitchers—and small cups. After a while, four Japanese gentlemen came from a steamy room, sat down—and were served the biggest strawberries I have ever seen, with a little cream, and powdered sugar. Then we understood the "conference": we'd asked for sake in a room set aside for dessert. Even George and George's attractive wife didn't know that rite.

The management was polite about our faux pas and the four gentlemen regarded us amiably—as if they, too, had taken their sake in this wrong room. Nobody snickered, nobody raised an eyebrow; not then, or at any subsequent blunder; so for a while I wondered uncomfortably if their conscious courtesy rose from the fact that they were conquered people and we, the conquerors. I learned later that they lack such sentiment of conquest and merely have remarkable manners.

In due course we were conducted to a counter and seated in a row, on stools. There were no other white people in the restaurant. Facing us stood a chef. Laid out in neat rows beside him was almost every type of raw sea food one could name.

Bowls were put in front of us by the bowing girls.

(Within a day or two, I found that I bowed my way through the hotel and in and out of eating places. Many tourists complained that "all their bowing and scraping" was "craven" or "servile." Those were, of course, tourists who could not change themselves enough to bow back. For there's nothing servile or craven about politeness, even in forms unfamiliar to people from Bucyrus.)

On George's instructions, we put soy sauce and grated radish in our bowls. The chef held up—on chopsticks—one morsel of seafood after another. George nodded, after questioning us, our serial acceptance of lobster, shrimp, smelts, strips of larger fish, squid, octopus, crab fragments, mussels and eel.

"Our chef," George said with relish, "is one of the best tempura cooks in Japan. He's published a book about it."

The chef smiled, though I do not believe he understood. Morsels of the selected delicacies bubbled in stainless steel kettles of hot fat.

Ricky and I stirred together the soy sauce and ground radish, emulating the Smiths. We used chopsticks. Knives and forks were not part of the restaurant equipment.

On little plates covered with paper, deep-fried bits of seafood were set out by the chef. We'd each be served a mouthful or two of lobster. Then a shrimp apiece, or two. Then a strip of squid. These were dipped in the sauce and eaten, very hot. And all were delicious. The Smiths watched covertly to see how Ricky and I would react to certain items of this menu: octopus, for example.

Many Americans are modest gastronomes who willingly, or at least gingerly, experiment with new foods. Our country is made up of diverse peoples and divided into distinct regions. So the man from Iowa may be as fond of "Southern cooking" as his own. He doubtless enjoys chop suey, relishes an occasional Italian dinner and may lunch on chopped lamb with rice, cooked in olive oil and wrapped in grape leaves—consuming it with gusto, as if born in Asia Minor. Furthermore, modern methods are bringing into every domestic supermarket more and more different foods—exotic, but delicious and increasingly popular.

But a great many Americans, unfortunately for the travelers among them, are finicky, palate-bound, even neurotic, about foods. They will eat potatoes, say, but only French fried or mashed and with ketchup. When such persons go abroad they will find (to their horror and hunger) great cities without mashed or French fried potatoes and whole nations without ketchup. A variety of viands will be offered—highly palatable to most, but to them, repugnant. So their trip will be ceaselessly blighted and they may, owing to that single prejudice, take home a poor opinion of everything abroad.

I used to be just such a narrow eater—a ketchup compulsive, revolted by any unfamiliar dish. Long months spent in the North Country where we hunted meat for food, cured me of a repugnance for liver, brains, sweetbreads. A trip through Russia in 1936 made me able to eat anything in extremis: food there was often odd—and filthy. Helping to test survival gear for lifeboats and rafts during the war gave me a taste even for raw fish. So my stomach is at home abroad. And Ricky is not just enthusiastic but almost reckless in the business of trying new foods—even agave grubs! So we easily passed the "Smith test."

While we were devouring tempura, a small thing happened that gave me an unexpected sense of Oriental affinity.

The chef, who had been beaming at our enthusiastic consumption, suddenly beamed even more, pointed at me—and spoke to George.

"He says," George told me, leaning around Ricky, "that he's almost never seen a Westerner use chopsticks so well."

"Me?"

"You. He says you hold them perfectly. He says he watched you pick up a bit of lobster as small as a rice grain." The chef's head bobbed and he spoke more Japanese. George went on. "He wants to know where you learned."

I was pleased—and baffled. I hadn't had chopsticks in my

hand for years—and then rarely. Maybe the sake had relaxed my anxiousness about table manners and my reflexes had done the rest. "Tell him that anybody can eat with chopsticks after a minute's effort. I've tried it a few times in New York."

George told him but the chef wasn't satisfied. He kept watching me eat with an expression at once perplexed and pleased. We'd been in Tokyo a week—and chopsticks had become casually familiar to Ricky, too—before I remembered.

When I was about eight years old, missionaries from China had stayed at the manse while they raised money for their work, in father's church. Either to show off their Oriental lore, or to amuse the Wylie youngsters, those missionaries had broken out chopsticks and taught us to use them. My brother and sister, younger than I, had soon wearied of the pastime. But I'd stuck to it until it proved (some forty-five years later) I'd mastered the etiquette. And from such trifling things can come the beginning of a liking for alien customs—and people. . . .

We went home that night through the Ginza, which is a district, though there's a Ginza Street, too. It swarmed with humanity. Signs on the fantastic-topped stores and theaters were beautiful, as are all electric signs when you cannot read them. Our stomachs were full of good food; our heads, with oddments of new information of which some did seem fairly peculiar.

The oddest was the fact that, until our armies occupied Japan, even Tokyo had virtually no street names. The army put up signs and gave certain thoroughfares lettered names. But even today, nobody "knows" Tokyo. Only districts are named and while maps are to be had they chart a wordless, numberless labyrinth. If you take a cab in Tokyo, you generally have to be able not only to speak Japanese but to direct your driver precisely to the address you wish to reach. A cabdriver may be picked up a mile from it—and not know where your hotel is! Not even the Imperial Hotel, I discovered—and not even if you'd learned to pronounce it: "Tai-koku."

I still do not understand that! The average Japanese city dweller must know mere trails through his metropolis: the way to get to work, the route to his friends' homes, the road to shops

273366

LIBRARY
FLORIDA STATE UNIVERSITY
TALLAHASSEE, FLORIDA

and markets and a few other byways essential to his living. The rest of the city is evidently wilderness, as is pathless jungle to wild animals.

We slept well. The morning was blue and sunny; the sky, as we opened the French windows of our spacious room, polka-dotted by colored advertising balloons that rode above the fanciful tops of Tokyo's big buildings. Here and there were tall towers. I assumed they were left over from the war: emplacements for antiaircraft guns. But that was wrong; they were for fire watching.

Tokyo is, largely, a wooden city with paper walls and windows—fragile, save where it is modernized and westernized. Some eight million persons live there, in the crowded squalor of poverty and the still-crowded splendor of riches. The bamboo, rice paper and teak houses burn quickly, even when not purposely set afire by napalm. Comparatively few citizens have telephones. So the towers serve for fire spotting just as similar towers in America are used to spot "smokes" in forests.

Ricky and I dressed, had an American breakfast in our room and went forth to see. The guidebooks said that just walking anywhere in Japan was itself an adventure. In that, they understated; we spent a day and an evening Tokyo-gazing, agog as any tourist.

Mr. Io was a rare Japanese, a self-made man. Though the Japanese are not rigidly locked in life stations, like Hindus owing to their caste system, prewar Japan was feudal. No ready path existed by which even an accomplished individual could rise. But Mr. Io had made a beginning before the war; and afterward, he achieved thoroughgoing success. His progress stemmed partly from the fact that he had learned good English as a boy. Early in our occupation he noted various products which our troops employed and the Japanese admired. He set up, at first in a small way, to manufacture copies for domestic use. That enterprise led to the ownership of several factories and dominion over numerous home industries.

Mr. Io had also made the reverse observation: certain Japanese goods and gadgets unfamiliar to American soldiers were much appreciated by them. Again, he profited.

Ricky and I met him in his offices because he was a friend of a Mrs. Cane—an American woman to whom we had a letter. Mr. Io liked to entertain visiting Americans, she said. Furthermore, to my astonishment, he had read, and he treasured in his library, three of my fishing books. His office was like that of an American executive. Probably he had copied the business quarters of a customer in the United States. His secretary and clerks spoke English almost as well as he.

We had a cup of tea. Then, with Mrs. Cane and Mr. Io's secretary, a Miss (I think) Gamoshishi (whom we were told to call "Lu"), we were escorted to Mr. Io's limousine (a Cadillac) and taken on a tour of the city.

Mr. Io and I sat with the driver, in front.

He was a tall man—considerably taller than I: perhaps six feet two. He had an austere face with a square chin and a long, somewhat thin nose. His eyelids bore the fold of tissue that gives an impression of slant; but his eyes were as wide and open as a Westerner's and not quite as brown as mine. He was lean and hard; it showed in the smooth way he walked.

"Lu," as tall as Ricky, which is fairly tall, was flower-pretty. She helped to answer our queries—and subsequently, on loan from our host, became our part-time interpreter and social secretary.

Mr. Io talked with me about fishing as we drove through the now-familiar downtown section of Tokyo. He had fished in many places in the world and caught as many big ones as I. . . .

He was not a typical Japanese. But since our relations with Mr. Io were to make several contributions to Ricky's and my understanding, it is useful to consider the common and stupid connotation of "typical," where it refers to foreigners. There are many tall Japanese, for example. Many do not have the slightly compressed noses associated with Orientals. Not a few have eyes that slant less than the eyes of certain American models, in great demand by fashion photographers. Moreover, Mr. Io was certainly not yellow in color.

How, and why, white people came to call others red and
yellow I can comprehend—but not condone. "Yellow" races are
not yellow at all, as any American could see in any Chinatown.
Most of them merely have, in their skins, more of a pigment
called melanin than most of us. But they are sometimes whiter
than many sallow Americans; and they are seldom as dark as the
average sun-tanned lifeguard.

I do not mean that Mr. Io looked like Gary Cooper. But I
do mean that if he sat on a Coney Island (or California) beach,
in Jantzen swim trunks, wearing a rayon sports shirt with a
bathing-beauty pattern, eating a hot dog on a bun and holding a
bottle of beer, a hundred good Americans would pass him by,
dozens noting he was a fine figure of manhood but only one or
two observing the slight signs which showed his relationship to
the "yellow" race. And those who noticed would doubtless be unable to say whether the revealed "blood" was Japanese, Chinese,
Korean, Filipino, Hawaiian, or what. Only the Negro (alas for
us!) is so heavily pigmented that others can usually distinguish
him. But no Negro, no person, is "typical" . . . !

By the time we reached a certain market street which Mr. Io
wanted us to visit, he and I were well acquainted. Fishermen have
that faculty.

He ordered the car parked. We walked down a wide, cement-
paved "street" where traffic was forbidden and people streamed
between two rows of gaudy shops. Ricky said, "It makes me think
of something at home." I guessed: a carnival midway. She answered that I was right—and noticed some hand-carved tortoise
shell in a window. She investigated with Mrs. Cane and Lu.

"Not far from here," Mr. Io said to me, "is a very beautiful
Shinto shrine. Would you like to see it?"

I went into a shop where Ricky already had two bowing
women busy with tortoise shell adornments and said we were
going on to the shrine.

A long flight of steps led up to an immense, pagoda-roofed
structure. Its roof was scarlet, the frieze beneath, gold. We
climbed the steps slowly. I looked back at the midway—a pageant
of men and women in kimonos and a medley of voices, tempo set

by the geta-sound which is like the rattle of bamboos in wind. Mr. Io led the way amongst people milling in the shrine.

He had fallen silent. Under the ornate roof at what corresponded to an altar, he bowed gravely.

So I bowed.

Mr. Io scowled a little and moved to a group of golden symbols inside a red-roped square. Above them, folded paper hung over a central image. Whether the image was gold, or gilded, I do not know. It was a sculptural abstraction that resembled an Alexander Calder stabile. Mr. Io bowed again.

And I did.

Now, his discomfiture was plain: he thought my emulation a mockery. Nevertheless, he went solemnly to the place for contributions, took out a pocketbook and tossed a folded yen-note amongst the heaped offering which consisted mainly of coins.

So I took out my bill clip and I, too, added a paper bill.

Like Mr. Io, I bowed again and backed away.

He strode angrily to the head of the colossal staircase and waited, iron-faced.

I said, "I hope you don't mind that I, also, made your ancestors an honoring bow? They must have been fine people."

His face relaxed slightly. "Of course I did not mind."

"Or added my small offering? After all—there is, in your religion—the great principle I believe."

"You know anything about my religion?"

"Something," I said. "Wait a minute." I thought and then quoted: " 'There exists no highest deity beyond that in the human mind.' "

He muttered, "Shinto-Denji!"

I nodded.

He looked back at the shrine symbols and said, almost as if confessionally, "I also go, at times, to the Buddhist temples."

"Why not?"

His eyes then lifted. For an instant, they searched mine. He asked, presently, "How do you—an American—quote Shinto-Denji?"

"A man," I said, "is born, first. Next, he asks, *Who am I?*

From that, he must soon ask, *Who is God?* His parents—that is to say, his ancestors—will have given him one, particular answer. But if he is man enough, he will look as best he is able at *all* the answers of *all* men. And he will look within himself, also, for answers that may be there."

My arm was seized by fingers like wrenches. "Do you believe in God?"

"I believe I am *part* of God."

"So do I!" His voice was almost exultant. "It is the same! I believe my *conscience* is part of God."

"Then we agree. And that is why . . ." I looked back at the golden mandala on the altar to finish my statement.

"My friend," the Japanese whispered, "I thank you."

He bowed toward the icons again—and then at *me*.

So I bowed to him.

The words, perhaps, give no concept of his tension, of his initial fear that he was being shamed or of his astonishment that I was not making obscure fun of his worship.

He started down the steps rather stumblingly, stopped midway and muttered, "I *still* do not understand. *Shinto!* An American!"

"There is the state aspect of Shinto that I think is limiting," I said. "The pantheism, I feel in my way. The animistic part— I cannot sense in the Shinto way. The ethics—I honor. The symbols—that crisscross paper, the abstract image—that represent integration of the contradictions by meditation—I understand them, Mr. Io, very well. And the lotos, the sun symbol—the reconciliation of opposites, life source—all the others——"

He had been nodding jerkily. "I see you do."

We walked quite a distance before either of us said anything more. Then, as if he were weary, he leaned on a fence made of peeled logs and looked toward a grove of winter-bare trees. Beyond, was a covered street and sprawling bazaar, where Japanese were sitting, cross-legged, selling at auction bright-dyed everlasting flowers, ball-point pens, fans, beads, candy, cakes, neckties, geta, Western footgear. I also looked, and pondered.

No experience in life moves me so much as understanding

that comes from the love that is life and opposes the fear that is, not just death, but also worse: our human destructiveness, our vengeance for mortality. By such understanding I mean, also, that rise of appreciation, that affection which follows shared awareness, whether it involve a pair of persons—or millions. Some new, thitherto unconscious truth is born and divided among people, by that phenomenon.

But if I was touched, Mr. Io was touched even more.

The small experience also seemed sad to me, in a way, and slightly incredible. He was a very well-educated man. Surely, he knew there were hundreds of Americans who had a far more elaborate learning in the religions and philosophies of the East, than I! And—surely—some American he'd known must have been able to behave with him, in his place of worship, as Mr. Io would undoubtedly have behaved in that American's holy edifice.

But maybe not.

Maybe not . . . !

For most men it is a long, inconceivable way from a Shinto shrine to a Christian church. A long (and usually presumed impossible way) from Hashai Io to Philip Wylie, even though, as Elmer Davis says, "We were *born* free." The distance is not actual, however, but only a space invented by pride and measured with the cruelty of pride: *my God is truer so I am your superior and untouchable by you.*

Mr. Io began to talk, quietly. "It is attractive here. The people shopping—and just enjoying the sunshine—in so pleasant a place! These new stalls and the gay things people can buy. The bazaar—and the pretty covered street, which I will show you. Yes. Attractive!"

"So many things in Japan are attractive that, in my country, wouldn't be. They'd be utilitarian, perhaps, and clean. But nobody would plant that tree there—and nobody would make a little garden in such a spot as—" I gestured.

"You burned it," he said flatly, coldly.

"The war?"

His strong arm swept the colorful district. "You cannot possibly imagine! My shrine—that gorgeous, peaceful place—is all

new. It was burned to the ground! This market—the bazaar—
the flower market—homes—everything! And there were only narrow streets leading out. So most of the people who were here
burned with this area. To death. Fire poured from the sky. Tokyo
shook with bombs from 'Mr. B.' and smelled like a forgotten fry-
ing pan. Smoke and burnt people. *You did that!*"

"I know." I looked up at the sky. "Quite a few young men I
was friendly with were also killed here—by you. They flew those
B29's. They doubtless fell—some of them—right here—in their
planes that *you* set afire."

"We were defending ourselves." He spoke frigidly.

I knew what was happening within him.

By showing repect for his religion and by revealing I understood what I respected, I had made him happy in a new-found
way. So, now, he was emboldened to test on me another agony
that under ordinary circumstances he might not have acknowledged in a lifetime's acquaintanceship. My insight had given him
a pleasure he could not entirely trust, hence could not bear:
surely, you Americans are not capable of complete sympathy?
That doubt had caused this attempt to raise a doubt—and pain
—in me: to anger me, as a further probe.

But, in this new connection, I had an understanding that
was appalled by the picture his words evoked but lacked "complete sympathy."

So I replied, speaking as flatly as he, "About ten days ago,
Mr. Io, I was standing on a small area of buckled steel that
barely rose above high tide. It had been put there by Japanese
bombers, on the bottom of Pearl Harbor, without warning and
while your statesmen in Washington were pledging peace. That
steel was the top of a coffin under which a lot of our sailors lie.
Near it were the sunken wrecks of other ships. I don't like war.
I think it shows, not that we are still primitive—that's too easy.
I think war shows we are somewhat insane; for we could be
men now, not beasts. We could have and know Selves. But we
Americans have 'face' too. We are generous—more so than anybody, I believe." I looked straight at him. "You shouldn't have
sunk the *Arizona* that way, Mr. Io—or all those other ships. When

you mention the horror here—the dead, the frenzy—and tell me how you remade it all so beautifully—you should also tell yourselves about the crime that got your sky full of Americans. You made the mistake of angering America."

He didn't answer at all.

By and by I looked at him. He was crying.

Japanese do not weep easily.

But I do not believe that they are "inscrutable," either—that their emotions invariably turn their faces to blank bronze. I think, instead, that they have a useful way of hiding feeling when they are sure—or even when they fear—that what they feel will not be understood. "Oriental impassivity," I think is but that. And every culture has a comparable way of dealing with dread-of-ridicule, or even incomprehension.

Many Americans laugh off all such distress, as if they were empty within, idle-minded, trivial, unhurtable or stupid. Englishmen outstare the discomfitor, eyes glacial, lips stiff. Latins rage aloud and in public, blowing off the hurt in what seems uncontrolled emotion and is but ritual.

One process, only, underlies those varied responses.

After a while, rather gingerly, he took my arm. "Let us find the ladies," he said.

We drove past some of Tokyo's great public buildings that afternoon. As we rode, we talked about the problem of population in Japan. There are so many people on the islands already that not every mouth can be filled and the number of those people is rapidly increasing. The land is already used for agriculture to a degree unimaginable in America. But land is not enough. The sea remains. But waters in which Japanese are permitted to fish are constantly diminished by ourselves, by Canadians, Russians and Red Chinese. Prewar trade with China, which would yield food if restored, is now restricted.

"We widely advocate, we teach birth control," Mr. Io said. "We practice abortion in Japan—cheap, hygienic, safe abortion. But the population still rises. We are beginning to want to eat, far more than to want additional Japanese. So we are beginning to fear ourselves a little. The next step is to hate each other, is it not? I often wonder"—he smiled faintly—"what the Roman Catholics would do, if their faith obliged their members to tear down less-necessary-cathedrals so as to use the land for more-necessary-gardens."

Mr. Io's remark was another psychological venture toward intimacy: he could, of course, be sure by then that I was either no Catholic or an odd and liberal one; but he could not be sure of Ricky's religion. What he wanted to achieve was further insight into the dimensions of our belief. In that effort, he had also inadvertently implied certain limits of his own.

When he asked his rueful, ironic question, he was gesturing our attention toward the exterior of a Japanese traditional theater. But his eyes flicked toward mine to see how I'd respond to an implication that Catholics are less rational than Shintoists.

I laughed.

There is something preposterous to me (as to many Catholics) in the detail and rigidity of their dogma—something a little embarrassing to them (and ominous-seeming to me) about the too-common Catholic custom of insisting that all sex mores and laws in their environment correspond with compulsions and tabus which they regard (like most "true believers") as beyond assail and as the law of God: for it is the "righteous," alas, who push more people around than the "wicked."

I had laughed.

But I said, "It took me a long, long time, Mr. Io, to discover it was possible for any Catholic to use his rites and symbols as a means to higher awareness and a way toward truer truth. It once seemed to me the Catholic style of conscience—which you call your Godly essence—belonged too much to the Church and too little to its members. Catholics generally confuse self-righteousness with rights. So do most Protestants, most pious people. They are often compassionate; but where conflict with reality is concerned, they usually do not know the meaning of truth or tolerance."

"You hold faith in pretty low regard."

"Not really." I thought that over as Mr. Io described classical Nipponese theater for Ricky, and until the car stopped again.

Mrs. Cane, Lu, Ricky, our host and I, then walked down a "covered" street, a long thoroughfare with a glass roof, a street not unlike a vast and lofty greenhouse. Beneath it were shops and markets patronized, or merely appraised, by crowds of bright-clad women and dun-clad men—people who were hungry, needed clothing, wanted ornaments to wear, or flowers, or sought artificial home decorations—a thousand things to purchase there, or covet.

After we had admired this stagy, but practical street, I talked again for I realized Mr. Io wanted me to do so. "Religions have been man's principal means toward increased awareness of cosmos and himself until science and its methods became an even more powerful way to learn the universe, and, lately, the human Self, too. Ever since science brought honesty to objectivity, religion has been obliged steadily to yield in that province. Now that man has begun to explore and learn himself by scientific means—by faith in the human brain coupled with an equal doubt of all past assumptions of that brain—classical religion has become steadily more obsolete in its remaining province: subjectivity. Always religious differences have been the source of human hate, conflict, intolerance and war. Of course, to say that today, I have to include emotional beliefs like Communism as 'religions'—and I do. There is a deep difference between every precise doctrine and the inner nature of every man; that discrepancy makes the believer fear, hence hate, *himself*. In that terrible truth about belief, the honest mind will discern the deepest source of our human difficulty. Our animal instinct is repressed by religion, but then it rules men *through* its dogma. Logic is repressed by rituals in the same way, for the same ends that are served by instinct—a force with purpose but no awareness, hence 'unreasoning.'"

"I wish," Mr. Io said rather wistfully, "you'd write that down."

"I've written it many ways. I'll send you the books when I

get home." Thinking of the distance ahead, I almost added, if I get home. "And other men have written it better, before me."

He repeated the words I'd quoted to him: " 'There exists no highest deity beyond that in the human mind.' You mean *that?*"

I said, "I'll settle for that."

Ricky caught up with us and exclaimed, "Look at the cat!"

I thought she was trying to tell me I'd been conducting one of my "interminable, boring monologues." She wasn't—at least, not entirely.

The "cat," which we thereupon stopped to observe, was a drawing-in-oil—a tall, narrow picture by a Japanese artist, framed in unfinished wood and displayed in the window of an art shop. The cat was huge and white. He stalked down the canvas, top to bottom. But his head was lifted and his yellow eyes stared up with implacable concentration at the beholder—like eyes photographed while focused on a camera lens that see you forever and from any angle. The draftsmanship was adroit, even brilliant. The picture had a touch of violence and a hint of the near-comic. No one would expect such feral fixity in a house cat. The simply drawn cat portrait seemed to illustrate all of animal nature that is not inimical to man and not precisely hostile, either, but merely itself and implacable, wherefore extrahuman and, so, *formidable.*

Ricky laughed at the painting. "How *wonderful!*"

"We have," Mr. Io smiled, "some rather clever artists."

Lu, his secretary, gazed earnestly at the cat and her right shoulder shivered visibly. "Whatever it's doing is *bad!* I—sometimes I'm afraid of cats!"

Mrs. Cane had to evade two kimono-wearing Japanese gentlemen, to look. (She often had to do that. For Mrs. Cane, a widow who worked for one of the air lines, is very blonde, very handsome—and six feet tall. Oriental gentlemen, for all their courtesy, often stepped close to her and stared as if she were a female breed they had heard of, but never before seen.)

She examined the cat in the shopwindow—after smiling vaguely at, and side-stepping, the awed men. "It's the work of— I forget everybody's name!—but he's a new one, and a comer.

He'll give a race, in American art stores, to the Jap who makes those marvelous brush drawings of horses!"

I hadn't been aware that Evelyn Cane, who seemed an un-aesthetic, matter-of-fact person, was knowledgeable in modern, Japanese art. But people continually present such pleasant disil-lusionments. I was also interested that she, who knew both Mr. Io and Lu, could say "Jap," which I'd been told was offensive. She didn't offend them. I never took the risk.

Meanwhile, Ricky had been studiously watching me. I realized why, and grinned. "You know that space over the tea table? You always wanted something narrow and high for it."

She gave me two more chances.

"How in the world can we ship it home? It's at least three feet long."

"Must be a way."

"Maybe it costs too much."

"We'll see."

I started for the shop door. Inside, the lady clerks had al-ready commenced their first bows.

Mrs. Cane offered aid. "If you buy it—in fact, whatever you buy—I'll be glad to have mailed for you. Our company has a sensational wrapping service."

The price of the cat portrait, translated from yen, was eight American dollars! We bought it forthwith and waited while it was covered with colored paper and tied with bright ribbon. Mr. Io had his chauffeur carry our purchase to the Cadillac.

"And, of course," Mrs. Cane reminded us, as we came out of the shop, "you won't need to put it in your customs declara-tion."

We hadn't thought of that but in the weeks and countries ahead, we often used the opportunity.

Congress, chary about taxes where imports are concerned, has recently passed a law which enables the tourist to send home, duty free and undeclared, any number of gifts—providing each costs less than ten dollars and no recipient gets more from a single sender than one gift a week. I do not believe our Con-gress minds if such "gifts" are occasionally exchanged later for some other present. We could thus give our cat to a relative—and get it back—or to our maid, who probably would be alarmed by the stalking beast, anyhow, and let us keep it at home.

That piece of legislation has lost little in revenue to USA. But it has given jobs to perhaps a million artisans in other lands.

In every foreign city and town visited by American tourists, there are shops and departments of stores which sell these less-than-ten-dollar gifts. Many such articles are extraordinary. For ten American dollars will buy an incredible amount of Hong Kong embroidery, Thai silk, Indian weaving, of brass hammering in the Arabian countries, or—as here—brushwork by a witty artist.

Ricky found out the secret of the cat's fascination and the reason for the picture when we had hung it at home: "Don't you see?" she said. "That cat is stalking *you!*" I once watched a huge, well-tended cat stalk a Frenchman down a narrow street—to amuse itself, or for practice, or maybe in cold hate. The sight is funny—and disquieting. So is our painting.

Mr. Io said, "It gives me, always, pleasure, to see what foreigners buy in Japan. May I congratulate you, Mrs. Wylie?"

We strolled on out into the diminishing sunlight.

A half-dozen teen-age girls—some in kimonos, two in bobby sox and jeans—loitered beyond the street at the side of a ramshackle building. Its bamboo decoration, once fancy, had partly fallen away and paint hung shredded from its staircase. As I came near, I discovered the girls were smiling at me in a bright, significant manner I couldn't fathom. Two wore their dark hair in pony tails. Like most Japanese kids, they were scrubbed, fresh and pretty. I slowed to observe what I thought were high school girls. They began laughingly to address me.

"What are they saying?"

Mr. Io glanced measuringly at me and warily back at Ricky. "They are asking you to go upstairs with them."

"You mean, they're prostitutes?"

He nodded.

"Be damned!"

"Attractive?" His voice was noncommittal.

"A couple of them—very. But they're just teen-agers!"

The kids began waving, calling, oscillating their lithe hips and pointing to the stairs. I hurried away.

A little farther on, we came to a row of big posters showing the backs of girls, nude to the waist. "What are they? Advertisements of available partners?" I asked.

"A"—Mr. Io sought the word—"burlesque show. Stripteasers."

Beyond the posters I then saw a theater lobby with a ticket booth. "Didn't know you had 'em here."

Again, our host looked back apprehensively. (In Japan, ladies *follow* men.) "It is a new thing," he answered. "The fact is, I myself, have never seen a strip tease."

"Suppose, in that case, I get some tickets and we go in for a minute?"

"Oh. Please. No."

"Why not? If you've never seen this sobering American contribution to aesthetics, you must."

"*Mrs.* Wylie . . . !" he expostulated.

"Mrs. Wylie," I answered, "was taken to many such shows before we married. I've taken her to some. One renowned stripteaser is a friend of ours. We've had her at parties and for dinner. Mrs. Wylie is also a sensational ballroom dancer—and I'm not bad, either—so we run into strip teases at night clubs where we go dancing. Besides," I added, since his anxiety was growing, "she's a doctor's daughter." That, I thought, should clinch it.

He repeated, almost gulping, "You have had a strip-teaser in your *home?* Did she . . . ?"

"Of course not. As a guest. Friend."

"We better not go." He was torn between a palpable wish to do so—and an apparent apprehension about Ricky. So I walked over to the wicket, handed out a yen note and held up five fingers.

The interesting feature of Japanese strip tease was the audience, for it consisted of entire families—Pop, Mom and kids from bobby-soxers to babies. All of them sat in stiff, bug-eyed wonder.

A succession of attractive Japanese girls sang songs or danced and simultaneously removed their kimonos and kimonolike underthings with the traditional tempo and insinuation. They introduced two novelties which our police, goaded by prurience seekers who call their vice the protection of public morals, would certainly ban: some of the girls stripped completely; and several finished their act by lying down on the stage floor on their backs. Their every movement and gesture had a quality almost innocent and those who lay down on the stage floor, in a way that would be regarded as anything but innocent by our censors, seemed the most naive of all. For what, when you think of it honestly, is strip teasing all about?

After fifteen minutes or so, we returned to the cold outdoors and the long, gilded sunlight.

Mr. Io approached his secretary while Ricky and Evelyn Cane evaluated the Nipponese copy of American public titillation. He asked worriedly, "Have you ever seen anything like that?"

Lu turned large, dark eyes up at her boss. "Only on that trip I took to New York."

The sigh of relief that escaped Mr. Io lingered large and steamy in the air. Lu came from an upper class Japanese family. And it was about her, not my renegade American wife or Mrs. Cane, that the Japanese gentleman had been so anxious!

After that, without query or other comment than that there was another place everybody wanted to see, Mr. Io had us driven to Yoshiwara—Tokyo's red light district. Both Mr. Io and his chauffeur held the usual debate about which streets to follow, what turns to take. We were accustomed to that enigma of transport by then. But it did occur to me that Mr. Io might have feigned a certain amount of his seeming uncertainty over the location of this area and that his chauffeur might subtly have conspired in such pretense. They finally got on the track, in any case.

We drove down a tidy street. At the doorways of each elegantly painted house, at least one girl stood—a padded silk coat over her kimono. Most of them had a square, businesslike build and expression; most were in their twenties. Some were attractive; most, not very. One of them—to make the Tokyo convention of living advertisement even more graphic—lay on a silk-draped cot or bench, in her doorway, with her knees spread wide apart. When we drove by, she tossed back her long, black hair and smiled through that "V" of invitation. Another, an extraordinarily beautiful girl who was certainly not more than sixteen and probably younger, watched us pass with the serenest of smiles.

"Most," Mr. Io said, "are mere country girls. In two or three years they will go back to the farms with the dowry they have earned—and marry. But that young one—she is not a country girl."

I said, "If I were twenty—and in Tokyo alone—I'd have jotted down a description of that place, so I couldn't miss it. *Her*."

"Louse!" Ricky exclaimed. "If you were here *alone* and eighty . . . !"

Mr. Io glanced at Ricky's reflection in the rearview mirror.

Ricky went on, "She was certainly young, and lovely as some one in a dream!"

Mr. Io's expression became one of amazement.

Presently he chuckled—almost giggled—and took up a related topic: geisha girls.

It was getting dark, so we started back to Tai-koku, the Imperial. For most of the distance he rhapsodized over the beauty, charm, wonder, fun, stimulation and general joy of a geisha party. He also explained that high-class geishas were moral, which meant that they were devoted to the man of their choice. He added, further, that there were very gorgeous, less-high-class geishas "one can play tricks on."

"They enjoy having tricks played on them," he said, and the thought greatly pleased him.

Our host also sighingly deplored the cost of even the deceivable geishas—which turned out to be thirty or forty dollars per girl, per evening. About par, I thought, for the American call girl.

We thanked Mr. Io and Lu under the porte-cochere of the

Imperial—holding up other hotel guests in taxicabs. We promised to see them again, soon. (And as I've said, Lu attached herself to us whenever we needed her, after that.) "Perhaps," Mr. Io murmured to me from the window of his Cadillac, as it started, "I shall be able to arrange something."

There was, on his fine face only relish, certainly not a lewd or guilty look—the expression, I thought, that one man should wear if he mentions the pleasures of sex to another—but an expression seldom seen on American male faces when sex is discussed under any circumstances!

Since I've been back at home, a dozen Americans who'd been officers and G.I.'s in Japan during the Occupation—most of them friends or acquaintances but a few, complete strangers —have approached me furtively, with some such words as these:

"I see in the paper where you went around the world. Get to Japan?"

"Well—Tokyo. And Nikko."

They then enquire, with a significant drop in their voices and a hidden note of worry mixed with wonder, "How *is* it?"

The first time I was puzzled. "What do you mean—how is it?"

"Has it changed much?" The anxiety represented a fear Japan had somehow deteriorated.

"Has what changed? And how could I tell? I never saw Japan until last winter."

That was the way I responded to the earliest, ardent questioner—a lawyer whom I knew slightly.

He replied with a barrister's obliquity, "We used to sort of hate the Japanese men. After all, they put on a terrific, devilish war. But the *women* . . . !"

I got the point.

To the rest I said, "Nope. No change."

If I have time, I talk on. But not of the traditional geishas who still powder their faces chalk-white and wear their hair in a mound of what looks like black-enameled boat propellers. I describe the modern geishas who look like other Tokyo

girls, but prettier, on the whole. I mention the young girl who
stood beside that doorway in the Yoshiwara District and also
tell about the dance hall girls, whom the unattached Western
young men seem to prefer.

They act as table-hostesses in the dance halls, as partners
for the fox trots and rumbas, and they "take you home if they
like you."

"Brother!" one Australian flying officer volunteered, "they
make the kind of love, for marbles, that you can't win or buy,
down under!"

If asked by eager friends, I also report they still run in the
Tokyo papers unabashed ads commending the beauty, sophistication, friendliness, charm and "obedience" of the girls in the dance
halls. Such ads also note, in good-sized type, that the halls serve
ideal American drinks—and close at eleven or twelve o'clock,
every night: that is, conveniently early.

I do not say to the nostalgic enquirers that my knowledge is
hearsay—except for what I read in the English language papers.
Why should I jar their dreams?

The foregoing may have given the reader an impression
that I endorse the Japanese peonage of womanhood and also
favor prostitution. It may even have caused some to imagine that
Ricky is indifferent to—or abnormally broadminded about—ex-
tramarital sex adventures, and bawdry.

That is far from the case.

But the alien attitudes toward sexuality which I wish to
state or, at least, to imply in this book, will concern our own
customs more than those of other lands and peoples. Foreign
sex attitudes are difficult to express, because our responses to
other customs are conditioned by an American dogma that
defines what is "right" and "Christian." We are conditioned,
that is, by standards developed in the minds of fanatics, neurotics and hysterics: Saints and prophets, Puritans and prissy
Victorians who had less access to reality and less contact with
truth than any pragmatic pagan.

The Japanese way of treating a woman politely, yet as a
kind of servant to males, is appalling to me. I found it, in fact,

even more shocking than did my wife—or various other American wives, though all of them seemed to be somewhat distressed by it.

Questions on that matter rose in my mind as Ricky and I traveled—and after we came home:

Why—for example—did some American women react with less dismay than most American men to the total disenfranchisement of Japanese females, to their culturally imbued servitude and their obedience? Do American women perhaps feel a lack of dominance, of wanted authority, of what might be called male command in American husbands, mates and boy friends? Does the trained, ingrained humility of the Japanese woman toward men strike a note like envy in our females? Do they regard us as weak?

If that is even partially true, most American males are failing in some obscure, psychological way to act toward women as women deeply desire. In such a case, American men (who presume they are somewhat spoiling their womenfolk) actually are spoiling themselves by refusing to accept an authority (and the responsibility that accompanies all authority) that women wish they would assume.

In describing, and making a term for "momism," I've said elsewhere that mom's American sons are psychologically half-castrated in their youth, by mom. I've pointed out that the pants-wearing, American family boss is often a middle-aged mother who—by petting, wheedling, feigning illness, or by overt tyranny—limits individuation of a great many American males and sabotages their sense of independence. (Yet, to increase man's independence and individuation would seem the logical function of mature females.)

But I began to wonder, in Tokyo, if it were not American men-in-general who have created "momism" through default, cowardice, irresponsibility, and owing to libido oriented toward things rather than people, especially family. Greedy, infantile women, I have thought—though a common curse in America— may be more the victims of men than their victimizers. The difference between the attitudes of American men and women toward the feudal sex concepts of the Japanese suggests, not Japanese superiority but the nature of our own calamity.

What I have called momism rose in the nineteenth century when it became evident that immense resources of our continent and the torrent of technological development offered hope that the many might come to possess the good life thitherto enjoyed only by rulers and a "privileged few." In ever-increasing numbers men turned to production, distribution, sales, and other enterprises described as "business." Immigrants then swarming to the land of opportunity had as a common incentive the same, materialistic goal. Immigrating women, like American women, had been brought up to accept male authority. Males were expected to possess authority *within and over themselves*, and as husbands to furnish family leadership in all cultural and occupational matters. Most men led and many tyrannized over their wives, in that era.

As the New World males turned to the new goal of attaining as high as possible a degree of material welfare, females accepted the change. In itself, the aim is desirable. Owing to their orientation toward male authoritativeness, they did not consider disagreement, in any case. An historically unprecedented ratio of American energy, intelligence and effort was concentrated on one material purpose as males abandoned the intellectual pursuits, the arts, education—especially primary teaching—as well as religion and even the rearing of their own children. Ensuing voids were filled by women, by inferior men and a dedicated male remnant. Today, indeed, Americans in general consider the pursuits of art, intellect, education, and so on, as "sissy." And the man constantly concerned with home and family is regarded as merely henpecked—which, indeed, he may (or may not) be.

However, those very areas of interest and activity which were so largely ignored by men engaged in seeking a high living standard are the areas in and from which authority rises. The pursuits that were first widely abandoned and are today widely disdained as egghead, arty or effeminate, supply the ever-increasing knowledge and the evolving wisdom on which authority of every sort depends. The American male turned from the human mind, psyche, personality, spirit. He thus became intellectually out of touch, obsolete, empty of relevant knowledge—and even proud of it!

Furthermore, production and corporate systems devised to mass-produce and distribute his new abundance, put increasing multitudes of men under a new style of rule and their owr "authority" lessened as it depended upon job status, job securit and promotion. A new hierarchy, with a new subject people thus came into being. The coal miner and the corporation vice-president, having abandoned family authority and having never sought intellectual authority, now came under the hegemony of business.

What the Americans accomplished by that concentrated endeavor has astonished the world. But the cost is very high: the emotional independence, inner dignity, self-knowledge, uncompromised integrity and capacity for family leadership of America's males—in short, *masculinity itself!* Authority required for family headship went by default to women who took over its functions unwillingly and ineptly. They are not the natural and desired functions of females. One result was an uncomprehending (but expectable) demand by women for "equality." Another was momism: the reflex employment of tyranny to disguise or compensate for frustration and confusion.

Whose fault? The fault of men and women—who, together, gained the world and lost not just themselves, but each other!

The many men who have asked me, of Japan, "Has it changed?" and thereby referred with manifest nostalgia and marvel to Japanese women merely exhibit the same phenomenon in another way.

What is it they imagine they found, in sex feelings and sex relations in Japan, that they secretly remember with almost reverent pleasure? Is it the docility of the doll-like ladies? Is it some special physical expertise they display in sex activity? Or is it just a sense of biological irresponsibility for what they did in Japan that they cannot permit of themselves at home: the enjoyment of a double standard of a cruel sort? I tried to answer my question.

There are, in USA, many prostitutes, loose young women, nymphomaniacs and willing wives. Among them are many as giving, as abandoned and as adept in love-making as women anywhere. Of those women, many take every tangible responsibility for their acts. So they could and would assuage such wishes-about-women as those listed. Hence the remembering men have some other sort of wish.

Is that longing merely owing to the fact that Japanese girls are females of a different race? Novelty cannot explain the degree of their fascination, I am certain.

Is it, then, that American sex mores smother men at home with guilt and anxiety, so that the same things may be done in Japan (where induced shame and prudery does not exist) without an inner panic that prevails on the banks of the Delaware River, in the penthouses of Lake Shore Drive, under the boardwalks of California and in the bagnios of New Orleans?

Certainly, that may be a factor. To it, might be added another.

In Japan, a wife, a mother figure, a mom, grandma, aunt, woman teacher, mother-in-law (in sum, woman) traditionally has no authority over the way any man behaves with other women. The assumption of such authority, in Japan, is regarded as if immature: a "tragedy of young love"—as when a girl stabs her faithless lover; or a "ludicrous affront"—as when a wife scolds a husband for keeping a geisha girl, at whatever detriment to the welfare of his family.

Japan holds absolute the double standard that—before the emancipation of American womanhood—was partially accepted here. Man's the boss in Japan—and no argument is allowable.

For such causes, perhaps, some American women take satisfaction from observing Tokyo wives whose spouses are palpably their lords and masters. And such causes tend to show why American men remember with yearning a nationful of women who expected them to be and behave as lords, as masters, as men.

But there is no equality, justice, ethos or morality in the traditional Japanese man-woman relationship.

American women, who have slightly envied dominated Japanese wives, ignore that. They are, after all, not married to Japanese husbands! The American men who have such rosy recollections, did not have, at the same time, Japanese wives toward whom they would have felt ideals of Western morality which have been bred into them. Those few American women who have married Japanese men, and the numerous American men who have taken Japanese wives, appear to maintain their relationship on the American sex level of romantic love, equality and monogamy. (Some, for all I know, may of course live at that *other* level of American mores which tolerates promiscuity, though almost invariably in bitterness, hate, drunkenness, and every violence.)

The clue to a clearer answer lies, I think, in Ricky's open admiration of the pulchritude of a very young Yoshiwara prostitute—and in Mr. Io's astonishment at that behavior.

His wife would not likely be allowed as a dinner guest in Tokyo—even at a dinner attended by *my* wife. *His* wife certainly would not be driven by him through the red light district, or exposed to a discourse on the geisha system, or taken to a burlesque show—though the wives of what he called the peon class were sitting there. Mr. Io's wife, if such things happened to her, would feel only the deepest shame. But my wife was calmly interested—and plainly not ashamed.

Mr. Io apparently concluded that Ricky, being more worldly than his wife, was even more devoted. He thought it required the pressure of a culture to compel his wife to behave properly, while mine, being more sophisticated, no longer had to be hidden from (or to hide from herself) the fact that American husbands felt and behaved about other women as did Mr. Io.

But if he imagined that (as he seemed to), he was wrong about us both. . . .

No man, of course, knows what his wife thinks; and only the wisest can guess how she acts in his absence. But all decent men can sometimes perceive how women feel:

The world of our two sexes is immature. Our maleness and

femaleness, taken with our aware minds, should be the means to mutual and reciprocal understanding, to maturation, love and trust-of-love. Instead, so one sex may exploit the other and both may combine to exploit the objective world, people invent (or gradually evolve) systematic moral concepts, i.e., religions.

These systems are said to "reveal" (in differing but always inhumane and inhuman ways) what both sexes thereafter call good and evil, virtue and vice, natural and unnatural, reality and illusion, truth and falsehood. They apply their terms to what is called love. But all the systems are wrong—ours, everybody's—since one motive of their origin was to evade the fear that burns in any being capable of thought, who covets the outer world without regard for the inner, and another motive was to evade the fear of inescapable death.

But Ricky feels unwilling to condemn anybody or any system. To do that would be hypocritical. For even though she believes the acts of others are wrong, she usually withholds judgment, since she is equally aware that her own cultural mold was misshapen and would perhaps still prejudice her opinion.

Love, which she feels was naturally intended for all people, she sees as subdued by each special system: stunted, channeled and distorted in unsatisfactory ways. How can she, then, take too critical an attitude toward apparent perversions of love in others—even of merely physical love?

I think she feels more at home in the world than most persons—but still somewhat alien. That she feels more loving than most, and frequently more loved—but somewhat lonely here, nonetheless.

She neither regrets the past nor dreads the future. Yet her present song of living has a counterpoint of melancholy. Sometimes, that aloof sadness seems to convey a contrary rapture. However, it is not, I think (no matter how many sages disagree), a mere contrast, necessary to make discernible the joys of life. It is not any such mathematical abstraction or blank dynamic, echoing in all happy people because they could not perceive ecstasy if they did not also feel forlornness. It is not her way of bearing Original Sin, either.

The music of her moody bliss is the melody of what-might-have-been, in some truer world.

Now and again, for a few listeners, the contrabass of human melancholy is pierced by the music our systems have deafened out: the song of truth itself.

And that experience of what-is-lost-yet-real explains an enjoyment in certain sorts of sorrow which would otherwise be morbid. We have each been robbed by our system. The ensuing poverty—even when we call it virtue and godliness—grieves all, and enrages many. But that which religion has stolen can be perceived beyond lament, as serenade. The enraged (the fearful) cannot expect to hear the forfeited music, the symphony of truth. To those who do hear, grief over the loss is acknowledged in the hearing; but that regret is less than the affirmation: the undertone that assures truth abides still, beyond our sorrow. The name of this experience today is Hope. The name will be Freedom when mankind discards all systems that teach him he was born evil and must attain goodness by faith in the system— thus, by dishonorable instruction, making him forever the shackled puppet of that system!

So, I believe, Ricky *feels* though she would not try to say it. So she enjoys yet somewhat mourns—not self-pityingly, alone for Ricky, but for now-time and the human universe: you, me, us all.

Thus she goes on loving you, me—and the great world she and I were trying to see.

4
Tokyo and Nikko

On our second morning in Japan the reporters who had met us at the airport, and some who gate-crashed, began to phone for appointments. I'd already protested that a first-time visitor would have nothing to say; but there is one advantage in being interviewed which most people miss: *you* can interview the reporters.

Obviously, every reporter I saw in Japan or elsewhere, whether a citizen of the country, an American, a Briton, Turk or Italian, knew immeasurably more about each nation than I. My appointments therefore served to gain information.

I have never been a newspaper reporter; but I know a good many, well. I like reporters. Excepting in technical fields, most reporters are far better informed and much less prejudiced than most of the people they interview. And I've rarely encountered one who, after he'd obtained his story, was unwilling to talk if he had time.

Ricky has often told me that I'm too voluble, unreserved and incautious with reporters. But I hold the "no comment" response of a presumably free citizen of a free country, to a question asked by an agent of the free press, is proof of pompous asininity or lack of self-confidence or of dirty work that needs disclosure. Since my books have always been frank, and often intimate, I am an empirical authority on the effect of honest answering. The effect is excellent.

During the next few days I saw seven or eight reporters. They wanted to know why we were there. What I intended to write about the trip—or about Japan. Some had read remarks I'd recently made in the States about atomic stalemate and the probability that no major war would ever be fought. They asked about that. They asked a few questions about my books. They asked how I—or we, when Ricky was present—liked Japan.

Then I asked them how they liked Japan and the Japanese.

It was a cogent question. One New Zealander wholeheartedly detested the people, country, customs, climate and food. He thought the throngs on the street were beasts, holding them in about the same contempt that an ignorant, deep-South bigot has for Negroes. Most American reporters were enthusiastic about the place and the people. One or two seemed unimpressed. But further questions made me feel they were men who did not particularly care for any people—including their own fellow citizens. Humanity to them was mere raw material for their work—an attitude I believe they deemed "professional" and one far too common among scientists, doctors and engineers.

From reporters, I learned a number of things—and also obtained numerous opinions which I was able to verify to some extent by putting the same questions directly to many sorts of Japanese, or by giving them an opening in which to discuss the subjects.

In such a fashion, for instance, I was able to learn the psychological means the Japanese employed to salvage what they could of the "face" lost through military defeat. The means were two:

The first was the familiar use of a whipping boy or scapegoat.

We tried and punished many Japanese military men and political leaders for war crimes. Most Japanese have assented to that, believing they were led into catastrophe by a handful of evil (or stupid and overgrasping) leaders. Since, as a nation, they were more used to domination than many other peoples, that reaction is not unfounded: a feudal society professing a state religion could hardly be expected to create a sense of responsibility strong enough to cause the individual to disobey plainly immoral commands. Currently, the Japanese are not brass-crazed. . . .

One night in the lobby of the Imperial Hotel, Ricky and I met the Japanese Admiral who planned and commanded the attack on Leyte Gulf that very nearly wrecked our invasion of the Philippines. In the last possible moment, it became a rout for Japan which ended her big ship threat.

We met the Japanese officer by accident. He had lent his limousine and chauffeur to a retired American Admiral who had just arrived in Tokyo on a business errand. A Detroit man, whom Ricky and I knew slightly, was struggling with our ex-Admiral when we appeared in the lobby: the sea dog was drunk. He kept insisting that our Detroit acquaintance take him instantly to some place where "a man can find a few willing girls." At the same time, he nervously and incessantly deplored the theft, or loss, of his passport, money and spectacles.

It was a loud, unpretty scene and since we had a dinner date with the beleaguered tourist, I came to his assistance.

The weaving, retired American Admiral was introduced to Ricky and me. He kept talking about his missing money and his appetite for girls. So I said quickly that I was a friend of Admiral ———, believing the mention of an active officer who wore four stars might restore the dignity of our compatriot. It did, but not immediately or lastingly.

"F——— Admiral ———!" he bellowed, with Annapolis cheerleader volume. On second thought, however, he brought his eyes into focus, shook my hand, made a few joking but less drastic comments on my Navy friend—and found his missing valuables in a hitherto unexplored pocket.

He also released our dinner companion, whom he'd been using for support. Then he introduced a short, powerful-looking, tweed-jacketed Japanese of middle age who had been standing in the background. This was the Admiral who'd lost—but so nearly won—at Leyte Gulf. He bowed, smiled, shook hands and made a brief effort at polite conversation. As soon as opportunity offered, he hurried away.

I had been aware that every person in the lobby was watching our group. So had Ricky—though she endures such humiliations with extraordinary poise. I became aware, now, that every Japanese in the lobby recognized their departing Admiral. But nobody bowed to him, nobody looked awed and not even a desk clerk had come forward to aid in a plainly sticky situation. Half a hundred cold faces watched him go out into the cold night to summon a cab.

The Japanese Admiral had wealth enough to own a car and hire a chauffeur. If he'd been tried for war crimes, he had been released or served a sentence. But what was important to his fellow citizens seemed to be that he was among those who had led Japan to downfall. I would not say he was held in hatred. But the Japanese showed toward him the rudeness of overt nonrecognition. That attitude must have been deeply felt, for there was no reason, any longer, to feign because Americans were present.

Our retired Admiral had by now pulled himself together.

If he had not behaved so abominably, it would have been comical to see him begin to wonder exactly who I was, what I might say, and to whom. He tried a few more halfhearted jokes to camouflage his earlier, unfunny obscenities and at last marched out to the borrowed car.

We saw him some time later with three western-dressed, much-painted Japanese girls who tittered around him politely while he caroused in the bar. I daresay he woke up in the morning with his passport and spectacles but without the fat wad of yen he'd lost and found. This time, the money would be gone for good. . . .

So I saw that evidence of scapegoat psychology: a wealthy, intelligent-looking high officer whom all Japanese regarded icily. And I heard many Japanese voluntarily assert that their leaders had been foolish and betrayed the Emperor.

In that connection it is interesting to note how many Germans (who would resent being called a feudal people) make similar assertions: they were misled; they never really knew what was going on; and so on. Yet many Germans openly, and many more covertly, admire the leaders who were authors of their calamity. What such Germans do not realize is they, too, had a state religion as compelling as Shinto, no more logical or real and, at its profoundest, immeasurably less ethical.

We were shortly to find at least the grounds for suspecting that some few Japanese are still as jingoist as any Germans. . . .

The second and even more potent way of saving "face" among the Japanese is—the atomic bomb.

When it is mentioned in the Tokyo press—which is often— the two words are often accompanied by some such clause as ". . . which brought Japan to her knees."

The bomb is accorded by all Japan a power akin to legendary instruments—Thor's hammer, David's slingshot, Arthur's Excalibur. For who can resist that which is magically irresistible? No one—not even the Japanese! A beaten nation never had a better out, and the hue and cry raised in Japan today over radioactive tuna, the radiation sickness of the crew of the *Lucky Dragon* and the fall-out from subsequent experiments, reflects in part an unconscious will to sustain the idea that the war was lost owing to magic. That Japan was a defeated nation when the bombs were used is not generally acknowledged by the Japanese. Our own military men did not acknowledge it at the time either, although they have done so since the war's end.

They were planning to invade the main islands and had prepared, I've heard on excellent authority, for a million American casualties. They were contemplating, the same authorities tell me, a possible second million. They were not of a mind to wait for naval victories, blockade, the destruction of Japanese shipping and the continuing ruination of cities by the B29's, to bring down the enemy. But even those Japanese who could, or do, know the condition of their country on August 6, 1945, and know we were ready to invade, believe that only the A-bomb made further fighting futile.

They expected to fight back house by house and think of themselves, not as defeated in fair battle, but hexed. Japan to the Japanese is Loki, who was given a wrestling partner over whom he could not prevail though he had outwrestled all others; the Norse god finally learned his opponent's identity: Death. Who can beat death, then? Who can beat atomic bombs? Japanese see themselves as almost superhuman—but even supermen fail where the magic forces of legend are exerted. So they react with inordinate vehemence and fear to our Pacific bomb tests, keeping alive *their own myth.*

It is a circumstance the Communists neatly exploit. Japanese response to Soviet tests (which produce similar fall-out on the main islands) is not violent—evidence that the selective Communist tactic is effective. Japanese fear was naturally oriented toward the only users of atomic weapons in history, ourselves. Both propaganda and fact combine. For the Japanese know that America started atomic bomb warfare, so it is easy to persuade many (as the Reds do) that Soviet atomic tests are wholly defensive in nature.

America currently has no effective means to combat the Red strategy. We do not point in behalf of freedom, or of the self-determination of peoples, or of the UN, to the Red's history of aggression when Japan suffers Soviet fall-out. We do not make clear our motives in continuing the bomb tests. We do not talk effectively, as America, to Japan.

That kind of failure—the failure to bother to answer hostile propaganda that could readily be exposed—characterizes America everywhere. It is one of the main reasons we are losing the cold war. . . .

Shortly after our arrival Ricky and I were invited to a banquet at the foreign press club. The Scandinavian members of the club were in charge. We sat at a large table with a number of Americans, ate smörgåsbord and listened to Swedish singing and, if anything in Tokyo could have been more incongruent, we missed it. We danced to American fox trots played by American musicians. We drank aquavit. The air rang with continuous skoals. Several hundred people attended that "Scandinavian Night"; a chef had been air-imported from Oslo to assemble authentic viands. A very gay party—and informative, for I was introduced to an "expert" attached to our embassy, during an interlude in the speeches and songs. . . .

He was a man of about sixty, a former university professor of vast reputation, a pince-nez-bearing individual who resembled a heron. He had a heron's aptitude for standing at implausible angles and for haughty peering. After the dinner I could not recall whether he was an expert in sociology, economics or political science. I merely recalled that he was hired by our government to study Japan and its people and make policy suggestions from the standpoint of one of those several alleged branches of science.

They are not scientific, of course, since they rise from human psychology—a field not perfectly understood, as economists, sociologists and political scientists are wont gleefully to proclaim. In that glee, they usually ignore what we do understand about psychology; thus they indicate their discipline to be founded on an evasion of the known. True science, however, strives to stay aware of its blanks. It is a pity that our governments tend to rely on these pseudo scientists of society, politics and economics; for they do not agree upon a single principle even among themselves!

This man's first question was, "Well, Wylie, what do you think of it?"

Just for the hell of it, I answered with a thought that had been in my mind for a day or two: "Fabulous country! Fascinating people! When I think how much Western culture the Japanese have acquired in the bare century they have been open to it, I'm amazed."

He said, "Ah."

"Technology, I mean. The West was centuries ahead. The Japanese caught up in so many ways—so rapidly! Overtook us, in some."

"Great *imitators*," he admitted.

"Innovators, too. They've made some brilliant contributions to science." He was about to demur. His nose poked forward like a heron's bill. But I went on, "Even in applied science. If you doubt it, ask the pilots who fought the first Zeros with our best planes. Ask them, that is, if you can find any who survived."

He said, "Ah," again, and picked up his highball. I was to be allowed to continue. I did:

"So—what I've been wondering—is this. Isn't it possible that, in the years ahead, they might pick up other parts of Western culture? The ideals of freedom, of democracy, of individual importance and responsibility, for instance . . . ?"

The he-heron swigged and cut me off. "My dear Wylie! Your Japanese is utterly incapable of learning that sort of thing! Your Japanese will never change his traditional fealties. Your Japanese is fixated in a social system from which he cannot rise, incapable even of imagining liberty—" About then I developed an early strain of the antipathy already disclosed; for he went on and on about "your Japs."

They are not "my" Japanese. I dislike people who say, "your so-and-so's," anyway. It is a manner of generalizing intended to show that the speaker is an absolute authority, his listener is ignorant, and the people under discussion are inferior to both.

For a while I argued with the desiccated bird. I pointed out that many peoples as tradition-bound as the Japanese had thrown off, in the past, just such limiting conventions. I noted how certain people, like those of India, are engaged in the effort. I added that various nations, these days, are even being forcibly indoctrinated with new and different traditions—Soviet captive nations. I said that ample evidence showed forcible changes could become deep and lasting.

It did not budge him. "Your Japanese," he answered, "is constitutionally, culturally, and racially unfit to become a free person, ever!"

What is more irksome than this common but false conviction? What is stupider than the notion a nation or a race cannot change? If it were true, there would have been no history nor any evolution. And what could be a bigger folly on the part of the government of a free nation than to send to another, desired as a friend, an "expert" who was certain no change could be

expected, when continuing American-Japanese amity is dependent on drastic changes? Why send an expensive man to tackle a
job he believes impossible?

Furthermore, to assert people lack the capacity for change,
simply because they fail to exhibit change, is not scientific. It is
nutty. A man who has never heard of liberty, or one who has
heard of it but does not understand it, or one who understands
the theory but does not yet desire freedom for himself—and even
a man who understands freedom and seeks it for himself, but
does not believe it is practical for his fellows, will not have a real
sense of the whole meaning of freedom. But that failure has
nothing to do with any man's capacity. Given more time, education, opportunity, information, stimulation—and he may show as
much capacity for realizing liberty as George Washington. Men
can change and be changed by education—and by force. That is
a fact which the Communists know about people—but many
Americans do not seem to want to hear, any more, since it
suggests educational duties they have defaulted.

The man we'd deputized, like the New Zealand reporter, regarded the Japanese not just as culturally and intellectually
obtuse toward our ideals but as biologically limited in such a
way as to be forever unteachable. He believed—contrary to fact
—that their ability was limited to mimicry. In spite of visible
achievement, he deduced, by the application of illogical proc-
esses, an inherent Japanese inability to learn.

His fallacious techniques produced erroneous charts, graphs
or other opinion-forms as source material for his American superiors. Meantime, certain other skilled agents in Japan, holding
no such mistaken idea about the rigidity of people, were busy trying to teach Communism and—if they failed—to lie, bribe, blackmail, trap, betray or bludgeon the Japanese into Communism.
The bird-shaped, batbrained professor bore himself loftily from
my bog when I asked him why, even though the Japanese could
not appreciate liberty, they could not be taught to *mimic* it.

Of course, many persons working for our State Department
do take that view about other peoples which all free men must,
if freedom means anything: they assume others want and can

learn to be free. But there are too many like my soon-flown acquaintance who believe the color of a man's skin, and his current concept of nationalism, incapacitate him in perpetuity for wanting liberty, or learning what it is, or liberating himself.

Yet the fundamental appeal of Communist propaganda, and the most effective lure among its many specious claims, is that it will provide "liberation." That one word gives Communism success among millions who yearn to be free; and they are rarely told that Communists lie through their teeth every time they utter the syllable, "free."

Those of our minions abroad who are themselves so unacquainted with freedom that they regard it as a special privilege of the few are utterly incapable both of advancing America's cause and of combating Communism! There ought to be some easy Binet test for diplomatic candidates to find, before they pack their bags, whether or not they know for sure that they really are Americans. . . .

Some Japanese of power and importance apparently still cling to a hope of restoring their "Co-prosperity Sphere." That hope may not even be whispered about in high echelons; it may merely be a half-unconscious wish; and Ricky was the one who perceived its possible survival. But the datum should be noted.

She and I were invited to a mysterious luncheon soon after stories about us had appeared in the Tokyo papers.

We received a note at the Imperial desk saying a Mr. Mitomisha would like us to call. The desk clerk was plainly impressed by the name, which meant nothing to us. We phoned Lu.

"Mr. Mitomisha," she said, "is highly connected with the foreign ministry."

"How?"

"He is also a big businessman."

"Okay. Should we eat with him?"

"Absolutely! He's very big! I'll arrange it."

It was wise to let Lu arrange matters which involved using the phone, or trying to talk to secretaries—who often spoke less

English than they imagined, or none. Lu presently reported our date had been set for following noon.

A limousine picked us up. We were driven, on another fair but chilly day, to a restaurant surrounded by gardens, teahouses, stone lanterns, brooks, ponds and trees so carefully situated and tended they might have been handmade and hand-painted. In spring or summer or fall the gardens would have been magnificent; even in the dead center of winter, they had great beauty of design in dead-grass browns and the dark greens of pine and fir.

The usual bowing headwaiter met us as we arrived. Mr. Mitomisha, a short and smiling man, rushed from a door flanked by statues of samurai warriors in full armor. He was quite thin and elderly, with salt-and-pepper eyebrows, wide as moustaches. The eyes beneath had the aspect of cunning that propaganda and cartoons have led Western people to expect in Japanese. He introduced himself rather grandly and conducted us across a flagged reception room to a bar. There, we were caused to meet five other Japanese gentlemen.

They smiled and chuckled and bowed as they shook hands. All were dressed in well-tailored Western clothes. All of them looked as sharp, in different ways, as our host. We heard their names—and didn't actually learn one. So we had no idea what they did—and do not have, to this day. But, as we took bar stools, Ricky gave me a quick glance, concealed from the merry-seeming gentlemen—a glance that said, "This is serious!" or, maybe, "Watch yourself!" For we had expected to meet only the mysterious Mr. Mitomisha and perhaps somebody to interpret if he didn't speak English. He spoke it—and so did the other five gentlemen—better, perhaps, even than we were allowed to discover.

Ricky asked for a dry martini. So they did. I had a sherry. On this occasion, my sherry was a deliberate "ploy"—a gambit in one-upmanship. The round of drinks was soon repeated. Our six hosts seemed to regard the affair as of the utmost fascination, and the purest, most casual fun. There was a great deal of talk about transocean flying and, when Ricky showed interest, a pleasant discussion of formal gardens.

Then we were escorted to a private dining room where we sat around a beautiful brazier, consuming soup and sake and sukyaki—which, we learned, they pronounced, "ski-aki." Everybody made a great many jokes. I began to feel that Mr. Mitomisha and his imposing pals, like Mr. Io, merely enjoyed entertaining American visitors. . . .

Just how we began talking about war and atomic weapons, I could not afterward recall. Certainly, I did not make the remark that led to the subject. But since I soon had a quiet, apparently interested audience, I did talk. We'd finished the rice course (and had a second helping we didn't want—to indicate a zenith of pleasure in the repast). There was no reason why I shouldn't have talked about weapons and war.

I realized only afterward that I'd told one of the reporters I'd witnessed the testing of an atomic bomb—a fact duly printed and doubtless duly translated, by one or another of the six gentlemen present, to reveal my Q-clearance and presumptive access to inside information in the field. I have written a now-obsolete novel about an imaginary atomic attack on the United States. And I serve as an expert consultant to our Federal Civil Defense Administration. But if they had expected to learn from me any restricted data, they must have been thoroughly disappointed. For it was merely published information—that most American laymen and even most American military men do not add up sensibly—which I used to hold their attention.

I made, indeed, my usual pitch; it need only be summarized here—a train of thought that went as follows:

We Americans and the Soviets have for a considerable time possessed H-bombs triggered by ordinary fission bombs which, in turn, will cause fission in cheap, plentiful Uranium 238. The radioactive fall-out from one such bomb can make areas of thousands of downwind square miles so hot that for a day or more after the shot an exposed person would receive a lethal dose of radiation in a few minutes.

Such bombs can be made of almost any desired power. The limiting factor is the weight of the atmosphere. Lethal crop-dusting in areas of thousands of square miles can be done by medium bombers. What a submarineful of such stuff would do, if detonated off a coast when the high altitude winds blew on shore, can be imagined—at least by some minds. A hundred such subloads could doubtless wipe out most life on a large segment of a continent. The same sort of weapon can be shot in missiles, used in mines, launched in supertorpedoes of long range, aimed at coastal cities from far at sea, etc., etc., ad nauseam.

People who possess such weapons are not likely to wage wars with other owners. The side that determined on total war would certainly exterminate the other—while, simultaneously, committing national suicide as its expiring foe retaliated in kind. Everything the Soviets are doing in Russia, and outside, suggests they have evaluated that fact and are now planning their conquests of the world by other means than force of arms.

The common thought that a "conventional war" might be fought while atomic weapons were withheld or outlawed is not tenable, not a trustworthy basis for comfort. For a loser in a conventional war would be tempted to recoup by employing "tactical" atomic weapons; then the enemy would copy him—and "tactical" nuclear weapons would assuredly rise in caliber, step by step, till H-bombs and H-devices were employed. A do-or-die (and suicidal) effort with all atomic equipment would be the certain Götterdämmerung of a future Hitler, or any council of defeated or defiant men whose fanaticism was like madness.

The argument that we didn't use gas in World War II because it was so deadly and outlawed as well is nonsensical. We did not use gas because it was not so effective and manageable, pound for pound, as high explosives and fire bombs. The fact that gas was outlawed has no weight. Sinking ships without warning and bombing open cities had been outlawed *by the same covenant* which the United States hadn't even signed! Nations waging war, these days, run the additional risk of encountering some brand-new and fearsome weapon that might be "legal" no matter how many covenants were signed. For it might not have been dreamed of earlier!

Furthermore, not only are USA, England, and Russia in possession of the annihilating H-weapons, and not only is offense today unimaginably far ahead of defense, but it is easy to see that the "continental broom effect" of offense will *increase* while defense grows steadily and relatively weaker. Intercontinental missiles and other gadgets can never be surely intercepted. Electronic and mechanical gear that might somewhat protect a nation from such fantastic spreaders of mass annihilation would cost, moreover, unguessable billions to install and would need a million technicians to make and to keep in order, around the clock, from here on into eternity.

The ecological aftereffects of the use of fission-fusion-fission (and other) weapons has hardly been considered. Granted the United States survived such instruments, with a few million people and homes intact, the ensuing years would see countless lower organisms pick up and accumulate hot isotopes. These, in turn, would be the food of certain algae, molds, bacteria, viruses and plankton. They would next become the basic nutriments of various insects and, finally, birds and animals. Many forms of vegetation also concentrate radioactive materials. In the end, mammals, including man, would find the food chain (and the chain of countless other essential raw materials) either broken by the radio-annihilation of supportive species or rendered so hot that it might be impossible to raise hogs or corn(or boys and girls) in or near a fall-out area, even after a quarter century.

Finally, nations and lands lying between such battlefields might be exterminated as their weather and terrain became poisoned. Japan itself, though a noncombatant, might so perish in an "all-out" Russia-vs.-America war.

I said I did not believe that Russian Communism proposed to commit suicide to win the world and have nothing. It was winning without war in any case. So there will probably never be a Third World War. War has become too risky for the Reds to start, except in limited areas on a conventional basis. And the USA would never start one.

Many, *many* other arguments just as cogent can be brought to the support of that viewpoint.

My luncheon discourse gradually made the six Japanese

listeners so glum that I blurted, "Is it bad manners in Japan to talk of serious topics at mealtime?"

They assured me one could talk of whatever one wished at any meal, in Japan. But when we parted from the six Japanese gentlemen, they were far less jubilant than when we met.

I said to Ricky, "I wish I'd never started that palaver about fission-fusion-fission. It ruined the party!"

"It sure did!"

"But they seemed to want to listen. Was that just politeness?"

"Not exactly, I'd say. Apparently, you explained a number of things they hadn't clearly understood before. After all, they were politicians or government officials or big businessmen—not scientists—and so, just as bomb-dumb as their opposite numbers at home." She looked at me thoughtfully. "Didn't you realize what their actual reaction was?" When I shook my head, she went on, "They seemed to me—hideously *disappointed*."

"Disappointed?"

"Sure. Every word you said made them see more clearly that—maybe you were right. Maybe there wouldn't be an all-out USA-Soviet war. That is—maybe Russia and the United States were not going to destroy each other, so maybe Japan could not regain strength in an ensuing power vacuum, and take over Asia, as Japan once planned. That's my guess. But I think it's worth considering."

I daresay Ricky had the answer. Six men in that stone-flagged, bamboo-and-rice-paper dining room ate delicious fruit and thin slices of broiled meat, sipped aromatic tea and conventionally admired the flower arrangements. They also *listened* —and their faces grew steadily more downcast. Were they wondering if the hidden, long-range hope of "certain persons" in Japan was a foolish dream? I bet they were . . . !

I did not know then—but I learned as we traveled in other countries—that my position is that of nearly every other major government but our own. We Americans are almost alone in imagining that we or any nation can win an all-out war in the future. We are almost alone in thinking a world war could be conducted without ultimate world devastation. Alone in presuming that arms equal strength and it is still sane to risk big war. And, of course, not all American officials (not even all our high brass) believe there will be another war, or that USA would win if there should be. The mere theory should alter our policy!

Though we had a lugubrious lunch with those six strangers whose Mikadolike glee, courtesy and, possibly, cunning turned o blank depression while I talked, Ricky and I had a festive evening soon afterward, with four other gentlemen of Japan.

One was a professor of ichthyology to whom I had a letter from mutual friends in Manhattan. Another was a retired government official who had served as the Tokyo representative of the International Game Fish Association. A third was a gentleman who'd spent much time in consular service abroad, including many years in America. A fourth was a tall, imposing man with a fabulous sense of humor whose name and profession—(again!)—I did not catch.

We were invited by the retired official (through the ever-gracious Lu) to a tempura restaurant for dinner. We were escorted there by the professor who had (for reasons already explained) great difficulty in locating the restaurant, even with the taxi driver's help.

One American stranger, with wife, was conducted through another lovely garden by extremely lovely girls dressed in a modern kimono style. In a bright-colored, mat-covered and breathtaking reception room we exchanged our shoes for felt scuffs. From there, we were led to a bar and introduced to everybody present, including a middle-aged woman who appeared to be the restaurant manager.

We had cocktails. And I made a remarkable faux pas.

The Japanese sometimes supply dinner guests with washcloths wrung out in warm water. The custom is comparable to our use of finger bowls. But the washcloths are "served" elegantly—and before a meal instead of afterward.

The bar of the restaurant was furnished with modernistic

American metal-and-plastic chairs and love seats. A magnificent over-the-bar oil painting of a nude was descried by dim vapor-tube lights—in the American tradition. And as male guest of honor, I was tended the first washcloth—on a small, silver tray. It was folded so it looked like a flower or a confection. I swiftly decided it was a fancy pastry intended to be eaten with the cocktails.

So I took the little silver plate from the handsome serving girl and asked, "Do I just pick it up and eat it—or break it first—or should I pass it?"

"Eat it?" murmured the professor in an odd tone.

Ricky giggled, "It's a *hot, wet washcloth*, dear! You wipe your *face* with it."

I laughed. Who wouldn't?

Then—everybody laughed long and uproariously.

We then moved across another garden to the dining room. An exquisite girl took a position behind each chair to pour sake as fast as it was consumed.

Sake is not very strong, by American cocktail standards, but one learns that it isn't a bad idea to let the small, eggshell-thin cups stand awhile before drinking and automatic refill—especially after the first five or six, and particularly when those follow manhattans.

My faux pas, and our united laughter, had wholly dispelled the tension of such first meetings.

Ricky asked, as the soup was served, why sake was drunk hot—a question she'd been thitherto unwilling to put to any Japanese for fear of offending in some unenvisaged way.

The heavy-set, white-haired ex-official chuckled. "There is only this reason—to make us think it is stronger, and that we are getting very drunk. We Japanese get drunk easily—and when we are drunk, we titter and are foolish."

"Let's," Ricky said, "titter and be foolish."

I have never had more fun.

Even the lovely waitresses joined in the jokes and laughter, for some spoke a little English—some quite a good deal.

I told our hosts not to hesitate to speak Japanese, as Ricky and I liked to hear it and would not mind: a courtesy foreigners such as ourselves too often fail to show.

We ate a score of different, delicately cooked seafoods, rice —and fruit more beautiful, big and flavorsome than I'd seen before. Finally, tea was served.

It was then stated that the professor had perfected a way of painting fresh-caught fish with a layer of natural color and pressing their bodies against paper in a fashion that produced a remarkably perfect and very beautiful "picture" of the fish. Sets of his alleged imprints were now unrolled and displayed by the girl waitresses. Each scroll was a presumed self-portrait of several fish; each such composition was arranged as a Japanese alone knows how; the colors of the fish imaginatively contrasted, or harmonized; the scrolls were leafed through one by one. The work was at once so exquisite and dazzling that I was sure our hosts, knowing my interest in fish, were regaling us with the work of some great artist. I assumed the "self-portrait" explanation was a joke, in keeping with the mood of the party— and said so, which brought general laughter. That only increased my belief the fish had been painted by some great Japanese—and Ricky and I were being kidded as well, perhaps, as subtly tested for aesthetic judgment. It even occurred to me that we might be viewing some great art treasure collected by one of our hosts.

But presently the professor called for paper, paint and a plate of fish. The fresh-caught fish soon provided were an art work! The chef had chosen a handsome platter, half a dozen different, brilliant fish—and "arranged" *them* to make a picture! Amidst much amusement—and to my surprise—the materials for brush drawing were provided and the professor proceeded to make a fish imprint right there, at the tempura counter!

We six sat in a happy row—unshod feet warm on little stoves, stomachs full, eyes possibly overbright, and the glamorous girls behind watching breathlessly. He painted and pressed on paper a realistic yet artistic black-and-white portrait of a snapper-like subject. My skepticism was thus annihilated.

Then he invited *me* to try it!

I did.

The hilarity of our hosts, the waitresses, the lady manager, other female attendants, and Ricky became almost apoplectic. I watered black pigment with professional calm, selected a large, grouperlike fish from the platterful and proceeded to paint it up, with the assured gusto of Leonardo.

But when I then pressed my handiwork on a large, rice paper sheet, the result was less than a chef d'oeuvre. Unmistakably a fish, it somehow looked like a fish cooked almost to pieces. And I said so—to a suddenly silent audience that, sensitively, feared my grisly boggle would embarrass me.

The room shook with laughter.

I had neglected to put paint on the eye of the fish so, now, on my print, I painted an "X"—the cartoonist's "eye" that indicates a person is drunk or knocked out.

That delighted all of us even more.

We went into the night at long last, happily, and the restaurant ladies followed us, smiling, bowing almost to their knees, their laughter white in the cold, waving when we drove away.

"I *never* had more fun," Ricky said, when we were alone again. "So gay and happy! And so *democratic!* I didn't know the Japanese were capable of letting their hair down that much! They even included the cook and the sake girls in every conversation! And the *presents* . . . !"

Ricky referred to three scrolls bearing imprinted compositions of tropic fish which had been formally presented to us after proof (by the professor, not me!) that they were produced as claimed and not masterpieces of water color. We treasure them at home. And their artisan, Professor Hiyama of Tokyo University, subsequently had a one-man show of his work at the American Museum of Natural History in New York City.

A day or two before we left Tokyo, we were having lunch with Mrs. Cane and Lu at Chinzan-So, another pixilated garden restaurant, when I happened to say, "I had hoped we could go to a geisha house before we left. But we won't have time, now. Too bad."

Mrs. Cane stared and Lu almost lost her chopsticks. "You didn't *know?*" Lu murmured. "They said it was a *restaurant?* I suppose they did! On account of Mrs. Wylie."

I didn't get it. "*What* restaurant . . . ?"

"The professor who drew the fish—and the other men—took you to one of the finest modern geisha houses in Tokyo! That's where you had dinner!

We met another professor of whom I took a poor view, though perhaps it was owing to internal distress. That Tokyo night I had the common malady: *enteritis touristis.* We often had it. But Ricky is a doctor's daughter and like the well-trained offspring of most physicians, conservative about self-medication. If Ricky takes a pill you can be sure something has been giving her a rough time for some hours. She is skeptical about the efficacy of medicines, besides; she uses them not only rarely but pessimistically.

Ricky's husband, on the other hand, is an advanced hypochondriac—with specialties. It is my feeling that there is (or ought to be) a pill or potion capable of providing relief from *any* symptom. I am a pill taker and a new-pill-trier.

With a round-the-world tour in view, however, even Ricky had assented to the offer of a doctor-friend to make up a "kit" for medical needs putative and imputative. He had provided, in astonishingly small compass, antibiotics, sulfa drugs, concentrated paregoric, antiseptics, unguents, and the like. Still another doctor-friend left at our home a carton of assorted medicaments which he felt to be the indispensable world minimum. I spent an afternoon decanting some pounds of liquids and pills into plastic containers and thereby reduced the weight to half.

A third friend, a surgeon, upon chancing to see the collection, made this suggestion: "Let me toss in a few instruments and then, with what you have, you can practice medicine clear around the world!"

So we had that equipment. But on the night we had dinner with our second professor, in spite of vague warnings, I neglected to take or to bring along a single remedy.

I sat on a mat-covered floor. It is a posture I find becomes quickly uncomfortable and eventually excruciating. I suffered. Two ways. Mrs. Cane and Lu, Ricky and the prof (English) watched a kimonoed girl—no geisha and not pretty—stew up green vegetables and chicken with indecipherable oddments in a clay pot on a fire in front of us. Meantime we drank some sake.

It did me no good.

The professor, an emir from a southern city, visiting in Tokyo, had ardently desired this meeting. His name, I believe, was Ishishi, or very near that: a short, fattish man, wattled, pale, with hair that fell into his eyes and had to be raked back by skinny, long fingers, bizarre on so obese a character.

He talked about Hemingway.

I said I knew Hemingway. I said I thought he was the finest living American writer in the area of feeling, emotion and instinct. I said——

But Professor Ishishi turned to John O'Hara.

I said I knew John. I said——

He asked quickly if I had known James Joyce.

No, I said. I thought to ask if he knew Eddie Guest—but not a chance. He was already deep into the genius of Joyce, going like a Jaguar on a toll road.

Those who believe that second-rate straight man of Dublin improved his status merely by complicating prose impress me no more than such other compulsive collectors as auctioneers and the salesmen of junk, remnants and lost-and-not-found luggage. Faulkner is much admired abroad solely because his translators have rendered his *meanings* from their curry-thick inscrutability in English.

I said so, when the Professor finally paused to eat.

I could see—everybody could, by then—that as far as Ishishi was concerned, I was a moron.

He tried Ezra Pound.

I have tried Pound—and abandoned him.

T. S. Eliot.

Another, who has too much noodle for me—or vice versa.

Ishishi next rattled off half a dozen names I never heard of.

"You don't know those great, young American *poets* and *poetesses!*"

I said, "Nix," hating letters and longing to burp.

"Don't you realize that Ogriver, Collenney and Hatrell have *changed the lyric form?*" His meager eye fixed on me with plain amazement.

"Have they?"

"You don't read *Jaune*, the poetry monthly of Arkwell, Arizona?"

I shook my head.

There was silence. We ate awhile. Yesterday's octopus put forth its tentacles in my viscera—and writhed them. One of my knees fainted.

"Willa Cather—did you care for *her* works?"

I said, "Yes." Partly true. I have read and admired books by the late Willa Cather. Unfortunately, I frequently forget who wrote what. I could at the moment call to mind nothing of Miss Cather's useful for counterattack.

"Mark Twain . . ." he labored on.

I thought we could get together on Twain. But the Japanese pinfeather of the American wing of the French avant-garde deemed Mark Twain a "mere journalist."

I was becoming sore in more places than the knees and the small, large, ascending, transverse and descending colons. I nonetheless tried a riposte: "Are you interested in *science*, Professor?"

He snapped his fingers. "Science! Mere data."

"Much new knowledge on many subjects, as well as ancient wisdom, stem from science. Art, too. It's merely—contemporary knowledge. Classical authors kept up with science. Is there a possible, *real* aesthetic, for the half-educated, half-witted, scientifically ignorant and half-baked——"

"I am considered," he interrupted, "an *authority* on American slang! Half-baked! *Ha!* But there are a few terms I still cannot latch onto—or dig, you might say."

I brightened. I am no authority on slang or anything else much, but I do know a bit of the argot.

However, Professor Ishishi proceeded to bring forth sundry

terms that must have been used by Lydia Pinkham's grandpa. It even occurred to me that he might have invented them. Again, he had me.

"Speaking of poetry of the modern sort," I therefore said, "I suppose you're familiar with Hughvalyn Danger?"

It got him. He didn't say no; he didn't say yes. He merely cocked an attentive brow and stuffed his mouth so full he couldn't answer.

I filled in: "Convict. Attica Prison in New York. Lesbian." (There are, I happened to know, only men at Attica.) "Writes poems on brickbats—poor woman's not allowed mail privileges. Throws them over the wall. Only way she can get her work printed in that great, new medium, Esperanto Braille. Surely you know *its* 'bible'? *Banjo Veuve*, published in Wiscoy, New York."

Ishishi said, "You jest!"

So I got up to look for the Men's. Had to.

As I separated myself from my spasms, I reflected that young Professor Ishishi stood, even in 1956, about where many liberal intellectuals had, in the United States, some quarter century ago. Art-dazed college graduates, they firmly believed that any-thing they could not grasp must be profound (or trivial) where-fore they must pretend to grasp (or dismiss) it. There was un-conscious validity in the pose. For they were unable—or at least unwilling—to grasp mathematics, physics, chemistry, biology, psychology and the like. So they fell behind the main human show of their era. But in the arts, where meaning is often opaque, or nil, or deliberately addled, anybody can play even-Steven at "understanding" and, hence, at critique. So, there, they intellectualized with might and main, and also liberally, of course.

The gag even continues. Learned curators still hang, in good museums, paintings that could be duplicated by nervous horses micturating on clean snow. I can kick a brass spittoon into as good a "sculptured head" as has brought fame to several latter-day clay-kneaders. Musicians of skill still offer a thing called, probably, *Grape Nuts Suite*, and where the score calls for tack hammers to play piano keys, they follow.

American "liberal intellectuals" have vanished, pretty much.

It turned out that many weren't liberal at all: they were taken in by economics, another no-rules subject, and some even joined or sympathized with those "economists" who want to free man by taking his freedom away, and all's fair in the endeavor. Not liberal, such dopes; and, as I noted, not intellectual, either, unless the evolved purpose of mind is self-deceit.

Now, in Tokyo, in the winter of 1956, sat Professor Ishishi, talking the same old Left Bank lingo that had irked even me in the Twenties and Thirties. Primed to the gills with the phony and determined to lead his students astray in all new fruitless directions, he was a man, I thought, who made a point of knowing everything not worth knowing at all and teaching it as the academic Essence.

After that reminiscent, but in no way nostalgic, evening, I paid the check, went with Ricky to our hotel, and took paregoric. . . .

I was eating a poached breakfast egg the next morning, wondering if it would digest, when I murmured almost to myself, "That *jerk!*"

"What jerk?" Ricky asked.

"Our Left Bank boy wonder from lower Honshu."

"Professor Ishishi? I though he was *sweet!*"

"*Hunh?*" The grunt betokened naked horror.

"You were so mean to him! What little you did say——"

"I was preoccupied. Also—interrupted."

"I know. You ate too much squid the other day. He wanted you to talk—but you wouldn't."

"I talked to him a lot!"

But Ricky sat on me—fair enough when I'm about to defend a prejudice. "Don't you see what he feels? He wants to teach *American* literature. He's sick of the Japanese university custom of teaching 'English' literature as wholly British. He wants to be American! He wants his classes to become Americanized! *That's* why he follows the latest fads and fashions——"

"*Latest?* The forgotten Methuselahs of free verse . . . !"

Ricky set her coffee cup down. "Sure. But why? He's never been in America, or even Europe. All he's learned, he's learned from books. He *corresponds* with some American professors of English——"

"I'll bet! Men scared of toads, who think it's commando brave to omit adverbs. Profs who yearn to write in baboon blood! Columbia——"

"Quite a few American professors of English are like that, still. And you know it."

I said, "I remember meeting a couple at Cornell like that."

Dirty tennis, for Ricky went to Cornell and so did Karen. Besides, I very much admire good profs: a teacher is what I try mainly to be, myself—even if I'm not very good at it.

Ricky went on hotly. "Of course he writes to our college profs! How *else* is Professor Ishishi to learn? And how can *he* tell that some liberal intellectual stuff, or some new criticism, is for the birds? Didn't you hear his pitiful story about how difficult it was to get books? *American books?* Didn't you hear him say our government ought to print cheap Japanese translations of best-selling American novelists, essayists, playwrights, poets—the way the *Reds* are doing? His students can get tons of Communist 'Literature' for peanuts. But if they want *The Grapes of Wrath* or *Moby Dick* or *The Red Badge of Courage*, they either can't get them, or they're asked more yen than students dream of! *You* sneer—at a perfectly wonderful guy, because his knowledge is *dated!* He just had the bad luck to hit a couple of avant-garde professors—and they passed his letters along to their arty pals. It's so tragic it breaks my heart. What have *you* done, pray tell, to help get knowledge that's up-to-date to eager guys like him? Think what he *has* accomplished—even if it's mistaken! Then ask yourself if *you* could learn Japanese, in America, and make yourself an authority on Japanese slang with no more outside help than a few books and records. Sometimes, you give me a pain in the behind. When you're so damned *righteous*—and so damned wrong!"

Every day, near the Imperial Hotel, I saw a woman kneeling on the sidewalk. She wore a cotton-wadded coat so ragged it exposed her mercilessly to the strong street winds, snow and raw rain. Beside her lay a little dog that looked eagerly at every passer-by and, when each went on, lowered its head sadly. A cushion insulated it from the frigid cement; the woman used gunny sacks. All day long she read books—a very pretty woman about thirty years old who knelt, read and petted a dog behind the brushes and paste tins of a shoeshiner.

In all the times I passed I never saw her at work. The few daily pairs of shoes she may have shined could hardly have provided money enough for food. She doubtless thus sacrificed herself to add a bitter-won jot to some household on the brink of utmost destitution. That she was well enough educated to read books, and had heart enough to minister tenderly to a little dog, yet could find no better work, appalled me.

What sort of world is this that births so fair a person, teaches her so much, then sets her shining shoes on winter streets?

Yet millions, millions and tens of millions are like her. Millions and millions and millions have less: no shoeshine gear, no pretty face, no little Sheba at their sides, nor literacy.

It wasn't my business.

What does it matter?

My guilt at being unable to "do anything" merely reflected an American sentimentality, didn't it?

Or *did* it?

What about the convinced, dedicated person who, someday, somehow, would say (in effect) to the kneeling woman (and all the millions like her): "If your country became a Peoples Socialist Soviet Republic, you could work indoors, in a warm shoe *factory*, with a clean white uniform and meat for your dog?"

Lies?

Not by the standards of that ice-cold street!

That ice-cold street, where the ice-cold war is being lost by us, the world's free men. Cold streets—and the burning streets of Indo-China, Indonesia, Ceylon, Calcutta, Bombay, Alexandria— and even comfortable Mediterranean streets—as well as Congo River banks and South American alleys. . . .

We decided to go to Nikko. We had intended, in the few-days-over-a-week set aside for Japan, to make a longer side trip including Kyoto, like other tourists, but Ricky and I couldn't.

There were too many people that George knew, and Mrs. Cane and Lu—Japanese people, in Tokyo. Too many lunches and dinners. Too many shops that would send home interesting gifts for less than ten dollars.

Too many little dramas. For example. . . .

Mrs. Cane said, one morning as Ricky and I tramped through miles of open-air market, "This is where I shop for my food. Reasonable prices and excellent fresh fish, meat, everything. A few blocks away are several hundred American families. Military people. But I've never seen one wife or one soldier in this whole area. They go to the PX."

The Japanese marketmen and marketwomen pushed loaded bikes and motorcycles through the crowds of customers. On every street food of every imaginable sort was sold, including American brands in familiar tin cans and glass containers. Food—and baskets and silverware, hardware, clothing cloth, dishes, cooking utensils, pottery, rope: the house gear of humanity.

A boy of about eight, standing near his father, looked at Ricky and me with a strange expression—one of willingness to like and be liked, but of anxiety, too, as if he did not know whether such a thing was possible. I winked at him.

The effect was incredible. He burst into a joyful laugh, jumped a foot into the air, clapped his hands and babbled the news to his busy dad: *The man winked!* His father smiled at us. A young man on a bike saw or heard, nudged me and pointed at an open vessel in a stall. It held what looked like cole slaw. "Salad," he proudly, unmistakably announced.

"Salad," Ricky repeated.

The young man tried to think of more English words and could not. But just up the street a vendor tapped a glass jar filled with candy made to resemble miniature fruits. "Cherry," he called. So we added to his vocabulary by naming the rest: Apple. Plum. Peach. Grape.

He pronounced the words, all of us pointing to appropriate candy jars.

Everybody near was smiling then and saying English words.

The smiles, nods, word-at-a-time communication followed us up and down the streets.

You don't have to know the language to meet people. You have only to wink at a kid. It is like that almost anywhere on earth. . . .

The train to Nikko was electric.

It loitered through the wooden slums of Tokyo and went on north, at seventy miles an hour. A hostess addressed us in Japanese on a loud-speaker, making us welcome. Music was played. Two teen-age girls in uniforms pushed a cart up and down the aisles and sold oranges and sandwiches, candy, crackers, beer, sake and brandy. The girls seemed surprised every time they passed us because neither Ricky nor I wanted to buy the packages of Spearmint gum they held out.

Most of the passengers were Japanese—farmers, merchants, business people, wives, children, relatives. The rest—Americans, in the main—were going north to ski. There were two honeymoon couples from the States or from our forces stationed in Japan, and everybody seemed happy on that train.

Four young Americans across from us bought beer, set a suitcase on their laps, drank and played bridge all the way to Nikko. From overheard conversation, I gathered it was their first time in Japan. (From overheard argument, I also learned they played bridge very badly, indeed.) They never once looked out the window.

Farms fled past us, bunkered against the north winds by hedges of bamboo. Rectangular rice paddies appeared and vanished—rivers, villages, shrines, big towns, people working in the fields by hand and with animals—women and men and kids—scenes Ricky and I had read about. And we, anyhow, could hardly take our eyes from the fast-changing vista outdoors. It was easy to imagine how lovely the countryside would be when the brown fields and skeletal trees were green again and the thoughtfully planted flowers bloomed.

By and by, in the distance, we could see hills, then snow-covered mountains. The track became sinuous and steep; eroded vales closed around us. We came to Nikko.

There weren't many people in the hotel.

Our room was enormous and its windows gave a dazzling view of the high mountains and the village street winding toward them. Indoors, a big log burned with a small fire and we had lunch in a dining room that could accommodate a hundred, where a dozen people sat now at half as many tables, eating excellent "European" food. Nikko is the Emperor's summer resort and winter business is slow.

After lunch we met our guide, Mr. Okima—a thin man with a sensitive face who wore a very old felt hat, a threadbare topcoat and a business suit inadequate even when it had been new —long ago, and probably in some other country.

A rural quiet lay over the town; distant, individual voices could be heard on the crisp air. But one steady sound, the rush of water, played a constant undertone. Water surged beneath covered gutters down the town's main street and here and there the gutter lids were broken so that walking demanded caution.

The car climbed a switchback road, an engineering masterpiece, where plough-piled snow obliged us to stop at intervals so busloads of Japanese tourists could creep past. School kids, mostly.

Lake Chuzenji lies near the crest of these mountains, blue and cold in wintertime, and we visited Buddhist temples on its shore—walking on clean matting cold as ice among shrines, paintings, statues and holy relics—in our socks. Gentle Mr. Okima lost his breath easily, I perceived, and he coughed a good deal—always apologetically. His thin shoes soon became soaked by the snow and mud and wetness.

By an elevator that plunges several hundred feet through a shaft cut in solid rock we visited the base of Nikko's Kegon Falls, watching them shatter and leap on in boiling cascade. We drove in slush part way around the lake, gawking at winter-dressed citizens, the lobbies of Japanese hotels where rows of shoes and geta were ranged on matted floors and at huge launches snowbound on the shore. . . .

We were just tourists, that day, away by ourselves and alone —except for Mr. Okima who quietly explained, softly suggested— and coughed. We sent the somewhat bedraggled Pontiac back down the mountain and took a cable car. Larger and more attractive than any cable car I'd seen before, it dived inchmeal down its awesome track, disclosing mountainscapes which changed dramatically with every few rods of descent. In sullen afternoon we drove on roads that were green-thatched by stupendous cedars, all but walled in by century-expanded trunks. These cryptomerias planted long ago not only line certain roads but soar in solemnity above Nikko's renowned temples, above rock staircases, gates, pagodas, carved gods and demons and dragons, imperial gifts, stone lanterns and labyrinthine halls that led to holy-dim chambers and kneeling shadows who murmurously praise various gods. A heavenly heathen dazzlement of gold, scarlet, that blue the Moslems favor and every hue—the whole set about with wondrous sculpture overembossed by tons of semiprecious jewels.

With icing feet, in mummy silence, at a benumbed pace, we went through all those stagy, gaud-heaped tunnels-of-love of Believers who are called nonbelievers.

Dusk fell. Dun birds abandoned the uncheerful pickings on the snow-matted earth and sought refuge among the cedars. We, too, were tired and cold and hungry. Mr. Okima led us, before we were obliged to ask, toward our car and the hotel.

Here is his story:

His family came from Nikko but he had been brought up in Tokyo. As a young boy, he had shown musical talent and soon he became a cellist. A place in a symphony orchestra was waiting for him when the war had come. Mr. Okima was found unfit for military service: he had tuberculosis. So he took a war plant job—but went on studying cello. In one of our air raids, his district had been burned. His father, mother, brothers and sisters had been consumed. And his cello.

After the war, finding no work in Tokyo, he had gone back to the family home in Nikko—where he is sporadically employed as a guide.

A cynical reader of that bleak synopsis might imagine Mr. Okima created it, in the hope of being given alms, or even the price of a cello, by a kindly hearted tourist.

"All wogs, Japs, and Chinks," a tourist once told me, "give you a hard luck story. That's why they learn English."

But the sensitive, soft-coughing, self-effacing guide hadn't the slightest thought that we—or anybody—might be led, by his account, to offer money. He no longer expected or even dreamed he could become the cellist he had once been. He was a man in frail health, perhaps even a dying man—without wife, children or family. He needed but to pay his way in the world as best he could for as long as possible. Of that, we both were sure.

Our tip was generous but not lavish; it surprised him: "If you would give me your address," he smiled, "I will send you a card next Christmas."

(His card came as I proofread these lines!)

Several times in the night we got up to stand at the window and watch the moonlight select vistas through cloud irises: often, the great mountains seemed to float in spectral, bluish air—— and one could see why temple builders had chosen Nikko long ago: it is the kind of place where people have always imagined gods live.

A morning train whirled us back to Tokyo. . . .

At a party the next night, Ricky and I had a last but best opportunity to discuss, with American men married to Japanese girls and a Japanese man who had an American wife, the many things we'd seen, thought of, wondered about and guessed in our busy stay.

Then a car came for us.

It had been snowing all evening. The trip to the airport was a cold, chain-clanking ride past indecipherable lights, with frequent skids in trolley tracks. Passengers waited in the echoing terminal with that nervous silence which characterizes air travelers in uncertain weather. George had accompanied us and he introduced us to an air line official who took us to a modernistic, warm room where a Japanese in a white coat brought sandwiches for us. Outside, the wind spiraled over an airfield that tapered to white impenetrability. By and by, we learned that a flight already three hours out, toward Hawaii, was coming back: icing up. Later still, we and some sixty other people were sent back to hastily booked space at the Imperial.

We were given the same rooms. We didn't unpack but just swallowed sleeping pills and pulled up the Imperial's heavy blankets. A knock came on the door in what seemed no time; it was seven o'clock. The handsome young chambermaid we'd had all week brought in two pots of coffee, bowed—and grinned sympathetically.

The snow had stopped.

At the airport, an American salesman who had a bad sore throat and a worse hangover, was trying to get a pick-me-up. The chief of India's travel bureau (on his way to the coronation in Cambodia) sat down on a bench and argued about "neutralism." Ricky gave the salesman antibiotic lozenges for his throat. I persuaded the air line official whom we had met through George to arrange a special bar opening for the salesman. But since I didn't then understand "neutralism," I got nowhere with the Indian.

Our flight was finally announced but I heard a tall, well-heeled, elderly American cursing. I looked where he was looking. I saw that Japanese mechanics, breathing steam as they labored in the slush, were removing a wheel from our plane: *flat tire!* The well-dressed American was so indignant and voluble that I found myself defending air travel:

"Obviously, the tire was observed to be going flat just now. Better they change it, than try to take off and have a blowout or land on a soft tire. Sure, we were held up all night! So what? Man, you are crossing hunks of the Pacific Ocean—in the dead of winter. In less than twenty-four hours, *counting* the delay, we'll *still* do what takes the best boat a week. And everything you're griping at is done to insure your safety."

Somewhat to my astonishment, the austere, elderly citizen said, "You know, pal, you're *right!*" And he wandered away, whistling to himself.

An hour or two later, we were looking down at the bay-indented coast of the southern islands. The captain of the plane came up and introduced himself to Ricky and me: "May have to return to Tokyo," he said. "That's inside dope, just for you two. One compressor's quit."

When he'd gone, I exploded in plain American profanity.

Ricky calmly quoted my earlier remarks: " 'Everything you're griping at is done to insure your safety.' "

"But—damn it to hell!—this is our fifth delay!"

She continued to quote: " 'Crossing hunks of the Pacific Ocean—in the dead of winter——' "

"Okay," I said. "*Okay!*"

5
China is no more

Guidebooks agree that Hong Kong harbor is among the world's three most spectacular. One treatise adds that the ideal manner of first viewing it is by air at sunset on a clear day. In late winter Hong Kong is often fogbound and a plane bound there from Japan may land instead at Manila. But when we arrived, the sun's edge stood on China's hills. And the books were right. Leather-hued islets along the coast floated sharp-shored on the blue sea; there was no haze. The Crown Colony, Hong Kong and Kowloon, swept below us and every building and wharf, hovel, sampan and junk, every ocean liner at anchor in the roadstead glowed brilliant and many-colored as the stained glass of cathedral windows.

Of course, Ricky's and mine was no longer a mere *Sentimental Journey*, like Sterne's. Ricky may, indeed, have sometimes felt her trip more nearly resembled *Travels with a Donkey*. We saw what the guidebooks said we would—and no book could describe. What lexicon is adequate, though? A good preparation for Hong Kong, for instance, would include reading the works of Marx, Lenin and Stalin, as well as texts explaining British enterprise, British colonial policy and the temperament of Britons. Poets could take it from there. . . .

I'd been wondering on the plane where my own "prepara-

tion" for this region had begun. The answer was: *postage stamps.*
Owing to a childhood hospitalization of several months' duration,
stamp collecting became my hobby. And one of the best ways
to begin an interest in the world is to collect its stamps. Father
brought to the hospital from Cleveland a Scott Stamp Album.
He'd gone there to earn by extra preaching extra dollars for my
medical bills. Citizens of Delaware, Ohio, then dug out en-
velopes and copybooks filled with stamps gathered by themselves
in childhood, or by deceased parents and grandparents. So I had
a somewhat valuable collection that went back to the begin-
nings of postal service in the United States. (Precisely *how* valuable, I have no idea. Years after I'd forgotten the album
existed, my brother Ted came upon it in an attic and sold it,
for what sum he never said. And I never asked: he was in college
and ministers' sons in college need every dime they can lay hands
on.)

One pasted-up copybook given to me contained many Hong
Kong stamps—carefully removed from missionary mail, no
doubt. These I soaked off to affix with paper hinges in my album. I was dismayed to find the colors ran. Afterward, pages of
British queens had individual auras in tints of unforgettable
philatelic nomenclature—ultramarine, carmine, lilac, lake, ver-
million, and so on.

So, even at ten, to me Hong Kong was a far-off place with
stamps that ran. The album, furthermore, contained a description
of each country, its inhabitants, government and the like. I also
knew, therefore, that it was a British Crown Colony, a free port
which included several islands and some mainland territory, that
the capital was actually called Victoria City though "Hong
Kong" was the name usually employed for it, and I knew the
population was overwhelmingly Chinese. I also knew its location
on the map.

In fact, from stamps I learned that sort of thing about every
country: Transvaal, Bosnia, Bohemia, Montenegro. The great
wars have changed not just the stamps but the maps, however,
and now and again I think momentarily of the globe as it was
before Woodrow Wilson rearranged it, or Hitler, Lenin and the

others. Still—the hobby has value: too many travelers thought geography dull, forgot their sixth grade lessons, and in middle age arrive at this or that fabulous region, hardly knowing where they are. Stamp collectors remember. . . .

The plane thumped down. We were whisked through port protocol and a taxi carried us along Chinese streets. Its Chinese driver smiled often and said nothing. The drive was short but I gave our chauffeur an American dollar—all I had for a tip—and was startled by thanks in comprehensible pidgin English. It is a language of brief nouns, pronouns and short verbs. As time went on, Ricky used it so constantly and effectively that she would say to *me*, "You send shirts wash?" or "Eat lunch one clock? Two?"

The airport is on the Kowloon, or mainland, side; so is the Peninsula Hotel and a taut-faced English clerk received us there, gave us our mail, and helped us change Express checks into Hong Kong dollars, at about six for one. A Chinese in seedy blue serge uniform and a neat blouse took us up in an elevator. With us came luggage-bearing Chinese porters so young I insulted one by offering to carry our heaviest bag which he could barely lift from the floor. A Chinese hall porter in a white shirt and white duck trousers ushered us into our room.

We let the luggage sit, and, for a long while, stood at a casement window watching junks and sampans plod amongst big ships and ferries cross the harbor to Hong Kong, busy shuttles that wove white wakes in a blue bay. Across the water, signs with Chinese characters lit up: cerise, jade green, yellow—and indecipherable as those above the Ginza.

By and by, a knock came. An elderly, bent Chinese in soiled white entered, smiled, said something and turned on the bath. He hung up large towels, smiled again, wagged his finger at a printed sign as he departed. Water was available in Hong Kong only from five thirty to eight, the sign said.

"That was the bath coolie." Ricky started to unbutton her dress and soon I heard her splashing in the big tub.

I ordered some bottled water. A different "coolie" brought it, for here, even more elaborately than in Japan, is endless specialization. Each small job is done at low pay or for small tips so that the largest possible number of people can wrest their daily rice from every activity. A day later, we found that the bath coolie also polished shoes; but that was because the first task did not pay enough to keep him from starving.

There was about that bent, shy, sweet old man, a look of humble amity, of love, that instantly touched both Ricky and me, though neither of us mentioned it until near the end of our visit. Emily Hahn and Pearl Buck and the rest have not yet quite shown how lovable the Chinese can be. I think I never saw people easier to like. You looked at them, they at you. You exchanged a smile and perhaps noticed some slight oddity together—such as my Indian moccasins, which the bath coolie couldn't polish and I washed with soap, an act he found inordinately amusing. You thus found you had made a contact more than casual. The twelve or fifteen boys came when we left, to thank us: everyone—not bowing, like the Japanese, but standing courteously, glad of their tips, perhaps glad we hadn't scolded them as some do, but happiest because we'd noticed them as individuals. To be so perceived was, I think, the point of their manners—manners which expressed the meaning of their inner values.

Sometimes, though, the very number of those who attended to our wants secretly irritated me. I liked each one: but they could become too many. And I was not reconciled to Asia's surfeit of eager aides until, one day on the road from Delhi to Agra, I watched a number of men spread bluestone for the foundation of a wide shoulder. They squatted wherever the trucks had dumped the material. They had no tools and simply took the fragments from the heaps by hand, carrying or tossing them one by one to the roadbed. The waste appalled me for an instant; then I saw the horror of its meaning. Here were turbaned, bearded, human men, men with Old Testament faces, noble-looking, who lived so meagerly they could support themselves (and for all I knew, their families) by handling one small bit of stone at a time, all day, every day, till death.

After that, I bore with better grace the incessant invasions of our quarters by multitudes of servitors. For in the Asian world a grown man gladly waits an hour or three or four to carry to you—proudly—one small tray. It was not waste, not inefficiency, but a naked sorrow. . . .

While Ricky bathed I continued for a time to admire night-spangled Hong Kong across the way. By and by I went to the bureau in search of a radiogram I'd noticed in a bundle of precious letters from home: familiar handwritings and scripts of recognizable typewriters. Probably, I thought, the radiogram would say that Harold Ober, my long-time literary representative (and beloved friend) has had an offer for movie rights, or wants to know if I will accept a writing commission. That is the most frequent content of such communications with me.

I opened the envelope:

BOB DIED THIS MORNING HATE TO HURT YOUR TRIP WITH SUCH BAD NEWS.   ARTHUR.

If you have lived very long and loved at all, you know. . . .

Death is not the worst thing—only the last, and love makes it necessary. One was not, is—and will not be, so others may follow. Death is one price of Evolution. It cannot be evaded, should not usually be sought, and never partakes of evil. It is each person's required gift to the rest and says: I yield now, that you may continue. The contented add: I have made the world some small bit better in my fashion; I have given you my life as an imperfect example; pursue and enhance the best of me, for you are now in my stead.

It is our function to evolve consciously as no beast could, before us. And immortality is the essence of instinct—our own and that of the beasts who begot us. Immortality belongs to the newborn and the unborn—all future generations: men's *children*. In beasts, the egoless, time-forever-present immortality was but *acts*: feeding and breeding and pup rearing; in men, it can be that and the immortal *awareness*, also. Only the arrogant steal the intent of Life and meaning of Nature to furnish heavens for their vanity and hells for those whom they cannot bring to subjugate agreement in that vanity.

Immortal Christians, Mussulmen, Brahmins—whosoever believeth in life everlasting for his own nebulous person rather than for his children and their children! Posterity is the immortal fact and to create it, instinct's meaning. But every purpose of instinct is stolen from Man, Nature and God Himself by those who use the passion of instinct entire to sustain the dull dream that Eternity's designed to perpetuate status quo: their own shabby selves.

I have heard the temples and cathedrals of the earth resound —heard them murmur, chant, moan, clap, sing, bellow and whimper for every Paradise, while all about their streets the inhabitants of Hereafter ran in tatters picking over garbage to fill their mortal bellies.

"Suffer little children to come unto me, . . . for of such is the Kingdom of Heaven."

That was the Truth He spoke.

The greedy disciples, the arrogant apostles never knew.

They built churches.

The churches built Heaven. Heaven's shape evolved as men, reluctant, faced new truths of necessity and cast aside reluctantly the catacombs and roaming ghouls of prior faith.

But every brainwashed devotee clung as long as he could to his ticket to Heaven and accepted on "faith" as long as possible, every vile dogma—spending a lifetime in animal rites, raising up idols and edifices in many-styled attempts to grab the natural heritage of his own children. The eyes of children then were let to fester, their limbs to decay and their bellies to bulge with famine. But these abandoned young, Heaven itself, were "compensated"; they were instructed in the faith so they, too, could dote on their deathlessness and let life die around them. Only those few who serve God with the brain He gave, and His love of truth and the courage, and instinct, have ever defied the holy shamans—who use fear to capture the immortal instinct and promise Heaven so as to rule here in Hell. It is proof of God's

Reality that among the few are even some of the "faithful": a Moslem here; a brave Presbyterian; a Roman Catholic, yonder; and there—men and women who say they are atheist. Thus Truth sometimes masters creed and creedlessness.

Yet how hard is comprehension even for modern man!

He could discern with his mind's eye, learn his Reality, from Holy Writ itself. He could discover why the instinct he inherits from more-loving, more-honorable beasts is still the dynamic of immortality—the omnipresent, infinite Will of God! He could find out that death is this reward: a restoration of you, of me, to the shape no man fears, which was his before conception. From Science, stars, a contemplated navel!

Who bravely learns? Few—few.

I put the radiogram on the bureau, pressing it smooth, and went to look across the harbor at an invisible city, aware in my way of death.

I remembered a hundred nights at Bob's home, brilliant guests and guests with warm hearts, as well as some—patients— unable to shake hands. I remembered people who entered that home and sat in aureoles of acceptance, happily: old patients. Long since, they'd stretched out on Bob Lindner's psychoanalytical couch as if it were the rack. They had at last walked away to be and do that which they had once been unable even to contemplate.

Frenetic Florida nights exploded in my reverie . . . and calm nights under the slow stellar pinwheel that turned above a northern coast where he and I had talked to one another as men too rarely do—withholding nothing, saying all, fearing no lapse and sure of understanding: *friends*.

Halfway around the world his corpse now lay while his father wept—who had so recently wept at the death of Bob's younger brother. I could not help to carry the bier or comfort his widow by recalling Bob's flaming integrity and his courage. I could not take his kids for a walk in a Sunday Park and say:

"This is the way I felt when my mother died. I learned what we all must do. You will act as you know Bob would have had you—here now, and tomorrow, and in all your childhood forever."

Bob's children! The stabbing grief for Bob was for *me* and would diminish in its time; but I knew from knowing myself (a knowledge he had most helped me to gain) I had but *begun* my contemplation of Bob's immortality, his three kids.

My mood overspilled.

Hong Kong! Far-off, unknown, it grew hideous. Chinese characters across the harbor danced with demonic malice before my bleeding eyes. The rage of the living, at death, surged over me. Helplessness mounted. Space as well as time had cut me off —and Ricky—who also loved Bob. We had exiled ourselves even from the passion of loved ones and from our own compassion. We were alone.

The glistered harbor hooted at me, shook its incomprehensible emblems in my face. I heard the fifes and drums, and saw the banners, of all paraders to Hell. They beckoned. I held back flinching—and read the lesson to myself he'd shown the way to learn: what would you have you do? Immediately, I knew *husbandliness.* I found, too, that quality my family attributes to being Scottish, Jews ascribe to Jewishness, which Hindus, Moslems, men, women, East, West, correctly and proudly acknowledge as the ancestral gift: temper.

Ricky came.

Her handsome, lithe body had been tubbed beige-pink. Her washed hair—black-seeming, now—curled like ebony shavings at her brow and the neat nape of her neck. She saw a cocktail I'd ordered, its cold glass opaque from waiting. "Oh, thanks!"

She drank. I waited, then.

"There's a radiogram," I soon said. She caught the inflection, held the glass still an instant, set it down. "It's very rugged, Ricky. *Rough.*" I read it to her.

We didn't say anything.

She rose slowly.

We kissed each other.

She walked to the window where I'd been and looked at the same alien witchery. I knew this:

She was thinking of her kind, versatile, not old mother who'd died only weeks ago—suddenly. And of my father. He had wound up the scroll of seventy-nine years—hard learning, brave achievement, bitterness, and yet an outpouring love restored to him in the end, that promised manifold. My father had gone two weeks before her mother so Ricky was thinking, *There is too much dying.*

She and I are similar in this way:

To immediate crisis, we generally respond as if, not crisis but a mere intellectual problem were present. We do the useful, sensible things, withholding emotion. Only when the necessary is finished do we run our separate risks of extravaganzas in sentiment and feeling, jousting with uncertain instincts that lance about with pain and sadness.

"I better wire Harold," I said. "Don't know just how Bob's estate stands, at the moment. Sometimes, a family is completely without cash. Remember when Hervey . . . ?" I wrote out the message.

We discussed the wife and children of another author, another friend. They woke one morning to find husband-and-father dead on the floor, access to funds shut off by mean law, and not five dollars in their combined, trembling purses. I'd happened to have a pocketful of bills that day. For we must eat, drink, purchase, pay the paper boy and milkman—even while trying to compose unexpected epitaphs.

"And we'll have to wire Johnnie."

"I'll get Max to phone, too. Ask if he can do anything."

"And you better wire Verona and John Slater. They're wonderful help, too, in times like . . ."

So I riffled in drawers, found more blanks and started writing more messages in the spidery scraggle that often is the penmanship of those who use pens principally to sign checks or scribble autographs. Love. Sympathy. The goddamned words. As if they were business wires.

She dressed. I bathed hurriedly: the eight o'clock faucets would soon shut off. The bath coolie cleaned out the tub and filled a covered metal jar with cold water. A bed coolie turned down the beds. We went to the Swiss-managed restaurant in the Peninsula Hotel and ate our dinner. We went to bed, talked about Bob awhile—and fell asleep.

The next day we hired a car and a guide: Portuguese, it turned out, a man who'd been in the Hong Kong militia and was captured by the Japanese. He spent some years on their main islands, watching his fellow prisoners die. He told us about it all —in detail.

We covered Kowloon, each playing at "tourist" for the other, not noticing our spirits were becoming insecure and despair dragged at every feigned enthusiasm. Beneath the attention I forced on sight-seeing I kept telling myself that, surely, I was accustomed to the facts of life—including the great stone fact of death: I'd seen enough—myself come near enough; but perhaps *Ricky* was suffering secretly and overmuch.

We drove as close to the Red Chinese mountains as we could and stared at their empty, arid contours. We photographed a long, modern-looking train as it came from the Red border into this small, free zone. We took pictures of Chinese women with heavy pails on shoulder yokes wading ashore after gathering clams and seaweed in one of many azure-surfaced indentures, where sea invades barren superdunes. We inspected a sampan village: a swarm of overswarmed small boats where whole families lived, ate, copulated, gave birth and died—in pup-tent spaces. It smelled like that. We took the classical photograph of a junk with a saffron sail tacking across blue water past a distant hill town.

We drove down Chinese city streets lined with post-supported, rectilinear upper storeys: shops below and apartments above. The square posts colonnaded the curbs and were marked from top to bottom with crimson characters advertising wares for sale—an effect that big, square barberpoles might give a street: lively and bright. But every cement façade was time-stained and dank. Up-yawning stairs behind each entry penetrated dim regions where eternity devoted itself to the cultivation of mold and the perfection of hallway halitosis.

We rode in rickshaws—after the common, conscience-ridden debate as to whether it is degrading to support the abuse of men as beasts of burden or a lesser evil to give gainful employment to human beings who not only sought continuously and clamorously to haul us, but manifestly needed work of any sort. Ricky and I rode. Some tourists wouldn't.

By car, we went along miles of wide streets in the center of which dwelt thousands on thousands on thousands of human beings who had fled Red China, leaving behind friends and possessions and, often, families—to escape Communism at whatever risk or penalty. There they were, in a continuous strip of lesser Hoovervilles—"houses" made of old boards, rusty galvanized iron, bits of used linoleum, matting, tar paper, flattened-out tin cans, sides and ends of cartons—anything with surface that might hang together for a while and fend off the coldness of the winter, the rain, and the sun besides. We drove rather quickly amidst streaming bikes, rickshaws, hand-pulled carts, head-loaded men and women who trotted as if driven by clockwork, buses, vans, trucks, English cars, and American.

We saw the shanty-and-vegetable-garden projects devised for refugees and the new but bunker-bleak apartments being built for them in the area where fire had destroyed acres of sub-human beetle-warrens where thousands had sought liberty only to be again evicted by holocaust.

We watched the British deploy regiments of tough-looking troops—together with tanks, motorcycles and mobile guns. Our guide made us hear for the first time—but not the last—that Hong Kong was indefensible and the Reds "any time they wished, could take it in a fortnight." Its value as a free port merely postponed, they all said, ultimate certain onslaught. And that value, we gathered, was owing as much to opportunities for illicit trade as for commerce permissible by treaty and UN declaration.

We saw the immense nets that blocked harbors opening toward the sea—a British effort to impede smugglers and, in particular, opium smugglers. . . .

We went over to the "Hong Kong side" by ferry on another day and drove about that big, insular city. Some of its main shopping streets are as gloomy, narrow, dingy and somberly over-hung by massed masonry as to be indistinguishable from London thoroughfares. The signs of shops, offices and stores are English, too. Trotting rickshawmen and Chinese pedestrians (along —perhaps—with an implausible hence hazardous system of traffic light control and trolley procedure) alone served to remind us on some corners that this was English once-removed—and rather far removed, distance-wise.

We were driven near the summit of Signal Mountain and along a handsome coast to Repulse Bay.

We visited the incredible Tiger Balm Gardens. Aw Boon Haw, a Chinese who made his heap by selling a nostrum with that Oriental-magic brand name, had caused to be built in the rock terraces of his back yard a zoo-circus—a menagerie of concrete animals and legendary figures, painted with such harsh pigments as are found on dime store counters. Among heroes and monsters familiar in myths of both East and West, among snakes a hundred feet long and other bizarre plaster horrors, rose the exquisite White Pagoda, marking a family burial place.

Children swarmed in the terraced rocks—ignoring the perfervid petrified monsters and murmurously, monotonously demanding-proffering shoeshines on a descending scale of terms. Other guided tourists in close-knit hordes stared at the profligate display of cement sculpturings. They were like waxworks commingled with the gay images of grue that suddenly appear before boaters in dark "Tunnels of Love," horrid junk intended to make ladies squeal—for hugging's sake. Outdoors, they seemed banal.

The magnate's house, or "Haw Par Mansion," was open to privileged visitors that day. So our guide arranged for Ricky and me to see its different, but equally ornate, interior. Oil portraits of Tiger Balm potentates, their wives, heirs and assigns yanked the visitor's dizzy attention from huge porcelain pots bedizened with dragons—and vied vertiginously for notice with magnificent silk screens set about glass cabinets that contained what was said to be the finest collection of carved jade on earth.

It may have been. I have a miserable eye for sculptured

form. But some of the small jade objects were lovely even to my
flawed perceptions. I was also amazed that jade came in various
colors. And I marveled even more at the ornaments in Mr.
Haw's cases, because they had surely used up the lifetimes of
many thousands of men—first in learning the art and subsequently in chipping rock and tenderly polishing the shaped,
precious residue. . . .

The night after that excursion Ricky and I quarreled. Our
arguments are rare and mostly symbolic. They may even concern matters of fact that either of us could establish by a quick
look in an encyclopedia. But if we feel conflict, we do not look;
we debate, since neither of us is occupied with the actual subject. Instead, we are trying to make sounds that represent some
inner discontent. That discontent may be nonverbal. It may
be unconscious, repressed, guilty, censorious, or merely something we don't want to state. But *it* is as real as the quarrel is
often itself absurd.

Husbands and wives, arguing in pulpit tones over the exact
height of the Washington Monument, very rarely thereby come
to learn that he's annoyed because she cut her hair short while she
is vexed because he has forgotten their anniversary. So their
reconciliation, too, is also symbolic. Yet it resolves the whole
dispute—the unreal one that was spoken and the real anxiety
concealed. For reconciliation reminds both partners of their relationship which transcends petty acts, transient grievances and
even genuine injuries which we all, in our imperfectness, do one
another. The quarrel tests love; the reconciliation affirms it.

I cannot remember the subject of our argument.

But we reached a point at which Ricky was vowing through
sobs that she would go home, if we did not share one passport.

Bathed, still bickering, we nevertheless went out to search
for a different eating place. We found one not far away. But a
trip hammer, apparently working on an all-night shift, so shook
the building that we walked on grimly for blocks and at last
came to a dubious Chinese place. We were escorted to a balcony.
There were no other Westerners in the floor-and-a-half—but the

waiter understood English. The food was excellent, but we ate dolorously.

During that dismal meal, I began to realize that the grim word of Bob's death had crushed Ricky by redoubling the torrent of grief she felt for her mother and which she had not had a day—let alone the needed weeks and months—to face, assimilate and come to bear. Then—and I guess only then—I could unburden some of my own pent-up distress.

After that, we were able to giggle at the infinite care of a man Ricky called a "band coolie" as he produced musical instruments, polished them lovingly, set up music stands and at last proudly gave way to a Chinese jazz band. The men played so badly, yet with such unction, and with so many approval-seeking glances our way, that we applauded as if it were Goodman leading his boys with his seraphic clarinet.

When we rode home—pounding side by side down the cold main street in rickshaws—I happened to see the electric sign of a tattoo emporium. I pointed to it and asked Ricky if she wanted to be embellished. The rickshaw boys caught on and broke into wonderful laughter while they ran with us.

So, when we came "home" to the big room high above the ferryhouse and the harbor, having eaten and laughed, we were able to speak calmly again.

We seriously discussed returning to America.

We were very tired. Our vacation was turning out to be strenuous. I'd been asked to make a tape recording for a Hong Kong radio station the next day. We had invitations to meet the Governor—and many other people. The letters we carried to Chinese and Americans in the city would surely result in further invitations if we presented them.

Air travel itself is not conducive to relaxation. Few people can sleep long or restfully in public view and nobody is used to sleeping in a half-sitting posture. Lights wink on and off, too; people smoke and read and grunt and snore; stewardesses and restless passengers constantly bustle up and down the aisles. And a landing, whether for refueling or at some scheduled stop, will jar anyone awake; if one soon falls back to sleep, the roaring take-off rouses one. Yet our vacation program called for half a world more of such travel.

We might, we thought, be able to turn in our tickets, go home by boat—and rest. Repeated sky strides also confuse. There's not time enough between, say, Greece and Italy, to cease musing on Plato and prepare for Pompey or to forget Phidias and substitute Leonardo. One is air-borne: one then endeavors to obliterate this morning's exchange rate and commit to memory an unfamiliar coinage with a disturbingly different relation to the dollar. That done, one merely starts to list sights that must be seen and to hunt up a restaurant where a first meal may be had; but as those needed chores are initiated, the plane lands bumpily. Bewildered and unready, one stands in a high Roman noon, still licking from one's lips the taste of an Athenian breakfast. . . .

And our grief—now made nearly unbearable by Bob's death—added an overwhelming burden. . . .

But there were opposed factors:

We could not return in time for Bob's funeral. Even had we been able to emplane when the radiogram arrived, we would have been too late. We had done all we could and our swift return might not even give consolation but be taken, instead, as a vain or emotional and therefore embarrassing response.

Certainly, our shared passport was no obstacle to either of us: our embassy could issue separate passports. But we knew again that, whatever we decided, we would do it together.

We were halfway round the world. It might be our only trip of such magnitude. Ahead, lay realms we'd never seen or ever expected to see. The tickets were paid for. The expense money lay in the Peninsula Hotel safe in travelers' checks and a letter of credit—money saved up, after taxes—money earned in a lucky year, by writing one word, then another.

When would my writing produce such money again?

Next year? The year after? In five years? Maybe *never*.

Meantime, we'd grow older.

When would we be willing again to carve such a chunk of time out of my constant writing schedule?

Would we be well enough, sturdy enough—in some indeterminate later year?

What, above all, would we think of ourselves, later on, if we gave up this great journey owing to private sorrows—and were never able to undertake it?

By the time we asked ourselves that question, in those terms, we both knew we would go on. We looked at each other, smiling, because we knew that each had wanted first to be certain of the other's true feelings. Somehow, we had managed to reveal them reciprocally, before making a commitment.

We went to bed early.

I woke up before dawn, however, and I remembered abruptly the walk my Washington friends had suggested. I dressed and hurried quietly from the room where Ricky slept. The informed men had said that if I made a dawn trip, I'd find out for myself something which, when I'd discovered it, would of itself disclose its meaning. I rode down in the Peninsula Hotel elevator anxiously.

For who has undertaken an errand grimly commanded by grim men that involves going he knows not where in search of he knows not what?

My "missions" have been few. I was never a soldier and I am not brave. The quality I possess that some regard as "courage" is a mere mingling of recklessness with tentative conviction— and the belief that my feelings for my fellow men usually will be reflected by them.

That what I was now about to see would somehow involve Communism, I knew. No more.

Two days before, I'd actually stood near the Red border and stared at the drab Communist mountains beyond, without any experience of that anxiety which had pierced me for twenty years whenever I'd thought of far journeys. But my nonchalance on that spot was a response, perhaps, to the visible fact that some million and a half Britishers, Americans, Chinese citizens and Chinese refugees calmly accepted this proximity of the Scarlet Squid. In part, too, I'd been stunned by Bob's death, preoccupied with Ricky's and my sorrow. Even a cold wind that blew dust from Communist territory against my face could not, perhaps, penetrate that mood with old, ingrained alarms.

But now, I was going to seek the source of my dread—in a foreign and unknown city, amongst a desperate, beggared people whose language I could not understand and whose temper I did not know.

There had been little time to wonder what circumstances or acts my friends had wanted me to see; but in occasional hours of night flying I'd tried to guess:

One might find what is called "Communist activity" in the Hong Kong streets, amongst the refugees, before the employed population woke: street-corner harangues, perhaps—the furtive or open distribution of Red pamphlets, or the circulation of petitions and organizational lists, for signatures—with, maybe, coercion. Maybe, too, outlawed posters hung at night, to be scraped away by police in daytime. Violence, or vice. Women used for bait. Or opium. *What?* I knew the foul boundlessness of Red methods.

And what about me? A Westerner, walking along in a clean, costly flight coat with a gaudy wool plaid lining—a man with expensive (if dirty) shoes. What would they think? Say to me? Do to me? Would I—for instance—come upon some act of intimidation I could not endure and quixotically involve myself in a fight that would end—at best!—in some hospital or jail? (I'd done precisely that, on savage impulse, long ago, in New York; and jail was where I had landed, that time.)

Would they sneer at me aloud? Would implacable hate scarily pursue me down every street and alley? Would they spit on me—as a group of Senegalese had spat, when I foolhardily walked the length of a gated, forbidden street in Marseilles . . . ?

Dirty light came from a scudding sky as I stepped from the hotel door. It was cold. Except for the middle hours of our first day in the city, it had always been cold, for us—fifty-five or sixty degrees by day and ten degrees less, at night. Not many people were abroad in the vicinity of the hotel.

I walked—quickly—along a few blocks of streets with which

I was familiar, rehearsing a turn into unknown routes and roads. Shops were shuttered with steel, or boarded up, and heavily locked, for Hong Kong is not a city where things of value may be lightly guarded. Too many people live on the rim of starvation. Too many have too little, have nothing, have that less-than-something which erodes away all conscience and sets raging necessity in its place.

In gutters, presently, I saw old women with brooms, pails—rudimentary equipment. They were sweeping up and shoveling into handcarts, the squalor of the day before—garbage, straw, paper soaked by night rain. They looked up at me with trouble-engraved faces; surprised, I could see, by the very fact that they concealed all emotion.

Come on, Wylie, I said to myself. I swung toward the waterfront.

Here was a thoroughfare that is conventional in the whole world's ports: broad and cobblestoned, with wharfheads on one hand, warehouses and saloons on the other. The rigging of ships rose on my left—funnels, masts, booms—webbed rigidly against the ashy saffron of approaching dawn. A truck went by, full of inert stevedores in trade-blackened cotton garments. They lost their jiggling ennui for a moment to stare at me.

On the next corner, I saw a building wall freshly stuck with paper posters.

This would be it.

I stared at photographs with Chinese and English captions. Not Red. These were posters put up by the Colonial Government, urging all refugees to register, to learn where they could get help, to practice hygiene, and to seek education for their children. Pictures retold the content of the bilingual captions. Here, English common sense was using a common Russian method to call attention to opportunities offered and services rendered by the State—and to give simple, down-to-earth advice.

I went on.

Street lights still shone; vehicles carried wan lights. The sky was vaguely alight but the changing densities of wind-tumbled clouds produced a variable chiaroscuro on cobbled street and blank building walls. All ships lay dead. Save for the occasional clanging passage of a load of men bound toward early, menial employment—save for whispering brooms of the aged street sweepers and the tentative toot of a whistle that came now and again from the roadsteads—the place was silent. My rubber heels made sounds that are rarely audible to me on city pavements: I am somewhat deaf.

But there were no Communist agitators on that waterfront, no refugees at whom to sermonize; no opium dens, saloons, places of prostitution or other establishments. Just shops, boarded tight as jewelry stores, and wharfheads and the things called godowns by the British.

There were no policemen, either. I did not see one during that morning's walk.

The selection of the waterfront as a first place to look was foolish—and doubtless related to my American association of stevedoring with Red connivance. This was a day-busy place; at night, a tomb. I turned into the central part of Kowloon and strode swiftly, to reach the area I knew to be inhabited by refugees before any of their mysterious daybreak activities should be halted by broad light.

For block after block I walked on wide, ordinary thorough-fares—until I came to Chinese buildings with square, scarlet-emblazoned supporting posts ranked along the curb so that the wide sidewalks were sheltered by the floors overhead. For some further blocks, tight-jawed shop fronts continued on one hand and on the other, an occasional truck, cyclist, cab or bus rattled past. I became aware, as I walked near the posts, looking at every-thing my eyes could make out, peering into every murky alley and recess—of an occasional cascade beside me. Something would rain down in the gutter every hundred feet or so—splash, thump, squash, plop. I investigated. Chinese families, tenanted in the floors above, were wakening and dumping yesterday's debris down their house fronts.

I continued, keeping closer to the buildings, for the spatter of these garbagefalls was considerable: the stuff was mostly liquid and contained remnants of pulpy fruits and vegetables.

The women sweeps were certainly vital to Kowloon's (and probably Hong Kong's) health—and even its traffic, since the accumulation of a few days' dumpage would choke broad boulevards.

Now, abruptly, a young Chinese stepped from a doorway in front of me. I thought it might be a beginning of the elusive, grim whatever that I was to see face to face. But it proved a familiar gambit of the Orient, one I'd experienced in the Ginza with Ricky walking at my side:

"Singsong girl?" the man murmured ardently. "Dancing girl?"

I shook my head and tried to walk around him.

"Very nice, very pretty, very hot-hot. Still awake. Right here." A neatly dressed, nice-looking youth. "Only walk one block. No customers all night—very clean. She make you happy all ways, all kinds, do it."

I passed him.

"Very cheap. You not like this girl, get more. Many more. Take two. Blonde hair? Get one, gold color hair. You say."

His voice was waning but still audible:

"You go corner around street. I make girl look out door. Long hair. Pretty eyes . . . you see her first. . . ."

The refugees began, soon after. A corner turned, and another, and a new street that was old.

Many were still asleep—men and women and children—asleep on the chill-sweated sidewalks in the clothes they always wore, the only clothes they had. Tired and dirty people with early morning flies prospecting their eyelids and open mouths. I came to a group who were cooking breakfast—three children, a mother and an old man. They sat silently around a stick-fire on the sidewalk. Over it, in a large tin can on bricks they were warming gray sludge—not enough to make one hearty meal, and not, I thought, bearable even to consider tasting.

The numbers of refugees increased. I tried a different street and reached a region where the overhang of the sour-smelling, shoddy buildings ended. Here, the refugees did not have shelter. They camped, instead, between doorways, on the roofless walk, and in the center of the street, and in clusters in open squares or on vacant lots.

Their abodes were such as I have already described: igloos of rubble, tepees of trash: big cartons lidded with anything that would shed water. Hundreds, thousands, tens of thousands, hundreds of thousands lived that way. Even one such "house"—hardly bigger than the kennel of a mastiff but lodging a man and wife and perhaps several children—could hardly be described in detail: an inventory of the scraps and bits that composed it, held it together, and made it somewhat weatherproof would include fifty oddments ranging from discarded coconut-fiber doormats to pieces of old umbrellas—and many would not be identifiable at all.

In this Dantean setting, which stretched out of sight in various directions, children were playing. Queues of people were waiting for government rations—women who had been pretty and a few pretty women, old men, youths, kids—wearing for the most part the Chinese version of poverty's least garments, but, in some few cases, the street-stained, climate-faded, tragedy-imbued remains of brilliant silks.

They looked at me amicably, if surprisedly. Some even smiled. In their hands, the ration seekers held every sort of vessel that could be recovered from a city dump as well as parts of anything useful that could be found in one: discarded pots and pans, handleless china and earthenware, the bottoms of oil lamps, deep trays, tin cans, pails, even reclaimed wax-paper containers. With these, they brought their morning food home, each refugee carrying his own portion—another's only if that other was unable to stand in line.

There were many infants, some recently born. Many, many children and many people who were old. Around occasional damp little fires that heated extra food—food begged, stolen, scrounged, donated, or earned—these pitiable beings ate.

There were sick refugees. . . .

On a hard-packed dirt area, across from a coal- and woodyard, under the metal door canopy of a warehouse not yet open for business, I came upon a large Chinese of about thirty who lay on his back inertly. Hundreds of people stirred nearby but no one, at the moment, was near him. He saw me. He realized, gradually, that a human being had approached. With effort he raised his head an inch or so and murmured syllables with fever-thick lips—through a throat capable of mere wet gargle.

He was dying.

His effort to attract my attention left him panting. Fresh sweat broke out on a puffy face where old sweat had traced in dirt the seams of agony. A foul and alarming odor exuded from him and hung about, fetidly. His skin was yellow—not with the hue attributed to his race, but owing to bile in his blood. His eyes had the already-dead glare of terminal disease. And when his air-gulping diminished, his breathing came in Cheyne-Stokes crescendo-diminuendo. Now and again he coughed phlegmily. I noticed, beneath his rags and body-dirt, irregular dark blotches.

I stood there for a minute, but he did not try to speak again or seem to know I stayed. The man certainly would die in hours or even minutes. Still, I thought, someone from among the refugees ought to offer him water, ought even to attempt to get aid for him—unless, of course, the Crown Colony had no facilities for a man of such sorts in such straits.

A middle-aged Chinese approached, saw the man lying at my feet, came a step or two closer, looked carefully, then jumped away from the warehouse and hurried around us on a wide circuit. An old man and a woman came next; they, too, reacted with horror and what seemed recognition—skirting the dying man distantly.

I didn't know what disease he had. The others *seemed* to know—and avoided him and his horrible illness like plague itself. After a while, not able to think what to do, I left.

The light was an even gray; the time, nearing seven. I'd gone many miles on foot with not so much as a cup of coffee. But still I went on, street after street, looking, trying to discover why certain astute men at home had insisted this pilgrimage through Hades must be made by me.

Everyone looked at me. Everyone was surprised to see me there. A few spoke—pleasantly, I thought. Maybe they were saying "Good morning," in Cantonese. I did not know. But, certainly, in those hordes of human beings living as larvae, as maggots, nobody was hostile or menacing. And, certainly, the Red International was not proselytizing them.

I came after a while to a row of houses backed up against a long, limed wall. These were made of boards, and had fairly substantial roofs of galvanized iron, wood, or big pieces of linoleum. Not many people moved in front of them, or within them, as in other quarters. So I guessed that this was the "Sugar Hill" of Hell, where refugee squatters who had jobs spent their nights.

As I came near these houses, a child appeared at the drapery door of one—a very pretty girl of eleven or twelve. Her blouse was freshly laundered and her over-large, black trousers were clean. She looked at me shyly and called into the house with delicate, childish excitement.

An old woman bobbed to the entrance and focused old eyes at me. Then she smiled—showing random yellow teeth. She pointed an arthritic finger at the child. "Very prettee," she said.

"Very pretty," I agreed, with enthusiasm.

"Ten dolla?" the crone asked, her face tense with expectation.

I didn't instantly understand.

"Ten dolla," the old woman repeated. "Hong Kong dolla." She suddenly snatched at the blouse of the little girl who, as suddenly, grew scared. Yet she also became passive. The old woman pulled up the blouse so I could see the burgeon of young breasts. "Ten dolla?" She pointed toward the dark doorhole. "Clean mat. Nice girl. Young."

The child's eyes met mine fearfully.

"No," I said. I said it again, violently. "*No!*"

"*Five* dolla," the ancient slut countered. She began to fiddle with bony fingers at the cord supporting the pants of the submissive child. I was to be shown other charms.

I ran from there.

Tears burned in my eyes.

Rage shook me so hard I had to stop, presently, and overcome it—a fury I have never before experienced.

All the rest of my days I'll hear, now and again, that avaricious, cracked, hopeful old voice urge, "Ten dolla . . . *five* dolla . . . clean mat."

After a while, I threaded my way back to a main street and by luck soon found an empty cab. I gave the name of the Peninsula.

The driver grinned at me knowingly: Europeans never appeared in that area at that hour save after sleeping off a night of sport in some room to which a pimp—or maybe a hungry father, brother or husband—had brought them. The cab driver thought he knew about me.

I rode toward the less-hideous, more Western part of Kowloon, trying to think.

That little girl. . . .

She would have assented—knew she must. Maybe she'd assented before, for the small fortune of five dolla, Hong Kong. Or maybe that was the fixed price of preadolescent virginity. . . .

And the dying man. . . .

Why had his fellow refugees reacted with self-preserving avoidance . . . and horror?

(Some two weeks after we left Hong Kong, the port was closed for a while owing to an outbreak of bubonic plague. I have subsequently described the man's symptoms for several American doctors. It could have been plague, the physicians said; or half a dozen other things. The most meaningful symptom, in their opinion, was the behavior of the passers-by who had doubtless seen plague. None of my medical countrymen ever had.)

On the long cab-ride back to the hotel I wondered again, with irritation and perplexity, why those men had asked me to take that walk.

Was it, simply, to see poverty's abyss?

I'd seen it before, in the squalid out-boundaries of South Russian cities.

Seen worse.

Certainly, there was no intrinsic "Red reason"—no evidence that the Crown Colony faces an openly planned Red "Bastille Day."

I did learn, later, that the Colonial Government is not sure of the politics of its overwhelming burden of refugees. It is the last stand possible to the fugitives. If the Colony falls to Red China, they not surprisingly wish to avoid capture under circumstances more deathsome than those incurred by their mere flight—desperate enough. They appreciate protection and hope it lasts; but I daresay many abstain from open enthusiasms for democracy so as to be less vulnerable under different auspices.

Myriads of these people did stage a murderous three-day riot, and looting spree, in Kowloon, eight months after our stay. But the inciting event was the hauldown of a *Chinese Nationalist* Flag by a British official. And I think I have made clear the incentive which led a mob of angered refugees to start *looting!*

There is no place for the British Government to send those people. Who wants Chinese in hundreds of thousands? Not America—so fearful of the "yellow peril." I've even heard American businessmen who have visited Caribbean lands—Rotarians and good fellows—mutter nervously at the numbers of "Chinks" in West Indian enterprises, at their prosperity in Havana and the "mysterious wealth" that enables "too many" Chinese to ride around on airplanes. They repeat the commercial superstition that any Chinese merchant can wreck the business of any competitor of whatever other race or nationality. That myth is part of the folklore of the Western world, so the British have found few lands that will take even a small, sifted handful of those among the refugees who have special skills. *Nobody else.*

Formosa—which is all that remains of free China—couldn't accommodate a tithe of the fugitives.

The British Colonial Government doesn't even know how many people have entered its inadequate territory. The fugitives from tyranny come by night—men and women and kids escaping by way of cities and hidden harbors up and down China's immense coast. The flea-thick, unwatchable sampans bring them to Hong Kong. Some may even swim the last miles. They also steal ashore from hiding-holes amidst the bales in freightholds; and they are landed in dead night by fishing junks. They push rafts into the "free-waters-called-fragrant" (the meaning of Hong Kong). Most have no skills to vend and bring nothing but themselves; untutored hands and limbs for hire in a glutted market.

Yet . . . they fled from the foulest antagonist in human history: Communism; they had that much pride, dignity, spirit, humanity and the British, like ourselves, pose as the committed enemy of their enemy—sustainers of free men and men who would gain liberty.

The Crown Colony—with outside help—does feed them as best it can, endeavors to house them as rapidly as possible, and tries to teach trades to as many as they can so they will have market worth. But the Colony long refused outside help in that task, because it would involve public inspection which—in turn— would have appeared to reflect badly on a beleaguered and overburdened Government. Hong Kong still fails to rejoice when scrutiny is given its method of asylum for its tragic wards. There are *so many!* And so many new ones keep coming! The mere order of magnitude of the arriving numbers is only guessable— and by grisly means: Red China's accurate monthly report of how many would-be escapees are caught by the searchlights inside the Red border, machine-gunned, tracked down by dogs, impaled on the barbed-wire thickets, betrayed and prevented from attaining liberty by other barbaric methods, which Communists have to apply everywhere to keep people within their boundaries. That execution list is the only basis of colonial conjecture about those who escape and reach free territory. Lately, moreover, liberty under the squalid conditions in Kowloon has proven less tolerable than Red rule to some—and little wonder! Refugees, notably a large group of fishermen, have voluntarily, if sadly, sailed back to Communist China. Here is the Free World's *actual* "gift" to men loving freedom!

And I decided, long after my walk, that what the Washington men wanted me to see was neither more nor less than the eye-burning evidence of the unimportance of *people* to Communists. (Which, too, I knew already.) Here were myriads who had not been allowed to choose their government, not been permitted to leave their land and, usually, despoiled of whatever they had, before they risked torture and hideous death by fleeing. In the Communist Faith they became what infidels are to Moslem fanatics: mere prey whose murder insures salvation—vermin, as surely doomed to Hell as were Unitarians—according to my Covenanter grandmother. The Reds, with equally dogmatic absolutes, merely provide Hell for heretics right here and right now—with far more effectiveness than they provide the similarly earthly Heaven Marx promised!

Not men and women and children, these refugees—but *less* than that: mockers of the Word of Marx. Exterminate them!

There could not have been any other reason for asking me to take that trek.

And it was (as I've observed) not a *necessary* lesson—to me, though the walk would certainly be valuable for every single American who has not looked with his own eyes on the living debris of the new Religion; and for every isolationist, too; and every American who thinks "Christians" will beat Communists just because Christians are "right."

It would—apparently—have been a valuable experience even for most of the Britishers and other Westerners *in Hong Kong*. Why? Because a reporter, hearing that same day how I had spent the morning, wrote about it in a Hong Kong paper. The subsequent headline announced in glaring type that an American author had strolled among the refugees at daybreak! Such behavior was phenomenal and newsworthy in the Colony, where nobody lived more than a mile or two from some teeming refugee anthill—but where white men did not go save for official reasons.

Ricky was having breakfast when I returned.

"I see you went," she said. She poured a cup of the coffee she'd kept hot for me. "See anything?"

I told her.

"Can't we *do* anything? *You!* Can't you *write* about it? Why doesn't Mr. *Dulles* do something? The *State* Department?"

"Why," I asked her bitterly, "don't the glorious free people of the United States realize they are getting closer every day, *themselves*, to living like that?" I thought of Russia. "Or *worse*." I thought again: "The survivors of the American people, I mean."

Ricky had gone shopping—an act in Hong Kong magnetic to both sexes! I was, myself, keeping appointments for fittings at the establishment of Jimmy Chen, a refugee tailor. He used the untaxed best of British materials—and the labor of English-trained Shanghai refugees. There were so many that round-the-clock suitmaking is a Hong Kong tradition. A man can procure the finest suits, coats, custom-made shirts or cashmere sweaters—at a price that would give my New York tailor apoplexy.

For two hundred and twenty-five American dollars, my tailor in Rockefeller Center makes for me (though not very often) a handsome suit—one that is effective for TV appearance and admired at editorial conferences. But, for two hundred and twenty-two American dollars, at Jimmy Chen's, I had made (and sent home duty-free under my customs allowance) one tailored wool and cashmere winter overcoat, one cashmere and one tweed jacket, deftly handmade, four made-to-measure shirts, and the following items from ready-to-wear stock: two silk neckties, two cashmere sweaters and four pairs of all-wool Scotch Argyle socks. All—for less than the price of one first-rate suit, handmade in Manhattan.

Women, however, may have certain difficulties (and some men, too) if their purchases extend beyond tailor-made clothing of British fabric. Our Customs require a "certificate of origin" for Hong Kong purchases—thus excluding most brocade, jewelry and divers other wares brought, or smuggled, from Red China.

The rule applies even to jade, jewels and sundry resplendent materials that had their true "origin" long before China became Communist. Assorted treasures and works of art are carried into the Colony by refugees. Selling them at a shocking loss, they still may thus start life in our free world, with capital. Other nationals can buy those treasures and take them home. Our Congress, however, keeps the Hong Kong gate to Red China shut tightly.

A Mr. Windover arrived that day to tape-record an interview while Ricky shopped. He seemed to be a nice chap—like most minor-league, versatile, news announcers. We ran over the questions he would ask and I would answer, in the recorded eleven minutes he had graciously offered me. He ruled out any impressions I might want to broadcast concerning refugees, and, finally, turned on his portable gadgets. We made the recording he had pre-edited. Afterward, just chatting with each other, he chanced to learn I fish in the sea, and write about it. So we made another tape recording, for his sports hour.

Thereafter, I sent for tea and learned about Mr. Windover's background and B.B.C. training—as well as his motive for leaving London: "restlessness." I then found (with no surprise) that he desired a sponsor who would subsidize him while he became a Great American Writer. He alternatively wanted an "in" with some Hollywood picture company that would assure such overnight stardom as Byron experienced. An influential American connection who would use guile and "pull" to arrange for the immigration of self, wife and kiddies, to USA, was a third hope of Mr. Windover.

Perhaps that's not entirely fair. For he also stated he would settle for bit parts in Hollywood—or for a part-time radio job in the United States, where he might "impersonate an Englishman." I doubted if he could have "impersonated" anything else but he did look like a movie actor—as Englishmen often do. Occasional foreigners naively imagine that if they could only reach our land, the superiority of their foreign culture guarantees they have only to meet a corporation mogul to become rich. That galls me because the very people who want our visa and mazuma often freely state we are bums. Now, few Americans have called their fellow citizens more names than I. But my motive in so doing is, quite simply, to use criticism to improve the breed I think finest of all. And no patriot is quicker to resent, in other lands, the slander of USA by some envious ignoramus.

I listened to Mr. Windover's romantic-avaricious concept of USA—and a knock came on my door, just as I grew dangerously tense. I assumed it would be Ricky—sans key and package-laden.

It was a tall Chinese dressed in tweedy brown herringbone with a snap-brim hat on his head—the conventional garb of successful Chinese in the area. Only a modest light reached our doorway, from the harbor-facing French windows at the corridor-end. In that turgid illumination, the Chinese towered over me. His face was nonexpressive. He might be there to invite us to a Cantonese hoedown or to arrest us.

He then began to talk—volubly and in a soft voice.

Why in hell, I wondered, should the man imagine I could understand Chinese? Few white Americans speak Chinese—and I am unmistakably "white" and, experience shows, obviously American to most people of other countries.

My evident confusion caused the Chinese to talk faster, and nervously. I shook my head and stretched out my hands, palms up: there would be no meeting of minds as long as he kept jabbering in Cantonese, or whatever. He comprehended my lack of comprehension. From his coat breast pocket, he drew a letter which he handed to me. I backed into our room to read.

"Dear Phil," the letter began—startlingly. I looked up at the letterhead and down at the signature to see who had indited a "Dear Phil" epistle to me, in the strange province of Hong Kong. It proved to be George Beebe, managing editor of the Miami *Herald*—one of my two home-town papers. An old friend.

I read on, with confoundment:

"This will introduce Eddie Gong, a graduate of Miami High School and Harvard, who grew up near your house in South Miami. He is now doing features for a paper owned by the Tiger Balm people in Hong Kong and also looking (aided by his grandma and according to old Chinese custom) for a Chinese wife. Eddie has worked on the *Herald* and I thought, maybe, you'd find a Chinese-speaking Miamian useful in Hong Kong. He's a nice guy. We get feature stuff from him while he wife-hunts. Have a sensational trip! Best to Ricky. Yours, George."

I was stupefied!

The tall guy had been speaking English all the time!

But—because he was Chinese, I'd assumed he had used that language! I am certainly not *that* deaf. So my failure to understand had been a matter of suggestibility—that slaphappy process of the minds of human beings:

There at a Hong Kong hotel door stood a tall, young, Chinese; *ergo*, when he spoke, he spoke Chinese. I'd seen countless men who looked the same, on the Kowloon-Hong Kong ferryboat, on the street, in restaurants, shops, bars—everywhere—and *they* didn't speak English. So why should this one?

That ridiculous blunder I shall never forget. And I've explained it here because nobody should fail to reckon on such fallibility. The mind draws myriads of false inferences. So many, that unless we verify all we think we know and understand, we cannot be certain of what we believe or what we claim to know. Our world is swayed far more by the convictions of uncritical, suggestible people, than by truth.

A man professes to be a Baptist Fundamentalist—so he, alone, is "saved." A man is a Negro—so white womenfolk are not safe around him. A man is a citizen of Russia—wherefore he is a commie and not even exactly human.

An "ism" is an *arbitrary* set of ideas—yet there is a true "Americanism." He is Ivy League, Banker's Trust, Republican, Episcopal, and plays good golf—so he's okay.

Absurd, incorrect, unwarranted, misleading, bigoted near-criminal and truly criminal inferences, made from familial or cultural suggestion—and ruinous to us all!

We evaluate others by such dimness, alone, as a rule!

Our conscious personality—brain, mind, soul, spirit—call it what you will, is capable, of course, *only* of "inference." Where its inference is false, the result may merely be ridiculous or embarrassing. But think, even here, how many of us waste our lives! There is, for instance, not one tangible fragment of evidence for "flying saucers"; their alleged reality is altogether a matter of inference. Yet, how many have a silly "faith-in-saucers"? How many regard the rejection of criticism as truth's best approach and—in the flying saucer mythology—even take dogged, scientific and official *denials* as further "evidence" that saucers exist, arguing that the government is keeping them "secret"! How many, that is, would rather oppose thought itself—than think? How many believed—till the notion was shattered by overwhelming disproof—that a reincarnated American housewife lived years ago in Ireland as Bridey Murphy and could remember her "other" life, under hypnosis?

Who takes the trouble to widen his inferences to his utmost capacity by critical study and self-study—even his *cardinal* concepts, his inferred "convictions" about God, Nature, Man and Reality? What person, having taken his ideas from the inferences of others, or from a credulous use of magic thinking that infers the world miraculous, then gathers all differing and contrary data to see if what he believes is even up-to-date, even informed —hence, even *sensible?*

Who—in sum—-lays a common claim to reason and actually uses it? Who among us is that real, that honest, that appropriate an embodiment of what he says God made him?

Who is that *alive!*

I shall not forget the day a Chinese youth stood at my door, talking the flawless Miami-American I've heard for a quarter century, which I inferred to be Chinese just because *he* was.

I learned, at least, that my habit of brain-use in the universal region of inference needed tightening up—learned it through a Florida Cracker named Eddie Gong. . . .

From then on, our fortunes changed. The tall man in the corridor was more than an omen; he was the product, good luck itself. When I had read the letter (and, of course, before I'd done much of the above reflection), I opened my door and said, "Come in, Eddie."

Mr. Windover, not altogether pleased at the interruption of his fantasied triumphs in America, nevertheless recognized a newsgathering colleague. "Hi, Eddie!" he said amiably.

Mr. Gong came in, tossed his hat, sprawled in a chair and we began to gossip about Florida and its citizens—the glinting but notorious as well as the brilliant and renowned. I had been in Miami much more recently than Mr. Gong.

Mr. Windover soon departed with his tape, profile and cupidity. . . .

In Eddie Gong, Ricky and I thenceforward had a guide with a realistic knowledge of Hong Kong, a buoyant companion and a perfect translater—though Eddie claimed he was the only Chinese in Hong Kong who "spoke Cantonese with a Dixie accent."

From Eddie we learned much about local government, politics, Red China and the refugees. Through him, we were shown sights we would not otherwise have known of.

With an American acquaintance, we dined on the famed floating restaurants. These aquatic dining rooms serve excellent sea food. However, sampans take out customers via the green and festering cloaca that flows around a sampan village—the least appetizing approach to epicurean pleasure in my experience.

Because of Eddie—and because of a sensation that had grown in me since Waikiki, when I finished a promised article on a rented typewriter and mailed it to *Look*—I broke a vow made before our departure from Miami: no typewriter on this trip. I had, to be sure, notes jotted, in blankbooks, in my execrable hand; but impressions and facts compounded faster than I could record them. Not only that, but my notes lacked the detail I thought I'd entered. Besides, I, myself, could not make out everything I'd written—hardly surprising since I had not depended on handwriting for more than a week or two at a time since my trip through Russia in 1936.

"I need," I said to Ricky, "a typewriter."

"Like acne, blisters and bunions!"

"No fooling. I feel as if I had no hands. It gets worse every week!"

"You said you wanted to get *away* from your typewriters."

"Just for notes, I mean."

"It'll put us over the airplane weight limit. Cost a fortune."

"I'm getting frustrated from no typewriter!"

"Well. Buy one." Ricky knows that a genuine claim of frustration is an honest man's red flag.

So, with Eddie bursting into cataracts of Chinese such as

I had imagined his first words to be, I bought a Hermes—and at a discount. . . .

Eddie made every day as productive as a week of ordinary touring. He took us to certain unfrequented places where Kowloon amuses and decays itself (as all the world does). He invited us to the press club so I could interview newspaper professionals.

He also played host, at a small tea, for a lady of about thirty employed by an English paper—the name of which I do not remember. She also wrote for the *Manchester Guardian*. Moreover, she had just returned safe and whole from a long trip in Red China—which was the reason for the tea.

Unlike James Cameron, author of the valuable report, *Mandarin Red*, Miss T. either had not stayed long enough, or looked sharply enough, to see beneath the veneer of Communist "progress" and "tranquillity" the glue of human blood which invariably holds together the shams and props of Red renaissance.

I may be asked how I could know that fact. The answer is simple, though perhaps it is not simple enough for some Congressmen to grasp—even if they read it here. There is evidence —moreover (and alas)—that politicians in numbers do not read books—they merely legislate. . . .

This matter of book reading is more vital to America than our stockpile of nuclear weapons. Yet, certain Inside Men, who seem to know where Eisenhower is and more or less what he does, once jubilantly drew America's attention to the statement that even our *President* read few books: just "westerns" and, repeatedly, *Ivanhoe*, they boasted. As time passed (and elections neared) the antireading Inside Men observed that quite a few Americans *do* read books and not just books by Zane Grey. The Presidential Inside Men then reversed themselves. They asserted Ike read "westerns" only for relaxation and was actually a constant reader of deep books. To prove it, they offered the quotation in an old Eisenhower campaign speech, of a sentence or two from Eric Hofer's remarkable, if addled, essay, *The True Believer*.

But since we have not had a President in a generation who has written his own speeches, some ghost may have supplied the esoteric quote. A further report that Eisenhower was devoted to Civil War history left me uncertain: Civil War history is a compulsory course at West Point (or was when Ike attended— though physics might, in the end, have proven more valuable to him).

Ever since, I've wondered what the President does read and has read. The issue's now so confused, we'll probably never know. But the original pride of the Inside Men in Ike's claimed distate for serious reading augmented a national mood of opposition to "intellectuals," including men of intelligence. Congressmen could say: "If the President sticks to 'westerns,' why should I read Marx or the Smythe Report, a life of Jefferson, or Lincoln's speeches?" Everybody could say as much—and most do!

For we have gradually become a nation of exultant ignoramuses. Because we read so little (and that little is mostly of little significance) we do not understand our era. Yet if we are to escape dilemma we must have a leadership that comprehends reality, and a public that can follow debate—owing to equal knowledge. Our first intellectual need is to understand *what Communism is* and thus to see the trap it has constructed around us. But today, most Americans are ignorant of the subject. So each is like a man who has inadvertently stumbled—blindfolded—into a snakepit.

By luck, the space where he lands is momentarily clear of all reptiles, both harmless and venomous. As the man sits up, shaken but as yet unhurt, his first act will be to remove the blindfold. *That is what most individual Americans have not yet done!* In this analogue the act is comparable to studying Communism as it is, not as Americans blindly imagine it. But suppose enough of us read, and think, and observe, to comprehend? Suppose—in this fitting illustration—we do remove the blindfold?

The man in the pit sees daylight. Then he sees a high wall surrounding him. Possibly he can scale it, but the attempt will involve a risk of falling back a time or two. Does the man now ignore everything but the wall and simply rush at it . . . through rattling vipers, and cobras with painted hoods spread loath-somely? Does he rely, in other words, on the impromptu use of his mere physical strength? (If so, he is doomed! Yet some of our present leaders seem to think America should hit the wall imme-diately and with all our strength. They believe that military power employed as nations used it before the Atomic Age will still serve to get us out of our dilemma. They have not seen the novel realities—the serpents, that is.)

Suppose, however, the man in the pit hears a sickening sibilance all around and the frightful pizzicato of the great vipers—and then *sees* them, alert and hideous? Only if he knows a great deal about herpetology will he now have a chance for life. If he does know, he will know whether to wait till the reptiles quiet down—or take advantage of the surprise his fall occasioned. He will know which snakes are harmless—and perhaps be able to pick a path to the wall, and scale it, in a place occupied only by nonvenomous reptiles. He will know which deadly breeds can be made to retreat and by what means—and know, in any close, critical encounter, which lethal kinds might perhaps be killed with a nervy leap and down-pounding shoes.

But suppose the man knows little or nothing of snakes? At last, seeing his true and horrible situation, he will know what most Americans don't yet: he's facing murder itself.

In frenzy, such a man may stamp upon harmless domestic reptiles and set the whole lot moving so his one path to escape is closed. He may "optimistically" decide this pit contains only harmless specimens and march with bravado—to agony and death. Or he may panic and thereafter—whether he shrieks and leaps about hysterically or hysterically freezes rigid—he is done for. He may even go utterly mad, asserting to himself (and to a world he insanely believes will hear) that these are not poisonous snakes but birds, or that they are rapidly turning from cobras and bushmasters into goldfish, so there soon will be no danger. And then he will die, also, though perhaps in the rapt, joyful and smug ecstasy of lunacy.

To men who read and think and understand our antagonist, it is plain that most Americans, so far and often, *have behaved in exactly those ways!* All are suicidal, in the end. It is plain to the knowers-of-the-enemy that even most Americans in the highest places do not yet understand the nature of our danger well enough to design appropriate counter-measures. For Communism is like a snake pit closing around us. Muscle—even nuclear muscle—will never save us. Only comprehension can save us—and then only if it is a sufficient public understanding to give us nerve for appropriate stratagems and efforts. . . .

The British Miss Talbott, with whom Ricky and I took tea in Hong Kong, had actually lived awhile with the serpents. But the serpents lulled her and persuaded her that they were ministering angels. Someday, doubtless, she will waken—but *when?* That is your question, too! Little time is left for the reveille of free men.

In his book, *Your Most Enchanted Listener*, Wendel Johnson says, "We believe what we see because most of what we see is there because of what we believe." That humiliating but proper postulate is apt for people in their homeland. It needs emendation, however, for many people who visit other lands:

They just don't *see*, because their belief prevents them from *looking!*

Miss Talbott, I felt sure, was at that time possessed of prior beliefs and concepts which—all unconsciously—prevented her from "seeing" what too many of us have certainly seen, in every Communist domain.

An hour or so of question-answering disclosed that she had nothing derogatory to say of Red China. Any criticism of that slave state was called (by her) "Western propaganda." What she believed was being achieved in China was what the Communist press claimed. (She needn't have made so uncomfortable a trek to find that out!) The way she said the Chinese people felt was the way their Communist masters made them say they felt. The Red alternative was, is, and will be: "chop-chop," and the pidgin term refers, not to victuals, but human necks.

Miss Talbott was a British Socialist. She must not have read enough books about either freedom or Soviet Russia, I thought.

For her inferences, in my opinion, came from uninformed emotion—not from reason. She was young and so, forgivable.

But I have witnessed slaphappy junkets in Soviet Russia itself, by countless fellow-traveling travelers and even people who imagine they are open-minded. Human butchery that occurs before their eyes is presented as a "defense against the enemies of the proletariat," by their indoctrinated guides. Leprosy will be called prickly heat by such guides, even if their charges see Russians die of it. It is one more matter of "inference, information and fallibility." I am afraid I am prejudiced against, and often rude to, people who talk as if the books they have not read did not exist—and truth is exclusively what they believe.

Mr. Gong—anyhow—made it possible for us to meet this British woman who exuded Mao's day-old breath and insisted neither Mao nor the five or six hundred million impounded Chinese had halitosis, despite the reek. I attacked her. If Red China was Paradise, why the Hong Kong refugees? Why the Manchurian slave camps? Why did the English reporter, James Cameron, as he toured China, slowly exchange a viewpoint like her own—for one of understated but livid loathing?

Only when I became courteous did she somewhat recall the decent postulates of her forebears and behave as if I were a pleasant human being—however sadly unlearned in the Red Reality.

For months thereafter, I cited Miss Talbott as the classic contemporary example of that "intellectual liberalism" I felt flawed and faulty, from my youth—from Greenwich Village days, from nights in Theodore Dreiser's big studio on Central Park South, when I listened to literary men and women who were going to "change the world by changing the system." (Later, I saw the land that *had* changed the system and felt my early doubt to be correct. When treachery or force is used to alter a way of life, ever more formidable force is necessary to maintain even the semblance of the change. I learned how Soviet Russia became despotism, not just at the top, but despotism in the grass roots, a tyranny even among tots.)

Years passed, and capitalism has changed itself, while Communism solidified. Thus, now, even the gentle, brave Norman Thomas can say that the major aims of his "socialism" have been realized in America.

To me, however, it has always seemed that if a system needs changing, the people themselves must first be changed by education that causes them to want a new way of life. I have felt that the exponent of liberty who worked toward change, would work at such education, teaching his fellow men their blunders, their sins and the superior opportunities he had descried—and letting them determine a new course, freely, when they had assimilated his lesson. My vendetta with my own loved countrymen has thus concerned hypocrisies and self-deceits, smug pretensions to vast virtues actually not discernible and, particularly, our American loss of individuality, of a sense of being, of higher values and of real happiness—through our concentration on the increase of a "living standard" entirely material.

To be sure, it is capitalism that created our material demand and our ever-augmented supply. But too many of the old "liberal intellectuals"—in my view—wanted to jump the step of education and—by fiat, by demagoguery, even by tricks and violence, or perhaps by miracle—desired to thrust a new economic system on a capitalist America. Too many—I thought—were like Miss Talbott. They could see an imaginary Heaven, but not that the road to it led into, and ended, in Hell. And too many of those giants, rampant for social reform in the Twenties and Thirties, seemed to me to be motivated by the belief that capitalist America did not sufficiently appreciate—or adequately recompense—their private genius.

It was Ricky who finally pointed out that those militant sophisticates (amongst whom I was a small-time and dissident bystander) had now changed, also. They have seen the human calamity implicit in the use of amoral means to achieve putatively noble ends. They still see our American preoccupation with capitalism, its fruits and process, as destructive of the same values I hold most dear, and in America, most neglected. But the majority of Americans, Ricky argued, also view life as an "economic" process—wherefore, the liberals and intellectuals in America to-day who seek the ends I seek merely use a different semantic. Their terms may be more readily perceived than my psychological terms, she argued.

The wrongs Miss Talbott saw would be seen as wrongs by me. The downgrading of man's psyche by corporate structures and machines is real and hideous. It creates anti-intellectualism: people unaware of the sources of authority and, because of that, unaware even of the true nature of masculinity; people who call scientists "eggheads," artists "sissies," and boast of their very ignorance; people with a President who perhaps may not even read books!

So my quarrel with Miss Talbott is half semantical—and half owing to opinions she may yet alter, as our liberals have done, when she finally sees that not freedom or enhanced human dignity or any other value can be lawed on and gunned into humanity.

Ricky's point—to put it another way—is this:

No man or woman who would stay free can afford to be deaf to any dissident voice discussing new facts or ideas in a humane tone.

For my sins in that region (and many exercises in public scorn), I owe some liberals and intellectuals an apology. We have an identical end; and I think, nowadays, the difference between our means is one of definitions: I oppose the forfeit of human stature and the default in "being" itself—the decerebration and willful ignorance of the people along with the danger that brings increasingly to America. I oppose those *neglects* and *lacks*—and so oppose our concentration on material benefits to life now so great that life itself is steadily narrowed, stupidified and made anxious. The liberals and intellectuals make the same criticism and similarly, today, would teach better values. We differ only in that they criticize *capitalism itself* while I deplore our *preoccupation with it,* to the increasing exclusion of all else.

On our own, a night or two later, Ricky and I had a quite different adventure.

She phoned a Mrs. Wong, wife of a rich Chinese business-man to whom we had a letter of introduction. Mrs. Wong turned out to be the first truly inscrutable Oriental we had encountered. Whatever Ricky said, she answered with, "Hello?"—or silence.

So I tried Mr. Wong, at his place of business—and found myself talking to a graduate of Stanford! We were invited to dinner. And many aspects of the ensuing evening were unusual.

The various Wongs and their in-laws lived in a half-dozen houses on one large tract of scenic land. As the dinner guests gathered, Wongs kept arriving. (Emily Hahn has brilliantly described the nature of Chinese family-love.)

The first Wong to greet us was the pater familias, a man who possessed a large fortune in Shanghai. Stripped of it by the Japanese (who set him, his wife, and sundry Wongs on forced marches to prison camps), Grandpa Wong endured and some relatives also survived. Several made their way to Hong Kong, when victory brought release. They soon had new fortunes. Among the in-laws, too, was a Doctor Hu, famed for his contribution to biology made at Chicago University. I had read of Dr. Hu—in *Time*. His former Chicago research partner received a Nobel Prize, not long ago.

Besides ourselves, the many Wongs had invited a Dr. and Mrs. Pelp (Dr. Pelp was a retired professor of some sort) and an American banker with his wife, a Mr. Rockefeller (no kin), retired vice-president of a New York bank.

The Pelps appeared in blue serge. The Manhattan banker was clad in a thin, gray dinner jacket—mohair. His wife wore evening clothes. Mrs. Wong, Jr., was dressed in a red, silken *cheongsam*—the beautiful, conventional Chinese dress, suitable for a clambake or the St. Regis. She was pretty and sweet. More than pretty: she had the Shanghai version of what Marilyn Monroe is said by man to have in excelsis: sex appeal.

The world-renowned scientist, Dr. Hu, appeared in a sweat shirt and gray flannels that still bore what might have been the stigmata of Chicago squash courts, labs, bowling alleys or the like.

The New England-born Rockefellers (as well as the Pelps) were inadvertent visitors to Hong Kong. They had been enjoying a world tour on a freighter equipped with de luxe accommodations for a small complement of frugal but adventurous passengers. The Wongs were local agents for the line and the boat carrying the Pelps and Rockefellers made an unscheduled stop at the Crown Colony because a Chinese Nationalist stowaway had been found on board after she'd left Formosa. The Wongs had invited the eminent American couples to dinner. Otherwise, they would probably have been obliged to stay on their ship. Chinese are thoughtful, kindly, and fantastically hospitable.

Most people think Hong Kong is always, not just mostly, hot. Thus the costumes of the freighter-borne Americans were what they imagined would be correct. Ricky and I wore sweaters under our warmest daytime clothes: Chinese homes are unheated. Eddie Gong had taught us that. And it is a good idea, in any alien land, to ask some Eddie-Gong-equivalent about proper dress for sundry occasions—not just to be correct, but to avoid melting, or icing up—ignominiously. This was a cool, starlit night in the mid-fifties.

Two hours of convivial drinking from bottles on a tea wagon pushed about by a proud Chinese servant started off the evening.

I asked several Chinese people, then, the question I'd been told to explore: What would be the reaction of mainland Chinese if Formosa were attacked—and America replied with A-bombs that annihilated the Red bases, along with a million Chinese civilians, more or less.

Grandpa Wong, a wondrous cagey and wondrous merry old man, never did let himself get around to answering. Dr. Hu felt such heinous assault would forever alienate the Red Chinese, along with all other Asians, from the free world. Everybody else I asked agreed with Dr. Hu, though one or two dodged the question, as had Grandfather Wong.

I liked Dr. Hu very much. So did Ricky. In looks, he was less than handsome—a squat, fierce-eyed man, with crew-cut hair—a man who was so muscular and at first so boisterously aggressive he might have been taken for a retired wrestler or even a thug.

I sat beside him at dinner. He was boyishly, wrigglingly modest about his world-wide fame. He was equally humble about his modern, self-sacrificing medical practice in Hong Kong. And he shamed me, in a way I shall try henceforth not to deserve again. For I described the symptoms of the dying refugee I'd seen.

"What did you *do?*" Dr. Hu asked.

"What could I? Walked on, sadly."

His eyes blazed. He became Hippocrates, swearing his first class to the Oath: "Not get *help?* Not call *police?* Not even bring water? Not even ask some refugee if someone *could* get help? My Jesus! Here, you only find a phone, call Number 999, and all such poor fellows have the ambulance in a second! It is a British *law.*"

I murmured that I did not know.

"Of *course* you do not *know!* But all *others* know—and did you ask a one? *Nixie!* You are a nice, amazing-bright fellow, Mister Wylie, and to us Chinese you also pull, not a Good Samaritan, but the Pharisee! So, how do you Americans teach Asia that freedom makes you humane and knowledge, kind—which we already know Communism does not?" He saw the devastation I felt. He patted my hand apologetically and went on, "It is a mere lesson. If I were no doctor, in an odd land like this, I'd do what you did. I only wish more from *you.* I know, love, believe in America!" A real Joe! I wish he lived nearer Miami.

Earlier, while Grandpa drank orange pop and Mr. Rockefeller ever more uneasily consumed scotch—I had noted a catholicity in Wong aesthetic taste. Any niche might contain a lapis lazuli carving, or a magnificent jade jar. But, on a conspicuous window sill, stood a more plebeian artifact: the two plaster pups which, in store windows or on counters, advertise Black and White whisky. Of course, the Wongs perhaps represented Black and White in the Colony. Still, the statuette—brand name clearly marked, life-size and as realistic as all such commercial art—made a sensational contrast with Ming ceramics.

We dined at a huge, circular table, proceeding through some two dozen courses—courses which increasingly embarrassed the

Pelps and Rockefellers: intermittent soups were served with porcelain spoons, but chopsticks only were provided for the rest. That disconcerted our American coguests.

Soon, a housefly buzzed our viands, touched our thin, beautiful chinaware, and examined the increasingly spattered damask tablecloth. Nonchalantly, Grandpa Wong drew from some recess under the table an ordinary fly swatter. With great aplomb, he reached far across the Arthurian table, and got the fly neatly—but to the discomfiture of the conventional, retired banker, who was already distressed by chopstick difficulties and appalled by the growing sabotage of the tablecloth. Enthusiastic splatter is good manners in China; besides, neat eating is out of the question. Mr. Rockefeller didn't know.

All travel accounts disclose the vicissitudes, even hardships, attendant on dining-out with alien people. Justice William O. Douglas, in his recent and superb book about his Russian tour, reported in almost overpowering detail his difficulty, as a guest of Arabs, in eating a sheep's eye and his nearly disastrous effort to simulate the anticipated relish, while masticating sheep's ear. He also told of his long dread but ultimate pleasure in the matter of camel's milk.

I am therefore glad to report, in this same area, a notable triumph for banking and the American character. Justice Douglas is, after all, a pretty tough cookie in any territory; but Manhattan bank executives lack, as a rule, the build-up of a rugged, outdoor past.

We were embarked on our fifth or sixth soup, our tenth or twelfth course. We had been served soups of chicken, shark fin, fish, and God knows what else. Ricky had already lamented not yet trying a "thousand-year-old egg"—an egg, that is, which has been buried in lime for a month or so, after which, chemically cooked and coal-black, it is exhumed—and eaten by the Chinese with éclat. Mr. Wong, Jr., had immediately summoned a servitor who soon produced such an egg. Ricky dug in and said then— says still—it was rich and delicious. Mrs. Pelp gingerly, gamely tried a morsel—and agreed.

Now, however, as another soup was served in another style

and hue of thin porcelain bowl, Mr. Rockefeller—already put out of countenance by his trifling miscalculations and things like Ricky's taste for antiqued eggs—foolhardily asked, "What is *this* kind?" None of his trouble was of his own making. He was thinly garbed and chilled to the marrow as a result. If the servants had not kept filling his highball glass with potions stiff enough to rock Pantagruel, he would have had to exercise or burn papers.

"Bird's-nest soup," Mr. Wong, Jr., replied, easily yet attentively.

The Manhattan banker stared at and stirred the delicacy. "I don't see any straw or twigs," he quipped—or thought he quipped.

"The nests," Mr. Wong, Jr., replied genially—and possibly with concealed curiosity—"are made from the saliva of swallows. We hunt up such nests after the young birds have flown. The swallows have a gland that excretes this substance—" Smilingly, Mr. Wong, Jr., lifted on chopsticks a sample of the transparent, gelatinous material of this certain swallow's "saliva" nest.

It dawned horridly on Mr. Rockefeller that the ornithology and cookery were true as stated. He glanced feverishly around the table. Ricky and I—like our Chinese friends—were spooning up the soup, which we like greatly.

Mr. Rockefeller shuddered, and all but hid the spasm.

He searched out his new-filled highball, a deep topaz mix, and drank it down. Then he picked up a porcelain spoon—looked into the soup bowl again—and put down the spoon. He clenched his jaws and repressed a hard abdominal lunge that anybody could note. He smiled.

This was a Life Crisis for him—an East-meets-West challenge. Mr. Wong, Jr., watched covertly; Grandpa lifted an occasional eye to discern whether will power or nausea would win the battle. I wondered myself. Groton and Harvard were being put to a test for which neither well-rounded school had prepared this illustrious grad.

Mr. Rockefeller grew pale.

I all but retched for him. Yet I *hoped*.

The man had what it takes.

Our compatriot abruptly snatched up the bowl in both hands and gulped its contents down.

During the next ninety or a hundred seconds, Mr. Rockefeller sat still. Pretty still. From my angle I could see his abdomen repeatedly try to explode. His Adam's apple made several risky up-and-down trips. But his New England will repressed every signal, every time.

Pretty soon he could speak; and he did so: *"Delicious!"*

It was triumph—as clear a case of one-upmanship as I've witnessed. No wonder his folks won at Bunker Hill!

Americans and Europeans resident in other lands display a generosity that often leaves the traveler as amazed as he is grateful. We had a letter of introduction to a Mr. Paul Lutey in Hong Kong. His business is shipping, but he and his wife, Virginia, made our concerns their principal activity, for several days. They accompanied us to the shops best for our purse and purposes. They entertained us. When they heard of my interest in the refugees, they arranged dinners and parties so we could meet and question UN representatives, government people, directors of refugee-aid sponsored privately in America, newspaper publishers and editors—anybody, everybody.

(I hope, some day, they—and many Japanese, Chinese, Thais, Indians, Arabs, and touring Turks—will give Ricky and me a chance at quid pro quo. But I fear our domestic best would fall far short of theirs.)

A wise and witty American, and his wise and pretty wife, thus gave me a chance to glean a really significant amount of opinion on the putative effect of atom-bombing the Red China bases. The men and women who discussed the subject at the various Lutey soirees and luncheons were Americans and Europeans; but they had been chosen because of current knowledge gained through recently arrived refugees or trips in Red China.

All but one—an English editor—agreed (and could not be shaken from the opinion) that any such assault by this nation would cost the free world the last shred of a diminishing sympathy, in the Orient and all Asia.

The Englishman thought that the "Paper Tiger" tag given USA in the Far East would be ripped off by such a measure and the Red Chinese, though doubtless at first enraged, would ultimately react with respect for the Atomic Tiger—and a new hope for their own liberation. That was the view taken at home by a few self-styled "old China hands."

When we left Hong Kong, I was certain it was a mistaken view.

Eddie Gong, after deliberating the same question, decided his viewpoint was wholly American and he could not and did not react like a Chinese. So he took a poll amongst numbers of the relatives and friends of his wife-hunting grandmother. These people were citizens of Hong Kong and many were descendants of Chinese who had been established in the Colony for generations. They agreed to a man and woman that A-bombing Red China would bring absolute calamity to America's reputation and give Communism the automatic fealty of hundreds of millions of still neutral people.

My question, of course, always assumed that USA first used such weapons. For no one would deny America the military right (though many asserted it would be morally and intellectually insane) to reply with nuclear weapons to nuclear attack.

But we Americans are prone to disregard the simple fact that USA has *already* once atomically assaulted a nation—and a nation that had no atomic counter. Asia and the Orient have *not* disregarded that truth—and never will forget it. A *second* nuclear holocaust deemed unprovoked would certify to the world that the ethics and humanitarianism of Washington were lower even than Moscow's.

Here, then, I report a sample of the kindnesses that three Americans showered on us. And this brief notice represents many similar acts not here reported at all!

We have no way to express the thanks we owe . . . unless,

as I hope, in some instances, this volume will be regarded as an expression of gratitude, intense and remembering—albeit oblique.

Walking on the sunny, cold street the next morning, Ricky and I saw a Chinese boy of about three, a cute child dressed in a red cotton suit, also walking—gravely. For he was eating, too—eating with happy appetite, but seriously, from a wooden bowl. He used chopsticks and his small meal was rice. Just rice.

He stumbled and fell.

The bowl clattered on the pavement spilling nearly all of its contents.

The little kid got up on his feet, wobbling like a tumble-toy. He was plainly hurt—but he did not cry.

He looked at the bowl. Then he picked it up to appraise the trifle of rice that still stuck to its sides. An expression of childhood distress—of almost unbearable regret—briefly crossed his small face, turned his mouth down.

The countenance became stoical again.

He retrieved the chopsticks and commenced eating the few grains of rice left to him, philosophically.

And he walked away slowly but bravely at his previous pace.

6
the "childishly friendly" Thais

The flight from Hong Kong to Bangkok was "uneventful": we climbed into a cumulus sky above the South China Sea and sat down in due course at one more airport like the rest.

But no flight is uneventful to the mind. It sees special possibilities for odd events in air travel. An engine can take fire, fall off, or hurl its propeller into the lavatory. A maniac can shoot up a Constellation. Planes can go to gas-fire glory because vexed or venial relations of some passenger put a time-bomb in the luggage.

On this particular hop, there were even possibilities of a yet more dramatic sort: a MIG, operated by a Sino-Stalinist jet-jockey, might let go with his fifties. We might then escape, crash in flames, or land on the sea safely. At that point, we might be captured and killed, held as hostages, brainwashed, put to those old Chinese tortures or even politely sent back home, by the freedom-professing soldiers, workers and peasants of the Pigtail Satellite.

Such hazards, peculiar to flying, have kept untold numbers of Americans out of the best medium for travel—air. And such potentials show why commercial lines do not seek in pilots that degree of age and putative maturity which railroads want in

engineers, shipping lines in skippers. It takes adult savoir faire
and also—sometimes—youth's brave *so what.*

But so far as I know, not the slightest incident occurred on
our Hong Kong-Bangkok hop. It was routine.

Yet Ricky and I do not remember it as tedious!

Did you expect, when you studied geography in Grade
Seven, ever to fly down the South China Sea? Can you recall
the locus and map-look of such Seas? And would you find it
uneventful to fly a course, on a clear day, which brought you
to the realm where English Anna met that exotic King? Would
you not find it Adventure, if a low coastal plain, come suddenly
under your wing, was Indo-China—lands called Vietnam, Laos
and Thailand?

The jungle rivers were map-designated Nam, Menam and
Mekong. And as we looked down at hills precipitous under a
green jungle robe, we followed other watercourses to alluvial
widenings where mud-hut, thatch-roofed villages lay in small
squares alongside pale green oblongs of growing rice.

By and by, Ricky began to read in a paperback book we'd
found at Hong Kong—an early novel of mine so long out of
print that she'd never seen it before. So I took up my favorite
hobby. In America, it is called "daydreaming" or "musing" and
universally regarded as a vice.

What started me musing was the geometry of the Indo-Chinese villages that floated under us a moment and then vanished
in hills steep and chaotic as some green sea petrified in its most
tumultuous form. Petrified? Only in human time. Like a storm-
wrought sea, this land would smooth to level calm some eons
hence. Eons ago, it had tossed at human tempo: a tempest in
lava preparing crags for other elements to reduce. I noted the
illusory permanence of hills—a fact unknown to the Psalmist.
Then I mused on the engineering of the villages—primitive but
perceptible.

Their thatched roofs lay along fairly straight lines; the inter-
secting paths showed rectangular intent. Greater precision appeared in the squared corners of rice paddies. There, property

was concerned, not mere urban convenience. Men—even the Vietnamese (and their forebears who probably had staked out the fields centuries ago)—survey whatever concerns their pocket-books with care. . . .

How perfect the act of daydreaming for those impounded in airplanes or other vehicles! For people in hammocks, sitting beside ponds, ill or well, fed or hungry—all people alive!

Imagining does not even call for paper and pencil. No game-board need be spread or cards shuffled; no poker chips (or matches as substitutes) must be brought by any stewardess. This game of musing can even be played naked in a bathtub—a recommended locus, found profitable by Archimedes. Yet note how we Americans choose shower over tub. We dare not risk silence and recumbence. Rather, we stand, ready to run should Thought invade our minds, insulated against it by hiss, spatter and sudden, arbitrary shifts of temperature.

But Man Thinking, as old Ralph Waldo forgot to note, is usually something else before that. He is Man Stationary, or, at least, man engaged in some automatic task that asks nothing of his brain. But it is virtually against the law in all our Forty-eight States to be Stationary.

Doers are never sitters we say, and call ourselves doers.

We do our work and practice our professions. And the central purpose of our culture undoubtedly is to make it easier to provide the essentials of living—and then the comforts and luxuries—so we may have leisure for life's enjoyment. Well?

How shall Americans learn again the lost art of dreaming, before some differently limited but perhaps more determined "doers" erase that-which-isn't-yet: the American Dream? Does the very phrase not mean we intended to remain dreamers?

To hold fantasy self-destructive simply because it does not tan leather, nail boxtops, clean streets or invariably unriddle cosmos, is an error. To fear dreaming, as many do these days—even teachers!—is but to fear one's true self!

The dreamer, having access to Eternal Time, to Freedom of Mind (that absolute of eternity and infinity) need impose upon his human act no objective or boundary, need set no goal, require no task to be accomplished. He muses simply to *be* again.

If one dream in a billion produces a valuable insight, supplies a new contact with Natural Reality, provides a fresh comprehension of self or others, or merely sets a man going in some path which (when he again becomes Man Doing) benefits his fellows or even himself in a truly practical way, why, dreaming has at least advanced him and thereby all of us.

So I thought, there in the Siamese sky. Wylie, the dream-peddler. And I thought:

When men came from their caves, scratched out streets between such huts as lay below us—when men planted and owned (and defended) their fields, engineers soon came with straight lines and right angle boundaries.

So engineers began early to dominate our consciousness.

Their technique doubtless begat the rectilinear mind. This modern mind believed that boundaries, by promulgating an efficient here and now, also expanded the total nature of humanity. Ridiculous! Man became increasingly bounded, to attain ease. He desired ease so that he would finally have leisure—in which he could become his unbound self again! So the doer-owner lost touch with the dreamer. So the self became but a property of dogma.

Engineers, in short, gave rise to what we call Economic Man —man who imagines life, being, Nature and the cosmos and imagination itself exist to be exploited.

Man the artist lost his human art and became a wretched parasite with a planet for his host and all his various gods to keep him from the art of being—to keep him a doer opposed most of all to the doer's sin: awareness.

Age after age, man grew more and more to be the mirror image of his engineered machines. His gods became the unwitting reflection of a nonhuman dream only an animal would wholly enjoy. Not man-the-artist—not man-being, man-musing— but man-the-engineer, man the thing-of-things at last demoted God Almighty to cabinet status—an equal in the company of engineers. Boundaries became his delusion of power and growth. The smaller the "tolerance" of his mechanisms, the more efficient. Machines are mere means to ends but man now saw his body as the end, not letting himself muse beyond.

His inner "tolerances" were correspondingly diminished, of course. He thus became conformist, expecting solace by dehumanizing himself to stereotypes. For conformity—or "standardization"—is the efficient means to mass-produce objects. Intolerant, too!

It was, in its way, a fairly good muse—and it got me to Bangkok.

Ricky interrupted, offering a penny for my thoughts, as we approached the airport.

"I was just thinking that those primitive village streets back in Vietnam are *already* too straight, for my money!"

She handed me a penny. "If they aren't," she said, "the Red Chinese will fix it, when they take over."

A loud-speaker cleared its throat. Our captain began to chat with his passengers and between each of his assertions came a long pause, as usual. At first, I'd thought those pauses were due to operational demands on skippers who had to talk and fly. But I decided they were more in the nature of that abuse of time (for thought-collection and for keeping a captive audience in suspense) which characterizes amateur public speakers, everywhere.

He said we could not fly over Bangkok although he would like to show us the town: The King of Siam had forbidden it. He said the visibility was unlimited. He told us what to do about customs. And he added that the shade temperature on the ground was ninety-four degrees—long pause—Fahrenheit.

The passengers set up a murmur audible above the slowing motors.

The plane bumped, reversed props, halted—and we filed out.

I drew in a good, deep breath and started for the terminal on the hot concrete—carrying two coats, a camera and my on-board bag. I overtook a lady passenger.

"Swell day," I said.

She turned with angry eyes. Her one coat and small canvas satchel had already brought perspiration to her face. She

thought, for a moment, that I was speaking ironically. "Isn't it
hideous! And they said March was a good month for Siam!"

Ricky said delightedly, "Smells like Miami!"

I then noticed that Ricky and I were rapidly overhauling
most of the passengers. Mere announcement of the outside temperature had slowed them down, in their heads, before the fact
could possibly affect them. So I dropped back and offered to
carry the lady's coat and satchel. My heart had revved up, to tide
me over the snows of Chicago, wintry fog in San Francisco, sub-
seventy rains of Oahu, Tokyo blizzards and the tweed-and-
sweater frigor that doubtless the insentient British have imported
to the Crown Colony. Now, my pulse was gratefully returning to
its easy Caribbean beat.

The woman would not let me like warmth. She panted, "I,
for one, am going to go straight to the air-line office and get *out*
of here. I can't *stand* this!"

Presently, we were ranged in health and passport queues.
And I addressed a sermon to my perpetually captive audience,
Ricky, saying—in effect—that thermal discomfort is neurotic.

People who live in the North—from Jacksonville, Florida, to
the subtundra of Milwaukee and beyond—almost always come
"close to perishing" in tropic lands, I pointed out. It takes them
days, weeks, even years, to become "acclimatized." Some never
manage. Yet it is the observation of a very shrewd and psychoso-
matically alert witness (me) that their rolling perspiration, hard
breathing, sleeplessness or coma, pseudoasthma and general ma-
laise, in hot countries, is induced by the mind.

Take Bangkok. (Ricky took Bangkok.) Ninety-four is not an
unusual temperature—in summer—for Bismarck, North Dakota.
It is possible, if Gulf weather moves up our map, to have high
humidity with the heat. Bismarckians may complain about such
damp elevations of their local temperature; but they generally
endure them casually.

Heat occurring in New York or Chicago (and the constant
steaminess of estivating Washington, D. C.) does few natives
harm and is the expected thing. That is the simple fact, although the American press—devoted to the evasion of good news

and the exaggeration of all evil and misfortune—has a summer custom of calling the statistically expectable demise of every senile twerp and hypertensive executive a direct result of "heat waves."

In short, I asserted, the discomfort, frenzy and collapse of Northerners in the tropics arises from causes which are, conservatively, 99% imaginary. What they bear at home, and perhaps do not even notice, prostrates them the moment they encounter coconut palms standing in vertical shade. They have been taught, in prejudiced geography classes and by Hollywood, that below Cancer and above Capricorn it is not only torrid but white men fall prey to gin, miscegenative coition, and early death, accelerated by a host of awesome diseases. Yet I have spent far more tedious, bed-soaking nights in Delaware, Ohio, than ever in Maughamland.

I have further noticed that stricken, near-hysterical individuals in hot countries become their normal selves the instant their attention is captured by some outer phenomenon—a game of bridge, a highball, a horse race, a Dixieland band, a good steak, a hooked fish, a blonde, a rare wildflower or whatever especially interests them. That fact cinched my opinion.

Ricky said, "Move up, dear. You're blocking the line." And she added, after weighing the words, "Too bad your principle doesn't work in reverse. I mean—you suffered so in Japan, from the cold."

Ricky relished as much as I the mold-spiced midday of Siam. But most of our companions, as a disillusioned official of the air line presently predicted, hied—or dragged themselves—to travel agencies, canceled their five or ten days' stay, and got out of the region by the earliest plane available. . . .

A taxi rolled us along macadam on which two cars could barely pass and wooden-wheeled carts drawn by assorted beasts forced the cab to a shoulder. The way was lined for some distance by queen's crepe myrtle trees—in bloom. A canal bordered the thoroughfare; and in Thailand, canals are called klongs.

The klong was lined with unpainted wooden homes that had shrines on posts instead of letter boxes. In the klongs, kids swam and men paddled desultory boats. Above the klongs monkeypod and bo (or po) trees slanted—and banana trees dangled ripe fruit in easy reach. Jacarandas, golden shower trees of sundry species, royal poincianas, *cochlospermum variatum,* mangoes, and half a hundred other trees furnished a perfumed shade and laid petal carpets on the water, amongst lotuses.

In retrospect, Thailand still seems familiar in that one way: South Florida has "klongs," too; and similar trees that engineers want to cut down to straighten streets in Coconut Grove.

But here (whatever my wife says!) is another psychological source of dismay in some Northerners who brave the tropics. The verdure is alien and of the jungle. In consequence, any vista of aligned pink cassias nested with air plants and orchids conjures up fauna—creatures that literary men have always used to panic cold-country readers: tigers, perhaps—certainly boas and pythons and towering king cobras (which do live in forested Thailand) as well as scorpions, centipedes (commoner in that ocean annex of Manhattan, Bermuda), herds of stampeding elephants and, of course, lizards. How suggestible and fearful we often are!

Our taxi was soon dodging amongst rickshaws, samlors (a kind of rickshaw-bike), motorized samlors, trucks and cars from all the world, and brown people who wore those "hats like plates" Noel Coward ascribes to the Malay States.

We turned finally into quite narrow streets, between quite ordinary buildings—and our taxi reached the King's Hotel. Its doorman was an outsized Thai in what seemed the residue of a military uniform. He did not notice us until we had carried our own luggage halfway from cab to portal: an earnest discussion with loitering friends had taken his attention from his job. Now he saw us and leaped, all one grin. He used every limb and muscle to welcome us, so that he seemed to dance.

The lobby was very dark and its "desk" almost indiscernible, after the sun-dazed outdoors. The murk rang with hammering. We could dimly see a patio where carpenters sawed teak with

Iron Age tools and masons were pouring concrete, one bucket at a time. We read (nobody was in a hurry to greet us) a rudely lettered sign. When the workmen were done and the now-tattered garden was replaced, it stated, the patio would be "European." Shade and tables "would everywhere prevail." Thai girls would bring frosted drinks; flowers would emblazon the day and perfume the night: and there would be a "sensational American swimming pool."

We registered. Boy-sized, faun-hued men picked up our bags and our accommodating eyes now saw that the foyer opened into a bar, a restaurant, a money-changer's emporium, a place that sold black sapphires, the patio and a hall. Several sapphires gleamed dully above a ten-watt bulb in a glass case hung on the wall. I made a brief stop at the money-changer's and then went up two long, broad flights of unwalled but roofed stairs, meditating ticals. I found our door. I tipped our porters—too much, I immediately felt certain. Ticals are tough.

Ricky was by then standing bemusedly in our room.

"Jeanne Eagels slept here," she said.

I took a look:

Two beds, twin, low, nubbly-appearing—their heads against a frowsy wall that once had been painted manila and now was dun and spider-webbed with cracks. The furniture was bamboo, with some upholstering freshly renewed according to a concept of color harmony that eluded me—and some looking as if the place had just been looted. Chairs, desks, divans, floor lamps and table lamps abounded—so much furniture that passage seemed impossible. The chamber was booby-trapped, besides, with electrical wires, frayed at many points.

The only window was small, and could not be opened. Its panes, muddied by many monsoons, gave an occluded rear-end view of ramshackle flats where Thai women leaned on sills and suckled babies. In the bare compound below, men naked to the waist (but sheltered by the flat cones of coolie hats) hung out wet, but not clean, laundry.

Numerous lizards waited for bugs on our wall—lizards up to eight inches in length, beige to ash-gray. They looked much

like chameleons, which are familiar to Floridians. And chameleons, I reflected, bite only each other, and only males, and only
at mating time; besides, there are almost no poisonous lizards.
One rare exception is an American species.

Beyond the room, which one ceiling bulb lighted—beyond
its dark, cracked floor that I thought was painted cement but
Ricky says was linoleum—I presently descried the bath. A vesti-
bule led to it. I tried the light switch there and another bare
bulb disclosed a new hazard. En route to the bath, one had to
skirt a deep pit excavated (or eroded) from a floor that plainly
was concrete. I employed the facilities. Experimentally, I also
turned on the shower. The plumbing bayed, burped, backfired;
an orgasm of rust followed and the flow resumed at a rate only
fair for a medicine dropper.

"Any hundred-and-sixty-pound man," I called, "could get
a nice bath here—in three or four hours." I looked about. "If
there were soap, I mean."

Ricky did not answer. Possibly already dead of cobra bite. I
went back to the bed-living-chamber.

She stood amidst the pretty random of those things a
woman puts on top of a suitcase: yesterday's blue lace bra, a
hairbrush, tomorrow's pale peach panties, a sewing kit of crimson
damask, tonight's red-and-white pajamas, the kimono bought in
Japan. Her eyes moved from a single object to another, back—
away—and back again. She'd spotted the telephone—and the
air conditioner.

I never learned what nation fabricated the phone. Albania,
at a guess. But if Alexander Graham Bell had lived in the Dark
Ages, all phones would have had its look. A large, clumsy instrument, apparently fashioned in a gravel mold, the uncouth gadget,
moreover, had suffered such vicissitudes as time and kicking-
about stamp on medieval artifacts. Repairs had been made with
plaster of Paris, rubber bands, string, glue, shoelace and adhesive
plaster. A shambles of hard rubber, held together by magic. I
next scrutinized the air conditioner. "The total effect," I said,
"is called by decorators, 'Transition-Asia.'"

"Joseph Conrad also slept here," Ricky murmured. "Pierre

Loti. Robert Louis Stevenson. Captain Cook. Bligh of the
Bounty——"

"Ghosts," I agreed. "But the phone is a miracle: Resurrec-
tion."

"It'll probably give you a shock." Ricky is not exactly
afraid of electricity, but she is—conservatively suspicious. A sound
attitude in Bangkok, I felt.

"We have many close friends in Siam whom we must call
instantly." My irony did not escape her. As usual, it merely
seemed inappropriate.

"I do want to phone the Smiths——"

"Smiths? What Smiths?"

"He's something in USIS, or CARE, or UNICEF." She
remembered. "It's UNICEF."

"Do we know these particular Smiths?"

"They're English."

"You have their number?"

"Oh, yes. Bangkok 4455-9."

"Copied, no doubt, from a package of matches you picked
up in some Jap geisha house?"

"Mrs. King Gordon gave it to me. In Tokyo."

That's the way it is. Maybe you don't know a soul in Siam.
Maybe you've been looking forward to a country where you'd
be a complete stranger and could go sight-seeing all day every
day without having to shoulder through wretched refugees, turn
down bids to kill yourself marlin-fishing, or talk about the cold
war with admirals and generals. Then you find you've been
"passed along":

Somebody you've met in Coconut Grove has a cousin in
Calcutta—who looks you up. Or an old pal you encounter in the
Ginza obliges you to phone the Bangkok Smiths.

I was daunted and it is a state I detest: I longed to be, or at
least seem, dauntless. There could be a way:

Without further hesitation—without enquiring whether the
voltage was 110 or 440 or examining the threadbare insulation—
I stepped up to the intrusive, beat-up box that was our air
conditioner and threw its switch. It began to hum as smoothly

as a new model on a Schenectady sales floor. Cool air smote me.
The atmosphere of the room—not unlike that of a kitchen where
a boiled dinner has reached the serving point—rapidly became
less calid, even somewhat less spicy. The lizards, feeling the glacial breeze, crawled into cracks.

Ricky was impressed. In her view, I had risked electrocution.

"What are we supposed to do with the Smiths?" I asked,
from my position of authority-regained. "Meet more Red China
refugees? Talk with the King of Siam?"

"He's in mourning. His mother died recently. Anyhow, you
can't see him without a black dress and I didn't bring one, so
we'll miss that."

I sat on the bed—jumped up—and found a less cobby place.
"Too bad. I went to Princeton with—I *think*—the Crown Prince
of Siam. He may be King, by now. We could have gotten together for a few locomotives in the palace. Maybe an orange-
and-black dress would do."

"That King is dead," she said. (Ricky has a way of knowing
such things. I suspect it is owing to the fact that she reads many
books I put aside.) "The present one is another."

"Princeton, also?"

"Sorbonne, I think. Maybe Penn, though. He writes popular songs."

"Then the Smiths want us to help rid their compound——"

"——kampong. Remember your Fairchild!"

"Kampong—of kraits."

"Kraits?"

"Snakes. One dropped on my brother Max when he was in
India. Didn't bite, though. That's why he's now in TV."

"They'll take us through the native children's hospitals."

"Bully!"

"And help us buy black sapphires—so we won't get stuck."

"Just what I want. A black-sapphire-studded belt."

"And—if we want—we can get some Chinese stuff. I mean,
jade, semiprecious stones—in old settings. The refugees keep
bringing it in. And some is smuggled." Ricky had once again
commenced to unpack.

So I began. "You can't get a Certificate of Origin for such things. U. S. Customs doesn't let you bring them in."

"No." Ricky sorted nylons. "But everybody——"

"——smuggles. Everybody but us, dear. Do you think I want you arrested at Idlewild? I mean—if we ever see Idlewild again? Imagine the headlines! WIFE OF PROMINENT AUTHOR JAILED FOR SMUGGLING COMMUNIST LOOT."

"I got a few things in Hong Kong"—Ricky sounded sad—"only a few dollars' worth. Shall I throw them away?"

"When we leave France. They're legal till we get home."

"Everybody brings them back, Phil! Even *Senators*' wives. They aren't worth a lot. But they're simply beautiful!"

"I'll miss you," I said, "while you do your two years." Ricky looked so despondent that I quit. "It's four o'clock. Would you like some coffee. Or, maybe, a chottapeg?"

"That's India."

"Singapore gin sling, then?"

"Yes."

The next days we spent in tourism. . . .

We visited the Temple of the Golden Buddha where a figure of that great man, some hundred-and-umpteen feet long, lies in gilded glory—beneath a leaky roof and between walls from which ancient murals have scaled like decals on the legs of wading kids. The sandals on that image are taller by far than I —and their soles are scored, I noted approvingly. For Buddha needed traction: his work, like every good man's, was uphill all the way.

We also paid our respects to the Temple of the Emerald Buddha, having by then hired a tall, thin, odd-looking guide named Charlie. He was, I would guess, part Chinese and part Swedish, but all Thai insofar as attitude, manner and accent were concerned. He told us—when we asked—that he was a Christian. His wife, he added, was Buddhist. He volunteered, further, that, if he had to do it all over, he, too, would be a Buddhist: "Christianity interferes too much with your private life," he said ruefully, "but a Buddhist doesn't have to worry if a pretty girl interests him."

You could see him react to that amenable thought with Christian guilt.

Charlie tiptoed about all Buddhist temples reverently, though. And when we stood before the Emerald image, he waited till he thought we weren't looking and hurriedly pressed his hands together in front of his chest, like a prayerful Covenanter—and bowed. So I am no more certain of Charlie's Christian authenticity than I am of his fidelity. Perhaps such occasional obeisances to the Buddhas make up for occasional flirtations . . . or whatever they call them in Thailand.

We saw the Marble Temple. And one morning we rashly decided to climb the outside of the tallest "prang" of Wat Arun, a tower called the "Temple of the Dawn," or the "Porcelain Pagoda." We were told by Charlie we'd get a fine view of the city, the river and the palace. He didn't go with us and I soon saw why.

A giddy caper, that Temple ascent proved. Two hundred feet high, or more—and leaning, slightly—it was a crumbling structure of stone and mortar in which were set millions of bits of chinaware—some of it, apparently, the broken dishes of upper-class Thais. Steps led up its near-vertical exterior, steps about six inches wide but irregular and often narrower, with risers of eighteen inches or more . . . the steepest staircase I ever saw. Iron pipe handrails, rusted and sleazy-looking, were dubiously fastened on both sides. Eighty or ninety feet of such an escalade towered before us.

I was nervous. Ricky went first and I pursued, thinking that someday, when the handrail rusted a bit more, a couple of idiot Americans like us would abruptly become a richer dust concealed in the rich dust of Siam.

Above that grooved precipice we found another, even steeper stone stairway.

Ricky hesitated. "Breather?" she asked, not troubling to turn her head for fear she might unbalance herself—or perhaps loosen a step and bring down the whole vast, venerable edifice.

"Keep going." I said it somewhat grimly—and for my own sake.

Time was—before I spent years in psychoanalysis—when I suffered agonies owing to acrophobia. Ricky, however, had never shown a sign of being "high shy" in her life.

I urged her to go straight on up, not because of a relapse of my phobia or because of worry about its likelihood in her: my feeling was, merely, that this scramble on the Porcelain Pagoda —though very like a fireman's climb up an extension ladder over the heads of a shuddering crowd—held hazards unknown to fire fighters. The rotten rocks and shaky, rust-bitten iron looked as if they should have been condemned by the Bangkok Safety Commission a century before. So the less time we spent there, the better. The gigantic porcelain-studded phallus might hang together for another thirty minutes, but not forty.

Ricky hesitated a little—and started up the second flight. As I followed, I gave the iron banisters a test yank. It sent ripples up the bars, but they did not quite come away in my hands.

Ricky stopped dead. Her heavy, red-leather pocketbook slid back to her shoulder. *"Don't do that!"*

"Just making sure," I answered.

She didn't say anything—but climbed, slowly, steadily.

A walled walk allowed us to visit all four sides of the holy organ and to look out from every compass point. A glance down the double set of stairs was alarming: they were steep enough to give pause to a Pueblo and descent—more difficult—cried for pitons, rope and a trusty ice axe.

Far, far below us, on a scaffold of twitchy bamboo, Thai artisans were giving a new gilding to a stupa—a tower a good hundred feet high. Watching them, noting the flimsy nature of their support, made my stomach shrink.

Beyond them was the Chao Phraya River; across that, the stalagmite fantasy that is the Royal Palace; all around it—Bangkok.

I had, for once, brought along our Kodak. Like Ricky's pocketbook (so-called), it had bobbed and banged against me all the way up. Now, I photographed the Thai steeplejacks, the Royal Palace and the riverscape with its chuffling traffic. I snapped the temple-toothed skyline to its last gold cap—in Kodacolor.

Bangkok is strange beyond dreaming. I thought Frank L. Baum surely saw the city, or pictures of it, before he had his first inkling of Oz.

Buddha, I also thought, would be astounded by what these Southern, Oriental people had done for him. Done with architecture and decoration, with swirling incense and tinkling temple bells—even though his magnificent philosophy (like Christ's) had long been largely lost amongst its grandiose mnemonics. Lost in gold and glittering porcelain, lost in the genital-and-mammary-shaped edifices, in green, ochre, peacock, scarlet, purple and gilded halls, in labyrinths both mural-lined and mosaic-adorned—lost amidst infinite friezes inset with a million tiny mirrors, in eye-hurting dazzlement and the cantanabulation of ten thousand miniature brass bells rung by the wind—in the ritual roar of gongs—drowned by drums and obscured by minty smoke. Buddha might not have scoffed—for he was knowing and preached mercy. But he would surely have repeated his apothegms sadly, for here and elsewhere they have been honored in the breach, the pixilated extravagant breach. It all made me wonder, as I often do, what Jesus would say of my culture, that imagines itself Christian.

I took it in, that morning, and kodaked it as I walked with Ricky around the scary obelisk. I had her pose for a picture against the enchanted city and the temples, too—the resplendent images of reverence which millions of men and women used up centuries to paint, grave, inlay, bemirror, emboss, gild, bell, scent and set nagas against the tropic sky to guard.

Here, therefore, were more engineers, more doers, people who ignored the lovely dreams Buddha tried to share with his nightmared world—people who made objects to symbolize the dreams and forgot what was represented.

I took Ricky's picture again—and suddenly noticed she'd gone chalk white.

"Sick?"

"I've never been high-shy anywhere in my life before!" she whispered, in a voice that appalled me. "Isn't it *awful!*"

A man lucky enough to possess a wife like Ricky (or to be possessed by her—it does not matter which) seldom has the opportunity to display that manhood which is supposed to complement femininity. I can recall only two instances: once, at night, we had heard a prowler downstairs in a lonely, unfamiliar house. I'd descended first. Once, Ricky woke me from a nap and asked me to kill a rattlesnake in our yard on which, a moment before, she had very nearly stepped.

Now, she was saying, "I *can't* go back down, Phil! I don't know how I'll make it!"

She laughed at herself, a brave parry at hysteria. "I'm like a cat in a tall elm! You'll have to send for the fire department to rescue me!"

So I rescued Ricky. Testing the iron rails again, taking her cumbersome handbag, I went to the head of the top flight of stairs, turned my back on its mail-chute pitch and gripped both rails.

"Now. You turn around. Take both rails. Start down. I'll be right in back of you and my arms will be on both sides." I decided not to add that, even if she fainted from vertigo, I could and would catch her.

Tremulously, she turned. Anxiously, she lowered a sandal-shod foot and felt for the narrow step below. It was a long reach —nearly two feet—to that step.

With the second, slow-reaching step, Ricky lied: "I'm fine, now!"

We learned, afterward, that climbing the Temple of the Dawn was, for Buddhists, a spiritual rite; the steps had deliberately been made very risky to point a moral: the way to heaven is not easy.

"Sure, you're okay," I said then.

Down we went. Ten feet, fifty. A hundred feet. And down. Charlie had watched uneasily.

"I do not have heart for this climb," he said when we reached the ground. "The view was handsome, modom?"

Ricky said it was and we returned to our boat on the river. . . .

I noticed in Siam, and elsewhere in Asia, that guides almost invariably address their remarks to madame and pronounce it "modom." In such countries, guides are usually men, and men are considered important—women, their mere adjunct. So the practice puzzled me.

I never figured it out, but I tried.

Perhaps all questions are asked of "modom," all sights pointed out to "modom," in an effort to emulate Western chivalry. But the greatest percentage of tourist sight-seers may be women; so possibly the more frequent form of address becomes habit.

It could be, though, that Eastern men do not like to address their Western opposite numbers by any term correlative with "modom," as, for example, "sir." Certainly, only beggars addressed me anywhere as "sahib." And "sirs" were few. If that is the explanation, I approve. For the refusal to concede higher status to anybody is the first step toward individuation and independence—even if Europeans and Americans too often seem unable to appreciate what liberty must mean to the other fellow.

It means each man's right and duty (and each nation's) to make choices and establish values without suasion or pressure. It means an end to cap-touching and appeasement. It means a rejection of the "authority" of others—social, political or moral.

The final fate of man, perhaps, will turn on a single idea; and it will then turn (if liberty is that crucial concept) on the *American* attitude toward it—lip-served at home so proudly and served so badly abroad. For the American idea of freedom is not projected. In Thailand, I began to see why. There I had some time in which to think; and my thinking concerned the widespread Oriental discontent with Mr. Dulles.

I do not know Mr. Dulles. I know something about his

beliefs, however, as he was an elder in my late father's church. Our longtime, much-traveled, clarion-speaking Secretary of State was a symbol of a specific odiousness to millions everywhere we journeyed. *What* he symbolized to them goes generally unnoticed in America, for it is the commonest attitude of Christian Americans—who believe they are decent people and freedom lovers, as well—toward that great human majority for whom our kinder names are "backward" or "underprivileged." That attitude underlies a process that is destroying our nation from the outside. If I can here make clear its nature and fallacy I shall feel this book was worth all my endeavor. The attitude is unconscious but it produces an "unfreeness" in most "free" people.

It has many evil results. It gives rise to a psychological continuation of colonialism. The Reds can and do exploit it constantly to "prove" that America is the colonial menace of the future. The Reds shout Freedom (and even defend it) until they win control. But we seem able to share Freedom only after aliens have sworn themselves to our side. Thus Liberty, our one effective weapon in the world struggle, is seized falsely by our foe, while often abandoned or misused by us.

Our other weapon, "economic aid," is inadequate itself and blunted by Red propaganda besides. The real economic gains in Soviet Russia (as Justice Douglas has pointed out) seem princely to the ordinary Asian. Furthermore they are achievements of people in part Asian, themselves. The technological blessedness of the West (and America in particular) is to Asians the feat of an alien people—a people who colonized and suborned them, humiliated, despoiled and terrorized them for centuries and who *go on* telling them what is "morally" right!

Almost every Asian therefore sees American Freedom as inferior to, or no better than Soviet "freedom." He knows he could improve on either brand. If, finally, he must choose between the two, why should he select the "freedom" of Americans? They are distant, incomprehensible relatives of the very Europeans who so long kept him miserable and impotent; and these Americans are now demanding he do this or not do that on moral grounds. Thus they deny him the very essence of liberty: *self-determination.* People more like himself, under the Soviet "freedom," he notes, have made advances in a short period of a kind he can imagine gaining for himself. When Khrushchev tours Asia, rejoicing in its independence—while Dulles and Nixon call signals, the moment they arrive—why should America be followed?

This is the question Africa is asking. So are multitudes in Latin America. Russia and Red China today are supplying all the answers, and mostly by lies. Yet men like Dulles *seem* to affirm every syllable of criminal Communist lies and to repudiate —by word, act and policy—not just the American ideal but American history and American reality. For America is not a colonial nation and does not have ambitions for colonies. America has helped many nations to self-determined freedom—to independence like its own. Why, then, are we blundering toward impotent isolation and the ultimate calamity?

Even in Japan and Hong Kong, I began to see at first hand how much our statecraft thwarts our real aims and ill serves our desperate necessity. Dulles was but spokesman and symbol of our appalling error.

A strange, shocking insight occurred to me here:

"Ethically" and "morally," of course, Mr. Dulles was abstractly correct. To remain free, the individual and the nation must certainly avoid Communism: a rigid dogma and liberty's antithesis. From his standpoint as a devout Presbyterian, our Secretary of State could easily discern that fact. Communism has even outlawed God and is *that* unfree. But—perhaps because of *his own* dogmatism—Dulles could not see that to be free, men must first be free to make *their own* "moral" and "ethical" choices. That requirement he skipped, and even arrogantly rejected.

Why?

Other men besides me have long tried to show that Communism, while "atheistic," is still a "religion." It is an intellectual system which provides a complete doctrine for private and social behavior and an all-embracing "belief."

I have also elsewhere attempted to disclose why it is that

men who unite and foreswear God inexorably produce credo that matches at every point the "godliest" fiats of any faith.

This is a process, I have said, which will go on till the day we understand our natures sufficiently to transcend our present blindness to the drives of animal instinct. For such drives, acting on human forms, are the source of our religions. Potentially, they are also our means to rise to something more aware, and awarely directed, than our common animal today.

An "instinct of the brain," I have suggested, is to *use time*. The human brain evolved, took shape, for that function: time-use. Man, far more than any other creature, can use yesterday's lessons, today, on behalf of tomorrow. But the conscious detachment implicit in such activities has supplied man with an *ego*.

The ego thus seems able to ignore its present self, or to behold little else, at will. What a man calls "I" may seem forgotten while his brain, moving in the dimension of time, perceives a problem, appraises it, criticizes the appraisal, dreams, and finally reaches a solution. In the process he "thinks" (or feels he thinks) and afterward he acts. In his action, his ego returns from limbo—and he assures himself that he was "conscious" the whole while and, so, not instinct-motivated like all lesser beings.

As primitive man's ego emerged, he saw that his thinking brain gave him superiority over all lesser living things. His biological identities with them, however, reminded him of an apparent inferiority which he desired to transcend. Since he could detach, think, reason—he was not *all* animal, i.e., wholly the creature of instinct. In time, he decided he was not animal *at all* —or that his residual similarities were evil, and demon-caused. His brain (having the "instinct-of-the-brain" I hypothesized) now had to explain the biological drives that still affected him. His brain had somehow to create adequate patterns for living that satisfied both the reasoning capacity of brain and the biological demands of body. Those "patterns" were, at first, myths and legends and finally "formal" religions. To sustain man's new egotism, the force of instinct itself thus came to support the "going godliness"—whether "god" was Ra, Moloch, Jehovah,

Wotan or Atheist State. Not to think much, but to think much of ourselves, we misused time! We ordered our "animal" instincts according to "beliefs." Belief changed, and progressed in insight, only as man himself learned enough about Nature to make each prior belief obsolete. But the goal of all such belief remained: conviction of the ego, through "faith" and by rules for all animal acts, that Man is not animal but God.

Believers in the "truth" of their system for biological acts and their particular way of identifying ego with "god" cannot acknowledge other or different "truth," where other Faiths are involved. The True Presbyterian *can* see the unfreeness—the infamy, amorality, arrogance and brutal subhumanity—of the True Communist. But the True Presbyterian cannot discern what "freedom" means, in relation to True Communism, when the word is simultaneously related to, say, a True Buddhist, or a True Brahmin. Neither can a True Communist make such discernments. For both are Believers. Both have absolutes of inner "right" and "wrong," of inner "truth" and "falsehood." Both are ruled within by dogma. The very firmness of their Faith, which wilfully excludes from their conscious minds the possibility of moral error or ethical inferiority, makes them unable to note identities in the basic structure of all faiths, beliefs, creeds, doctrines—in short, all religions.

The ego that accepts Faith on faith is ruled thereafter by whatever pattern that Faith claims "right" for the management of all the instincts including, of course, the brain's own instinct. Since the brain can think—whether or not it is used for reasoning—its instinct is the instinct to *be* right. But the man who accepts a dogma cannot so use his brain. To make his ego seem big—and to evade self-determinations of the conflicting urges of instinct—he not only accepts some God or gods (or a socialist state and a Non-god) but he agrees never again to *doubt*. Doubt is sin to a Presbyterian; to a Soviet citizen it means Siberia or a firing squad; yet where a man will not doubt he cannot think with free, true logic.

The price paid for cerebral detachment was, of course, a potential loss of touch with timeless, authoritarian instinct. Who knows himself, has ego; who has ego, is aware of yesterday and tomorrow and no longer lives in the animal's eternal present. Moreover, he who can call himself "I" must deal also with an appended insight: *mortality*. The time-using brain will see its own end in time! Our primitive forebears, however, worked out systems for that: "We do not die," they said, "we have immortal souls."

The brain's pure "instinct" knew better. But ego betrayed reason: and since no test-for-soul could be repeated at will, some other device was needed. The invention of "faith" provided it. It said, "Nobody's soul will become immortal *until he first has faith*." That gimmick accomplished much. It gave man means to sustain the illusion of complete superiority to animals: if he agreed to believe it, he would become part of eternity and never die. It gave him a way to pacify his frightened, frantic ego. It set up a channel in which he could at once obey instinct and yet attribute his obedience to the needs of his "soul." In a channel of faith, he could gain all those varied ego-boons by following the Polynesian moral system, Peruvian, or Presbyterian. His newest instinct—to criticize, reason, create: the "instinct of the brain"—was infinitely less potent (in most individuals) than the sum-total of all other biological drives, because it *was* "new," a rudimentary thing, not far evolved. Besides, this device called "faith," if fully incorporated in the ego, *gave back to man a conscious sensation of his lost, precerebral timeless state.*

I can hardly continue, here, a discussion of so esoteric an idea as the "instinct" of *parts*, such as the brain. It would lead us to a discussion of the identity of form and function in living wholes and their parts—an obvious realm for inquiry only now beguiling certain biologists. It would lead to a consideration of those parts, like hearts, which work involuntarily, or lungs, which we can consciously somewhat control—and thence to a contemplation of brains. We would have to consider the chains of synapses and also examine dynamic psychology. And then we would have but begun!

Instead, let us note that "faith" makes any man willing to ignore his brain's best effort, imagine himself immortal, i.e., faith returns him, or at least his ego, to some special status in some special sort of "eternity," which was the likely *seeming of being* before brains grew in animals. Since the brain supplied the ego in the first place, and was evolved to abet survival, that gambit was (and is) highly acceptable to most of most brains! *Its* "cost" will be noted presently.

We might also observe that the Communist faith, denying immortality to the individual, is *not even an unconscious attempt to include instinct in a self-description of man. Rather*, it consciously denies any instinctual nature in man, such as has given rise to religions. But religious belief was perfectly natural until now—even if perfectly mistaken. So the religiosity of Communism is not "heretical" as some say, or merely "regressive" as others claim, or "nonexistent," as our Presbyterian would hold. It is, in the terms given above, far more horrible: a system of compulsion and taboo rising automatically from an unconscious effort of man-the-animal to destroy utterly man-the-mind, man-the-artist! In the Communist Faith, Man, Brain, Instinct and the Gods are one: fleshy mechanism. Naught is but Beast. Humanity is the Illusion!

A categorical Presbyterian, when he would oppose categorical Communism, cannot see *that* horror. Communism revolts him because it claims to be in revolt against his God. So, to a Dulles, atheism may become the focal antagonism. If he makes that error, theism (preferably the Presbyterian version) will then become the suitable means for opposing the Soviet religion. But, actually, God is irrelevant to the struggle.

The process underlying man's faith is involved, not the semantical terms of its sundry "highest" descriptions in conscious minds.

Our categorical Presbyterian—or a Catholic—sometimes dimly discerns the faithlike shape of Communism, even calls it a "Christian heresy." (For does it not purport to end the evils of greed, as Jesus tried to end them—and to share material benefits fairly, as He commended?) It is no mere religious heresy, however.

For this nonworship of Non-god is accompanied by the

same rejection of the right to doubt that all godly faith requires. So, like the godly beliefs, it needs a structure of rules by which to control the drives of instinct (aside from already abandoned instinct of the brain to be right). For all men who agree not to doubt, or are forced not to doubt, or denied access to ideas and facts contrary to a ruling belief, *must*, by their very situation, be *told* what is "right" and "wrong." They have in those ways been deprived of access to their own reason, or conscience—to half the potential functioning-in-time of their individual brains. Dogma thus makes mere followers even of those who administer it!

The *difference* between a Dulles and a Molotov is that the former can tolerate, still love, dissenters from his belief to whom he cannot extend an equal right of belief. But a Molotov lacks any rationalization for his instinct—even a Presbyterian's. He *eschews instinct* along with every God and Faith and religion. A Molotov's religion, therefore, is unknown to him *altogether;* he is not just atheistic—he is *ahuman!* Our Presbyterian cannot see what faith *or* freedom means to a Brahmin or to a Bangkok Buddhist, because he cannot see the inner mechanics of his own dogma—its source, its error, its relation to man-as-animal and man-as-mind.

The Presbyterian is most blind to his most selfish error. He cannot see that all Faith like his appropriates the instinct of love, of fatherhood and motherhood, the instinct toward familyship and the suitable devotion of man to children and to posterity—in order that the faithful should win an immortality *of ego!* Immortality through man's children is, truly, the natural end and means for mankind; and all other species serve that procreative drive. Only man has brazenly imagined he can appropriate to himself the time that belongs to his children. The Presbyterian (or any other Believer) cannot allow himself to see he has stolen man's instinctual birthright for ego ends. He cannot see that the Hindu has done it, too—though Hindu immortality is achieved by successive reincarnations.

Any scrutiny of man's bad performances in all his civilizations and under all their faiths, back through recorded history and far beyond, reveals how man corrupted the massive impulses, or instincts, which have oriented the course of every living individual thing in two billion years of evolution, and must sway us today. That force, that urge toward orientation and acts was exerted in behalf of the living, toward the future, through the medium of offspring, of posterity, *for the purpose of evolution itself*—till man came.

To appropriate the changeless drive of past evolution for one's self—to invent a "religion" that presumes each unit in the cosmic process will perpetuate every ego in some eternal heaven (or hell), some Paradise, Valhall, Happy Hunting Ground, Elysian Field or Nirvana—is surely to pervert the meaning of life and to exploit instinct itself for the imagined grandeur (the mere vanity) of each individual instrument! It is also to rob the future —*all children*—of the aim-of-life incorporated in the parents. For, once instinct is fixated by faith and established in its particular dogma, all contrary inner truth is lost and all different inner reality is rejected. Men live, thereafter, in an absolute arrogance. "My duty," becomes the task of Everyman, and love and life and all meaning save the temporal are sacrificed. If men happen to do what is right, but lies outside their faith, they do not know it, or cannot explain it. For even if the Believer's "duty" demands "self-sacrifice" the deed's done to gain heaven for ego and not to gain it through posterity for evolution.

Since men do not yet much understand the "immortal" wonder actually incorporated in them, as "love"—and since they do not perceive that the conscious control of instinct rests upon understanding *love* (and thereby, themselves)—the effort of individual, creed or state to exploit the drive and aim of evolution in each of us becomes blind—and dependent upon empirical trial-and-error for its acts and its evolved dogma.

A *state* so founded, though it denies God and instinct, must set up symbols to evoke responses from that which it does not consciously know it deals with, denies, yet rises from. Back, therefore, come the symbols, ikons, hierarchies, hagiologies, totems, tabus, litanies, shrines, cults, parades of devotees, sacrifices and what not. A Red Russia is soon ipso facto "holier" than anything the Czars knew—holier, which is to say, narrower, more dogmatic, more compulsive about "right" (even when it is now stated as "the morality of all successful means") and more phobicly zealous against contrary belief—i.e., "evil." When they were ignorant of their evolution, men had excuse for their endless efforts to explain awareness by legend and superstition. They have put too high a value on ego in the process. But to use the ill-assimilated findings of century-old science as proof that the whole motivation of belief was but passing nonsense is, itself, nonsense.

Men are designed, I think, so that, some day, by understanding themselves, they will take charge of the great orbit of their own evolution. Their attention will once again focus on its preconscious goal: *the next generation and those beyond.* To achieve that level of awareness, men will have abandoned *all* the old, unconscious systems set up to insist men are not animals but subgods who command their animal for the soul's sake. To achieve a proper human concept of humanity and restore, in human terms, the drive and orientation of Nature, men will have yielded all private claim on the immortality of individual—thus, finally, expressing in conscious being the meaning of Time to the real Mind.

That insight shows, I feel, why *no* religious man—Presbyterian or Communist—can even imagine freedom for another: they are themselves unfree, temporal in conscious orientation, and so cut off from the purpose of being.

It shows, too, why so many devotees of one faith, upon becoming disillusioned, leap to another as absolute. Communists and fascists have interchangeable psychic parts. The Communist whose "eyes are opened" often becomes the most doctrinairian Roman Catholic or joins some Protestant sect as authoritarian as Marxism.

For whether a man's "faith" refers to some "God" who controls heaven and hell (future time, for ego) or to some state or group or social system regarded as the "ideal" for our human future, that man has faith. He has perverted what he is *to seem greater to himself*—and so become lesser.

Freedom, the mind's one infinite and eternal dimension, is not knowable to him, any more. Even when the mind employs it with "objectivity"—as in science—the man who has, through faith, borrowed eternity and absolute truth, from Nature, for his ego, cannot explore beyond temporal bounds. When such a man becomes alarmed, he repudiates his scientific method, as old Galileo did and as the Soviet scientists did under Lysenkoism. And when such a perjured or self-saving "scientist" scrutinizes the human subject—himself—he has a deep impulse to deny access to all freedom to himself—and all others. For, somewhere within himself, the believer-by-preconviction knows he is an utter liar, and utterly guilty for having damned his progeny, forever, by instructing them in his faith.

His children are Nature's future, Nature's "immortality." But he has taken that from them by teaching them that his faith *now* is their absolute. His *ego*, his vanity, is, alone, the absolute!

That, in truth, is the Original Sin.

Whoever says he knows all inner truth now, through faith, and whoever makes that status quo of mind the obligation of posterity, sins indeed. For a mere illusion of his own eternal being, he has robbed human eternity of freedom to be more than he. His ego has "bought" all the time there is, to support itself; no more or other time is left for his children. So awareness is forced to stand still, and evolution is frustrate, while the stolen forces of instinct sustain local, temporal illusions that cut off families, nations, eras of history from the very purposes of life and being.

Think what it would mean to mankind if the human goal became the upward evolution of each next generation!

The Golden Rule that lies at the core of all great religions would thereby be elevated into that level of awareness where the brain could use its entire time-capacity for thought. Man could doubt as much as believe. He could accept his true situation, for his being would involve all future human being. He would be content—no, exultant—to know that plans and concepts and truths lay beyond his ken, beyond his faith, beyond his religion, and beyond the law of his state.

Do unto others as you would be done by, *in their future*.

Leave them free! Make them free! Let them become themselves!

Do not saddle them with ego-bred faiths, clad in the garments of ignorant and even legendary men. Corrupt none with *your* corruption. Instill none with your dogma.

Free them!

Communism, alas, is nihilism, indeed, and conveys a heritage of man's utter nothingness. It has lost whatever love man learned from his instincts as his ego molded them into faiths. Yet the arrogance, the oppression, the intellectual follies, the lies, cruelties and bestiality of the Believers—yes, Christians too oftentimes!—has so sickened men that this religion-of-nothingness is the most successful dogma the world has ever had to contend against! It has compelled and converted more millions in a third of a century than there are living Christians. It wants *you*—whether by persuasion or Inquisition—and wants you, if you resist, dead! In that sense, no Believer can oppose another: both are bound by identical fetters of pride. And pride will let neither perceive the chains, let alone a need to sunder them if man is to evolve. ALAS. Both would move toward freedom if either struck off his own proud shackles—the only links in his reach! While their faith lasts, each can but cut at the unreachable irons that hold the other.

Ricky and I boated through the floating market of Bangkok in a low-powered, double-prowed craft with a brass engine that looked like Japanese handiwork. A wooden awning shaded us; we had a boy aboard to help with landings, a man to steer—and Charlie to tell all.

I will not ever forget those people who lived on water streets. Everybody bathed and all the kids swam at their own doorsteps. Each merchant—seller of hot coffee or ice, yard goods, coal, wood or hardware—had a small boat painted an identifying color. Each also had a gong, bell, drum or rattle that announced his type of wares, as he approached. The supermarket in Bangkok comes to *you*.

Some canal-fronting homes bore street numbers; and there were electric "street lights" overhead. We even witnessed the house-to-house calls of a meter reader from the local power company: he also was water-borne.

Greybeards and grandmas, infants, teen-agers, lovely girls smiled as we passed, laughed with us, and waved until our arms were weary from waving back, our faces stiff from smiling.

To go out on the veranda, work a while at a collection of potted orchids and then descend, clothes and all, into the warm, muddy water—washing self and garments in the same bath . . . what a life! Boys and girls performed show-off tricks for us like kids everywhere—diving from a porch rail, swimming under water, catching hold of our boat and letting it tow them. And in that verdant Venice no one appeared destitute, yet none was rich. There seemed to be no sad people. No people stricken with the rest of the world's city malady, the grimness, the look of ambition riding some sea of nameless fear—which is the nowadays meaning of "urbanity." Coolies loading rice, laborers in pottery yards, men sawing lumber or making reed furniture, women dipping water to cook lunch or weaving mats or nursing babies took time to print on our memories the affectionate smile of Siam, before resuming the task at hand.

We visited the Ceremonial Barges, great gilded canoes with seats for many oarsmen and all the Many-Colored Monkeys as figureheads. On blocks in a Royal Boathouse when we saw them, they were, plainly, Siam's parade floats, ready to adorn every Imperial ceremony of importance.

We . . .

But enough! Siam is a place not to read about or see in movies but a place to be.

The books say the Siamese are "childishly friendly."

I'm not sure about the childishness.

Is warmth and affection proffered to everybody, childish? If so, reticence, or suspicion or even hostility on any first encounter must be evidence of maturity! Why are they so amiable?

Living is easy in Thailand as living is—or used to be—in Samoa: not much shelter is needed—or clothing. Food grows abundantly. Rice-rich Siam has by far the greatest favorable per capita trade balance of any Asian country. Such factors create a human condition of contentment that makes friendliness the natural approach of people to people.

Still, the British, in their greatest days of Empire when *they* had the trade balance, were they known the world around as "childishly friendly"?

There was nothing friendly, on the other hand, about Thai feeling toward the first people ever to conquer them: the Japanese. Thai eyes burned when the occupation was mentioned. Thais pointed out with grim pride regions of Bangkok that had been wrecked by American bombs—Jap-aimed. And one of the principal Thai sports is a kind of boxing, elaborated by mayhem —not a sport of *passive* or *timid* people. Even Siamese kite-fighting has symbolical undertones which suggest the Thais are perhaps not quite so naïve as the authors of the books imagine. . . .

Charlie explained, as Ricky and I stood at the edge of a great field and saw smaller "female" kites dancing against the afternoon-blue sky. Up went a male kite and the "fight" began. Half-controlled, half-driven by antic breezes, the big males assailed the smaller—now capturing one, two or more female trophies and reeling them to earth (on the winning side of the dividing line that crossed the field) now being themselves dashed down by the diving, scissoring females. Cheers rose from the proponents of (and bettors on) both kite sexes—such yelling as you might hear at Yankee Stadium. But whenever the females brought a male to earth, there was also sympathetic laughter in the shouts.

A chapter of psychology, written on the sky in a language of kites! The aggressor males swept forth to seize as many females as they might. But the females had a cutting edge that could sever the male kite's guideline, set it oscillating and in the end cause it to dash itself to earth. I could hardly tear Ricky away from the kite-fights! Taken with the audience reaction, they meant more to her, I suspect, than even to me.

Friendly—they are. Naïve . . . ?

The first evening, I stood in a dim street fumbling with unfamiliar tical notes. We had just come back in a motorized samlor from a fine dinner in an Austrian restaurant that was a replica of any brauhaus in Yorkville, in Manhattan. The ride in the three-wheeled vehicle had been exhilarating—a popping, lurching, tire-chattering surge through moonlit streets past fragrant gardens and over bridges that crossed populous water-streets. Now, I could not make out the price my driver asked or decide what bill to tender.

From the curb, suddenly, a Thai stepped. He took my banknotes from my hand, politely, asked my driver a question, sorted out the smallest bill and paid my man, who smiled and drove away—satisfied. When I turned to thank the stranger he hurried off with a smile—hurried, I'm sure, for fear I might offer to tip him, as he had tipped my driver. He could have stolen my money and run away or taken some of it, and I would not have realized.

But that was not his idea. . . .

Thais are easily amused; and fun is a major goal in their pattern of living.

Perhaps that is childish. But perhaps our Western ideas of efficiency and progress are not so much mature as compulsive. Could it be, that life is meant to be enjoyed as it occurs—and not according to plane schedules, time clocks and an annual two weeks at some seashore resort? Is it, perchance, more meaningful to live at a leisured pace that leaves room now for innocent curiosity, laughter, watching things designed for watching . . . ?

We wanted to see the Siamese temple dancers and learned that two girls were giving demonstrations of that art at one of the night-club-restaurants near our hotel. So we had dinner there and watched closely while the young women danced classic fables to the drums, twanging strings and primitive xylophones. The dances demanded an odd, taut control of their performers. The carefully placed hands with bent-back fingers, the languorously assumed stances, the balancing and peculiar but expressive head-motions required such effort that the girls trembled constantly—despite an apprenticeship that began in childhood.

That night I had "European" food and Ricky ordered the regular Thai blue plate. I tasted it and found the food too strangely spiced for my palate; even Ricky, the cosmopolitan eater, felt it would take time to learn to like Siamese savors.

A dance band played during dinner. In the Orient, dance orchestras are usually Filipino. A lush Cuban girl sang Havana style with this one, and it played rumbas the way Cubans do, making us homesick. We were tired that night, as always, but the immaculate, nostalgic rhythm brought us to our feet. We danced a slow rumba and a medium rumba and a fast one—and we know how.

Rumba in Bangkok!

The room was low ceilinged, dim lighted; a hundred diners sat at the crowded tables and scores moved on the dance floor. But not one among the small, beautiful Thai girls and their Thai partners, the Chinese men and their women, the brown couples of indecipherable race or American tourists or young Britons from some embassy or UN post—not one pair could rumba. The girl sang again. No one rose to dance. I looked inquiringly at the night club entrepreneur. He was a goateed Eurasian who could have played villain for all the half-caste movies ever made—a man whose smile was more alarming than his krisslike frown, Bangkok's favorite restaurateur, actually as amiable as any klong-side greeter. The man nodded—so we danced.

No one else did. They watched us through three numbers and when we sat down, Thais, Chinese, Eurasians, Britons and our countrymen applauded!

Tommy Salinas, Arthur and Kathryn Murray, and a host of patient lady teachers would have burst with pride . . . !

The readiness of Thais to interrupt any task for the sake of pleasure is deemed reprehensible by most Westerners. One afternoon, an American in charge of a construction project told us, "These damned people don't *like* work! They learn easily enough. You can train 'em as electricians, carpenters, what not! But they have no sense of time! They'll take a day off, or a week off, for some crumby festival, or the wedding of a fifth cousin twice removed—and come back on the job without even an apology. Hell of a thing! They'll stop work for half an hour just to fool with a passing elephant. Go off for lunch and forget they were supposed to come back. Children? They're absolute morons! Thousands have little houses on the klongs outside of town. They plant gardens they don't even have to cultivate. Things grow here like Jack's beanstalk. They raise a few banana trees. When they want a little dough, their husbands come in town and run samlors for a while. Then—back home till the cash gives out. How can you get anywhere that way? No sense of time! No sense, period!"

But maybe the Thais do have a sense of time—and *we* don't. Maybe, for them, time is life's most spacious dimension—not, as with people in a hurry, its most cramped. We hurriers rarely attain the commonest state of Thais: contentment. But, then, like everybody, the Siamese are being at least somewhat westernized. Time's being closed in on them—because, lacking a proper sense of it, they're "morons."

Ricky and I left the restaurant that night after our meal, the temple dancers and the rumbas; we wanted to avoid the main feature of the floor show: a strip teaser whose blonde, bawdy body posed naked on a poster outside the place. Chinese businessmen, we were told, loved strip-tease; the Thais didn't seem to mind it, either.

In matters of sex and sex love, the Thais appear to be what the Behaviorists call "permissive."

People attribute that word to Freud, who would have disavowed it since he wanted a new morality congruent with our natures—but a morality, not an amoral "permissiveness."

The Thais doubtless have their aesthetic, and ethos, for sex behavior, though they enjoy candidly the fundamental needs and nature of mankind. Doubtless, too, their standards are being corrupted by the West. For we have distributed our ashamed dirty-thinkers everywhere, as missionaries and diplomats and as reformers. However profligate some of these may be in their sex behavior, they convey the righteous American sensation that sex itself is guilty and vile.

But part of the Thai friendliness may be owing to their

sentiments anent sexuality. Puritanism plus Victoria may partly explain, too, why the Britons brought no joy abroad and took no warmth from Empire. Psychologists have said as much. Our guide's forlorn admission—that Christianity too much restricted his private life—implies as much.

So it must distress the Thais (and all other "semicivilized" people) who thought sex a fine aspect of nature, to learn that Western men believe the acquisition of their cultural artifacts goes hand in hand with a denigration of self in respect to sexuality. It seems a high price even for antibiotics, atom bombs and Buicks.

To take for granted that the facts unearthed by the late, intrepid Dr. Kinsey are universal and more acts than American law allows are harmless and delightful, seems not unreasonable. I am not prepared to accept, however, a bit of dialectic by a western-educated Oriental who held that America is a "ludicrously *un*free nation" because it outlaws prostitution. (A couple of blocks down the street from our Bangkok hotel stood a luxurious bordello of extensive frontage that was five stories high.) The gentleman's argument ran about as follows:

Prostitutes become degraded by three factors: public prejudice, the local living standard, and any necessity of operating illegally. Where odalisques are fairly dealt with and honored (as he said they should be) they perform a noble service. In the gentleman's opinion, that service amounted to maintaining the peace of mind of the human race. He took a disgusted view (and so do I) of our notion that prostitutes "sell their bodies." They are, he said, (under favorable conditions) "artisans" or highly skilled workers, the ablest of whom should be revered just after poets, painters and composers.

A country, he said, that has so high a living standard as the United States and so admires skill should have the finest, most numerous courtesans on earth. Instead, it produces thousands of sly women who try to advance private concerns by what they call "cheating"—when the art is anything but that! He added (not without accuracy) that tens of thousands more American ladies —models and actresses—publicly strip their bodies, or pose for tantalizing pictures, with the sole object of inciting males to noble passions—which, then, are frustrated by custom and the law. This, he said, was the way psychologists drove experimental animals insane.

What woman, he finally enquired, imagines she lives in liberty when she is not only forbidden to accept payment for her most divine attainment—the one she, too, most enjoys—especially in a country (USA, again) where there are so many more women than men as to prohibit marriage for hundreds of thousands of ladies? What woman is free that is unfree to conduct her amours as she sees fit, as long as her behavior rewards and pleases her, saves males from countless evil deeds as well as ill health, and benefits the public weal? What man, with money in his purse and no wife or a wife who is cold, indisposed or occupied with a lover, calls himself free when he cannot enjoy a woman's favors without degrading himself in his own eyes (not to mention the woman!) and risking jail besides?

If that is freedom, he continued, most Asians are *already* too advanced to be interested in an American "freedom" that forbids profitable loving, so that prostitution, like drinking during Prohibition, is made dismal by the ban, not the indulgence—and breeds other evils and miseries not because of itself, but because it is not allowed.

And he concluded that no churchman or barrister could so define the ideal of liberty—and still make sense—as to exclude what he called the "inalienable right" of a woman to determine, herself, what she would and would not do with her own person. (I, too, shall leave that one up to the churchmen and barristers.)

We finally called the Smiths, and were not electrocuted by our Albanian room phone. They came to see us.

But we bought no black sapphires. After days of watching tourists stand in the streets gazing perplexedly at onyxlike stones in cumbersome rings, we decided that gem-purchasing was for experts. Anyway, the only stones we really liked—stones, I think, from Burma—were as costly in Bangkok as at Tiffany's and, so, much too costly for us.

What we did buy was silk.

The weaving of silk is a Siamese "home industry." Their native fabric is heavy and brilliantly colored. Its patterns used to follow the classical Court styles—too exotic for Western taste. All that has changed. Thereon hangs a tale the Smiths told us. . . .

Once upon a time, probably during the Japanese Occupation, an American (whose name, I think, was Thompson) paddled (or parachuted) into the environs of Bangkok to do undercover work for the OSS. When the war was over and his hazardous mission ended, Mr. Thompson had come so to like Siam that he decided to remain—and, perforce, cast about for an occupation which would support him amidst the temple windbells and beauties ubiquitously bathing. Noting the proficiency of the natives at silk weaving (and the apathy of tourists towards the patterns), this man sent to America (or, maybe, France) for fabric designers. And so, gradually, he put the home weavers to work with their vivid threads, on looms set to reproduce stripes, plaids, checks and mere solid color—styles which might attract the gaze and purse of passing Occidentals.

That is why "Thai silk" is becoming as much an American household word as was "Chinese embroidery" when I was a boy.

Ricky and I went to Mr. Thompson's store. And I wanted to buy every glittering bolt of yard goods, every necktie, shirt and shawl it held. Our friends at home are still grateful for what we did buy, and we, still brilliantly swathed.

Mr. Smith, Englishman and Quaker—and his very pretty wife—entertained us, translated for us and briefed us in many aspects of this odd, enchanted culture. They also arranged for us to see some of the work to which they were dedicated: UNICEF's effort to improve the health of children.

One morning, shortly before we were to leave Thailand, we were met at our hotel by a chauffeur and, as "guide," a Thai official in the UN who spoke English and had the remarkable name of Kraideb Devakul. All Thais have remarkable names.

We spent some hours at a large, clean "hospital" (actually a clinic), supported by the government but staffed with people trained by UN. We learned many things: Thailand is becoming a healthful country. The dread "tropic diseases"—like yaws and leprosy—are largely under control. The greatest present menace is tuberculosis. Childbirth is being managed better, every year, in Bangkok and in the "rice villages" and jungle towns outside.

We saw the equipment that doctors, nurses and midwives take, at a moment's notice, to women in labor in the city and its environs. We watched hundreds of youngsters being examined and treated. The medical doctors we saw—and, of course, all the trained nurses—were women. All spoke English. And a startling proportion of them had received their training, or at least some specialized course, at Columbia, or Chicago, or in some other American center of medical instruction.

The Thais, we discovered (without surprise), are immune to the water-borne diseases which make living in such regions a special problem for Occidentals. "If you were to go swimming in one of the klongs," a smiling nurse told me, "you'd land in a hospital with any of half a dozen diseases. Maybe all. You'd be —but sick!"

That distressed me because I happened to be suffering, right then, some steadily worsening internal pang.

But I managed to complete the hospital tour. My waxing symptoms were—after all—familiar: cramps, vague nausea, a tendency to sweat too much and general weakness. No traveler in the Orient or Asia escapes occasional attacks of that sort. It is, they say, the difference in water or the changing pH of water, or the cooking. And—they incessantly remind you—raw food that is not peeled must never be eaten: it is fertilized with "night soil" (a euphemism for human feces which irritates all honest men) and therefore dangerous.

Our guide-chauffeur had noticed that I was beginning to wilt and attributed it, I was sure, to the hospital sights—desquamation of lesions on children's faces, and the like. But I am familiar with and immune to queasiness from sights that involve medical wonders, and incidental grue. My certainty that Kraideb Devakul thought otherwise made me go on listening to the polite nurses—made me continue to inspect examining room after room, procedure after procedure.

Such is male pride. In the presence of strangers—the more alien, the more swiftly—our pride intensifies. For men see one another too much as challenge. Some students of our species even claim that the first, deepest reaction of every man to another is, "Can I kill him?" which, culturally translated, means most of us unconsciously wonder of another we meet, "Am I richer? Smarter? Better dressed? Driving a better car? Accompanied by a handsomer wife wearing costlier fur? Am I socially more important and a member of better clubs?" Few people would acknowledge such a going condition of their minds. But few fail, on encountering strangers, to show (even by the negative of lofty reserve) an awareness of our animal pecking orders and a sense of status, or its lack.

My pride there in Bangkok consisted, owing to the presence of a soft-voiced, reticent Thai, in trying not to vomit.

Kraideb Devakul was a challenge. He looked every inch the executive—the UN official he was—the man of influence and prestige. Take away a few shades of exotic skin color and he could have occupied a seat at any American directors' meeting. In his forties, moustached, broad-browed, wearing well-tailored, conservative clothes, he had only one other "trait" more common to Asians than Americans: he appeared to be exceedingly shy and when he spoke it was in a light, gentle, almost apologetic tone. Until you became acquainted.

Ricky, who saw more of him than I did, became acquainted with and charmed by our host. I had no chance. For we finally got back into the limousine and started on what was to be a tour of the countryside—something we had not yet seen. But as we went honking through the city thoroughfares, my cramps grew agonizing. I became sweat-drenched; nausea rose in me like an oily tide.

"Ricky," I said, "I'm sick. I guess you better drop me at the hotel. You take the grand tour with Mr. D."

She saw I was sick, for sure. Afterward, she told me that, in the space of a minute, I turned marble white and my skin went ice cold. At the time, she concealed her fright, quietly asked our host to go to the hotel, and produced from her big, red handbag a tiny bottle of the "concentrated paregoric" which had been provided by our doctor-friend in Miami.

I unscrewed the top—and held the bottle, feeling that I could not swallow anything.

On the contrary! I needed desperately to vomit, now, and to defecate. I searched the streets urgently to see where I might relieve myself. If I'd been alone (save only for the myriads of Thais), I would have used, publicly, the handiest canal-bank. But I tried to hold out.

The next few minutes were horrid—and astonishing.

It was bright day—high noon—and the sunlight was ferocious. Everything and everybody abruptly became abnormally vivid to me, as if my retina had trebled its sensitivity. My abdominal pains were now as severe as any I've ever had—and I've spent weeks with an open belly and peritonitis. I sensed (and yet somehow no longer felt) the gliding perspiration on my body. Under nausea's rotted hammering, I quailed and writhed. Then, suddenly, I could no longer see at all. In blaring daylight, I was completely blind! I knew I was an instant away from loss of consciousness. The sensation that I had to do something—anything—became overpowering.

I raised the little bottle and drank.

The alcohol-sting and licorice-savor revived me, somewhat. I began to see again, and I could bear my pain.

Ricky helped me up the long flights of stairs and unlocked our door. I ran for the bathroom.

When I came back and threw myself on a bed, she had a glass of stuff ready—chocolate-flavored sulfasuxadine: another gift from an apprehensive and thoughtful medical acquaintance.

I drank it—and somehow kept it inside me.

Ricky took my temperature. It was high.

I ached. My belly boiled with pain.

But after an hour or so, I was sufficiently recovered so that— on my insistence—Ricky went out and made the afternoon tour.

I stayed in bed. That evening, through our lucky knowing of the Smiths, we reached a German doctor. By then, our sulfa supply was low—and he prescribed more of the same. My bellyache was better but I still had chills that alternated with spells of feverish debility. There was nothing left inside me except sulfa drugs. We had booked seats on a BOAC plane for Calcutta, the next day. The doctor told me that I should not go unless I felt "perfectly well" by morning.

And, in the morning, to my astonishment, I did feel perfectly well—though weak.

We caught the plane. . . .

I have wondered since, what would have happened to me without the sulfa drug. I surely suffered an acute attack of some unidentified bacillary dysentery or some germ toxic enough, untreated, to flatten a man for weeks, perhaps even kill him. . . .

I often think of Bangkok—and I mean to go back.

It will probably be different, then.

It's changing. . . .

For instance, they're getting TV now. One afternoon when I stopped in a bar for a drink I watched a lovely Thai lass discourse on what I was sure was some very poetical theme: a TV set above the bar held her image. She was so gentle, so appealing, so courteous and so enchanting, I could almost imagine what she was saying: something wondrous, about love. Abruptly she reached out of the scene, and produced—a tube of Ipana toothpaste. . . .

7
the Un-American Indians

We flew too far north of Rangoon to see it from the air. We did see a road that evidently led to Mandalay, though I think it was not Kipling's. Over the Bay of Bengal hung a fine red dust and where ocean currents collected it, like pollen on a windy pond in autumn, it made rosy acres.

Here was another body of water I had not expected to cross in this world or any other! It set me to thinking of Jean Harlow, whom I used to know, and of the picture she and Gable made which was called *Red Dust*.

Long ago. . . .

Far away. . . .

Four gasoline motors, two wings, a humming in the head can bring "far away" so near! And then "long ago" becomes just yesterday. For crimson particles, suspended in the air—dust-dye from the plains of India—actually did blow in March (or, at least, in *this* March) to sweaty Indo-Chinese rubber plantations. Jean Harlow played tough on MGM's sound stages far away, long ago, in a film with a title I'd always assumed to be some writer's invention. But now, below, behold—red dust . . . !

In the twilight, like an aerial photograph rather than earth itself, the Sunderbunds appeared—vast swamps around the Ganges' many mouths.

Calcutta was immensity-in-lights, low keyed, smoke swathed, its airport that same airport—a pale crosshatching of concrete, parallel runway lights, an orbiting beacon, the fuzz-blue glow of a control tower. Cherry-red obstacle lights flashed beneath us like sparks. We saw the dull yellow squares of the terminal interior. Whoever wins the earth—free men or those who consent to tyranny—this much will *already* be standardized.

A Mr. Chidra was there to meet us. Always somebody! Somebody helpful, as Ricky and I were passed from hand to hand like registered mail. Tiredly, we stepped into the heated murk. Mr. Chidra was portly, brown, moustached and businesslike. He made it plain at once that customs, in India, would be difficult: Indians, independent at last, were perhaps making up a little for the infinitude of hardship they had endured under the bureaucracies of invaders.

At some point in the ensuing dim miscellany of inspection and passport checking, I was accosted by a thin, young man in a brown tweed suit whose name was Mr. Gudra. He wore steel-rimmed spectacles. Behind them black, high-gloss eyes held me with attention magnified. He began asking questions in rapid, perfect English—yet with a tone and with a manner that somehow provoked me. It had been a hard trip for a man who'd been as ill as I, the day before. I gathered Mr. Gudra represented the Calcutta press and I was as patient with him as I was able.

But finally the sticky-staccato questions in jew's-harp monotone upset me. I tried to get away. Every time I turned, Mr. Gudra anticipated, and set himself to block that side.

He had looked me up in *Who's Who in America*, I deduced. On and on his questions went in the tone of an importuning cicada.

Exhausted, leaning against the wall, shutting my eyes against the migrainous saffron glare of the place, I tried to think. Was Communist influence increasing in Siam and what did I mean by answering, "Quien sabe?"

I meant that Thailand had long been enthusiastically "pro" USA. But, evidently, Thailand was now getting in a position to try to play the Reds against the Americans, hoping to profit both ways.

Did I not believe the Thais had a right to do that? (He sounded hostile.)

Certainly, I believed they had the right. But I thought—indeed, I *knew*—the game was foolish.

How could I know that?

Anybody who understands Communism knows that.

What did I think of the Autherine Lucy outrage?

I could not recall what the "Autherine Lucy outrage" was. But Mr. Chidra bailed me out.

I went gladly—and with a faint grin. For I saw Mr. Gudra swing his long nose and gleaming spectacles on Ricky. She has more patience and humanity than I; but she was as weary; and when the need is dire she has a tartness which seems feather light on first touch but soon becomes a veritable bludgeon. Mr. G. was for it.

I found a beefy customs inspector in a dirty uniform eying our luggage as if he knew there was a time-bomb in it somewhere, or as if from long and repulsive experience he'd learned the suitcases of all Americans contained live maggots. But the painstaking search I'd expected—the opening of every talcum powder box—did not occur. Instead, to my immeasurable surprise, the big lugubrious pudge broke out a broad if sockety smile, reached across the customs bench, shook my hand, said, "Welcome to India, Mr. Wylie," and chalked my bags without lifting a lid.

And the drive into the city began.

It was dark except where rows of shabby shops, lit by kerosene lanterns, threw a feeble gleam into the crowded thoroughfare. Mr. Chidra drove at more than forty miles an hour. In obedience to some law I still regarded as insane, he used only his parking lights. When calamity was imminent he would lean forward, take his eyes from the highway, and momentarily switch on the beam of his headlamps.

It was a shocking ride.

A ride through night hot as hell, yet lacking the glare of Inferno.

People filled the road, gutter to gutter, and made the least possible room for us, at the last possible instant. Men constantly bounded in the chiaroscuro ahead, white turbans hurtling every which way, like popping corn. Animals everywhere budged slowly, or not at all—just turning enormous horns on us, and red fundi that glittered balefully. Brakes slammed then, and we whipped round the living roadblocks: sacred cattle and water buffaloes, goats, camels, dogs, cats, horses, burros, monkeys and night birds. Men in hundreds and women and children. People in white garments and burlap and dirty rags that once had been colored red or blue or yellow. Men and women and children and animals in *thousands*. And in *tens* of thousands. *Myriads* of beasts.

Every brief, emergency stab of the headlights showed a living river that ran infinitely ahead, its banks the crammed stalls where people ate, talked, bought, sold, and slept on the nude earth in the light of one lantern here and one lamp yonder.

Men rode bicycles and men on bicycles carried head trays loaded with baked goods, things in paper bags and tin cans, and dead chickens. Certain riders and walkers bore above headloads, flaming torches, which made holes in the night. Each such illuminated cavern disclosed a sample of the terrifying press of life through which we hurtled—braking, hooting, skidding, sluicing, evading a thousand human collisions by an inch each and the horns or rumps of as many cattle by less.

Mr. Chidra was a *nervous* driver, too. He obviously knew nothing of the mechanism of his vehicle excepting which lever or control had what effect, or was supposed to have it, for anyone who comprehended a car could never have let himself so wrack its machinery. Yet Chidra had a jittery accuracy of aim. Every time I shut my eyes, the better to hear the sound of heathen bones snapping or the bellow of bumper-gored bullocks—every time I braced against head-on collision with some car approaching on a similar, unpredictable zigzag—Mr. Chidra somehow found a spot just abandoned by ten men, two bikes and a camel where he squeaked past the onrushing parking lights.

This infernal rat race was run to the accompaniment of human tongues telling every emotion. From occasional loud-speakers also came blasts of incomprehensible music, rendered more obscure by the Doppler effect. Now and then we rocketed by a beating drum or the reedy semitones of what seemed tune-less flutes. Once, I heard American jazz. With this was mingled the groans, hoots and jibbering of beasts. And a smell . . . ! The hot, dusty atmosphere was damply impregnated with *the smell of India.*

Each Asian land had had its particular effluvium. Tokyo's streets are charcoal smoke, fat cooking and, in that pleasant mix, an undertone of incense. Chinese environs were subtly different. At night, a most strange sweetness rose unaccountably from Hong Kong's harbor. Thailand is pervaded by the odd minti-ness of its fundamental condiment.

But there is a sourness and a charred tang in India's air, stronger and more prevailing than its other essences—and the spice of it is curry. Indian food and places have a flat, faintly sour, tarlike underscent. I did not get entirely accustomed to it and I was almost on the point of leaving before I identified its basic ingredient: the pungent, punky stench of burning dung.

Fumes of India's fuel pervade Indian air—and every dish and garment and body in the land.

As we tore through that overpeopled night, India's smell blew upon us, saturating our garments. We inhaled it and would soon swallow it with every mouthful until, at last, we also surely smelled for a while like the smokes above millions of Hindu fires—even the industrial smokes above kilns. For pie-sized, pie-shaped cakes of hand-patted dung, mounded enor-mously by unimaginable man-days of endeavor, bake bricks as also they bake Hindu bread and Moslem cake.

The city grew up gradually around us—buildings, familiar yet vaguely different—crowds moving, yet curiously quiet. Low-keyed city lights were soon augmented by traffic lights. Our pace became less sweatily alarming. But still the jam of men and beasts was everywhere—men and sacred animals on sidewalks, and asleep beneath street signs, and busy smoking and mooing and spitting and defecating along miles of red-brick, sooty, gewgawed rows of apartment houses evidently put up by England in Victoria's reign.

Then an open area lay ahead on our right—the Maidan, Calcutta's proud park. Next—unimpressive in façade as a back street tavern in a Western slum—our hotel. The Indian room clerks talked English. So did the head porter. A dozen subordinate porters, in filthy turbans and brown rags tattered enough to be costumes, picked up our luggage—one man to each item, whatever its size.

I saw an Exchange window, quickly tore out some travelers' checks and gathered up a handful of new, unintelligible banknotes, along with assorted, unreadable coins.

Ricky and I followed a safari of porters across a lovely garden where a dance band played and women in saris danced—beyond tall dahlias standing in pots and citrus trees in blossom. A little elevator took us to a brass-faced door, hard to push open for good reason: the corridor beyond was air-conditioned. So was our high-ceilinged, handsome room!

I quickly calculated that my ten porters could hardly do with less than a dime each. I decided that a dime was too little for the long walk—doubled it in my mind—and, when the picturesque, pathetic band had set the luggage about, I paid them the rupees I guessed to be equivalent. Heads bent, foreheads were touched, the room susurrated with "Salaams." They went.

"You shouldn't tip them till we go," Ricky said.

"No?"

"It was in the guidebook. Didn't you read it?"

"No."

"How much did you give them?"

"About two bucks."

"They'll *haunt* us, from here on in!"

And they did. I never had such service—or hated "service" more: my tip had typed me as a rich American sucker. I could not drop a candy wrapper but a dozen heads would lunge and hands reach, to restore it to me. Then the hands would continue to reach—*out*. I did not get the situation under control, in Calcutta. To rid ourselves of swarming attention took a fresh start with new minions, in Benaras.

Our departure from Calcutta was spectacularly ignominious, in fact. For I made the opposite error, neglecting the baggage carriers because I told the head porter (to whom I gave my tenth or fifteenth exiting tip) to divide it with them. The man was incapable of the concept of spoils division, I guess. But when I saw yet more hands reach and heard yet more babble of demand, I decided I would rather fight all India in the street than buy my way another step closer to the waiting taxi. So Ricky and I were borne away in the early light while a dozen scrawny men chased our cab, palms out and up, pleading and praying loudly and soon, as we outdistanced them, stopping with fists shaking to fill the air with strange soprano oaths.

On our first night, we adopted what had become Standard Operating Procedure for arrival in a new city or land:

I had, already, changed some dollars into rupees and annas, the first step.

If our stay in a country was to be short, I tried to estimate closely what funds we'd need in local coinage and to cash a smaller number of dollars. If we needed more we would get it in driblets and would not be caught, on departure, with cash we could neither sell nor take out of the country. We next unpacked, to the degree our prospective stay warranted. If possible, we sent out laundry and dry cleaning, where it was recommended in the guidebooks. We had our shoes polished. We purchased American cigarettes, if needed. We obtained potable water—usually from Room Service, in bottles.

Next, at the hotel desk, or the nearest recommended travel agency, I hired a car, a chauffeur and, if necessary, an interpreter for the day following. I then purchased detailed maps of the city and region as well as such local pamphlets and guidebooks as were available. (On the margins of these, I scribbled notes which I thought might be of later use. When I was about to leave a country, I loaded a manila envelope with the material and sent it by first class mail to myself in Florida. That way, I had my kind of travel record—and our luggage was never increased by costly, excess weight.)

On our first evening—or day—we also usually tried the local food, and that night in Calcutta we had our first "real" curry. It was not, we felt, up to the standard of certain Indian restaurants in Manhattan—or to our own home standard, for Ricky makes superb curries. The meat, in India, of course, is not good. Animal-slaughter is offensive to Hindus; beef, lamb and the like usually come from Australia, frozen, and are kept in dubious ways until served. The vegetables are not safe to eat raw and those that have been cooked have usually been overcooked, according to the dismal conventions of the British. (Just after we left Calcutta an epidemic of cholera broke out. We had taken shots for cholera. But it reminded us trenchantly of the rule for care in eating, in Asia—if, by then, we required reminding.) Usually, after attending to our needs and trying the food, Ricky and I next took a long walk of a random, viewing nature.

That night, we were too tired. When we'd done our routine we went to bed in our spacious, cool room.

And the phone rang as we lay down!

Ricky answered.

Probably, I thought, it was the air line. Air lines alone (so far as I could see) knew we were in Calcutta. And air lines are forever phoning to ascertain if you are actually going to depart on the flight you've booked—a dismal comment on the habits of travelers everywhere! For people often book numerous passages and then use the one which suits them, at the last moment—leaving the air line with a residue of empty seats—for which, under capitalism or socialism, all of us pay in the end.

But it wasn't Air India. "Why, hello!" Ricky was saying warmly. "How nice of you to call!"

Mr. Chidra had put somebody on our trail, I thought.

But it wasn't that either. And it wasn't Mr. Gudra, Asia's press bearcat (and bumblebee). Ricky talked for quite a while, agreed on dinner the next night—and hung up.

"That was Ellen's aunt, Mrs. Orinkaur."

"Whose aunt? Mrs. Who?" I asked. "Oh," I said. "Ellen's."

Ellen, a friend of ours in Coconut Grove, has an aunt whom she regards as somewhat less than conventional owing to the fact that the aunt is married to an Indian. Years ago, she visited India. She became a student of Indian philosophy and her visit grew into residence. In due course, she fell in love with, and married, a Mr. Orinkaur, who—our friend Ellen said—"is a banker or something in Calcutta."

"They're coming to dinner?"

Ricky smiled. "No. We're going there. Isn't that swell?"

"I hope so."

"We won't have to wait for New Delhi and Agra to meet Indians at home."

"Ellen was vague about the aunt. And God knows what the guy will be like!"

"All you need," Ricky said, "is a sleeping pill. You're overtired."

No doctor, let alone doctor's daughter, ever made a neater diagnosis. I took the Seconal she handed me—and slept.

The next day, after coffee, rolls and jam, served in our room by approximately eight different, turbaned waiters and assistant waiters, we dressed—and our car was announced. A Sikh sat at its wheel and a Moslem (we soon learned) introduced himself as our guide. With them, we set forth to see Calcutta.

Ricky began the questioning, as usual, innocently: a few queries about local sights—for she had (as usual) boned up on them. We stopped to gaze at the Maidan Park—and the cattle herds dropping valuable fuel therein—and her questions grew more personal. As we viewed banks, bridges, refugees and hordes of people bathing in the Hooghly River, owing to the fact that this happened to be the birthday of Lord Shiva, Ricky found out the full name of the driver and the guide. (Unspellable.) The fact that both were married and had children. The number and sex of the latter. The fact that the Moslem had only one wife—and regarded Ricky's question about that with amusement. She also learned that the Sikh driver was born in Pakistan and had migrated to Bengal. Pakistan Moslems, he said, had made life intolerable for Hindus not only by direct persecution but by the passage of laws which, in effect, prevented them from continuing their religious customs.

That ought, we both thought, to have disturbed the Moslem guide, who had translated questions and answers—although we discovered that sundry Sikhs and others in India and other lands affected to speak no English but understood it well. The pretense of incomprehension doubled the work, the wages and the tips, I suppose. Also, it gave one of each pair of guides a chance to catch tourists in off-guard statements, providing they made any. Certainly the curiosity of Orientals and Asiatics about Americans was at least equal to the curiosity Ricky and I had concerning them.

Our guide, called something like—but not quite—Mohammed was not disturbed at the story of persecution by his co-religionists. He seemed annoyed at the Pakistanians, instead. "They are that way," he said. "No democracy at all."

"You, as a Moslem, aren't worried about the Hindu majority here?" I asked that.

"Not any," Mohammed said.

"But there were riots—right here in Calcutta—not too long ago."

He answered coolly, "It was political. The hotheads. I saw it. I did not participate. The gutters ran blood. Fifty thousand were killed."

"But now . . . ?"

"India is a great democracy. The freedom to worship is a foremost liberty. We are friends—Hindu, Moslem."

As far as I could see, they were.

It was quite a morning. Sociable sentiments sprang up amongst the four of us. The guide and the driver did their utmost to insure that nothing of interest in Calcutta would be missed by the sensitive, gracious American lady and her at-least-not-rude husband. We inspected parks and public buildings, the Coney-Island-like mobs of bathers in the sacred river, and temples—including a Jain Temple—a mother-of-pearl marvel with the kind of lighting skin-divers see on reefs. We took a tormented drive amongst the literally millions of East Pakistan refugees who have overpopulated already-gorged Calcutta: a city so boiling, so crawling with mankind I could not imagine how they even keep alive in the foetid subslums—even how they find air enough to breathe.

I made a further discovery here, about the basic smell of India. Its sour undercurrent had seemed tantalizingly familiar. On that drive, I remembered. When we were children, we made paste, of flour and water. It wasn't very good paste; and we were not very orderly children; sometimes, a dish of the stuff would stand until it had "turned." A sharp stench like that of sour flour-and-water paste pervaded the refugee areas. It came, certainly, from rancid messes of milled cereals and water—the staple of refugee diet. Sourness in some degree—that childhood odor—was always present in the dung-smoke-and-curry blend of Indian air. . . .

During lunch at the hotel a man in bizarre costume approached our table and set out on it three small pottery figures. I assumed he was trying to sell them—and waved him away. He protested but, believing I was onto such tactics, I all but bellowed at the man to beat it. He went—ruefully. Soon the bell captain appeared—an imposing bird whose station was embroidered in English on his white and gold uniform. He brought back the figurines, along with a paper the other man had showed me which described the pottery images. The bell captain explained:

"He was not trying to sell these to you, Mr. Wylie. They are a gift from a Mr. Gudra. They are copies of Mr. Gudra's mother's gods—and one small clay elephant, for a fun. This is the elephant." He set it on the tablecloth. "This is Lord Shiva." (Shiva had a fierce moustache and a white cloak.) "This is Juggernaut." (Black-skinned, in red, blue and yellow garments.) "Mr. Gudra's mother is from the Sunderbunds, where Juggernaut is worshiped. He would like you to let him talk with you this afternoon. He waits outside."

Juggernaut waits? No. He meant Mr. Gudra. I fingered the

rather horrid-looking idol in sunbonnet and striped blazer. So that was Juggernaut! The Vishnu of the tiger swamps whose statue used to be carried through these streets on a tremendous vehicle drawn by hundreds of men; and ecstatic devotees often threw themselves under it to be crushed to death. The British had stopped that—as they'd stopped suttee. Well. As they had, *in the main.*

I thanked—and tipped—the bell captain. I hefted the gods. "About a pound and a half," I said. "Nearly a kilo. How'n hell will we fly this junk around . . . ?"

I stopped, because Ricky looked guilty. She spoke uneasily. "I told Mr. Gudra, last night, you'd see them late this afternoon. Isn't it charming of him—to make you a gift?" She turned to the bell captain. "Tell him to bring his friends about five. Mr. Wylie will talk to them in the garden."

The captain beamed, salaamed—and departed.

"What in hell," I asked, "is *this*? That damned reporter was as sticky as flypaper——"

"Reporter?" Ricky echoed with surprise. "Mr. Gudra isn't a reporter!"

"Then what is he? Indian FBI?"

"He told you—straight off."

"Maybe so. I didn't get the first part of his palaver: had to accustom myself to his voice. After all, when I'm tired, I'm deafer than ever. . . ."

She was admiring the ceramic gods—and smiling. "Phil, you really do miss a lot. That Indian has met every Bangkok plane for three days. To greet *you*. He's a tremendous fan for your books! He is president of a *fan club* for your books."

"A fan club? In *Calcutta!* For me? Holy . . . jumping . . . God . . . Almighty!"

"Well. You know how Indians are. They always want you to feel fine. It could be—Mr. Gudra's crowd are fans for various writers and you're just one. But you *are* one. . . ."

I was dazed. "He did know a lot about my books. . . ."

"He knows every character in every novel! He can quote *Generation of Vipers*, by the page."

I said vaguely, "And he's not a—journalist—at all?"

"No. He works for the Five Borough Bank. Our Bank in New York City. And all he wants is to bring some of the fans to meet you. It'll be fun for you."

"Okay," I said. "Okay. I give up. In fact, maybe I ought to give up writing—if Calcutta Hindus are spying on me."

"They're quite literate."

And I'd thought—at the airport—that she would give Mr. G. the Ricky-Wylie brush-off. Instead, she had invited him to invite his friends! He'd been given the *opposite* Ricky treatment —like the Sikh and the Moslem that morning.

"You and your God-damned Valentine eyes," I said.

She chuckled. . . .

After lunch we told our driver and guide we wanted to go to the Botanical Garden. They were astonished, but they took us.

The way led through back streets where half-bare men and women toiled in workshops with mud walls and dust floors, ate in mud-walled shops, slept in dusty shade, washed garments in pans of muddy water . . . streets where men squatted in the gutters to urinate, turning their backs on traffic, children swarmed underwheel and flies swarmed on the children's faces . . . men and women and children in turbans, dhotis, shorts, pants made of gunny sacks and in nothing at all. They dipped cups of water from puddles in the gutters and drank and proudly brushed their teeth in gutter liquids.

All the while, as on the night before, the car horn blew, blew, honked and blew—hand-bulb and klaxon—and the radiator cap slurred; Ricky and I lurched apprehensively on the rear seat; human beings in literal thousands leaped out of our path in the last centimeter of time—often dropping baskets, trunks and cartons to escape. And beasts rumbled at us, budging with annoyed phlegm as a rule; if they did not stir, men put their bodies between the holy animals and our oncoming car, so they, not the cattle, would be hit—a million strangers playing Russian roulette with our weapon: the automobile.

The Botanical Garden was beautifully planted, extensive, and so nearly deserted I wondered why the sweltering crowds did not flow into it. People who lived in bee-swarms perhaps found a park (where one could look for a quarter of a mile and see only verdure) so unfamiliar as to be disturbing. We stopped to examine many flowering trees that were new to us and spent half an hour enjoying Calcutta's superb palm collection. We were halted later by an immense, unlabeled tree (we will never know what it was), at the base of which lay a small sheaf of rice heads.

"A dryad lives here," I said.

Mohammed didn't understand. He picked up the grain contemptuously. "Some of these people are tree worshippers." He handed the rice to Ricky. "Souvenir to take to America. Showing superstitious Indian custom."

Ricky would also have preferred to leave the offering untouched. She is interested in the beliefs of others and reluctant to scorn any Faith in public. And a few were watching us—people who might, themselves, revere sacred trees.

Like me, Ricky sees "worship" as one process and the difference between a rice offering to a great tree and a money offering at the foot of two cruciform pieces of a tree is virtually indistinguishable. It is a matter of relative sophistication (or relative naïvety), not a matter of "truth." A natural symbol—be it graven image or an image in the mind—when used to represent deity is of one essence that is human and inner. Western Christians, like all believers, can rarely discern the reality and value of so simple a fact. To all, their rites and images alone relate to God and everybody else's to Satan, folly, heresy or blasphemy.

Ricky tried to replace the rice at the base of the tree but our guide put it in the car.

We wandered from there to what was said to be the largest banyan in the world—acres of the thing—its aerial roots a maze of poles. We have banyans too, so the tree's growth habit was familiar to us; but not the extent.

A little beggar boy—snot-nosed, scab-freckled—followed us through the lone-tree grove, his hushy whine constant as migraine: "Salaam, sahib. Salaam mem-sahib. . . ." And after that, phrases repeated like a stuck phonograph record.

Mohammed angrily shooed him, as if the boy were a filthy cur. And I remembered a Chinese lad in the Tiger Balm Gardens who had offered to shine my shoes and accepted my refusal with so warm a grin I gave him the only coin I had: a Hong Kong dollar. Ten minutes later, he had clambered across a hundred yards of steep steps and rocky faces. I thought he would ask another. Instead, he said, smiling sweetly, "Thank you very much."

I wanted to escape this Indian boy—not appease him by a payment. When he persisted in his dreary, insectile whine, I weakened; but Mohammed grabbed my arm. "Give him money and twenty will be around us in a moment!" Two other people were visible in the root-maze. Yet I was certain Mohammed told the truth: given money, this child would signal, somehow, and we'd be hemmed in by leaky replicas of sick childhood, murmuring with the professional phrases of Indian begging. We'd feel their condition heartbreaking, horrifying. But they would use it to assault—almost to blackmail us—arousing our hostility and surging will to escape: pity would give way under their nagging to self-pity.

Ricky shook her head at the purulent boy and her eyes were a bereaved grey. "It's getting on toward four," she said.

At the hotel, I bathed, brushed my teeth and anointed my head from a small, precious stock of Yardley's Lavender Hair Tonic which I carried in a plastic phial. I put on a clean white shirt, a cashmere jacket I'd had tailored in Hong Kong and a brocade tie I'd bought there. Since a Philip Wylie Fan Club was to visit me, cosmopolites of Calcutta were going to see the Full Panoply.

Mr. Gudra was announced, by phone.

I went down, passing the garden, where music played for tea dancing and Sikhs in red, gold, white and blue uniforms with peacock feathers in their turbans served drinks and tea and crumpets. I had two big tables set aside for my guests:

The brilliant, sensitive Mr. Gudra would doubtless be accompanied by several learned students, a professor or so, and perhaps one or two dark, lovely girls in scarlet saris who, being oriented toward the Occident, would enjoy dancing.

Maybe Ricky had some inkling of that fantasy: she claimed to need rest and did not accompany me. Actually, no sane wife can long, or often, bear her spouse in the role of Great Man.

Mr. Gudra waited in the lobby.

Alone.

He was dressed in one of those mosquito-net things Ghandi used to wear, a loose garment, caught up at the crotch, draped over an arm and shoulder, but leaving bare the cobby shanks. Mr. Gudra was about as scrawny as Ghandi. Furthermore, his drapery, though once white, was now dirty—and quite damp.

"The others," he said as his June-bug eyes descried me, "could not come. It is, after all, Lord Shiva's birthday. They are bathing. I, myself, have just left the temple after ritual in the Hooghly River." His dhoti, or whatever the sleazy toga is called, was stained and dank. These people bathe in their shifts and dry out later, usually. He hadn't had time.

I led the way to the garden. I'd seen nobody in the hotel in Gudra's garb except sweepers and porters. The Sikh waiters took a palpably dim view of my guest as I signaled that we'd need one small table only.

My fan apologized for his fish-net costume, but with a smug expression. "I am not, myself, religious in any way," he informed me. "I do this merely to please my family."

I laughed somewhat hollowly at myself: how often we overanticipate an event—dress ourselves with expectant care—and find a romantic fantasy turns out to be three-legged races, indoor baseball and apple ducking! But since Mr. Gudra was ordering tea with meek aplomb I decided that no Hindu and no living Sikh could outpoise me. So I beamed at the man and thanked him for the little Bengal gods.

My guest seemed incredulous. "You really mean you like them?"

"Of course! Especially, the thoughtfulness."

His eyes shimmered. He launched into a god-by-god account of their history. "Of course," he concluded, "those are only miniatures—and cheap ones. My mother would fall down before your little Juggernaut. She would put him in the special mud room in our house and build a shrine for him."

Suddenly, I did like his gift. (And now Juggernaut stands in a proud place in my office, making me the only man, I daresay, who owns that deity in all Coral Gables.)

We talked about books for a while—and about India. He told many new and absorbing facts. And then he mentioned America:

"Things are pretty horrible there."

"Are they?" I asked.

His joy at our amity became abrupt regret.

"We are, my friend, not a black people," Gudra began loftily. "Not a Negro people. We have brown skins, however. Some of us—as from Kashmiri—not very brown: wheat-hued skins. We are *Aryan*. Related to you." Mr. Gudra gave me his profile. "Do our eyes slant? Are our lips thick? Our noses without bridges? We are white men in a sun-baked climate! Yet we cannot identify with you. Americans crucify all people of color."

Indians are exceedingly polite; they usually seem gentle and loving; they frequently yield their own attitudes, graciously, to accede to yours. But their emotions are often exaggerated.

Mr. Gudra had tar-hued, rather exophthalmic eyes. But his lips were about like mine; thin, yet thick enough to close on any mouthful of food. And I had to admit that, though my own nose is outsized, his was double in grandeur, as narrow, and beaked besides. Yet I liked the little character, all his ego and his fish-net costume notwithstanding.

"Crucify people of color?" I repeated. "*Do* we? Of course, we have race problems—religious bigotry—like everybody else——"

"Like Russia?" he asked softly.

"Ever been there?"

"I have never been outside Bengal."

"Well—go up, some time. They've had pogroms under

Stalin. They tell *you* everybody's equal. But I'd hate to try to be
a good Hindu—or a good anything else—in Russia. A few Negroes were around when I was there—big shots from other countries. They seemed to regard them as the French do: interesting
curiosities. Some Soviet women wanted to sleep with them—just
as white men like to try Chinese girls. But Russia never had a
great number of Negroes, left over from slavery. Or a large
group of the descendants of slaveowners who had been whupped
in a civil war. I mean, a group like poor Americans in the
South, trying to hide guilty feelings and yet maintain superiority
in the human pecking order. After all—no living Negro *accepted*
slavery. Not one white person, alive, ever *imported* a slave. It's a
sad inheritance, our problem. But in Communist Russia—they
still have slavery. They 'segregate' for mere differences of opinion
—not even color. They still persecute Jews. I've even talked to
people in Russia who had been 'segregated'—enslaved—and
escaped. I think what a free man despises is a man who'll *accept*
persecution, slavery, discrimination. Better *die* resisting."

"You've been in Russia." He breathed it reverently.

"It's not Mecca, pal! It's updated Dante."

"Drastic measures *must* be used to create a new world."

"Why?"

He changed the subject slightly: "The Autherine Lucy outrage——" he began.

I still liked this little botfly, but I was beginning to perceive his indoctrination. "You a Red?"

"I am apolitical."

"I see this Autherine Lucy stuff in the headlines of the local
leftist paper," I said. "And other papers pick up every slanted
item from the Red press!"

"We are brown people," he interrupted. "We—feel deeply.
That poor American girl! Her crime was to want to enter a university when she was merely . . . black! Which is like brown."

I tacked. "You call yourself 'apolitical.' Okay. You say you
have no religion, too! But you come in here Ganges-dunked and
call it filial piety. Maybe you are Communist in sympathy—but
not out loud. I see the Indian government takes a dim view of

Reds—and besides, you work for an American bank. But how can I tell what you believe? I wonder if you know, yourself?"

"Our papers of *every* kind are incensed. You Americans have stoned the automobile of a colored woman . . . !"

"Yeah. I skimmed about six newspapers in the bathtub, just now. The commie sheet set the line—and tossed in a few lies. The other papers followed."

"You deny this educated woman was refused admission to that Louisiana University? You deny her automobile was stoned?"

My own emotions became somewhat exaggerated at that point. "Look," I spoke so loudly that nearby heads turned, "don't ever mention Autherine Lucy to me again, Gudra. Not ever!" I picked up his teaspoon—the only noisemaker on the table—and beat with it: "I don't want and I will not let any Hindu or Moslem ever *mention* her name to me! After all, *I am an American.* I am proud of the distance my country has gone toward freedom. It is not perfect. But no alien slobs, covered with blood, can talk like that to an American!"

"Why—but—" he gasped. "Do you deny——"

"Of course, they didn't let her join the college! And they did dent the Cadillac she rode in, with rocks. *So what?* America has a racial problem—several—and religious intolerance—*sure!* But no *slaves.* Russia has maybe *twenty million.*" I half stood and leaned into the face of this Vedantic creep. "Only a short while ago, the gutters outside *this very hotel* ran scarlet with the blood of *fifty thousand Hindus and Moslems* who murdered each other in street riots! *Fifty thousand people!* And you have the incredible gall to sit there and talk to me in lofty, censorious terms because one American person has her car dented by a few brickbats! God damn it, are you crazy?"

I have a voice that can ape the tone my father used to shake big churches—and probably hell's fundament. I used it to go on: "What kind of hypocrites are you Indians, anyhow? *Look!* If fifty thousand Americans are ever murdered in race or religious riots in Detroit, or Philadelphia, *then* you Indian bastards can talk to *me* about Autherine Lucy! *But not till then!* Because we Americans, so help me, are a thousand times as close to liberty, decency, tolerance, brotherhood—as you mass-murdering Indians! And we're a *billion* times nearer than Russia even pretends to *want* to become! So shut up, you!"

Having temporarily finished, I shut up, too. I then saw that Mr. Gudra was shaking all over and panting. He took a portion of his mosquito-net garment in a quivering hand and wiped his brow. People stopped looking at us, one by one. The dance band began a loud number—evidently, in case I had more to say. I had, but I gave him the other barrel quietly:

"How, pal, can any Hindu mention *segregation* to an American, as an exclusively American sin? I never heard of any white American rushing to church to get 'cleansed' because a Negro's shadow fell on him. But some of you people do. You have millions upon millions of 'Untouchables' who are segregated and treated like dirt—who share your color and your gods! Yet you accuse *America* . . . !" I broke off.

He began to weep.

"You see," I murmured, "I, *too,* have deep feelings."

"Lord," he said hoarsely. "Lord. I *do* see! I never thought of it that way. Mr. Wylie—you have greatly illuminated the darkness of my mind! You have enlightened me!" He stopped sobbing the instant he perceived he was enlightened: Indians love enlightenment. His face lit up with joy. "I expected greatness of you!"

I skipped what was no compliment but a neat ploy to regain his self-assurance. I said grimly, "See that you *stay* enlightened."

"I shall not fail you!"

"Not *me,* pal: *yourself!* And go about enlightening some others will you? The Reds have your minds balled up in this country. Why don't you ball up the Reds for a change, if you love liberty? Every argument they have, that sounds good, is a lie—or a deformed fact, like the one about Autherine. That's the commie system for making you suckers."

"I shall never be the same."

"Have a drink."

He was startled. "It is against my"—he finished lamely—"health principles."

"Do you realize, Gudra, if you keep on *acting* Hindu, you will *remain* Hindu, no matter what you say you do, or don't believe? Saint Paul put it neatly: 'By their *acts* ye shall know them.' Why not start *acting* free?"

"Whiskey," he said faintly, "and water."

Ricky appeared soon after that—and we had a nice time.

I was relieved, to see that Mr. Gudra—when he took his leave—was calm, but thoughtful. And dry, too. In his gentle but impassioned way he might even start heckling Red-tinged compatriots.

In the darkness of a suburban street our puzzled taxi driver finally (though unwillingly) took to asking questions of the abundant people. We then found out where Saran Orinkaur lived and turned between his tall, brick-and-iron gates. We drove up his private, tree-roofed avenue and stopped at the veranda of his big house. We got out and paid the driver and rang the bell.

Through the large, unshaded and uncurtained door we saw the approach of our hostess. A tall woman with a fine figure and dark, wavy hair—about forty and very good looking. She wore a blue silk sari that left bare one strongly molded shoulder. It was beautiful. Her face was serene, though lighted with expectancy. She had hazel eyes, not unlike Ricky's. She wore sandals shining with jewels and on her long hands were many rings that glittered. She opened her front door.

"You're the Wylies! How terribly nice of you to come 'way out here. We'd have driven in—but my husband had a meeting that is not ended, yet. Come in!"

The rooms were stuccoed and seemed somewhat bare although they contained a number of large, rich-looking pieces of Western furniture. No pictures hung on the walls—though a huge, round, brass ornament adorned a chimney. Undraped, unscreened windows accented the general bareness.

She took my hat and Ricky's diaphanous Thai shawl. She asked us to sit down. "I'm Alice," she said. "You're——"

"I'm Ricky——"

"And Mr. Wylie's Phil. I've read some of his books—since Ellen wrote me you'd spend a day or two in Calcutta. Amazing!" She took away the hat, the shawl, and returned, walking softly yet with strength. "I have a cold," she said. "Summer colds are just as bad in Bengal as Boston. Another reason I hated to come in town—and consequently imposed on you. What would you like to drink?"

"Could I have a martini?"

Alice smiled. "But of course. Very dry, I bet?"

Ricky laughed. "Yes." Ricky liked this woman—and I did, too. She was American in everything but dress; she dressed, I thought, to please her husband. I have seen many American women who wore more jewelry to please themselves, or any man but their husbands.

Alice Orinkaur left the room again.

Across a broad hall was a dining room, its table set with crystal and silver, its walls covered with Oriental rugs; in the most conspicuous spot on the wall was an oar.

We looked at each other. We were both thinking: What would Orinkaur be like? A gnome, like Mr. Gudra? Old? Able to speak English?

Servants appeared with big silver trays. Again, with a dozen little silver dishes of peanuts, blanched almonds, candied ginger and various relishes, nuts and viands I could not name.

Alice returned and made drinks. We soon heard an easy, spaced tread and our host came in. He kissed his wife. He bowed to Ricky, kissed her hand and shook hands with me. As he did so, he tried the "hand game," I think. Hanging onto heavy rods bent by heavy fish is good for one's grip. I gave him a deep-sea fisherman's response. He seemed pleased.

Saran Orinkaur was six feet four. He had the build to stroke an Oxford crew, and had done so. He was about Alice's age and one of the handsomest men I've ever seen. He did not look "brown," as had Gudra, but a hawk-faced Briton with a tan. He had pale brown, very alive eyes. A neat moustache. He said, with his Oxford accent, "Decent of you to come out. My wife— has explained . . . ?"

So we began, rather uncertainly, to talk.

We covered the indicated ground: our trip to date, our future itinerary, how we'd reacted to various peoples and the state of Ellen, her husband and her four daughters, when last seen by us in Coconut Grove.

The Orinkaurs regretted greatly that, since it was March, Calcutta's social season was ended and Ricky and I had missed the balls, dances, fetes, carnivals and other revels to which the Orinkaurs would have taken us if it had been wintertime—and if we'd planned to stay longer in Calcutta. Dinner was announced by a muted gong.

The first course was creamed carrot soup—from their garden. The second, creamed salmon on toast. Then—roast lamb, oven-browned potatoes, Harvard beets (garden, again— Orinkaur was very proud of Alice's green thumb) and tomato-and-lettuce salad with real mayonnaise. "You can eat it," Alice smiled. "No night soil touches it—and the well water we use has been laboratory tested." We ate with the relish of salad-starved tourists.

"An *American* meal!" Ricky sighed happily.

Alice nodded. "I thought you'd be amused—and pleased. After all—I *am* American. And I know what it's like to go without eating green things for weeks and months! Even if you *do* stuff yourself with vitamin pills. In fact, that's why I started the vegetable garden." She reached down and slapped her ankle.

We had been doing it, too. Through the unscreened windows came the sweet scent of frangipani and night-blooming jasmine—also an army of mosquitoes. I don't know why they lacked screens. Certainly they could afford anything they wanted. And, certainly, screens could not have gone to storage or the dry cleaner—as had the paintings and draperies at the end of the social season—a fact we had been told, with apologies.

It slowly became apparent, and then too apparent, that Alice and Ricky were bearing the brunt of polite dinner chatter.

It became uncomfortably apparent. Saran Orinkaur was steadily attentive. His face made the proper responses. But he could not seem to think of anything to say.

I tried—looking at the oar. "See you rowed."

"Long while back." He told me where.

"You like sports?"

"Fond of them. Ride. Pigstickin'. Tigers. Hunt, I mean. Have some horses. You?"

"Nothing so dramatic. Swim. Used to dive. We have a pool, now, and I'm learning again. Fish. Tuna, marlin. . . ." I can give any Briton (or Indo-Briton) clip for clip in a clipped-speech dialogue.

"Skin-dive, by chance?"

"Used to. Not much, lately."

He warmed slightly to that and for a while, Saran and I compared sports notes.

It relaxed him—somewhat. But, when we'd run through enough anecdotes so that he felt the ladies should be included in the talk again, he returned to reticence and a seeming of hidden—what? Anxiety, I decided. He was uncertain, or even worried about us, in some way.

What way, I wondered? We'd worn the right things. We were doing the right things and saying them. By then, it must have been evident to him, as it was to his wife, that we "couldn't care less" that he was Brahmin and she ex-Congregationalist. Ricky and I usually like (or dislike) individuals according to their sense of reality, not according to prejudice. It wasn't that.

Then, *what*?

That we were American and his country and America were not seeing eye to eye?

Perhaps. . . .

I decided on a gambit. "Our Secretary of State's due in India, today, I believe."

He had been eating gracefully, but with slightly tensed shoulders. Now the shoulders grew more taut and he shot a glance of alarm at his wife.

"Mr. Dulles," he said. "Yes. He's to see Nehru, and some of the government people, for a few days, I believe."

"Been in Pakistan."

"Yes." The word came uneasily.

I said, "That *chucklehead!* That arrogant *dope!*"

Alice chortled.

Orinkaur's shoulders lost some of their rigidity. He smiled a bit. He turned and asked, "You know him?"

"No, I don't. My father did. My father thought he was 'a great Christian and a great mind'—until he became Secretary of State."

"Then?" Mr. Orinkauer was listening, not eating, his amber eyes fixed on me.

"Father blew his top. Said Dulles 'knew nothing of the Orient, less of the rest of Asia, didn't vaguely understand the Middle East, had no history, no psychology, no physics, no sense.' Father said Dulles 'talked Christian world freedom' until he was appointed . . . then 'practiced obsolete power politics.' He was pretty disappointed in Dulles. He even called him—one day when Dulles clumsily upset some applecart in the name of 'Christian morality'—a 'lawyer in his soul.' "

His laugh was as uninhibited as Alice's. "Quite a man, your father must be."

"Yes—he was. He—died, recently."

"A sad loss!"

"An irreplaceable loss. But not sad. He was seventy-nine. Rounded out a full life with mighty few regrets. Not to mention a lot of laughter."

"How did he understand this Dulles so well?"

"Father was a Presbyterian minister," I began—and saw his eyebrows shoot up involuntarily. I grinned inside myself. The Indian no doubt had formed his concept of ministers from the majority of missionaries sent to India.

"For quite a while," I went on, "Father had the Park Avenue Presbyterian Church in Manhattan. New York." Saran nodded, knowing what "Manhattan" meant and, evidently, "Park Avenue." Shaming me slightly. "Dulles was an elder or a trustee. He became fond of father. Also—vice versa. Mr. Dulles wrote me a very swell letter about my father, when he died. Dulles is a perfectly decent, sincere man." I could see a cobweb of skepticism in the other man's eyes. "I know. He's just— wrongly oriented. Outmoded. Hasn't the slightest concept of how to battle Communism."

Orinkaur's emotion became so intense that he resumed eating to conceal it. He said, "Ah? And does anybody . . . ?"

"Communism," I said, "is a religion. In my view."

His fork jerked. "How many Americans understand that? It's also Nehru's view. *Ours!*"

I started talking. . . .

"Would you, Phil," Ricky interrupted, "please give me a cigarette?"

Ricky's face, to my practiced eye, had become faintly annoyed. *One of my homilies.* She had reminded me by her interpolation that I was making a speech. (Like father!) I felt momentarily nettled: Orinkaur's attention was real, not simulated. But one must always think twice about Ricky's motives. On second thought (Mr. Orinkaur supplied me with a cigarette from a marble box inlaid with onyx while I still fumbled in my pocket), I realized there was no way to be sure our host was as absorbed as he seemed. Indians have good manners; Ricky had merely given them a chance to get off the hook. For I can talk about the blindness of the dogmatic mind all night.

"I'm a little bit obsessive about this," I said—to end the monologue. "I hope I didn't——"

"On the contrary." Orinkaur looked at me thoughtfully. "We never heard an American with precisely that insight."

"I told you," Alice broke in vehemently, "to read his books! I said you'd be amazed." She turned to Ricky. "My husband is in charge of petroleum distribution in Bengal—most of the shipping—and Air India, in this district. He has little time to read." (Ellen, I recalled with amusement, had vaguely described him as a banker.)

Saran Orinkaur gestured impatiently and turned to me

again. "You think *all* religious people have that 'block' for other religions and quasi religions?"

"Not all. Many very devout individuals have room enough in their minds to accept the right of others to differ. They understand the universality of religious *motivation*—the inner etiology. And some religions—like Buddhism—let the faithful include other religious concepts in their philosophy. Protestantism and even Catholicism are changing swiftly but almost without being aware of it, in America."

He nodded. "Hinduism—in nearly all its manifestations— allows its devotees to accept modern science. While Moslemism seemingly does not." He paused. "You think the rigid believer had still another disadvantage, owing to his convictions?"

"Just this. He cannot understand the psychodynamics of other convictions because the insight would destroy his own dogmatism. He is unable to analyze and to unmask faith in the materialist dialectic for that reason. He cannot see what it is— therefore, he is impotent to attack it at its psychological source. He can merely protest on moral or mystic grounds. His own dogma deprives him of a logic to transcend dogma."

He then startled me by leaping to his feet and applauding lightly.

Alice murmured, "*Darling*. I know this is very exciting for you. But—" She turned to Ricky. "Exciting for us both. We've yearned for years to hear an American say these things! But Saran has hypertension, and his doctors . . ."

The tall, lithe man laughed self-consciously and sat down again. His eyes now had an expression I'd not previously seen any Indian display. They twinkled.

"All right, Alice! No more politics—philosophy—psychology. Whatever you want to name it. Mr. Wylie, you give me a great deal of very stimulating encouragement. Even if only one American thinks as you do——"

"Good lord! There are hundreds of thousands! They may use different terms. But they feel the same way."

"I shall go back to my concerns for India tomorrow—for

liberty and democracy—quite a different man. *Hundreds of thousands of Americans.* I believe you. And I thank you."

Any sincere show of a real love of liberty knocks me for a loop. And it was stunning praise. I picked up a cigarette and lit it, dropped my lighter, bent to retrieve it and had my damnfool sentimentality under control.

When I straightened up, he was still gazing at me and I will always treasure the look in the tall man's eyes.

After that, we really had an evening! The Orinkaurs told us a great many things:

There were (for example) some four—perhaps more—millions of Hindu refugees in Bengal. These penniless people had been driven from East Pakistan by Moslem intolerance, hate, murder, menace and legislation that restricted their religious rites. The refugees presented a ghastly problem. All Bengal could not assimilate them or even sustain them adequately. "New Delhi" (the Government of India) had resettled about a million families in interior villages. Villages where up-to-date methods of agriculture, home industry and the like were being introduced and the fugitives would have some chance to reestablish themselves. But "inland" is hot, dry country—semi-desert. The people from East Pakistan longed for the humid climate they were used to—rainy forest, sweltering swamps and steaming verge of the sea. So most left the villages and returned to Calcutta—where they enjoyed a familiar climate and had some chance of foraging, of "relief"—but no real hope of adequate opportunity. . . .

The Orinkaurs told us this:

Independent India, thrilling with new life and new aim, was involved in a tremendous endeavor to show the world that a "free Asian republic" could make Asiatic Red China look inferior. "Not soon," Alice said. "In half a century's time, perhaps."

They told us we'd discover that every Indian outside the two split, widely separated Pakistans, had a sense of the new equality, democracy and social purpose. The Untouchable was starting to dream freedom—along with every rich industrialist or landowner, a few "reactionaries" and "intractable maharajas" excepted. They seemed inspired, dedicated people. I was moved by what they said—yet dubious. But I knew how little I knew. This man could be a Founding Father of a new India—a Burr or Hamilton of a currently unpromising but ultimately triumphant nation. Or just diplomatic.

Late that evening, we explained we had to go back to our hotel, as we were to leave Calcutta on an early morning plane. We asked if they would call a taxi. Our host insisted on driving us the dozen miles.

I was slightly apprehensive: he was a man of dash and emotion who'd taken a good many drinks that evening. In such circumstances I would not have elected myself to chauffeur through those packed, appalling streets. But he was adamant—and Alice said she'd go, too.

"But your cold, dear!" he protested.

She turned to Ricky and me. "Yes. My cold. It is better, though. You two have half-cured it. Besides, if Saran gets into town late, he is very likely to phone me he will sleep at his office. Of course, what he does, is visit a night club where there are several enchanting girls."

Saran laughed, and Ricky cocked an eyebrow. "I've known Phil to do as much."

Alice demurred. "It is not that I mind the girls. He should have other girls! Men are better husbands for it. But Saran works so hard he cannot, tonight, afford the stress." She smiled warmly at the splendid man. "Tonight, I shall go with you, Saran. I like these Wylies. I wish they would stay a year—or come back, soon. You can go out, Saran, night after tomorrow—if you sleep long this night and the next. At home!" Her laugh was musical.

I think she meant exactly what she said. But I am not quite sure our American mores make wives as sanguine as Alice—as incapable of jealousy. Only a long, ecstatic life with a Saran Orinkaur could—perhaps—dim the American doctrines of possession-by-marriage, of "sin," "rights," and all the dirty names we have for acts of most of us.

A servant brought a Jaguar to the porte-cochere. I sat

in front. Ricky and Alice talked softly in the rear seat. The Indian and I did not say much at first; his traffic problems required concentration. He drove rapidly, considering the press of man and beast, even at that late hour—but as expertly as if his Jaguar were a shotgun dead beaded on empty areas between skidding clay pigeons—thousands of them. We near-missed myriads, hit nobody.

During a moment of necessary halt, I asked if the traffic toll in Calcutta was tremendous.

"It used to be," he said. "Nowadays, though, if you can drive in Calcutta, you can drive anywhere on earth."

"I can believe that!"

He meant something else—and explained: "During the war, when there were bomber bases here—your Twentieth Air Force —as you may perhaps——"

"I wrote a history of our B29's."

He gave me another warm glance; then grinned. "*Anyhow*. The military people drove like demons—hit many—and left them lying. Had to. War. The refugees here now from Pakistan aren't town people. They don't know how to walk on streets. So they oftenest got hurt or killed. But everybody was sickened by the slaughter military vehicles caused, and, after the war, death incurred by plain citizens who followed the military lead. The crowds took to striking back, finally."

He started up, avoided a bullock cart, rounded a line of water buffaloes and bypassed a man squatting in the gutter. But he didn't go on talking. So when a chance came again I said, "You mean people started puncturing tires on parked cars? Such stuff?"

"This," he answered gently, "is *still* India, Phil. When somebody was hit, a crowd pressed around the car that did the damage. The people yanked out the driver. They burned the car. And they beat the driver insensible—often, to death. They *still* do—if they think a driver was careless. Every few weeks. . . ."

"Fairly drastic. What happens in such a case—to taxicab *passengers*?"

"Oh, the mobs are very nice to them. It's never the passenger's fault. They help you out politely—even get another cab for you, after the burning and the beating." He moved ahead, stopped. "In Afghanistan—" He broke off.

"Afghanistan?" I prompted.

"That sort of mob execution is illegal unless a policeman is present. So—up there—the lads hold the driver who has hit a person—or a sacred animal, which *all* crowds regard as an even worse offense—till the police arrive. Then—the police hold the *driver* and the crowd hacks off his head." Saran spun the wheel, braked smoothly, left behind another near miss. "I saw it happen—not too long ago."

"It would distress Ricky," I replied, after a while. "So I hope we have good chauffeurs while we're in India."

"You will," he said firmly. "Most bad ones have retired—or are dead."

Saran and Alice lingered at the curb in front of our hotel—lingered and in a warm, sorrowful-fond way, as if they hated to give us up. In fifty fashions, by asking fifty promises, they tried to ensure our return. We said we would come back some day to Calcutta. In the "season." Nice people.

They drove away and the Jaguar seemed reluctant to widen the distance between us. Ricky kept waving. She said, "What a *spectacular* evening." Then, seeing dim figures start up from recesses in buildings where they'd been sleeping, she added, "Beggars—even at this time of morning! Come on, Phil. We have only three hours left for sleep." And three hours later, she dug me out of my pillow and handed me a cup of coffee she'd already ordered. After a little while, she also produced a Dexadrine tablet. "Be a long ride to Benaras. And we'll want to take a tour when we arrive this afternoon."

"I love you."

For a moment, there was a lambency in her face, a dulcet but incandescent look. "You don't have to illustrate when we have so little time to sleep! But . . . !" She kissed me.

8
Ganges, Ghats and Grue

It was our first experience of Air India.

We had verified our reservation when we had arrived at the airport, from Siam. Moreover, Mr. Chidra had phoned to say he had double-checked. We reached the airport that morning—after a drive which Saran Orinkaur's data made no more comforting than our night ride into town. We were just in time! Ricky heard a terminal clerk tell a couple of men in fezes: "You can have the seats of two Americans, Mr. and Mrs. Wylie. They have not shown up."

It was *still* an hour before departure time!

Ricky bored into that situation like any lady tourist affronted by a mere male. The fez-topped men (who looked like Assassins or Thugs in search of work) blushed, quailed and oozed away under my wife's righteous fusillade. She got back our seats. Being deaf, I'd missed the clerk's treacherous words and realized only that my gal at the counter was somehow vexed.

The plane was a DC3—its stewardess a tall, angular young woman—very skinny—with fingers like jointed pencils and gorgeous black eyes. The pilot and copilot were high school boys, I surmised.

Like the Russian commercial pilots I'd nervously endured

in 1936, these casual kids felt that a passenger line was meant to furnish merry adventure—for them. They got the plane in the air.

Coffee, fruit and other comestibles in cartons and an American Army locker lay about. At every take-off and landing those stores, along with assorted luggage, freight, express, coats and privately owned junk parked anywhere, crashed about the plane. Sometimes, a cargo-shift occurred during flight—tilting the plane abruptly and causing an abrupt reflex at the controls. All in all, it was quite a change from Pan-Am and BOAC! We left the green lands and were soon flying over the plain of India. In the next hours, as in hours of other flights, I looked out and down. This time, I learned something of the meaning of the Indian village.

The land became sere, often naked; escarpments of colored rock rose from the March-brown terrain—crags like the wind-crenelated mesas of our Southwest. A sparse peppering of cattle could be seen, occasionally, or a strawstack; but the earth looked infertile. Yet there were villages. Hundreds. *Thousands.*

Even that inhospitable landscape was tessellated by villages, about so many per square mile, as if there had to be that many at such intervals, without regard to convenience or topography.

Footpaths led from each cluster of mud hutments to the next. These paths joined cart tracks at distances long for a man walking, or even bullock-hauled. Each such double rut ultimately connected with a meandering dirt road. So every village had at least pedestrian access to the outer world—though the way there was long and circuitous and though it went across semidesert. Sometimes, amidst spaced clusters of twenty, even fifty mud huts, a larger village appeared, a village showing some added, pitiful sign of its prestige: green tops of a few trees breasting a roof of red tile, an edifice that had been whitewashed or even some structure of painted boards. Still less frequently, one boasted a quonset hut, reflecting the sunshine with a shattering, silver glare.

I could understand why characters in Indian novels measure distance by village count: the mud hamlets are not mathematically located; but points "five" or "ten villages away" must be approximately equidistant, in whatever direction.

Some say India has five, and some, six hundred thousand of these villages; all say they *are* India.

The thought of people down there in the cinnamon-red dust (or the sodden monsoons), millions, millions, millions of almost literally "Iron Age people" or even "New Stone Age," brimmed my brain—choked it. For a time I felt as if Asia was meaningless to an Occidental: a human spawning-ground that might, in some next ten thousand years replace man—if, say, his civilized minority should blast and ray itself to extermination.

Horizon to horizon—villages! Here, there, parallel, across, and predictably to ever-oncoming rim of the upside-down blue bowl in which we flew—*villages!*

In Asian dust a feeble integration of the dust that forms us all. Here, not men exactly; rather, a plasm bank that could *become* humanity in time; not *quite* our dust: only its waiting rudiment. But these were not prairies a pioneer's plough could fruitfully slice. Just plains: infinite spaces with a cracked puddle-bottom here and, far off there, a russet rock castle; yet everywhere, *villages* in which people dwelt.

Ten thousand years of prior people, driven by hunger, had exhausted the soil. Time itself had sterilized the place, ages ago, and nobody, not even a Hindu—who can subsist on one lentil at a time—ought to inhabit this vastness. It would turn back locusts, bake the life from scorpions. This land, *had been*—but it *was no more.*

While Pithecanthropus stuffed bananas in his furry face, abler contemporaries perhaps broke sod below and planted. They flourished an eon, then endured their dust storms and departed! Pre-Hindu Okies surely had begun here, failed at length and trekked flivverless toward some rumored California-by-the-Ganges! By the time our cannibal sires in Britain squinted down crossed sticks to plat Stonehenge, this land had been lived in too long, too much, too often—by too many. How did it now sustain (bitterly and uncertainly) a pool of primitive human substance? Or was this, in true timescale, Man-vestigial: a revela-

tion of the going of us all—the means, manner and cause? Yet
—they lived on and on and on, below and all about, to the
sky edge: millions in villages.

The socially impotent. The illiterate. The famine-fated.
Plague people. Human beings—hardly.

That dreaming, I abruptly thought, was *not true:*

China had been the same. The Yellow River in flood was
no less decimation—Juggernaut—than the sun over this sun-
inundated cosmos of villages. The steppes of Siberia, with their
immemorial cold that impounded mammoths forever, were as inhospitable. Frosted crags of Caucasia! Foetid shores of the
Congo where life so proliferated that death was obliged to outdo
its man-reaping, all-harvesting prodigiousness.

Something was wrong with me—not with the imperishable
mud daubers below.

I fought against the knowledge of that wrong! I lost to
truth:

Around here, someplace, ten thousand years before this
morning, certain villagers built cities, invented algebra, learned
astronomy, wrote poetry, found how to smelt metals and even
iron. They evolved Sanskrit. They came to the edge of the cal-
culus. And they set spiders spinning ages ago to weave silk
cherished even by men who nowadays can weave lime and air
and coal into sheer fabric!

When our DC3 pushed its private sky-bowl to Benaras, we
would stand—furthermore—where (two thousand five hundred
years ago) one such villager announced most of the concepts
attributed by later people to Jesus. A person named Buddha.

So the infernal plain was not an epoch ended. Not a shot
biological bolt. Not human dust returning to sediments fingered
by the wind. I was *wrong.*

There had been, only, a long slumber here—as in China
since old Lao-tse had his day—Siberia, Africa.

Just—slumber? *Rest*—perhaps?

Then who will next awaken *what,* on this panoramic dust?
A fabulous fresh psychology? A new mathematic? An opened,
additional dimension? Charts of Jupiter? *Beyond question!*

For I knew, and I had to see *because* I knew, that those below, and the Red Chinese, men long tundra-bound and the fever-checked blacks were as other men, exactly. As ourselves— exactly. *They are we:*

I knew the genes, the chromosomes, and the history, the anthropology, the archeology and paleontology. I could not let myself be like many of my countrymen who also know these truths, yet talk, think, persecute, praise and have their being as if what they know were unknown! Their heads are bony bags wrapped around a madness. What these bare-landed people do in Vishnu's name is as real—and maybe realer than what they do often in Dixie—in Christ's.

I ached from the effort to muse justly.

Yet *to be* is first to acknowledge known truth. And I *am*— even if I'm less sure than Descartes that *I think.*

Technology has already set big engines humming on the tundra, the permafrost, the steppes. A billion men—sons of philosophers, artists and scientists who lived two and a half millenniums ago—are inspired by what is called the Revolution. Russians were; we can be. The great Chinese have taken up our technology (and abandoned the Christ we tried to teach, the liberty we said we embodied). Dams are rising in the Yellow River gorges; and in Cathay's villages, new wheels are turning.

A new faith . . . false as any old one!

A new great hope . . . perhaps less false?

And these *Indian* people . . . ?

The sluicing baggage tipped our plane and the playful pilot set it level again. My thoughts were jarred ahead:

These people also are evolving.

At the Muscovite gospel center they are learning to catch up. They are ahead in some ways. The West is possibly in eclipse. Relatively, indeed, and there is no other sane means for the measurement of most human doings, Red progress makes the present pace of free men slow and like a procession of the last dinosaurs tottering hungry, sick, too hot—or too cold—perhaps athirst—and surely blind to the cause, wherefore mad. Blind and mad and lurching toward the end of the line of a genus. No beast in all such parades realizes his course is preset on oblivion, or his kind is dying in himself. Each hopes to find new pastures beyond some next ice field or desiccated slough—and a mate—so as to regain the peace of eternity-in-his-present.

Instinct and appetite drive a procession that does not analyze desire or seek to know that a different direction might furnish survival. Hunger, thirst, cold, heat, quest of mates, compel them in a perpetual passion for the old, outer status quo that provided their fragile inner peace. Brainless reptiles! . . . But men *have* brains! Is it that we, the once-free, may have ceased to evolve?

Depressed for a while, I soon thought resolutely: we must see what we are not doing, and what others do. We must gain new capacity for growth, new will to change.

We had it once, gloriously! Shall we free men now conform-in-God, Dulles . . . and the vanished status quo . . . and die? *No!*

We landed in Patna with an alarming avalanche. The air, the heated sunlight, was welcome after that clattering skycoop where the management forbade even a cigarette. Smoking in air overbreathed, air acid with Asian sweat, might have smothered us all. (Soviet planes will replace India's DC3's—thinned by a high crash rate. So I've read, and I was never less amazed.)

Two American schoolteachers had also arrived at Patna, the only other foreigners. They had flown in—God alone knows in what!—from Nepal. There—and God alone knows why—they had made a ladylike (but doubtless learned) tour. The customs authorities had ransacked their beat, pitiful suitcases with minute, suspicious zeal—as if seeking a contraband grain of dust. And the wilted ladies argued in vain.

A young, fat Indian in a blue serge suit explained to Ricky that somebody was reported to have smuggled some item—opium, he assumed—from Nepal. So the word was out and these bureaucrats were not sure but that the pair of rusticated American lady grade-school teachers had hauled to Patna opium from Katmandu.

The inspectors did cease shaking out the bunion-sculptured

old shoes of those two elderly women while we were on the ground. Yes, they will have tales to tell as they vanish slowly, in the rocking chairs of some skimpy "home." This was their solitary, hard-earned recompense for their life investment in teaching your children. Hours of humiliating display of their underwear, in the withering heat—and Nepal! Their Tour— which the less-enterprising majority of ex-teachers would tire of hearing about in the thin pastures of your charity.

So here's one way you might become that plodding dinosaur I saw in my frightening reverie above the arid land. You have edited history and forced your mentors to teach wishful thinking. You have not been educated, but indoctrinated, by underpaid (and usually far-less-game than these) ciphers. For they who teach you, determine what you are—and are *not*. Do you imagine that you can purchase an American future with a nickel wage for teachers? Who but the foolish, the inferior, the afraid (and two gutty souls in two hundred) will take your farthings to teach your sons wisdom and save your daughters from public proof of private delinquency—your own!

In the bake-oven afternoon we saw your shame—and bargained with various Indians for transportation to town. They would talk awhile and then disappear, although there seemed to be no way to vanish: just airstrips, burnt grass, the little terminal and a few cars standing in the heat. (Ultimately, I realized that Indians "vanish" and "reappear," not because they use the rope trick but because you fail to identify them until you come to know them as individuals.)

Finally, I manhandled my own luggage from a cart, buttonholed the least disreputable-looking entrepreneur, tendered money—and we drove through the tidy countryside into the wide, shaded, pleasant streets of India's most sacred city. Our guide was by no means inscrutable or unapproachable or even disreputable. He had merely been trying to get for himself and his Sikh driver the most promising of the Calcutta passengers. We qualified—after he'd studied everyone. As we proceeded down a broad, neat thoroughfare of Benaras, we decided to hire this team permanently.

Once we had made the deal, our young guide's English improved remarkably. So did his general comprehension: he had seemed vague as fog, at the airport. Ricky found, before we reached our attractive hotel, that he was a law student in the University of Benaras, working his way as a guide, and attending lectures when he had funds. By the next evening, I think we had seen him at least through Torts.

His name was Bandra. He was loquacious, fascinating and appealing—especially after he learned our tipping habits (and also, I felt, our politics—or, more precisely, our philosophy where political concepts were concerned). But pretty much everyone in India wanted to know our sentiments about world relationships before becoming chummy.

The hotel "desk" opened on a long veranda where a score of American tourists and a few English travelers lounged around small tables. Beer, highballs, ice water and tea sat about to cool them, though it was shady and breezy.

Cross-legged men in turbans sat there, too: merchants who spread on the floor postcards, ivory, brass and wooden souvenirs. A large glass case contained specimens of the renowned Benaras saris and shawls; they glowed as richly as Thai silk, some of brocade, some of plain silk and some woven of the sheerest stuff I have seen: mere rainbows that one could almost inhale.

Ricky eyed them as we pursued our porters down the veranda past the faces that turn, serially, on all such porches in the world. There was a shallow, ornate lobby and, beyond it, a sizable dining room—tables covered with clean, white linen. The food smell was appetizing. Also, next to the lobby was the shop of a jewel merchant, tightly locked in this midday heat.

Then we were in our room—cool, dim, immaculate—with two four-poster beds. The posts supported cubes of mosquito netting. Were we not very near the Ganges, the hideous river where charnal pyres burnt corpses and widows sometimes still threw themselves into the flames (or were tossed into them by pious relations)? What place near that stinking, vile, heathen river could be so charming? But we needed mosquito nets, apparently. For pestilence must flit by night from that putrid cloaca. The spaciousness and cleanness of the part of Benaras we had viewed seemed incongruent; not the net-shrouded beds.

When we had unpacked a little and washed a little, careful that no polluted water should pass our lips, we went out on the sunny veranda. Two men with tight-tucked loincloths, turbans, and a bulbous flute, were waiting outside our door. Set about them were baskets. Undulating around the neck of one was a python about ten feet long. They began yelling for rupees.

But our guide came up quickly: "They are not snake charmers," Bandra said. "There are not many, in Benaras, now. In the villages—yes. Not here."

"What do they do, then?" I asked.

"Just show you snakes. More snakes, bigger, and more kinds —for the more paid them."

"Cobras?"

He was scornful. "Nothing poisonous! The hotel would forbid that! It is somewhat dangerous. Bystanders have been bitten—even watching good snake charmers."

The two men realized they were being undercut. One lifted a basket lid and an animal rushed out. A collar and leash stopped it. "Mongoose!" I exclaimed.

"They will let the mongoose eat a little snake—for a price. It is not worth it."

Ricky said, "Thanks, Bandra. We can see a better show a mile or two from home. South Miami."

"Anywhere, modom," he agreed—though I did not believe "Miami" rang a bell for him.

We walked on, sat and ordered cocktails from a towering Hindu who had the face of an Abraham or a Moses. We noticed bougainvillea and other familiar flowers in the garden.

I finally had to show the imposing but flustered bartender how to make a manhattan. More or less. I accompanied it back to our table, sipped, and said Clarke's Hotel could be any first-class spot in the West Indies. Ricky was watching bellboys, porters, room clerks and several self-important-but-not-identifiable men in business suits—and turbans. (They turned out to be minor hotel executives.) They didn't seem Bahaman—but

the wide streets we'd traversed, the setback, louvered homes, the
gardens and flowering trees were—again—familiar. So was the
hotel architecture: Bahama-British in our eyes. The heat-fagged
but rather noisy Britishers behave the same in Nassau.

Soon I noticed the bartender was watching me impassively
but fixedly. There had been no maraschino cherries in his stock
of cocktail fixings. He had substituted a peeled lychee nut, pre-
served in red syrup. It reduced the volume of whiskey and
vermouth—an advantage he may have considered—but I like
lychees. The patriarchal barman was wearing a tight gold-and-
black vest, a silver sash, and a Prince Albert-length silk coat cut
like Nehru's; but he was the coolest person on the porch—two
displaced Floridians excepted.

' I stuck a toothpick in the lychee nut, lifted it from the
drink and nibbled its lemon-and-raisin-flavored meat. Then I
made the international thumb-forefinger symbol of approval.
He thereupon broke into a smile that showed not a prophet's,
but a pixie's soul. Maybe that of a reincarnated Huckleberry
Finn. So I raised my stemmed glass in a toast to thank him further. You would have thought from that answering grin that he'd
been awarded a Nobel Prize for his solution of a bartender's
quandary.

Who can resist such people?

We made the acquaintance of some people named Brown,
from Gary, Indiana: man, wife—and their son, a university student taking time out to travel, or possibly employing a period
of suspension to continue learning by other means. I suspected
the latter owing to his discomfort when I tried talking about
college. So I didn't enquire. The Browns were nice people. He
owned a chain of stores. Baptists, but not the "Hard-Shell"
division.

In Hong Kong we'd spent time with another Indiana couple—a banker and his wife on a world tour. Very bright. Very
well read. Very happy with each other and the trip. At lunch
with the Browns I found myself reflecting that in gone-by years

I'd met dozens of Hoosier couples as pleasant, decently educated, familiar with the world and willing to consider ideas differing from their fairly conventional views. They must have better air out there, than some states! Two bachelors I admire also live in Indiana: Jesuits, department heads at Notre Dame.

After lunch the Browns took off for the Monkey Temple and other centers of that sort of worship most Americans regard as "pornographic." We were asked to go along but Ricky declined: She is one of the few pure to whom all things are pure. Most women of her background have been screened all their lives from the overt sexuality of mankind. Many take all opportunities for voyeurism which will not expose their frustrated curiosity. Half the big cities of Europe furnish live exhibits for these ladies, their husbands and their friends. More Americans than we were allowed to imagine patronize those demonstrations. And others, who never get abroad, pool their curiosity at some ladies' bridge; later, after an alcoholic gala at the country club, they join with their husbands in what the newspapers call "orgy." It satisfies an emptiness that the Rickys of the world investigated and outgrew at the proper time—in youth. Impure, indeed, is our Puritan husk!

Our religion, like most religions, derives its principal authority by administering sex conduct. The need of men for sex rules—"morals"—is implicit in the force and ubiquity of the drive. We need air to breathe, shelter, clothing, food, too; but those "animal appetites" are not subject to much arbitrary law. They are not amenable to gross restriction through religiously induced fears.

Yogi does use a breathing ritual. Monasticism is a sort of "administration" of the shelter-need by limitation. Ritual restriction of food is fairly common—as by Hebrew dietary law and on the Catholic's fishy Friday. But those rites administer hungers so immediate that they do not furnish priests with a strong enough semantic: *time for binding the mind.* The sex drive is the most potent of our common instincts which can be restrained enough by the application of fear to give vast authority over the fearful, to the frighteners.

Here in Benaras, of course, that hold on man could be seen in forms historically earlier than our own. Hinduism is still, like many ancient beliefs, not wholly antisexual. Some Old Faiths kept temple houris and encouraged bodily sex pleasure. Here some even furnished idols to pleasure devout but needy women— or used to do so.

But the faith in which we Americans were reared is opposite and has so indoctrinated our culture that even agnostic parents cannot save their offspring from it. It first discovered— pragmatically, I daresay, and long ago—that men and women can be more solidly and easily attached to authority by *fear* than by encouragement, i.e., *love*.

Ideally (if the motive of spiritual thrall may be thought of as ideal) the utmost power over a frightenable species could be gained by two steps:

First, by arousing *at the earliest possible moment* a deep fear toward a deep desire.

Second, by prohibiting every expression of that-which-is-feared, save a minimum essential to the survival of the species.

In the West, of course, what is called Christianity has attempted that through manipulation of the most powerful instinct amenable to such alarm (hence guilt). It makes incessant efforts to set up in the unconscious mind an indelible, *negative* semantic anent sex.

Thus the "Christian ideal" for sexual behavior is absolute chastity. The only allowable erotic act or sex relationship is confined to married couples. Some American sects even insist that they alone have the power to perform the marital rite. Others hold that even married love is vile: an act which demands shriving and cleansing, especially after a child's birth. Nearly all, furthermore, insist that physical love in marriage is sanctionable only when performed without erotic play and only when exclusively aimed at reproduction. American *laws* directly support the above ideology. Various acts of uninhibited love even of man and wife are called "crimes against Nature" (though it has been shown by Ford and Beach that such loving is a most natural act not only in men but also apes, mammals and reptiles down to and including some fishes)!

"Salvation" (inner security) is granted, under our morality, only to those who agree they are born vile, or cannot themselves avoid filthiness, and only those who also agree to follow rules of "purity" or "purge" laid down by neurotics ages ago.

What a somber day when authority learned it was easier (and quicker, hence more efficient) to take charge of humanity by inducing self-horror in the cradle than by encouragement, or love!

How dismal a disaster! Thenceforward, authority itself lost the means to note that when an instinct is corrupted to enslave a "soul," or frustrated for that purpose, it runs its course behind the scenes of consciousness. And when such grim-purposed defilement involves the reproductive instinct—the wellspring of procreation *and* creativity—believing man becomes their unaware but automatic bound-opposite: destructive—either of himself or his fellows.

Taught thus, to hate, shun, loathe, combat, dread and be shamed by his animal self, he cannot wholly love. Taught a vileness of self by cradle-slaps and parental voices before he is taught a speech, he remains rigid with unfathomable self-dread. His taboo, hence a compulsion, rests in ecclesiastical canons. He was given a new shape the day after his birth:

—they did not let him explore himself, so he never discovered himself and therefore does not know himself

—they did not let him explore others, so he does not know them either, and cannot love

—and when he could talk, they gave him word-symbols to explain the anxiety and guilt they had engendered—and to tell him how these might be mitigated (but never for long, and never explained) under an authority the words named

—not knowing himself, forever, he had no free choices and so lacked the pride for discipline of self

—and all this, they taught him, was called "morality"!

The name is "betrayal."

No wonder man has stolen the future from his offspring! He feels entitled to compensate himself for this dreadsome present pain. The vision of personal immortality itself (also designed and administered by authority) is hardly *sufficient!*

No wonder the symbol of many men for what they regard as "self-sacrifice" and as "humility" is a cross—instrument of torture—sign of man's greedy betrayal of man. It is not the sign of true humility as an animal, or of human love, that Christianity's Founder gave: the Light.

Yet—on torment is founded the morality of most of our religion. To it, we must subscribe, parent or child, for the Law is in agreement with our faith in Torment.

What mother in America—what father—would dare rear one child in a sense of erotic pride, of self-possessed self, of animal dignity and human also? What parent could say (and always act out the dictum): "*You* are the authority—through your individual access to your humanity and so to wisdom, instinct, love, mind and reason." That emancipating knowledge would set sons and daughters free of the inner machination by which the pens of piety are kept populous.

Such love-oriented sons and daughters, however, would be rebuked in kindergarten for lewdness; their parents would be ostracized or dismissed from jobs or locked up; and if such children reached maturity, there would be nothing for them but the penitentiary, since their mere openness would violate eight thousand American statutes.

The babe is born Eros. It's first erotic gesture receives the destroying, frightening, guiltmaking repression—Thanatos in action. Life's murdered. Belief lives on, corrupted. Life is for death's sake, now: pain, vengeance, suicide, every wickedness.

So Eros, the suckling, if he lives cannot mature; for he must conform and take society's shape—your authoritarian, blind society of love-eternally-perverted and hate-canonized. So your children are molded by shame—of social necessity; thereafter, few of them can speak of love with honor or even laughter. You have sentenced them guilty, for life!

That matrix-of-the-spirit takes form at birth. You shape it soon and shamefully before your offspring has a word with which to remodel or cleanse its mind. How can the youth, the adult even, trace back that hideous matrix in which you poured a living, trusting but preverbal infant?

Yet all True Believers have been the same (whether they worship Bo Trees or believe in the Tree of Knowledge of Good and Evil), as those who revere sadistically that other fragmented Tree. Among Hindus, for what is permitted, *other* taboos exist. So the individual's decision—even where his act seemingly transcends our Western "morality" and appears more real—remains compulsive. There is no more humanity in their compelled "love" than in the fear we generate for the same ends of piety.

Faith, without equal and constant Doubt, is the only road to immortal life in the ego. It is the only means whereby the individual can be cut off from biological time, from cosmic time, from the sinless, nontemporal instincts. It is the instinct-of-his-brain to understand and to administer both with a pure, incorporated ethic—a perfect morality which then will make of ego, not End, but a means. But faith-*without*-doubt, imbued by whatever method—compulsions to fornicate, or psychological emasculation in the cradle—orgy or monkhood—is the way to create the guilt-prone person, the anxious person, the authority server, the ever-lost joiner, the empty belonger.

That knowledge is not new. Alexander Pope was not the man who noted first that the inclination of the tree is caused by bending of the twig. And Sigmund Freud merely carried that observation forward a step. The cruel distortion which begins earlier than language remains as rigid and as unconscious and as powerful as that which, alone, is there to be warped: instinct. It is not describable by the victim in any symbol he likely "knows" or can discover: his burden of anxiety was seemingly "there," always. Therefore—to him—it seems innately true. But it was *Jesus* who noted that "little children" partake of the true substance of "Heaven"—a statement Jesus could not and would not make of little children, reared after Him, as Christians by that

sad lot who knuckle to Paul, kneel to Peter, acknowledge Mary
—and merely "interpret" Jesus.

What a world it would be if all "Christians," instead of one
in ten thousand, understood Jesus and followed His concept!

And I have long thought this: How much better off might
modern man be, if Jesus had never lived to furnish texts that
truly resurrected a *few*—and were so warped as to decerebrate
the rest, castrate them, make them bitter, set them forever in
search of physical comforts which would restore their amputated
peace of mind while they forever pretend they seek "spiritual"
immortality!

But, that day, I saw this also: If Jesus had not lived, but
since Buddha did, we would have: Benaras. We are little better
off for Jesus, so far. But we could be His, with true courage.

Ricky and I went to a better place than the Monkey Temple or, perhaps, any other. . . .

Sarnath.

At Sarnath is the Deer Park where Buddha first disclosed
to his five friends the "eightfold path" to *his* salvation. For a
thousand years, a broken stupa had domed up in a weedy pasture, here; and Lord Curzon had dug it out as well as a ruined
monastery that stood in Buddha's time (and before). A nearby
museum now contains more local archeological findings.

So we walked where Buddha had walked and I stood on the
very patch of grass where—they say—he spoke words that echo
still, like Jesus' talks—and preceded many of them in thought,
content and meaning.

Bandra told us about the place and its history. (Indeed, that
day and all the next, the young law student talked with earnest
brilliance about old India, and new, and about the world as he
saw it. He described the world the Indian Hindus saw, and the
Moslems—and discussed knowingly what Nehru and the government descried in their future.)

Sarnath was busier than it had been, perhaps, in all its history. For in another year—according to Buddhist calculations

in India and China, though not in Siam and Indo-China—precisely two thousand, five hundred years would have passed since Buddha had begun his teaching. The great stupa was under repair; hostels were going up; roads were being widened. Pilgrims would flock to Sarnath in 1957.

I cannot say I was "moved" by the experience of trying my shoes in Buddha's traces. Fascinated would be a better word. Yet my deepest respect goes to those men who add to the awareness of all through insight, talent or intuition (it may be said, through brave love of truth and so through the excursions of spirit such love demands). To contribute to mankind some major entity unknown before—music, painting, books—or to take a stride in science—or make a physical or philosophical discovery without which humanity would have been less wise, rich, aware of itself and the cosmos (and less aware that the two are the same)—to create and to discover—this is human essence!

The men who so employ it—and these alone—are the geniuses. New art, knowledge or new understanding gained by one and added to all: this is the Highest Goal.

Buddha had genius.

But till man's cleansed—till other millenniums go by and no one, any longer, imagines salvation comes through self-condemnation—will any Buddha (or Jesus) be properly recognized. Not till we adduce the truer religion that expunges original sin and makes each his own responsible authority, needing no psychological slave-chain to ease the very pain the fetters induce! Not till man needs no authority whose "heights" are, in solemn truth, often the abyss of human denigration! Probably not till women also are numbered equally among this scant company of the geniuses (for now they are most besmirched and therefore least free) will humanity be human and know what the wise man was trying to say at Sarnath. Jesus tried, too, in His fashion. But their meaning was snatched, inverted, perverted—and, by that act, the men-in-power regressed, keeping mere authority at whatever cost to truth, to mankind, to humanity and to love.

Curse them all . . . all except the *truly* holy: the few whose hearts were heresy and whose acts, in consequence, did show they'd caught sight of the eightfold way, or Christian charity—living men, who knew the faithless "faithful" had been crib-stripped of faith and were not even mortal (let alone immortal) but spiritual eunuchs. Men who did not practice magic so as to revel in death. Living men, whose *acts* revealed their knowledge of The Secret.

The geniuses tried to tell it. . . .

But vainer men edited their marvelous and meaningful images back into the old, subversive shapes, the horned scare-gods, demons, golden idols. So, once again, men knelt, who were built to stare straight at stars. God Almighty was done in the eye. Moloch was raised, with his sin for authority's sake, and God's latest name on his brass belly.

Has the incidence of genius fallen? Are the geniuses being destroyed in cradles (or mangers)? Can nobody see Moloch, now—but only the graved belly-word: God, God, God?

Is the secret lost?

In Sarnath, as everywhere, I recollected its words: THE TRUTH SHALL MAKE YOU FREE.

But truth is not the revelation of some ass—sainted after a hundred years of moldering. Truth is not dogma. As Jesus knew, truth is *method*—a method called *honesty*. He knew because He dissented from dogma and revelations that curdled his own religion. What disciple got that point?

Truth is a *method* called *honesty*. In fifteen hundred years of Christianity, men learned the method, a little. They applied honesty to objects and developed the relative truths of science. But the self-styled Christian authorities, who prevailed by dogma and by allegedly "revealed" and "divine" truths, first *denied* science and punished scientists, then relegated all such truth and such method to a "secular area" which their contemptible dishonesty "transcended," they said.

They still transcend—they say. Well, you know, the pain of lying to another: you lose, if nothing else, self-respect. Do you also know the price of lying to yourself, *about yourself?* You do? Then, tell me, who is God? You? Or God?

End of The Secret: Jesus'. Buddha's. Yours——?

The sun came slantwise, gilding all with mid-March luminosities: the wide, flower-bridged streets, tidy villages and the neat, rolling farms.

We went to a weavers' mill. We watched apprentice boys and cross-legged old men manipulate looms, filaments that furnished Benaras its silks, its shawls and saris. We smiled communication when one of the artisans burned a thread of gold to show how the fabric vanished but the metal remained, sun-bright.

In a salesroom, we sat down to buy, as men and their color-ravished wives have sat since Marco Polo's time—kings, queens, princes, concubines, Moguls, khans, Western emperors, go-getters from Gary, even writers. The seller perched cross-legged on a mattress and unspun folded raiment—gossamer flash of Asia, incandescence, gold, silver, colors that had made a village into Tyre, and Benaras.

The room was radiant with beauty—fabric flipped open and flicked upward, silk falling like a thistledown parachute before us—a hundred saris and two hundred, and as many shawls and scarves.

Like all the rest, we estimated our purse and selected—choice as near folly as choosing a handful of precious stones from barrels. When our interest flagged from dazzlement, we were revived by a turbaned minion who served us nepenthe he deemed suitable to the silk: Coca-Cola.

I wrote half a book of travelers' checks. . . .

We had dinner with the somewhat bemused Browns. Afterward, the jewel merchant's booth was open and we went there. The man from Gary, like most men of wealth, was attracted by the opulent rendering of Oriental gold and silver and the light-splashing facets of a thousand colored prisms. Old jewelry and new—heirlooms from other ages, trinkets hardly cool, precious stones and semiprecious, rings, toe-rings, bracelets, lavaliers, cuffs, breastplates, coronets and tiaras.

Mr. Brown picked them up and held them under lamps—talking quietly, with some knowledge of their nature and worth. But he had the dubiety of all traveling Americans; his eagerness to buy was tempered by the fear of being made a mark. A sad state, and one which can be avoided two ways: by having a trusted expert on hand, or by purchasing according to one's own values and not those of any market—be it guaranteed by government, or run by charlatans.

Ricky and I shop the latter way, and so we can never be cheated. We never pay more than we are willing, for something worth *that much* . . . *to us.* We trade money for what we—not they—consider of value.

At the jewelers', we bought nothing.

Mr. Brown—apparently presuming our restraint was a sign of Yankee shrewdness—affected to buy nothing. But after we'd gone to bed (in the two four-posters cubed around with mosquito netting), he went back and bought a sapphire ring he showed us later, a little sheepishly.

In the morning, we were driven by our chauffeur, along with Bandra, to the top of the ghats—for the trip that is the tourist pièce de résistance in Benaras. . . .

Almost as long ago as I can remember, I've heard about those ghats in the Holy City on the Ganges. Missionaries from India—horrified Sunday school texts—or outraged magazine accounts acquainted me, early, with the gruesome riverside and its ghastly practices.

Here the dead were burned over open fires! Here, still, a widow sometimes avoided official surveillance to burn alive in reverent agony. Here, in short, was the essence of grue—real-life tableau that outstripped the grisliest dream of Poe. Travelogue motion pictures have acquainted *all* good Americans with the awfulness:

Long shots of the deformed beggars. Medium shots of barbarians who came half around the world for redemption in the Ganges. Close-ups of half-consumed bodies on the fires. Books like *Mother India* have authenticated the grisliness of that fecal river. There, I'd somehow been led to believe, crocodiles snapped at the devotees, consumed with gluttonous, gnashing teeth the unburned residue of everybody—and caught a few pilgrims alive!

It just wasn't so. . . .

A cumbersome small boat took Ricky and me—with Bandra—out on the water on a morning overcast, cool and very windy. There aren't saurians in the river, which is fairly wide at Benaras and, compared to American city rivers, *clean*.

Once, I saw an unmistakable porpoise break and roll in the green, quite clear water. And porpoises do not frequent polluted water, in my experience. After we had rowed and drifted for a couple of hours, the sun came out.

On the city side, the ghats—stone-paved terraces—rose steeply for perhaps a hundred feet. Interspersed with them were temples, shrines and residences of devout, rich Hindus. Though the day was at first chilly, several thousand men and women were bathing in the water, drying their garments afterward, and dipping up brass jars of the sacred fluid to take to temples—or to homes both distant and nearby. Bandra, by looking at the saris of the women, could tell us from what parts of India most of the pilgrims had come.

Here, a man would stand, half stripped, taut, rapt, his eyes on Outer Space, his voice, in the timbre of a Jewish cantor, intoning Vedantic prayers.

Yonder, a bedraggled crone threw an offering of food into the Ganges—half a coconut and a handful of grain.

Further on, cheerful over neatly aligned flat stones at the water's edge, women *not* engaged in reverent activity were rubbing clothing to get it clean. They filled half the available places in a municipal laundry ghat.

I saw a silly thing:

A splendid mansion, perhaps a century or two in age, stood on a prodigious wall some seventy-five feet above the river. The wall—by which the mansion was supported—threatened to crack open and collapse owing to a tree that had sprouted in some minute cavity and been allowed to grow until its trunk and snaking roots were sundering the masonry.

"They better chop that down, soon," I said, "or else they won't have a house!"

Bandra looked at me with worried amazement. "They *can't* chop it down. It's a sacred bo tree."

"But . . . ?"

"Soon—the wall will fall into the river—and the house will go with it. It must be that way."

"If anybody's in it—at the time?"

He shrugged. "Probably they will leave before. If not—the tree is sacred."

Not the people. The tree.

I thought it silly but it is hardly "heathen." I've lived in Manhattan hotels where the thirteenth floor is numbered "fourteen"—as if that agent of bad luck so many Americans dread were unable to count up to its own number! To each man, the magic of others seems outrageous! A hotel will not collapse because (in the minds of the magic-thinkers) its "thirteenth floor" has been eliminated by the stroke of a paintbrush; but the minds of such people have certainly collapsed.

A procession of women, making I-forget-how-many scores (or hundreds) of circuits around another bo tree, did not much move me to disdain: I've seen too many friends cruise around a mere fraction of another tree (or parts of two) as they made the Stations of the Cross. So who is heathen?

To God, to the Purpose of Cosmos, this is all one. For when men speak of God, or their gods, they but bespeak themselves. That which is represented as God to *me* must surely see all silly rituals as one: as mere people, trying pitifully to shrive their sin and gain merit, under people-made rules of good and evil. If such men possess Truth, Nature lies, and is unjust also. If Nature is evil, or errs, why imagine God—or how?

The Ganges' opposite shore was low, sandy and without houses: an alluvial flat, flooded at times. But, as the morning warmed, people appeared there, too—set down baskets, doffed clothing behind reedy patches of brush, and swam. I assumed that they were holy-bathing; but when I asked Bandra, he shook his head. "They are Moslems. Having a picnic."

"The river isn't holy for them?"

"No. Just a good place to swim."

"Don't the Hindus mind?"

"Why? It is a big enough river for us all."

Occasionally, in the early morning, a drift of smoke from upstream ghats brought a faint odor like the fat-charred element in Tokyo's air.

We went there.

The burning ghats were as neat as the others. Scarce, expensive wood was corded in three sizes. Men kept the pyres level, and stoked; men raked the ashes in heaps—and dumped nothing in the Ganges that would have contaminated a reservoir. We watched a procession descend the terraces—stopping, turning and proceeding. The white-plastered mummy of a relative was borne on men's shoulders and their occasional pirouette was to delude demons, in behalf of the deceased. That sad march was escorted by the usual sorrowing stragglers that go to every funeral on earth.

We rowed closer.

In a hot land, every body must be disposed of quickly; the sanctity of a Ganges-side cremation was matched by its practicality. Where, in a tight-packed city, would you bury your dead? What stretch of arable farmland should be sacrificed for a cemetery? How would you carry a cadaver so far? Who'd pay the wagoneer? Why not do the cleaner and more sanitary thing: cremate those remains of humanity—that are exactly as abundant as humanity itself?

Chop the wood, just across the river. Carry it, by water, cheaply as you can, to a good spot. Burn the body—and its possible pestilence—saving the precious land for crops a hungry nation required, and sparing the usually impoverished survivors the lasting cost of grave rent, "perpetual care"—and potential epidemic.

I watched carefully.

On the fires, vague shapes of what had been human could be seen but only as things bigger than the logs. To get the necrophile travelogues you'd have to go ashore and spend hand-fuls of rupees. Then some bribed employee of this open-air crematory might stir—not the fire—but the residue of flesh. Only then would horror become manifest—and photogenic! Only then visceral organs would spill from scorched bellies and the fulsome teat (so much adored in America) might exhibit itself—globe red-roasted, nipple done to a turn.

The "ghastliness," in sum, was more manufactured than ac-tual: the Hindus were neat about it—till you paid them for messiness.

Of course, if some widow had thrown herself on one small, trim, rectangular, burning fire, I would have run or swum ashore to try to get her off. That would have been horrible! Yet—there is far more mutilation, burning and masochistic dying done daily to honor America's highway Juggernaut than along the Ganges in decades! I've seen quite a few people burned alive, and the guts of dozens on our streets—writhing ruins of the accident prone, of the inferior maddened by horsepower, of the exasper-ated, the unstable, the selfish, the arrogant, the unlucky, the sick and the poky—sacrifices to gods called Ford and General Mo-tors.

When we came back to the landing place we met the Browns who were also disembarking. They seemed more be-mused than they were after their temple-crawl. We five re-mained awhile on the quai, watching the nearest pilgrims bob and duck in the green water and pour it on their heads, while others, opisthotonoid with zeal, brayed prayers at the now-warm-ing sun.

"It's exactly the same thing," I said to the Browns, "that you Baptists do. For the same reasons."

They looked at me—the boy flushed in fury.

His mother clenched her throat for retort and paused, as if she could not find an equal violence.

But the father, after a startled moment, said, "Damn if you aren't right!"

He began to chuckle.

So the mother and the son remained silent till they, too, could at least smile. And I treasure that man's reply.

He represents something closer to Christianity than the Baptist version. Maybe, he had been truly—even if fleetingly—converted, there on the Ganges. Anyhow, he had a vision hard to come by, in Gary, for all its good Indiana air.

We went up the steps after that, bulled through the naked, ash-plastered beggars, ignored their induced or luckless deformities, and pushed back the sick babies they tried to stick on us.

Ricky and I, with Bandra, joined a horde that flowed both ways through a street hardly wider than my outstretched arms. Soon, half suffocated by the mob and its stenches, revolted by people eating in the shops that walled in this stinking flash flood of humanity, we came to a temple door where pilgrims and local people were entering and emerging: an aperture in stone no larger than the entrance to a big house.

Men crammed into it; others crowded out; now the enterers were ahead, and in command—now a bulge of exiting devotees won right-of-way and vomited the others back into an already-packed slot that was hardly street at all. From time to time, the whole mad, praying, glassy-eyed crowd was blocked both ways: the temple door filled with the body of a bullock which was eventually shoved into the multitude, outside. Then the tussle of ingress-egress recommenced.

Suddenly, I had a desire to be elsewhere.

Hundreds kept coming—legions bearing brass canisters of Ganges water. Thousands—above their heads ghee-lamps, saucers in which melted butter fed a feeble wick. Water spattered on me, from the jugs; sweat from the mob; ghee from the jerkily carried lamps. At knee-height, and at my knee-side, I saw a row of the most hideous beggars conceivable, their crooked backs and ulcerous skins against the wall. I looked for a way to get out. I was told to lean down and peer into a hole in the temple—an iron-grilled, square opening, made, I suppose, to let air into the place. Within, I saw unknown numbers of the dirty, white-robed devout tramping round and round something I could not see—that was thick spread with flowers, with marigolds. As they circled, chanting, some flew off toward the stoppered door, and the new worshipers joined the holy pinwheel.

The cobbles under my nose were dung thick, Ganges wet, vile and slippery. There was so little room for mere bending that people butted me this way and that; I was obliged to cling to the grille to look and to stand up, afterward.

And I saw that Bandra and Ricky were removing their shoes. It was the only time, then or ever, that I balked: "I am not going in!"

"Not in the *temple*," Bandra answered. "Up the stairs, here."

Had I known that, I'd have assented. But I thought we were slated to join the demented carousel inside the holy place, even amongst the bullocks that entered for no sacred reason but just to eat the marigolds, floral offerings which had served their sacred purpose and poor forage, but certainly the sole fodder on any downtown Benaras street.

That panicky balk cost me a good deal of face with Ricky. Bandra, too, for all I know or care!

We went up some steps half-ankle-deep in slime and beheld, for what it's worth, the dome of the Golden Temple, made (or claimed to be made) of I forget how many tons of gold of a fineness I don't recall. Bandra then found a way into an open space on the far side of the temple: a market. Heaps of crimson powder were on sale—the dye women use for caste markings. And there was air to breathe.

An old priest appeared, carrying marigold garlands. He proffered them to me—and I rebuffed him with the residue of my fear-fury—my horror at stinks and compressions too great for me to tolerate without rehearsal. (If Bandra had taken us into the temple, I believe I would have passed out cold!) But this belligerence toward the priest hurt our guide. "He wasn't trying to sell the flowers. He wanted to give you them, for a blessing."

So I was ashamed.

Fortunately, the old priest tracked us to our car—knowing, perhaps, that Bandra would explain. Ricky and I accepted his garlands then—and I gave him money—being a Presbyterian hence well-acquainted with that ecclesiastical quid pro quo which is not "selling" but a "gift" and "blessing" besides—and costs more than value received.

After lunch at Clarke's, we emplaned for Delhi. . . .

9
New Delhi: the
politics of privation

Max Wylie, my brother—two years younger to the day—graduated from Hamilton College in the late 1920's and, desiring to see the world but lacking means, accepted a job as a teacher of English in Fohrman Christian College, in Lahore, India. For something on the order of three years, he served on the faculty of that missionary institution.

Max loved the Indians. He learned some Hindi, and was often in the homes of his students—village houses and the palaces of maharajas. He wrote a book afterward called *Hindu Heaven* which showed an intense *lack* of love for certain sorts of missionaries and it rocked certain segments of Christendom. But "Christendom" is often rocked; it always settles back: this is the chief function of organized religion. Yet Max lost no Indian fealty by telling some truth about some evangelical fools.

In the quarter century that has passed since his teaching years in Lahore, my brother's apartment has been a port of call for Indians arriving in Manhattan. I have met many of them there and so has Ricky: Max never forgot his students. He kept up a desultory correspondence with a number. Not a few went on from Fohrman College to Cambridge, Oxford, the Sorbonne and other seats of learning. Not a few became wealthy; more took over parental empires of trade. Several became importantly associated with the new government, when the British had gone and India was free.

One of these is Arthur Lall, the gifted statesman and author who has for some time been India's permanent delegate to the United Nations, in New York. His novel, *The House at Adampur*, appeared between this writing and the air voyage it records —a story of fascination and informing values that made me wonder how many of our diplomats knew *America* as well, *felt* it as poignantly, or could articulate the pains and hopes of our patriotism with comparable skill.

From Max's quondam students, Ricky and I carried letters of introduction to several people in New Delhi; and we found that letters had been written concerning us and our arrival. I had no more than mentioned our name to the woman at the desk of the Hotel Imperial, when evidence of such letters materialized:

Her handsome brown eyes dilated in her caramel-colored countenance. "Mr. *Wylie! Philip* Wylie?" When I nodded, she cried, "Rajkumari Amrit Kaur has been phoning *incessantly* for you!"

That name meant nothing. I might have wisecracked, owing to sheer astonishment. But Ricky came to my side and spoke to the clerk. "Of course! It's so nice of Princess Amrit Kaur to phone."

The Indian lady's gills worked with awe. Other tourists and nearby Indians were staring at us. And it takes a high grade of celebrity to impress, let alone to overwhelm, a desk clerk in a first class hotel, *anywhere.*

Just then, a man who had been listening from an office recess hurried forward and said urgently, "The Princess' secretary is *again* on the phone, Mr. Wylie."

So—before I registered—I accepted an invitation to lunch with the "Princess."

The standard porter-safari conducted us through carpeted halls, past luxurious shops and big lounges, to the elevator. Turbaned men, stationed on our floor, unlocked a door.

We entered a living room decorated in French style. Which

Louis I no longer could determine, though I once ghost-wrote a book on interior decorating and, then, I knew. To the right of a tycoon-sized parlor was another exquisite room, with ceiling-to-floor windows, satin-draped and shuttered. The safari boys proudly threw back the shutters. We had a corner view, from there, of handsome gardens. On the other side of the central chamber was a large bedroom and beyond that a bathroom with space enough for a directors' meeting.

A platoon commander, speaking for his gold-braided, bowing aides, said, "It is one of our best suites—and none is better. Until the other day, the Australian Legation occupied it. Suitable houses for embassies are hard to locate in New Delhi. It took the Australians months."

Doors opened. Closets slammed. Luggage creaked as it was benched. The last turban marched away and we were alone.

I asked, "Who's this 'Princess' somebody?"

"She doesn't use the title any more. But I guess Indians still treasure it. She's Minister of Health. In Nehru's cabinet."

"How'd she know our estimated time of arrival?"

"Arthur Lall wrote her. Didn't you read his letter?"

"Sure. In Hong Kong. A jumble of Indian names. How could I remember Hindi when I was still trying to master pidgin English?"

I then took a considerable stroll, without leaving our suite. "Going to be nice here. Civilized. Comfortable. You could put about eight Statler-type parlor-bedroom-and-bath suites in the main part—and have a small skating rink left over. Wonder how much it's going to cost us? Hundred bucks a day? *Two* hundred?"

"For one day," Ricky answered, "let's not ask. Let's just live in it and relax. Golly—I could *stand* a little civilized ease!"

Down in the garden under our windows, a dance band commenced to play "Harbor Lights." *Very* civilized, I felt. "It's like the Westbury, for furniture, Miami Beach for entertainment, and for size—straight Mogul."

Ricky tried a khan-type divan, silently.

The phone rang.

A worried Indian hotel clerk told me he was not certain we could keep the suite for the week we planned to be in New Delhi. Would we be grievously discommoded—his phrase—if we were moved to another suite, not quite so elegant, in a day or so?

I thought of Ricky's delight over this first large luxury in a long spell. I also thought of my dwindling supply of travelers' checks. I wondered if we'd already been downgraded, after our royal arrival. Perhaps a discreet call to the Princess' secretary had vouchsafed the fact that Mr. Philip Wylie was only an American author and not even a journalist.

Ricky, presuming that I was balled up by some new name of a written-to Indian, handed me Arthur Lall's letter. I glanced at it automatically while the manager continued to explain the pressure on his limited accommodations.

And I decided that he was making a pitch in the hope of releasing his big suite without giving us offense. So I waited till he had rounded out his apologetic insistence and replied, coldly, "We would be very much distressed to move at all. We like this apartment. It is almost adequate. We are unpacking. We shall have a great deal to do in Delhi. We shall entertain. These rooms will do—*barely*. Please see to it that we keep this suite—!"

"It may be *impossible* . . ."

"Please see to it. And"—I scanned Lall's letter—"please have your telephone operator give me the number of B. K. Nehru—the Premier's nephew."

I thought maybe he was a cousin. But his name was there, and he was a big wheel in India's government.

The manager rang off, nervously.

I left a somewhat startled Ricky, used to my fumbling in crises where name-dropping will serve as does nothing else, and I took the elevator to the lobby. I'd seen a neon sign there—small, and discreetly glowing, on an arrow: three letters: PAA.

We had booked our round-the-world flight through Pan-American World Airways though our actual flights went by way of a dozen different air lines. In India, the local company has a monopoly. Trans-World and Pan-Am don't fly internal routes, so I had not expected to encounter Pan-Am, after we left Calcutta. But I wanted—now—to know how to nail down the apartment we precariously occupied. I had, furthermore, some rebooking to attend to. An error had been made in the scheduling of a flight to Agra. So I followed the neon arrow.

In the office I found a Mr. Seshadri, a speaker of seven languages and several dialects, movie-actor handsome—differing only in hazelnut skin, a man with intelligence and stores of that patient fortitude called courtesy. To Mr. Seshadri, I explained my desire to retain our rooms—and the problem of the Agra booking. He said he would investigate.

I went back. Ricky and I began to unpack.

Mr. Seshadri knocked ten minutes later. The suite would be ours. And he advised renting a car, driver and—while in Agra —a guide. The plane trips were crowded. The road was good. We would see dozens of Indian villages. He could hire an expert Sikh chauffeur and a Plymouth car in superb mechanical condition. If we preferred, at an advanced rate, a Cadillac. . . .

In the days that followed, Ricky and I came to know Mr. Seshadri very well—not so much owing to a need of further aid, but because he was a kind of Indian we otherwise might not have met: neither an official nor one of the less loftily employed people with whom we talked a great deal, but an educated man of middle class.

On the evening we left Delhi, by Air France, for Beirut, Mr. Seshadri escorted us to the airport. We sat out together a not-unusual delay of three hours. In that time, Mr. Seshadri and Ricky and I held one of those random, intimate discussions that occasionally occur when people with differing ways of life, who have come to like each other, break through ordinary reserve and openly state, ask and explain what truly concerns minds and hearts.

Mr. Seshadri had been in America, moreover, so we were not in the difficult position of trying to talk to a new friend in a far land who had no image of our background. By then, too, we'd spent a week in New Delhi, much of it with government people. The questions that came to our minds were, consequently, not of a superficial sort. Mr. Seshadri had the breadth, and the knowledge of his country and people, to grasp our residual incomprehensions.

But the greatest reason for that intimacy was that he, like us, had an almost desperate desire to know more about the American viewpoint in world relationships: he felt that his future, his family's, India's, the world's, depended on what soon would (or would not) happen in American minds and hearts. That one brilliant Indian as much as any other enabled us to gain insights that some people who have lived for years in India obviously miss. Of course, some don't care for insights but only for profits. Others, arriving in a heathen land, forever see nothing but the heathen.

But that talk was our *last* Indian adventure. . . .

The first was the luncheon to which Princess Amrit Kaur had invited us.

The way led along New Delhi's wide streets and through vast lawns, parks, fountains, pools, monuments and gigantic government buildings. There is no comparable capital in the world. The pink-buff sandstone and simple architecture of its public structures suits the landscape. Majesty is achieved by mass, and by the profligate use of open space around each building, each group of buildings, every monument and each memorial archway. There are vistas in New Delhi where, for a mile or more, nothing can be seen but an open extravaganza of federal property: mere scope implies the immensity of the land. The dusty-rose of stone and sculpturing is a crystallization of the red dust that drifts from the continental plains to the shore of Indo-China. The hue says "India," the pattern says, "Today." New Delhi has routes and room for a next century's traffic—beauty and spaciousness. There is not a sign of slum in miles, or of that middle-class conglomerate—apartments, residences and shops stacked and strung together without reciprocal consideration that is the usual city.

A *modern* city. Not one like your city—yours that lacks

proof all earth is anything but boards, bricks, stonework, dirty
glass, corroded metal, rust, dust, gum wrappers and refuse! Not
our common blight: streets without a flower, few trees and those
half perishing, grass gone—stinking slots where aspidistras die
indoors of gas fumes and potted palms or fiddle-leaf ficuses
wither behind curtains in symbol of the total extirpation of
vegetation! What an environ—our home town! Without proper
daylight, acquaintance with sun, full of roar, of iron-tired batter-
ing on cobbles and iron-wheeled scream on curved iron rails, of
chumbling motors, brake-squeaks, man-woman babble and jibbering whistles stuck in cop-mouths. The city, that filthies every
raindrop, soots each snowflake and beturds the unlikely stir of its
pre-exhausted air—its carboniferous, toxic, sulphuric, lung-tear-
ing, nylon-eroding air. Modern purlieus, civilization! Night cannot hush or hide it—since its very sores are displayed by regular
lamps, inadequate for mankind, and by random, tawdry shop-
signs—motile, hideous, confusing the perplexed angles and em-
phasizing in raw hues each defect and separate ugliness! Temporal cloaca—wherein man's bred, birthed, served, enslaved and
borne away in his body a whole lifetime after his essence boiled
away—in your city.

Of course, the part of New Delhi I admired was commenced by the British, who observed (after a couple of centuries) their seat in Calcutta was not near the center of this em-
pire-chunk, and had the climate of wet Hell, to boot. The
Indians have continued, in their little time of liberty, the original plan. And I admired only the federal portion of the place:
I am an enemy of cities, usually.

Indians will ask you if their capital is not "very nearly as
handsome as Washington." Washington . . . ! where every
avenue that runs from a serene edifice to become, in a block or
so, the great gutter just described. Washington should be moved.
It should be torn down. And if Washington is unwise, it will
be . . . torn down by the nothing-makers!

The residence of India's Minister of Health had its own
compound, set apart, on streets a mashie shot wide and a golf

course long. We were accosted by a mammoth turban. Told (by example) that in official India, "Princess" was now "Madam." Given a big portal to enter.

The rooms were large and Victorian.

Mme. Amrit Kaur was small, alert, wrinkled, poised and very learned.

(I would have been fascinated to see her compete on the "Sixty-four Thousand Dollar Challenge" with Oveta Culp Hobby or Mrs. Luce or Frances Perkins.)

Luncheon guests came quietly, one by one, and sat quietly talking till luncheon was served:

A Japanese interested in world peace;

A young English doctor conducting a village experiment in health reform and health education;

One English and one American diplomat,

Us.

Mme. Kaur sat at the head of a table of ambassadorial dimensions. Servants set elegant plates before us and served us a curry from massive silver dishes. With dessert, we were served silver itself: pastry flaked with metal which we ate for the first time. I presume that eating silver is a token of high station or wealth (power, now) which some old mogul introduced; so I wondered if gold taken internally were poisonous, or why we didn't eat ruby dust. Silver has no flavor I could detect, anyhow—and adds but shimmer to frosting. One might as well chew the tinfoil with one's gum.

The meal was delicious—and scarcely noticed, even the edible silver: enthusiasm for the new India was the food they relished:

. . . this "plague spot" was being cleaned up . . . the people in that "dust bowl" would soon have irrigation from the canal driving toward them . . . so many thousands of experts in so many myriad villages were teaching English, reading, writing, better agricultural methods, the culture of new crops, nutrition, baby care . . . and always, *always*—India was learning the principles, meaning and the purpose of democracy and freedom. . . .

I never heard the word used so often, or with more feeling! You'd think democracy was a new invention, one as revolutionary as what Jesus *tried* to say, yet one as fresh as atomic energy. . . .

. . . so many dams, power stations, hundreds of miles of paved roads, hospitals, clinics, midwife training schools . . . so many new secondary schools, high schools, colleges . . . so many miles of pipe, drains, sewers, wires, walks, ditches . . . so many power shovels, tons of dynamite, cubic yards of concrete, dynamite factories, cement mills. . . . Earthquake? So many million more man-shovel-hours to clear it . . . and the hell with impediments. . . .

It was like a war: excited logistics.

Progress.

. . . so many millions more people taught to read . . . so many radio towers put up, sets distributed, educational programs beamed on the dung-smoked, dusty Indian air. . . .

. . . so many flies killed, bedbugs, lice, fleas. . . .

. . . so many millions vaccinated, immunized, treated, hospitalized, surgically repaired. . . .

And such Augean chores ahead, with such titanic additional demands . . . !

They reminded me of the Soviets, in the days when the Czar had gone and the liberated Russians had not yet discovered that Marxism would out-Ivan all terrible authority.

Of Rome in the big days. Of deploying Phoenicia.

I sat at the right of the old lady and, mostly, listened, for every question I asked was fully, brilliantly answered. Mme. Amrit Kaur *knew*. She had spent a lifetime learning—after Gandhi, and with Nehru—learning, because of prison sentences and because of India's hunger and desperation and its unborn magnificence. . . .

A lifetime of *un*learning to be a princess. . . .

Two hours we dined, and talked.

I did not ask our hostess about her immediate problem. As Minister of Health, she was soon to face an angry Parliament. The Ganges had risen that winter and inundated the city water supply filtration beds. When the water receded, infectious hepatitis broke out in the city and two hundred thousand people had had, or were now suffering, that long-lasting illness that sometimes ends in death.

"Why are you so interested?" she asked me as we walked back to the drawing room for coffee.

"I like India."

"How does it happen that a novelist knows so much about sewers, disposal plants, water treatment and public health?"

I told her a little about my private campaign in Miami's two nervy newspapers. A long skirmish that helped change America's sickest and filthiest city to a community as healthful as modern sanitation and engineering make possible. In fact, the finally aroused citizens of South Florida not only purged their premises but pioneered in tropical public health. Today the Miamis are teaching the world between the tropic parallels how to live with new equivalents for Temperate Zone big-city technology. She persisted, however, in asking why a *novelist* should have so much scientific and engineering knowledge. I could answer only that either I am not much of a novelist, or, being a typical American who ran steam engines, made model planes, drove cars and compounded gunpowder before he was twelve, I was "brung up technical." But I sometimes wish informed people would stop asking authors how they happen to have educations!

It was after three o'clock when we departed.

In the following days, we read the blow-by-blow account of Mme. Kaur's defense of her administration before Parliament:

The Ganges Flood Control Plan had not yet been authorized by Parliament, she noted.

About two hundred thousand cases of infectious hepatitis had been reported. But, she asked tartly, had the disturbed representatives of India's far-flung provinces observed that the viral strain caused light cases and the fatalities were negligible? She admitted that not every rupee budgeted for the nation's health had been spent on the care and succor of New Delhi hepatitis

victims. However, gamma globulin was not to be had—the only
effective preventative. No funds for that existed! But did the
eminent representatives want exclusive use of Health monies in
Delhi, simply because they and their families were residents in
the area and directly menaced by this epidemic of minor nature?
Even if Parliament used every anna, the *total* funds for India
would not halt the sickness. Such monies as she had were being
used to halt, in its early stages, an outbreak of cholera in Calcutta. Would Parliament prefer national cholera to local hepatitis?

Was her ministry responsible for Acts of God until a more
sophisticated Parliament voted funds for human acts which
would modify God's—such as flood control?

She held her own, and more, with the hundreds of alarmed
delegates: an old, frail, wise woman! She won a vote of confidence. She went ahead afterward with her mammoth schemes
for the welfare of the new republic. Not even a doctor of
medicine, Amrit Kaur. Just . . . a princess with a brain who
found a Cause, and a need she could learn to help fulfill . . .
who found a leader and then *became* a leader—but only after
much learning, and the vicissitudes of British imprisonment.

I was proud when, three months later, my alma mater had
Rajkumari Amrit Kaur stand on Commencement Day beside one
other woman and several eminent scholars, scientists and successful men of affairs—to receive an Honorary Doctorate. The other
woman was Helen Hayes. . . .

Another Delhi day and another date for lunch. . . .

Mr. Lampur's house was modern. Adobe walls and a cactus
garden, set amidst other modernistic ranch house dwellings, it
might have been the Santa Fe home of a sun-worshiper with
good taste.

We arrived by taxi at one thirty. A young man—eighteen,
perhaps—answered the doorbell and took us into a living room
that—still—might have been a Chicagoan's. He sat us down on a
divan and asked if we'd like a drink. His mother, he added, had

not yet returned from "the committee." (I never learned what committee—only that she served on many.) His name was Curzon. So was his father's: Curzon Lampur, though only a few called him "Curzon": he was "very close to the Prime Minister," we'd been told. That proximity, we mistakenly assumed, bred hauteur.

The son brought orange juice and we understood why he had not asked us to make a choice of drinks. There seemed to be nothing Indian about him:

Gray eyes, brown, curly hair, a deep but shy voice, sallow complexion, and an air of seriousness that was awesome. He might have been any muscular, dedicated European teen-ager. His mother, we knew, was Parisian French. That made him a Eurasian—what the British had thought of as "half-caste," "racial hybrid," something inferior. The foreign service British, who rarely bothered to investigate genetics, or their own "mongrel" lineage, who rarely had any empirical thoughts—save of empire itself.

Young Curzon sipped his juice and glowered at us. I thought it was just the thistliness of adolescence and asked, "What do you do?"

"Attend the university."

"I mean—what are you going to do?"

"Scientist."

"What kind?"

"Physics."

"What sort?"

He stared at me bitterly. "Nuclear."

"How much math have you had?"

He seemed surprised—as if an intelligent question had come from an unlikely source. "Quantum theory—now."

"And you're—*twenty?*" (I guessed privately he was eighteen.)

"Eighteen." That up-grading of his age was to help my plainly poor status.

"And where are you in physics? Heat-light-electricity?"

"Radiation propagation."

I exclaimed, "For God's *sake!* You must be precocious as hell!" I added, "Nuclear physicists *usually* are."

A thought occurred to him. "*You* studied physics? Father said you were a——"

"Writer. I studied *elementary* physics. And kibitzed, ever since, on the field."

He thought. "Why do you have so many bomb tests?"

"Because the Soviets do."

"They've offered to stop."

"So have we. With certain guaranteed safeguards."

"They only made the bomb because yours was a threat."

I said, "*We* know—and you Indians *should* know—they started on bombs, during the war, without even being aware we were at work on them."

"Not according to my information!"

"Then you need better information."

"It's a question," the boy answered, "of who's being kidded —by whom. And so far, we've got a lot more truth out of Russia and China than the United States."

"You're a scientist," I answered. "Can you prove that statement?"

"You Americans say you're defending the free world. That includes India, if true. And you arm Pakistan." The assertion was obviously regarded as "proof" that nothing done or said by America was honest, honorable, true or decent.

"You don't like America?"

"No," he said.

"Or Americans?"

He stared stonily at me. "Have I reason to?"

I grinned. "Can't say. All I *can* say, is, if you have reason itself—a rational, open mind—I hope to God you will get reason to like us!"

His mother came crackling in: a rich-bodied woman of about forty with wind-blown, tinsel-blonde curls who was briefly, emotionally, apologetic about her tardiness. She asked us if we drank gimlets—and hurried out.

A Mr. Jundra and a Mme. Parta then arrived: two official-

looking, gray-haired, preoccupied, tired-but-pleasant people in
the government. They dressed in European clothes, good clothes.

Mrs. Lampur whizzed back with a tray of cocktails and
zoomed out again, to "change." A portable female dynamo looking for motors in need of current where she could usefully plug
herself in.

Ricky sipped her gimlet. She was regarding me somewhat
anxiously. I remembered. "What*ever* you do today," she'd
said in the taxi on the way from the Imperial, "*don't* talk
politics! These people *are* India's politics. They asked us to
lunch out of courtesy—because of Max. The *last* thing they'll
want to hear is your impression of India, theory of atomic stalemate, ideas about Communism and view of America in world
affairs!"

I'd agreed: this would be purely social!

But I'd already been started on a quasi-political talk by the
bright kid, Curzon. Ricky was justifiably afraid I'd carry on.

Curzon Lampur, senior, now walked into his home.

I was startled. Curzon Lampur may be the best-looking
man I have ever seen. Tall—perhaps six-two—and lean but hick-
ory-hard, like Saran Orinkaur. An adz-hewn profile—smoothed
later by Rodin.

He wore a frown of fatigue, not a scowl. He was about
fifty; and he was doing the work of twelve men. His eyes reflected light through the dark spectrum: blaze-black to topaz.
His hands looked capable of any skill: surgery, painting, black-
smithing. His voice, baritone, curt as an upper-class Briton's, but
not fogged by London affectation, and more staccato. He was
incredibly restless, almost unendurably impatient. He intercepted sentences because he guessed, accurately, nearly every
intended predicate. Yet that habit never had the rudeness that
characterizes most speech-stealers; rather, it gave the impression
of a man of brilliance, trying to help everybody communicate
—efficiently. His brain worked like an electronic calculator; he
understood people and cared about them. Interest, not hurry,
caused his invasion of their to-be-spoken thoughts. An odd attribute.

Since that day, I've heard it discussed by many who know him. They say, "He's so absorbed in everything, he doesn't realize he breaks in on you." Some also say, "A pity Gandhi didn't know him!" and add, "But *Nehru* does and Nehru has his eye on him."

He has, actually, more charm than any other one quality. He frowned, but he also smiled—at Ricky. Shook hands with me, bowing slightly. Then his other guests. He wore jodhpurs of a bluish-khaki material like safari-cloth; cool, durable and tailored. His blouse buttoned to the neck; it had a low mandarin collar, like a Chinese woman's dress.

A daughter showed up. She was about twenty-two.

Her mother had gone for another round of gimlets, so she introduced herself to us. Her father sat on a straight chair, watching her—abstractly—thinking of something else. Or, maybe, preparing to tell her, later, she'd smiled too much (or too little), had a stain in a fold of her light silk skirt, had pinned her flowers a half inch too low on her cashmere sweater. . . .

"My name," she said, "is—" and she spoke a dozen syllables. "But everybody calls me 'Ro.' "

I wanted to ask Ro if she'd entered the "Miss India" sweepstakes and add that I thought she would mop up. But I was afraid she wouldn't even understand the meaning of that clumsy compliment—which subsequently proved stupid.

Curzon—whom his father called "Junior"—was smirking like any brash preschool boy at my reaction to his gorgeous sister.

Mrs. Lampur came back. "Lunch," she said, "will be in about fifteen minutes." She smiled at Ricky. "If you'd like to refresh yourself?"

Ricky was prerefreshed.

Mr. Lampur was now intently regarding us. "Enjoying India?"

Ricky said, "It's wonderful! We're dazzled and uplifted and almost stupefied."

"Meaning what?"

She told him about our enthusiasm for India's effort to become a modern nation and, particularly, a land where liberty was comprehended and cherished.

I thought he seemed slightly surprised. "Where have you been?"

She told him.

His eyes twinkled. "Seen any elephants?" he asked—ridiculously, I thought.

"One," Ricky replied.

"Where?"

"Benaras."

"Bet it wasn't working!"

"But it was!" Ricky seemed puzzled.

"*There you are.*" Lampur shot to his feet swiftly and leaned against the wall. "You *couldn't* have seen an elephant at work in Benaras—because Hindus regard elephants as sacred and *don't* work them. That's my test of newcomers, for preconception or pragmatism."

Nobody calls Ricky a liar with impunity. It is usually risky to dispute her, or to claim she has made a mistake. She's quiet; but if she says anything, she means it and knows what she's talking about. So she just looked calmly at the Indian and answered. "It was being used as a ladder. Men were standing on the elephant to repair something on a telephone or power line."

Lampur laughed. "Of *course!* They *do* use elephants to *stand* on. Not called 'work.' Riding on 'em isn't classified as work, either . . . !"

"That's interesting. But I consider holding up a man is work. Am I going to be expected to say everything, here, according to some Punjabi definition of terms?"

Everybody laughed—Lampur most. Mr. Jundra and Mme. Parta hadn't said much; but now they both agreed Ricky had passed the test. I guessed that when Lampur was present, they usually kept quiet. But I was wrong. They were merely giving us a chance to reveal ourselves—studying us, before deciding where to take part in the conversation.

I said, "Our host has enquired whether we are seeing the

India of lurid lexicons—or just *seeing*. Shall we now put some questions to him—say, about native customs in El Paso?"

Lampur chuckled. His eyes left off an interested scrutiny of my wife and moved to me. I smiled at him and went on, "I think it would be simplest if I explained how we told three Baptists, from Gary, Indiana, that the Ganges-dunking in Benaras was exactly what went on in Harry Emerson Fosdick's Baptist Church in Montclair, New Jersey."

Lampur roared.

"One of them," I added, "agreed. The husband."

"I spent four years in America," Lampur replied. "And I *still* don't know anything, really, about you."

"There are quite a few of us. Almost half as many as there are of you. And we're not *all* alike!"

He smiled, looked at his empty glass, said, "Curzon!" in a sharp tone and at the same time, snapped his fingers.

I noticed he snapped his fingers to "brace" Ro, too. I suppose he copied that brusque mannerism from some don (or perhaps some prime minister) he met while he was polishing off his Ph.D., at Oxford. I never saw any other Indians who finger-snapped to call grown sons and daughters to order; and Americans don't do it. So it must have been an Englishman's parental way—and they are rude in such things—or his own idea.

After that, he again addressed Ricky. "How long have you been married to this discerning scribe?"

"Nearly twenty years."

He thought that over and abruptly said, "Let's stop beating around the bush and talk politics!"

So *I* laughed. "I was forbidden to bring up the topic."

"Why?"

"Ricky thought you'd be coming home from a political surfeit—for a restful lunch."

He glanced at Mrs. Lampur (whose name had turned out to be Jeanne) and then looked at me. "Very American. *She* forbids *you*."

I turned to his wife. "You, I daresay, have occasionally

given him—not commands—but, say, valuable recommendations
—which he has even acknowledged? Or does a Brahmin up-
bringing and a technological education in Christ Church produce infallibility?"

Everybody laughed.

"We have been talking"—Suddenly the pleasure in Lampur's face and voice were gone—"to your Mr. Dulles."

I said, "Yes. I know."

"What do you think of him?"

I sketched my theory that a True Believer is incapable of
complete, effective opposition to the True Beliefs of others.

"That about sums it up," Lampur said.

Young Curzon brought the third round of gimlets. I was
beginning to feel the first two. But Lampur had missed one,
and he took the second, with such a falconlike plunge of hand
that I thought it would spill. It didn't. I pretended to sip mine
and set it on a coaster beside my deep chair.

"We thought"—and he spoke meditatively, slowly for him,
so the full import of that "we" would register—"that Mr. Dulles
was playing a game of statecraft too complex and subtle for us
to fathom. For more than two years, I racked my brains. 'What,'
I kept asking myself, 'is the goal hidden behind these apparently
contradictory, seemingly ill-advised, ostensibly uncomprehending
—and if you'll pardon me, *stupid*—gambits of the American
Secretary of State?' And now we have spent some time talking to
him, face to face. And now we know the explanation. It is not
statecraft too masterful, farseeing, intricate—for our minds.
Nothing is hidden. Mr. Dulles is simply . . . sincere." I think
that was as mauling a use as I ever heard made of one word.

"Mr. Dulles," I said, "is not—after all—America."

"His so-called policies seem to be popular."

"Americans do not yet know there will be no world war."

"Then—how do *you*?"

"I've known it—since August, 1954." I glanced at young
Curzon, who was staring at me. "*Your* department," I said.

The boy grinned a little: "*Scientific* proof, please?" It had
been my challenge of him.

"—didn't appear till the Geneva business. The Soviet 'new look.' They know. They practically asserted the knowledge by their change of tactics, if you understand Red tactics. They acknowledged that we've come to stalemate. From now on, no H-bomb-armed nation is going into the old Clausewitz act. Nobody's going to try to continue political aims with force. Not unless they are willing to commit suicide. Unfortunately, Mr. Dulles got all his A-pluses in corporate or contract law—not nucleonics. He probably thinks—and most Americans still assume, though the idea has frightened them to a state of unconscious hysteria—that, in a pinch, America can still whip Russia."

"China?" Mr. Jundra murmured.

I faced him. "Mr. Jundra. Quite a few *Congressmen* still believe that if we put Chiang Kai-shek ashore he'll conquer Mao in a few weeks. That ought to calibrate American opinion on China, for you."

"Calibrate? Oh! Give me the measure." His face wrinkled with amused self-disparagement. "After Korea—they believe that?"

Lampur was going to say something but his son broke in—so he leaned back against the wall and listened:

"Your date refers to the first Soviet H-bomb. What do *you* know about those bombs?"

"Enough."

Scorn swept his face. "Only a few scientists, a few officials, your commanding generals and admirals——!"

"I was Q-cleared, six years ago, to learn all I needed to know to help plan civil defense measures. So you can judge for yourself what I know."

"A *writer?*" Lampur was surprised. Then he laughed. "You are—surely, then—not a Red suspect! If I understand correctly, you have what was taken from Doctor Oppenheimer."

"Yes."

"Why do you think you are at stalemate?" Curzon persisted.

So, as I had in Tokyo, I sketched some of the released but ignored or only-slightly-understood information, and some top-level theory, about fission that starts fusion and fusion that in turn splits U238. I made it just as technical as I could. I added some rather obscure but public data on genetic and ecological effects. I kept talking fast, and seemingly unrestrainedly. (What years of anguished practice I'd had in the tragic restraint imposed on us all!) Soon, I was certain I had given Curzon a bushel of scientific fact he'd not wholly understand (since biology was involved). And I had the rapt attention of the others —save Ricky: she knows that familiar set of unanswerable arguments and often hears me repeat them. Once, they so distressed me that I was no fit husband for any woman. She still worries about me—and the bombs.

But that did it:

Curzon was looking at me with an expression of awe.

"Eisenhower knows this?"

"He's told. Some of the brass disagree. I think Ike may listen to them more than the physicists. But he's been *told!*" I added, "Right now—the AEC is headed by a businessman. He believes passionately in military 'secrecy' and apparently takes a sort of 'wishful-thinking' view of scientific data. He isn't qualified to interpret it, out of his own knowledge, either."

Mme. Parta spoke tensely: "If your President, your generals and admirals, your heads of atomic energy do not thoroughly understand the subject . . . !" She sighed. "What a tragedy for the world! But I cannot *believe*——"

Curzon said indignantly, "We know, at the University, about the ignorance of your leaders. Not long ago, Eisenhower spoke of the 'secret of the atom bomb,' before UN. How could a man call it a 'secret,' when the Russians were making them? When, indeed—there never *was* a true secret!"

His father said, "That's hard on the American President——"

Curzon ignored that. "Eisenhower said to the world press, when the Americans tested their first, giant H-bomb, that it got 'out of control' and that it did things the 'scientists had not anticipated.' *Two* blunders an informed man simply could not have made!"

Indians, the "lesser breed without the law," were making shrewd, knowledgeable criticisms of public fumbles by an American President. "Ike," I said, "once referred, in the presence of a friend of mine, to the 'infamous' *Smythe Report!* He was that far off the beam, that out of date, that incomprehending. Nevertheless, not the President, but the people, make America's final decisions."

Mme. Parta breathed, "God save the world!"

Jeanne Lampur looked toward a door where a maid stood. "Lunch is served," she said softly.

The cooking was French—and excellent.

Lampur spooned soup and restarted the talk. "Why does Dulles arm Pakistan?"

"I guess he thinks the Arab League is the best buffer between free Asia, you included, and the Reds."

"Doesn't he know the Arabs can't stay in any league? Doesn't he realize that they only gang up for brief ends of their own—and hate each other? Does he really think Pakistan—or countries like that, no matter how well armed—menaces Russia? Doesn't Dulles know about Communist infiltration inside Arab countries? Doesn't he know he's going to lose Afghanistan and the Khyber Pass to the Reds, pretty soon? And Syria? Wasn't Iran any sort of lesson to him? Doesn't he know what Pakistan intends to *do* with its American gift of arms?"

"Fight you for Kashmir?" I asked.

Lampur nodded. "Dulles doesn't understand 'holy war.' And his own 'moral righteousness' insults *us*. But doesn't upset the Kremlin a bit more than Allah or Gog or Oom."

"He's still thinking like the Presbyterian Board of Foreign Missions. You're *still* heathen, who must be enlightened."

The striking Indian flushed. Then he chortled. "I believe you've got it, *exactly*. It will amuse Nehru! See here, Wylie. We are doing, in India, an operation in freedom comparable to the very trick Communists attempt everywhere: we are getting to the grass roots, the villages, the people—with a national program of education in liberty, democracy, technology, literacy, health, and so on. Yet Dulles calls our attitude 'neutralism.' In his mind, no free nation can be self-determined—for he doesn't grant others the right to disagree with Dulles. He doesn't even grant to another nation the right to stay out of his positive, or negative, *notions!* India must be with him, he says flatly, or it's against him. So an independent nation of three hundred and sixty million people has no independence, but only Mr. Dulles's duty to obey Dulles! Our whole program is to teach India the very freedom Dulles says he defends—but doesn't practice—before the Communist line can reach India's grass roots!"

"How long will it take?" Ricky asked.

Lampur shrugged. "Quarter of a century. Half a century. Depends. If India has to build a war machine to fend off Pakistan, it will cost so much that our educational program will be set back decades. We haven't funds for both! Your people don't seem to see that real danger."

"How real is it?" Ricky asked.

Lampur looked at her aggrievedly. "Pakistan is not, and will never be, a free nation and a defender of liberty. It could tie up with Russia as easily as with the United States, tomorrow. It's a holy Islamic dictatorship. Physically, it's split in two, by a big slice of Northern India, which includes the Kashmir. Our Moslem friends talk about a Kashmir plebiscite. It sounds reasonable. But what they want is not that. They want so much chaos in all of Northern India that we can't hold it unarmed as now. Only that would ruin our work and our democratic plans. Without North India, we'd *stay* a medieval nation—starving and forever impotent. *With* it, India can become the great bulwark of democracy in Asia. Don't you people, you Wylies, see signs that Indians know they are in a race to show the world a free democracy of Asiatics can make a Red Chinese tyranny look sick—given time?"

We both nodded. "Almost every Indian we've talked to," Ricky said, "is full of a will to show up Red China."

"Isn't *that* worth keeping on America's side?" Lampur grew angrier. "My God! Our laws against Communist treachery are ten times as strict as yours! *McCarthy* would approve of them.

Internally, India is the most anti-Communist nation in Asia!
But in international relations—we *have* to play neutral."

"Why?" I asked that.

He went on, harshly. "Look. Point Number One. The *only*
nation that could openly oppose and deadlock Russia, with any
meaning to Russia, is a nation that can deadlock Russia on the
matter of atomic holocaust! That means—USA. Not even England! Number Two. Nothing another nation says, powerwise, in
international relations, *actually* carries weight with Russia." He
paused while a little white wine was poured into his glass; he
tasted it, nodded assent, and went on while we were served.
"Number Three. India knows, and India knows that the Soviets
know—they can't take over India now, or soon.

"Don't bother to ask 'why.' I'll tell you." Lampur's dark
eyes shot toward Ricky, then me. His smile was sudden and almost affectionate. It vanished. "Some three hundred million Indians are Hindus. Every kind of force and violence has been
used by conquerors over the centuries to convert them. Nobody
succeeded. Now—as your Navy says—hear this: Point Four:

"The Moslem has an absolutist, fanatic belief—and in its
present corrupt form, it doesn't offer a single True Believer—
and you've read Hoffer?"—He saw we had—"even the potential
background for modern, scientific education. It offers even less
chance for the concept of liberty. It operates by inhibiting
knowledge and maintaining a depressed population. It is *the*
most totalitarian and intolerant of the 'great religions'—Communism excepted. Wylie, I accept that term. Arab countries,
though full of internecine hostilities, want a Moslem base for
all culture. That's the will of Allah. Hinduism is *different*. Different in this way: it is far more tolerant; Hindus are religiously
open to concepts of freedom and the facts of science. They're
teachable in the *modern* sense, even when they remain Hindus.
Moslems are not candidates for *any* defense of freedom."

I thought of Mr. Gudra, who was well educated, and yet
dunked himself in the Ganges. I thought of Bandra, whose law
studies were modern but who apparently believed it was right
and proper to let a sacred bo tree ruin a mansion and even

kill its inhabitants. Bandra—who had a better concept of liberty (and a far greater working knowledge of tolerance and brotherhood) than many of my American friends.

And my eye darted to young Curzon.

He understood, with a swiftness like his father's, and nodded at me, as if I'd asked. "I'm a Brahmin. The 'modern' kind, but that's my equivalent of what you called a 'faith,' a while ago. Christianity, after all, and science are things *India* originated, and exported—that you people——"

His father finished for him: "—bastardized in some ways—as we did, too. Our version of your Faith also dropped Science—our great contribution. For ages. All *right!* We think"—And again I detected official weight in the pronoun—"it would take Communism at least half a century to destroy Hinduism sufficiently to replace it with Marxism, Stalinism, Khrushchevism—whatever the then-current brand name might be. We know Russia would have to murder and torture perhaps a hundred million Indians, in order even to get *going* on a program of reindoctrination. So we have *time* in India! Time to beat the Reds to our people and win them for your side forever—*if* policies like yours don't force us to use the time, and money, to stave off Pakistan."

That was clear enough. Believable, too.

Ricky said, "I'd like to go back a little. *Why* would the loss of Northern India ruin your plan for a free, democratic India?"

"That will be Point Five," Jeanne answered. Lampur had been abruptly distracted by a ringing phone. "The Ganges and the Brahmaputra flow there. India must have the water for the hydroelectric power it needs. North India is crossed by the rivers we require to cease being a semiarid land, subject to famine and doomed to poverty. We must *irrigate*. Can we afford to let people who hate us and are sworn to destroy us seize and control our water supply? Simple as that!" She spoke as an Indian—but she shrugged and rolled her eyes like a French woman.

Lampur returned as his wife finished. "*Exactly.* You Americans are rotten geopoliticians. If Pakistan won control of North India, they could divert the rivers, contaminate them—anything. They would possess the physical hope of India, entire! Their so-called nation is divided, *yes*. Too bad! Too bad Moslems never will accept democracy! Too bad they left us——"

"What about the Moslems in India?" I interrupted.

"So long as Pakistan hopes to seize all northern India—some will intrigue. Not the majority, even today. Eventually, our program would show to them all, as it has to most, that 'believers' must live in freedom, tolerantly. *Meanwhile*, your people arm Pakistan as a 'buffer against Russia,' when no arms but atomic power constitute such a 'buffer.' That encourages Moslem dissent here in our nation. Finally, and we reach Point Six, your people doubt Pakistan wants your arms to hit us."

"How do you know?"

"Because," said Lampur slowly, "I come from Kashmir. So do the Nehrus. We went to school with many of the leaders of what is now Pakistan. We know them intimately. We see them often. And what do they say to us—openly and laughing at our impotence? They say, 'America is giving arms to us to make us strong against Communism. But *you* know whom we shall attack: *You! India!*' "

"Did Mr. Nehru explain that," Ricky asked, "to Mr. Dulles?"

Lampur nodded vigorously—cut the gesture off—laughed bitterly, and said, "Who can explain *anything* to Mr. Dulles that Dulles has not already clearly determined—*even though* he knows nothing about it whatsoever?" He shook his head, as if to clear it of dizziness. "Your Mr. Dulles, and many Congressmen, and millions of plain Americans seem to think a nation is like a corporation. Deal with the *head man!* Having done so, back *him*—fool or tyrant though he may be."

"Maybe the Paks," Ricky said, "are just bluffing you. After all, they *also* have economic problems—a messy government—political divisiveness——"

"*Paks!*" Lampur chuckled over the word. "We do not believe they are bluffing. We are sure they want more than a plebiscite. Sure they mean to create chaos in the North so as to seize our only good power-source, our water supply—and destroy our hope of becoming the *actual* bulwark of freedom between

Red Russia with Red China—and all humanity. And, *since we believe it—our belief will govern our actions.* It must! Not Mr. Dulles's prefabricated opinion of what he thinks we ought to believe, since *he* does."

"Must be a lot of kinetic energy in the rivers in Nepal," I suggested.

Curzon took that one: "And Nepal borders Red China! India has to consider the massive and growing power of Red China, as well as Russia. Beyond Nepal lies one; beyond Afghanistan, the other. Also—Nepal is not India's 'Goa'!"

"Mr. Dulles," I agreed, "sure put his foot in his mouth, there."

Mme. Parta began to speak—quietly, "I am from Bombay. This matter of the head of your State Department defending Portugal's Goa was horrible, in its effect, in Bombay. We Indians, with our bodies and our bravery and our passive resistance and the great Gandhi, have thrown off colonialism. We Indians who bled under it, a thousand years. Now—we are *free!* The English were beaten by our means; they had to withdraw. So— today they are equal, and as brothers! We won—we love them. We remember the good they did and forget the evil *because* we threw off their yoke. Very human of us, if not logical."

She smiled to herself. "But now the Red world tells all our people that America will be the next colonial power. The next greedy, crushing tyrant. The thing we fear most! The Red world says, 'Only Communism can save you weak Asian billion people from American colonialism.' So then what happens? Mr. Dulles guarantees Goa. He talks of 'power vacuums' still! To us, that means the United States *will* sustain colonialism. So—the billion people nod to themselves and agree: 'The Communists are right! America talks liberty—but America supports colonialism, the thing Asians hate most. You support Goa and Portugal's Salazar. Franco, even! Arab 'states'!"

Ro spoke, for the first time during the meal. "I do not believe even one of my medical school associates in fifty believes anything different!"

So she was a medical student! Seeing her, perhaps most

Americans would conceive it a waste. A doctor, even a good one, even a great medical research genius, would be thought a lesser achievement for a brunette so beautiful she could, with her face and figure, her voice and manner, earn millions in Hollywood or on TV. Why squander on medicine a bust-waist-bottom ratio that would finally satisfy all tape measures?

"What year are you in?" I asked Ro.

"Junior. I begin internship a year from this May."

For a while, the conversation concerned school and family. The Lampurs and their guests were delighted to learn that Ricky and I had started planning this journey solely to see a grandson. Our innocent lack of intent to engage in political observation amused them. Nevertheless, we had become involuntary emissaries from our country—ambassadors without portfolio, or even conventional briefing, reluctant diplomats and not at all diplomatic! Yet—who goes anywhere abroad that is not watched, questioned, judged as his nation's representative? Ricky and I had no doubt better opportunities than some. And more curiosity. And perhaps we picked up more cues.

I'd begun to think Mrs. Lampur was the least-talkative Parisienne I'd ever met. But she entered into the discussion of family and schooling with enthusiasm enough to make up for her reticence. It also occurred to me, later, that she'd let the talk go on because her husband, her son and Ricky and I were so interested in it and (since the luncheon was proving so "successful") perhaps to rest a weary mind. Ricky often does that, when some guest of ours runs with a topic, like a quarterback returning a punt. Jeanne Lampur, moreover, ran her household—and many large organizations outside it. She was probably always so tired she enjoyed not having to "make" conversation.

For coffee (and a cigar accepted only by Mr. Jundra) we moved to a screen porch. Ricky admired the cactus garden. She and Jeanne held a brief, murmured talk on horticulture—and other matters of concern to them.

I said to Lampur, who seemed suddenly sleepy, "About Pakistan. Grant all you say. Suppose we gave India a dozen atomic bombs. Mere fifty kilotoners. And let the world know?

Such an 'arms-to-*India* program' would not menace Russia or Red China. But it *would* insure India protection against Pakistan." He was listening with wide, delighted mirth, his sleepiness gone. I continued, "It seems to me a neighborly idea. I know quite a few very influential people in our government and I'll try to talk them into it. We could spare that many bombs. We'd never miss 'em."

He slapped his jodhpur-clad thigh. "Wonderful! That will certainly beguile my colleagues." Then he sobered. "Wylie, if America really did offer the bombs—and I hate to spoil your joke—we would refuse them."

"Why?"

"Because we, in the government, and most of our people do not believe in force. We believe education alone can make men free. *Remember* that! Take it home and *write* it, if you get the chance. We believe liberty is, above all, a condition of the inner man—and force, even its *menace*, diminishes that condition. If we must fight Pakistan, we will. Red China, Russia—we can never fight." He sighed slightly. "I daresay, if I—speaking just for myself—did not at least hope you Americans, with a force that cancels out Red force, *still* had that 'inner sense' of human freedom—I would not even try to make a great, free India! And often nowadays it is *only a hope*, in me."

"America," I said, repeating a statement I've made at home in print—one I kept making constantly on this journey— "doesn't yet know she's lost her physical might—and doesn't yet know she has to fight for her existence with the weapon of her ideal. When she learns that, you can *count on America*."

Lampur shut his eyes. "If India fails," he mused quietly, "Africa goes next. And you're in a worse position to represent freedom, for black Africans, than for us brown people—you Americans! After the Dark Continent, South America. Parts of Europe also. Finally, you and Britain, standing alone, will be facing defeat by starvation. By then, 'economic sanctions' will be run the other way. Don't your people see that the world of communism is equal to the 'West' in power, *now*? Don't they see *that* every nation that slips behind an iron curtain—or a bamboo curtain—thereupon 'has the H-bomb'? That is, no matter what it loses, it shares the power to smash the United States? Don't they see that?" His eyes opened, blazing.

"Not yet."

"It's true. And you Americans would benefit by musing over all such truth. In a sense, the 'colored people of the world' are 'getting the Bomb.' Or wanting it. Why? To make themselves equal to white men. So, whatever happens to liberty— 'white supremacy' is done for! The day of the supremacy of Western, Christian civilization is also ended. A Western civilization of free men associated with free Asians could defeat Communism—easily." His burning gaze held on me. "As you so wisely know. Freedom could achieve that victory more easily and less expensively than your world now pays to lose—with diplomacy and by trade, and by a delusion of superior might. But if you continue to insist on Western Christian 'triumph'— on a Dulles sort of 'morality' set ahead of freedom—you are doomed." He shrugged. "And so are we."

"I know," I answered, "that freedom's all we have to offer, that the non-Christian free world cares for—except trade."

"If you still have freedom!"

"I think we do."

Then Ricky made the most effective statement of the day. "What you don't realize, Mr. Lampur, is how much India is like America, when America was trying to become free and independent. You're too close to the struggle. You don't see—perhaps—what our 'heritage' will mean in India—and still means, to us."

"I don't quite understand." He seemed hurt—as if "not to understand" was painful.

Ricky's face was alight. "We've been reading the Delhi papers every day. Following all the debates in your Parliament. And do you know what they are? They are almost exact replicas of the arguments that went on in the First Continental Congress! And afterward. Fights among the Federalists and Whigs and the rest. Among delegates from the thirteen colonies. They said the same sort of things that delegates from your provinces say. For similar reasons. The problems of law, local rights, central authority—all that—were battled out in America, in the eighteenth century, as you are battling them, today. You have another religion, yes. But you're even getting puritanical—as we did! You're free—so you start outlawing and restricting. Vote for prohibition—all that. Does liberty scare people into repression?" She shrugged. "Anyhow—you Indians are very like Americans!"

She stopped. Lampur and the rest were silent. Finally our host said, "That's a most remarkable insight. Jefferson—Burr—Adams—Hamilton—!" His eyes shut again and seemed to be pulling out a file labeled: American History. "America, also, was organizing a nation after throwing off—colonial Great Britain!"

Mrs. Lampur laughed. "You mean, you people actually read the proceedings of our Parliament? How tiresome—and childish—it must seem!"

"I've heard the comparison made before," Ro said, speaking apologetically, to me. "Aren't the differences far greater than the similarities?"

"Ask Ricky," I said. "It's *her* idea. She never mentioned it before."

"The *point*," Ricky said, "is not the similarities or the differences. Not *detail*, at all. The *point* is that any Congress in session in USA *now* is no more agreed, or even any more sensible. It's still a bickering, childish process. Almost any *one* day's record, would sound like the talk of nitwits, bigots, even felons—and vaudeville actors. But—the *point* is, *that's* democracy. That's self-government. That's what you have, in Delhi's Parliament, and what we had, and it's how we'll govern ourselves as long as men are free. No sample sounds like much or looks efficient—but when you add it all up, for, say a hundred years—well . . . !"

Lampur said softly, "*Thanks*, Mrs. Wylie! And if I ever forget that—I hope *I* never speak again!" And he looked at her—looked, and looked, till she flushed.

And after a while, Ricky and I departed.

It was four o'clock. Rudely late—but our hosts and the guests had not noticed the time, either, though fatigue came in their faces like a quick curtain, when the hour was announced.

Other pressing duties surely awaited them; perhaps we'd cost Lampur his nap—or, perhaps, a half-dozen skipped appointments.

At the car, he said, "Know Mr. Cooper?"

"Our ambassador?"

He nodded. "Great man. Doing a fine job. Understands India. We were grateful for Bowles. Cooper's like him, and maybe more so. If State would only——"

"Only what?"

"Your State Department," he shrugged, "is a sort of one-man show, isn't it? I'd rather hate to be a discerning American ambassador, these days!" Then, as we thanked Jeanne, as I promised young Curzon to lunch with him and we bade the others good-bye, Lampur grabbed the handle of our taxi door, as if to detain it by force. "Thank you for an exhilarating lunch, Wylies! My spirit is higher, because of it! Would you . . . ?"

We waited.

"I don't suppose you *could* stay in India? A man like you, lecturing at Delhi University . . . ? We'd pay your expenses gladly! *Anything* . . . !"

I told him of the duties at home that would demand me, in a few more weeks.

"Then come *back* soon."

We said we'd try to; and when the car started, he clasped his hands and bowed over them in the benediction of namasker. . . .

Ricky and I had made the Agra trip without much expectation. We had not greatly anticipated the postcard-trite Taj. A splendid journey, though. With our murderous-looking Sikh we'd ridden the hundred and fifty miles, through the guidebook-advertised novelties. Amazed.

Here, for robins, they had green parrots on the road; for squirrels, monkeys; for Chevrolets, Chevrolets *and* camels, besides that—water buffaloes for Cadillacs—and, coming back, clear in the headlamps, a jackal for . . . whom?

We'd tarried in villages and looked—with book knowledge and the new knowledge imparted by India's doctors, teachers,

officials—into mud chambers and markets and upon the people
. . . well-going, pot-toting, dung-burning; babysitting, buying,
selling, courting, quarreling, gossiping and burping, even as you
and I.

The Taj, we'd thought, the damned Taj, would surely be
one of those things. One of those things you daren't miss because everybody will ask forever afterward, Did-you-see-it? And
you must say yes, to comfort them; for it may be the only "must"
they know of in all India! And did you kiss the Blarney Stone?
Proceed through the (icy, murky, chant-eroded cave called)
Notre Dame de Paris? Saunter in the Roman Forum? Climb
Eiffel Tower by elevator? You have to look at Niagara Falls,
God-knows-why, and the Taj, we imagined, "likewise": a check-
off line on a list, falling between Red Fort, The, and Akbar,
Tomb of.

Ricky didn't say anything. . . .
I sat down on a bench inside the gate.
A student we'd hired to show us Agra respected our silence. The Sikh driver we'd had for some days stayed in the
background although I believe he had come in to watch us behold.

The sky was blue: Shiva must have scrubbed the sky. The
time was noon. There was no water in the reflecting pools, as
they were being cleaned; but perhaps it was just as well. Attention was fixed on nothing but the Taj Mahal.

We had walked through the splendid entrance, contrived so
the visitor does not see the tomb until he sees it whole. It hit
me the way it has millions of others.

Ricky came to sit beside me on the stone bench. . . .

The latitude of Agra is about twenty-seven degrees; it lies
north of our home in Florida but not far enough north to matter much: at noon in March there are few shadows. Light falls
beautifully in early spring when there has been a sweep of north-
west weather in that latitude and the sun—pure white, not yellow—strikes through a lucid atmosphere that seems to magnify
objects, float them, and give besides a razor edge to every

boundary. Agra now had such weather—excepting that its blue, blue sky contained fewer clouds at greater intervals. Palace-sized clouds, white as the breasts of angels, sailing on a painted fable —as if the daydreaming Architect Himself, seeing what man had here contrived breathed an appropriate background on celestial canvas—not in Old Testament arrogance, but with indulgence, appreciation—even pride.

In the foreground of the Taj stood a bauhinia, a tall orchid tree, every blossom matched to the occasional big clouds, a full, spring-blooming explosion of wastrel beauty—rare, yet familiar to us as the pink, ordinary oleanders, ranked beside the long, drained pools.

Here was a lovely deliberate statement of the truth as true in reverse: here man had equaled Nature and affectionately mocked her, using Nature's hardness and heaviness to create an earth-anchored cloud not surpassed in the sky.

I have burst into tears on first reading a poem . . . not Homer's compulsory *Iliad* . . . a poem like, *These, in the day when heaven was falling* . . . on reading

on revelations of what-men-call-God

on seeing a sky

a certain child

on hearing music

occasionally (every week when I was young and maybe once in two years now that I am not)

I've bawled. . . .

I wept as I sat on that bench and looked at the Taj Mahal.

What it "said" took a moment to translate from the apperception of blood, glands, marrow and organs into words the brain needed.

This, I thought, states the love of man for woman.

Here in the medium of precious stone and marble, the medium of an utmost human skill which clothed a body of alabastrine rock with a rock lace, a man said in the whole of his best idiom:

Woman.

And that is one level of the message.

The next says:

Woman: ergo love.

There is nothing else to say. This way of saying was never attempted so truly before—let alone so well achieved—in the stony fiber of Mother Earth herself.

Here is the fable of it that is no fable:

Once upon a time there was a good Shah named Jahan whose wife was the most beautiful of women since Lilith. She was called Mumtaz Mahal. When she died he determined she should have a unique immortality, wherefore he summoned many architects who designed countless models of love—all of them transcendent. But only one satisfied Jahan and he commissioned its dreamer (who so deeply understood the Shah and the woman) to keep her forever living, on a marble couch, wooed forever by the phalluses of the four winds. Those were so erected that not the heaving jealousy of Earth herself could bring harm to Mumtaz by deflecting her four lovers in one. And they have been faithful to her for three hundred years, and more.

Woman, it says, and *love.*

It says, for this worth of woman, man loved this much and was this much loved in turn and kind.

And I wept.

The eager-beaver student guide, perhaps owing to sensibilities acquired from the West, looked away.

Ricky saw me and smiled, for there is no possible communion except by act.

The Sikh was different.

His doughty profile and black, box-shaped beard might have been chiseled from the boastful monument of some old Assyrian or Persian: image of Ashur-bani-pal, Tiglath-pileser, Sargon. His blue turban disclosed the upswept line of his sacred long black hair. And surely he had a Sikh's two souls. In him, his warrior-soul seemed to predominate until . . . until he would turn to answer a question or indicate any interesting thing. Then he showed us in his eyes his other soul. For these Sikh eyes were heartful, mild, whelmed with affection: his gaze was a philoso-

pher's stone, a gem (like the Tajstone) that translated the dross
of hostility and the emblazoned fire of courage to love consummate and consummated love.

Now, every Sikh has "Singh" in his name and it means
"Lion." This one, like many, asked in his scant English that we
call him just Singh. Singh, a driver of cars.

He stood diffidently, behind us, and even a pace behind
the brightboy guide from downtown Agra, and he watched me
weep with those mild, enwondered eyes (such as true Christians
will lift up on Judgment Day to see Truth).

He *knew*.

Perhaps there is no Hindu warrior-word for love; perhaps to
half a Sikh one word suffices for love and conflict.

But there are many other soul words for woman and for the
man-woman meaning.

He knew I did not wish to conceal tears or display tears. He
knew I did not mind his seeing any more than the marble
Mumtaz-woman minded the rain in the monsoons.

He looked to see and saw. I dare believe he expected what
he saw.

A nonword in the center of his dual vocabulary was perceived as that *same* word, phallus-written for me long ago in
Massachusetts on the living parchment of a mother's womb,
where he had learned it and all men learn it but so few remember, or recognize, when they see it again in any conscious language of whatever loveliness.

So I looked back at Singh with the passive part of the look-
that-understands-the-other. Then I snorted my nose to exorcise
the prelanguage phrase and to restate my mundane maleness—putting away my ceremonial handkerchief afterward, with care, for
it contained an indelible homage to one man and one woman
for knowing one another's love as all should, and for his saying
their wisdom in a marble reminder: God is ascetic in thought, in
doing aesthetic, but in being—ecstatic.

The college-talking guide took us on. We did what they all
do, buying a flower to lay on the pseudo sarcophagus and march-
ing flowerless around the true coffin below.

Then—the Red Fort and Kodaks, the jewelbox tomb that architects find more "perfect" who cannot discern how imperfection makes completeness, in a woman, as in cosmos.

We turned thence to the residence of the Commissioner of Agra. . . .

I have an English friend, much loved, brilliant, who writes books. He is a small man, bald, roundheaded, given to smiling and clipped understatement. Alec, his name is. I knew him for years before I knew that underneath the tweed that seemed to cover frailty was a knotted cricket champion. After I knew that, I was not astonished (only worried) to hear he gave his English answer to Hitler and the worshipers of Wotan, as a Commando. This bandy-legged, stooped, sparrow-voiced Briton helped ravish an oppressed continent, removing oppressors one at a time, or ten, with the bloodthirsty aplomb, the invincible poise of the too-long-tormented meek.

Alec has a leather chair at Lord's where he will watch out his old-age cricket unchanged; no matter what he does he looks as if he'd spent his life in sedentary rehearsal. There is, however, not room on his skimpy chest for his medals. He is, besides, wise in so many matters he would be a branded scholar had not his inner scamp refused all cramping kudos.

John Lall reminded me of Alec, once-removed, by a mere tint.

I did not merely like John, as we met: I knew John. His wife came in—wearing a dusky sari that flared with color when she moved, and Ricky and I had this identical thought: the blood of Mumtaz ran true, still. She was beautiful.

They had asked us for lunch. Because of Lampur, Amrit Kaur and others, and because I know an Alec now, whatever his costume or caste, I could talk as to a friend. So could Ricky, and they. Two lovely Lall children sat down with us. Questions came. We recited our experiences, reviewed such information as we'd gathered—and they added Alecian insights. They took our photograph in front of the sweet-pea vines.

They, too, urged us, as we reluctantly began grateful good-

byes, to stay in India, or come back—urged us to speak in universities, on park platforms, or anywhere, of the freedom America *was*, and may still *be*, that India would become. Also we
"talked Max"—the universally luminous topic of my brother,
whom John had not met but knew through Arthur Lall's enthusiasms that were a quarter-century old, yet almost as bright this
day, at secondhand, as then face-to-face.

When they found we intended to drive the hundred and
fifty miles back to New Delhi, they pressed us to stay for the
night and, at the least, for tea and when we would not stay,
they tried to furnish us with a Thermos of tea—just as Alec
would have, being unable to imagine how even an American
could make do in the afternoon with a Coke, or with nothing.

We in turn took colored photographs of the John Lalls
(though not, alas, of the enchanted Lall children), standing in
front of the sweet-pea trellis that is forever England, Alec, Lall,
liberty and some very brave wisdom.

Finally we drove away, parting as brothers and sisters.

We should go back to India!

If not Ricky and not I are able—other Ricky-Phils, from
America, must go to assure these people how our sires, at Bunker
Hill, Bloody Shiloh and Belleau Wood and elsewhere, shored up
with deeds a triumph not sufficiently defined as General Motors.
They need the exact news.

We stopped once more in Agra at a shop where the lineal
heirs of the ornamenters of the Taj used the same skill, six hundred years kept secret, to inlay marble boxes and dishes. We
watched them spin wheels with their toes, incise patterns and—
without measuring—shape stones to fit: jade, lapis lazuli, carnel-
ian, alabaster, agate, bloodstone, jasper, onyx. We bought a few
and then dismissed the pay-happy guide. Singh took us along the
slope of afternoon to Akbar's last residence, so we could see it;
and he waited with a soft smile so Ricky could romp with the
monkeys there.

North toward Delhi. . . .

A storm came up. Early, Singh said, for such a precursor of
monsoon.

We'd noticed, in the morning, that they were chopping down great trees which lined the narrow macadam. (So narrow that two cars could not pass and we rode the three-hundred-odd miles in fearful awareness of the means locally employed to keep fast-driving Singhs respectful of beast and man—but heedless that on an ordinary day at home, merely being in a car that long at that pace on such a road would have left us prostrate, heedless because learning India even a little is a process without ordinary days.)

The wind spun its tops across arid land: dust-devils that twirled through the villages, hit mud huts and collapsed. Rain soon fell. We could see the sad walls erode and watch people taking refuge in way stations and houses. Dark eyes flashing from darker glooms that sheltered men, women, children, domestic animals, haulage animals, all skinny, sacred beasts. Carts and loads were left exposed to the elements: nothing alive.

The wind rose. The rain increased. Human habitation began to melt and flow in human streets. Lightning skewered India a thousand times. As we sluiced through jet-stream gale and muddied rain, Singh ran off on a shoulder suddenly and stopped hard, casting back eyes no longer mild, but concerned for us. I was about to ask why he stopped when a huge tree tumbled onto the road. We might have been under it if our driver had not known that every sudden pickup of a gale turned these huge trees to menace: they were rotted in the heart and fell easily, often killing. That was why they were cutting them down in the morning, and also making places for new plantings of a safer shade.

Night came all at once, cutting vision as the breath's cut by garrote. But the car surged on; village after village continued.
Night villages.

Not towns lit up and garrulous like those passed on entering Calcutta. Different.

In some, a half-dozen feeble glints showed that one mud hut, in perhaps every dozen, contained a lamp or a candle. In others, illumination was but a single lantern hung in a central place under shelter so any villager who required light, with the

sun gone, could find that gleam and pick out his thorn or bear
her babe.

But many villages had no light at all—not kerosene enough,
tallow or sufficient dung to keep even one spark burning against
night. They stood like deserted places in the tar-paper dark. Our
headlights, alone, descried more than their silhouette:

Life-packed doorways, and mud walls dissolving into arbitrary drains.

The wind abated suddenly, as if choked; the deluge ceased;
but the huts did not disgorge a soul. A brief miracle of part-day
ensued: the clouds split to display a brick-red sunset. After
that, the absolute of night, and villages without means of motion, weird towns, primitive and haunted looking. They might
have been pueblos, rediscovered an eon after the water dried up
and the people perished. Or cliff dwellings that had stood in
vacant silence since massacre extinguished the last light and
human scream. India, bursting with life by day, seeming dead by
night and of a venerable death.

We didn't talk much.

We looked much.

The jackal trotted in our lights like a fox on a sudden-
rounded Adirondack road.

We saw few moving vehicles in all the hundred-and-a-half
miles. And all I remember that Ricky said, for hours, concerned
Mr. Dulles, and, later, a diamond:

Beginning with a sudden chuckle, she asked, "How do
you suppose the Lampurs and Lalls feel about Americans? People with the assorted M.A.'s and Ph.D.'s, of those Indians?
With open-mindedness and understanding and their command
of languages? Their comprehension of the sciences—history, too
—and statecraft? How do they feel when they try to deal with a
corporation lawyer and old-Princeton-grad who evidently thinks
troops, maybe accompanied by Presbyterian missionaries, could
win back Red China any day? How do they even remain *polite?*"

And she also said, much later, "You know, Britian an-
nexed the Punjab. At the time the Kohinoor belonged to Agra,

but it was 'surrendered'—as the English say—via the East India Company. The biggest diamond ever! Yet how very little poorer Agra was, with *that* gone. If the English knew *anything*, they'd have taken the Taj and left the jewel!" She sighed. "But I suppose, if Elgin had got beyond Athens, they'd now own both."

In short, she was thinking, on that interminable drive, about races: the White one, that for centuries imported loot from the Brown and exported—chiefly—contempt. To know some Indians, to think of India, and to be White, makes any journey hard. But after another silent hour or so, we came to a village that had a few electric lights—and another with more. . . .

There was a letter from Max at the Imperial Hotel.

He wrote that mutual friends, Betty and "Doc" Foster, had taken a year's leave of absence from their jobs (she is an associate editor and he, assistant to Rex Johnson, Board Chairman of Nationwide Publishing Corporation) to do "something or other for UN in Beirut." Max wasn't sure that the Fosters would be in Lebanon while we were there—but he thought so.

And we hoped so. We like the Fosters. "Doc" wears the grey-flannel suit and is an "exurbanite" besides. He and Betty help set the style of American production a year or so ahead of consumption and also the style of those American whims the general public calls chic or sophisticated.

But Doc has more heart than the grey flannel usually covers, more depth, a larger sense of responsibility and a larger empathy. That, of course, was why he had taken leave from the fifth most prosperous magazine and book publishing company in the world to give a year doing "something" for UN in the Near East. Betty was with him; and Betty is as modish, witty, well-educated and knowing as the grey flannel wife—and quite a bit more, too!

I sent a radiogram to Doc. He radioed back an incandescent invitation. So our hope was fulfilled.

Excepting the King Gordons in Tokyo, whom we'd seen briefly, we had not encountered a soul we knew since leaving

Hawaii. We were not homesick but we were (if there's such a thing) a little friendsick and the answer from Beirut was heart-warming.

There was, also, an invitation from Ambassador Cooper to visit with him at the Embassy. And more letters from home. (We were astonished at the number of people who followed our itinerary with faithful letters. And when we returned, we found that there had been even more letters—for about a quarter of the mail sent to us was not delivered. Far travelers should therefore not depend on alien postal service.)

We were very tired that night, so we decided after dinner that "paper work" was all we could attempt. Paper work meant several things. When we could, we wrote notes to many friends and to our families. We tried, on the trip, to mail at least one postcard to more than a hundred friends and acquaintances, checking off the names in Ricky's address book. In each new country, also, I bought an assortment of postage stamps, for my three nieces in Richmond.

"Paper work," too, meant posting accounts from cash expense jottings in a daybook and memoranda in travelers' check folders. It meant filing receipts and keeping our list of dutiable purchases up to date for American customs.

We duly called on Mr. Cooper and, after our call, were invited to luncheon at the Embassy. Mr. Cooper is a corporation lawyer, Eisenhower's choice for New Delhi: a man of poise, attractiveness and insight. During our "duty" call he learned what every ambassador and counsel doubtless enjoys most in junketing Americans: we didn't want anything. Not an introduction to some nabob, not help with the local authorities, not a check cashed or even an additional visa. He also learned something about where we'd been and whom we'd seen in India, as well as what we thought.

He understood the psychology of India's strategy versus Communism and India's herculean endeavor to lift itself by bootstraps from barbarism to modernity. We knew the Indians cherished him and swiftly found the reason: he liked and understood *them*. Our invitation to lunch probably rose from the fact that Ambassador Cooper shared many of our reactions to India—on his level of infinitely-more-detailed knowledge.

So we had lunch at the Embassy—formal and elegant. Two career diplomats from our State Department were present, and one or two other people. Mrs. Cooper was such an American wife as a president might conjure up, to complement his ideal ambassador: a beautiful, sophisticated woman with a talent for making every sort of person comfortable with every other sort.

Naturally, there was talk of Mr. Dulles's visit and—by me— of his longer and flamboyantly partisan stay in Pakistan, of his dictation to Nehru of what was (and wasn't) "moral" and his assertion anent Goa—which must have caused a Kremlin fireworks celebration.

Two British guests—specialists on India—were quite candid in their discussion of the man Eisenhower regarded as among the "great" Secretaries of State.

Mr. and Mrs. Cooper stayed out of that!

Mr. Cooper told us that he would soon take off on a speaking tour of all India, visiting every major city and large town, in a "public-appearance" effort to show a skeptical population that America was still on the side of freedom but that Russia and China were not, propaganda and appearances to the contrary.

Our Ambassador would have no cinch! "They throw Franco at me," he said. "Salazar. Peron. Other State Department dealings with other out-and-out tyrannies. But I'm going before this nation—and I'm going to tell the truth. I'm going to explain America as I know America—not as it sounds to Indians these days."

I then recounted my assault upon Mr. Gudra, in the matter of race prejudice and Autherine Lucy.

Mr. Cooper listened with a grin, asked questions, and finally said, "I wish *I* could talk like that, on my speaking trip."

"Why not?"

Everybody laughed: it wouldn't be very "diplomatic" of an American ambassador to go before the people to whom he was accredited and bawl them out as dupes, hypocrites, fools and

mass killers! "Just the same," a guest said, "the difference between getting our true story across and letting the commie line
prevail here could be the difference, in the long run, between
the success of the Communist international and a free world."

I appreciated the "out" he gave me. "Lampur said Africa
would go next, if India eventually went Red."

Some one replied, "Africa may be *first*, by decades!"

"Not enough of us"—The Ambassador began a thesis familiar to me—"know how to fight Communism. Most of us are just
'agin' it, like sin. Which achieves nothing. As a nation, we oppose Red physical power with power. But the strength of Communism comes from applied psychology. And *that*, we leave too
much unopposed. America should have, in India, means and
people to match the leftists, rupee for rupee, broadcast for broadcast, printed word for printed word, truth for lie."

"How much *do* we have?"

A grim chuckle went around the table and nobody answered for a while. Then one of the India experts said to me,
"Shall we say that we're making about one per cent of one per
cent of the effort here in India to apply psychology—as the Ambassador puts it—that Moscow-Peking is making?"

The other expert nodded. "And our one per cent of one
per cent is about one per cent as skillful."

"Congress?" I asked. There was an assenting silence. "And,
of course," I went on, "the Republican Party." They laughed
again. So I looked at the two British experts and said, "I'm like
you. I'm not party-bound. I was ashamed when Ike promised to
stop the Korea effort—just to get the vote of American moms.
Ricky and I have had that tossed at us by Japs, Chinese, the British in Hong Kong, Thais—Indians. 'The only realistic UN effort
to stop Red expansion was ratted on, by the United States, to help
win an election.' That's what they say. I don't know how Ike,
himself, felt. A great soldier who was the first American to walk
out on a war. Pekin said, 'Paper Tiger'—and the tiger acted like
pulp."

"Mr. Wylie." The Ambassador spoke quietly. "Did you
think Truman was a great President?"

"I thought that he was a man with principles and grit. I thought he had far too little education to be President. But I said, when Ike ran, that history would make Truman look a comparative genius if Ike won. I won't withdraw that." I knew it sounded rude. I added, "Truman, in Ike's shoes, might be as uncomprehending today. After all, neither of them seems to understand the Atomic Age. If you don't understand that, you don't know how to be president—don't know whom to trust, what to plan, how to perceive future moves of your adversary." I turned to an Indian expert. "It must be mighty rough to spend decades learning a country—and then see every marvelous possibility mauled and sabotaged by—people who won't even listen to what you know!"

No answer—just embarrassed silence.

After lunch, Ambassador Cooper gave us a letter to Ambassador Heath in Lebanon. "My wife and I stayed with the Heaths," the Kentuckian said, "on the way here. Didn't know them. Heath's a career man—and a fine person. Sitting on the Near East hot spot now. Couldn't have a more able brain, and you'll like him."

I thought it would be interesting to compare an Ambassador like Mr. Cooper, who went from big business to India, with Mr. Heath, a professional. And I also thought Mr. Heath would have to be quite a patriot and quite a "brain" to match my host.

For Mr. Cooper could have been outraged by my bluntness. He was not. Within the limits of protocol (and of the orders and the rejections of his superiors) he planned to do in India what I now vehemently believed should be done—in America's name.

He offered us a car but we'd kept our taxi. . . .

"Wonderful people, those Coopers," Ricky said.

"Sure are. I liked those experts on India, too! It isn't a lot of fun to be a 'Western man,' and live in India—or anywhere else, outside the allegedly free world. And they have to watch their best efforts go up the flue. Congress probably thinks ours are lobbying for money to 'empire-build,' like many gangs that feed off government. But what they want to do, desperately needs doing."

"I suppose," Ricky said sarcastically, "when you get home you can sit right down and show the people of America that they are now responsible for world freedom because———"

"——because they'll lose their own if they don't accept the load? Because they're the only people who *can* accept the challenge of the Reds? No, Ricky. I might try to write *something*. But the American people are going to have to discover their real danger personally, one by one. They're going to have to perceive hot war isn't on the schedule, and the cold war—the idea war— must be won. Or they'll just naturally sink into history as a Red province, in about fifty years. And they're going to have to act from ideals—not to save their hides—or the act will flop."

"Mr. Cooper's tour of India ought to be a big help," she said. "No wonder the Lampurs are crazy about him."

"Sometimes, one good Joe in the right spot can do more than armies. More than the majority of a hundred and seventy-odd million people who don't know the score yet and couldn't care less, at the moment. Cooper's tour will be *something!*"

But the Ambassador never made that tour: an election was approaching.

So, not long after we left India, the GOP decided Mr. Cooper was the Kentuckian likeliest to win a Senate race. Wherefore the President asked him to come home and run.

I was at first bitter (and unjust) about that. How could an *American*—who saw a vital need so clearly and who intended to fill it, give up, go home, and run for the Senate?

Ricky stopped that beef of mine—months later. "You're crazy, Phil! You think people in politics can do anything they believe ought to be done. But Mr. Cooper had no choice! He can't decide to stay in India—if the President wants him elsewhere. After all, who *appointed* him? *Ike!*"

"You mean—a Republican Senate win in Kentucky is more important to the White House, next fall, than India?"

"In a sense."

"Wonderful!"

"Don't you see? Maybe Mr. Cooper *is* the only man with a chance to win that Senate seat. But the politicians, not knowing what Mr. Cooper knows, would figure a dozen men could do as well, at New Delhi." She eyed me hotly. "And maybe some of them *could*. Have you ever thought of *that?*"

"No. What I was thinking is that winning an election and losing the world may be *politics*, but it sure as hell is the *short* form of politics."

"The Democrats do the same things!"

I had to agree. "We need, though, some Republicans *and* Democrats who are Americans *before* they're mere rooters for a local team."

"We always do."

"Damn all generals in the Presidency! All preparers for the war they won, which all generals are, practically. Besides, generals spend their lives dealing with, and kowtowing to, big businessmen—trying to get bigger cannon. So when they turn to politics they're precooked prey of tycoons. And what *tycoon* operates from the fact that every time a Malayan coolie decides the Russian way is better than the American, his Detroit or Cleveland production line is slowed up—his preferred stock is worth less—and he's a touch closer to a not-unimaginable directors' meeting assembled to decide whether to become corpses or commissars?"

Ricky said sadly, "We've heard several business big shots say that if USA goes behind the curtain they'll pop us commissars, in a week."

"Men like that would rather *run something* than *be anything*. Like the Nazis, who work on rockets for Russia, now—or us. All *they* care about is their God-damned 'prestige in their field.' They don't belong to a *nation*—even to the human race. . . . He-whores of technology!"

Ricky knew I could carry that far into the night. "You admire Mr. Cooper. Why not credit him with *all-around* brains? Perhaps he decided he could do *more* for India, and so for America, in the Senate."

I hadn't thought of that—and I felt ashamed. A typical sample of Mrs. W. being fairer than Mr. W.

The things we'd planned to do in each country were often left undone, or put off, owing to other things that cropped up: things bearing on the present state of the world. But sometimes we were just tourists.

Our driver was Singh, still. But our Delhi guide was a sort of Indian new to us. Another tall one and also a Sikh—though with beard, turban and mien of ferocity. He wore a brown business suit and clean white shirts. He was athletically built and "smooth," like some Ivy Leaguers who aim themselves at lucrative marriage —at Bar Harbor, Palm Beach, Cannes.

Mr. Dantu Singh Bomba (I think it was) proved—in short —the Hindu prototype of our "playboy." He knew the terms for the national ideals: democracy, liberty, equality and brotherhood. But to him, they seemed to have the aspect of fads: they were popular, so he conformed. His concern was a good life for *Dan*, as he wanted to be called. He'd graduated from a university, though he felt a diploma was merely a means to personal ends. He had tried several "occupations," but he said they had been too "complex," or too "arduous," or too "unrewarding." He was a guide in his "leisure"—which, I believe, meant any time he needed money.

Nevertheless, he was an excellent guide. His English was superb. He had memorized what other guides recited anent local sights, and history. I suspect that if Ricky had been alone (and a bit different) he would have hinted that Delhi's dancing places —or perhaps its moonlight drives—were more interesting than ruins. If I'd been alone, I believe Dan would have made much mention of the beauty, sophistication and availability of Indian womanhood.

Yet he was not disappointed in the diversions selected by Ricky and me: he was being driven about in a car—he was exhibiting his vast knowledge and charm—and for such pleasures he was being paid.

We toured Old Delhi and visited the refugees from Pakistan—kicked-out Hindus, who live beside crumbling segments of Delhi's ancient wall.

We inspected Kutb-Minar, an Indian Tower of Pisa, but taller, nonleaning, and made of sandstone shaded from orange to red. We saw the Iron Pillar in the ruined courtyard behind the Kutb—a venerable post that never rusts and is said to have been cast from a stainless iron alloy of meteoric origin. It is alleged to be a preventative of and cure for backache! Those who press their spines against the column and wrap their arms around it will never suffer lumbago, sacroiliac, et al. Indian visitors so engaged when we came to the scene were highly amused when one Western pragmatist took a turn. Let it be reported, then, that the curious column doesn't work for Yankees—or doesn't work.

We went to see Gandhi's "tomb"—a huge, low block of concrete, protected by a balustrade and set on a platform, that marks the spot where Gandhi's body was cremated. The number of people who visit it daily must equal the daily world total of people who enter all Woolworth stores! They buy flowers from squatting sellers to put on the slab. A man with a stick pushes the flowers into geometrical designs and as soon as one is complete, he wipes it off to make room for the next floral deluge.

A broad, paved walk leads to the place. As one nears it, shoes must come off. But the flower-disposers use hose to keep the blossom blizzard from blocking traffic. Europeans in that coming-going reverent river check their shoes. For leather is hard to come by in India; it would otherwise be easy to walk off with brogans and abandon cloth sandals. But your socks get soaked.

Something should be done about this no-shoes business! I've often had my feet soaked with cold rain in Tokyo. They've been half frozen by the snows of Nikko and near scorched by temple courtyards, in Bangkok. Plastered with scores of uncomfortable muds—and exposed to alien fungi, bacteria and viruses, my feet have suffered. Herewith, I consequently invent the P. Wylie disposable sock!

My sock is transparent, in order not to be called a shoe and disallowed by some finicky priest. It is thermally *insulating*. Waterproof. And it is cheap. There is often no good way and often no time to launder socks in transit. Yet, after a really busy day in antishoe regions, you can hardly bear to put shoes over your socks, or to take what your socks have accumulated to your hotel for laundering. Mine, you discard on the spot.

Ricky more than once did so dispose of nylons and sometimes went forward with bare, wet feet in wet shoes.

My invention is also lightweight, and highly compressible, as bulk and heft are important in travel. Were I head of public relations at Cooks, American Express, Pan-Am or TWA, in fact, I'd give away the P. Wylie Foot-Chux, suitably stamped with the company name and slogans. The Japanese do provide scuffs to tide you over; some shrines tie cloth-and-cardboard overshoes on you. But few Americans can wear scuffs without losing them; and the overshoes make you clomp through torchlit catacombs feeling like a lead-shod deep-sea diver!

We inspected the Great Mosque that day and, for ten rupees, took a look at Mohammed's prayerbook (tattered), a single filament of his hair (auburn), and his footprint—made in the sand as he drank from a spring and later miraculously converted to stone. (Twelve triple A, approx.)

We studied the mysteries of several Hindu temples popular with tourists, and canvassed Delhi's Red Fort. This establishment contains the home, baths and harem of Akbar—who built another such fort in Agra, just in case.

I was by then deeply oppressed with the luxury and splendor, gaud-piled-on-gaud, which the Asiatic few have long enjoyed at the slavish expense of the many.

On recent similar expeditions my thoughts had become compromising to all-out appreciation of grandeur in dome, minaret, spire, chamber, court, ornament of precious stone or gold, and ornament inlaid in precious stone, or gold or in bas relief: decorated-decor, loud as colored feathers on a macaw. Toomuchness annoys most of us.

And above all the other show of Ind, Cathay or Nippon, the uses and pleasures of concubinage, though discernible to me as a youth, have lost, in the endless seeing of their chambers, the savor they once had. But let me not thus suggest I hold, as many of us do, that concubines are in nature Oriental and/or passée. (Though why men who say they "take the Bible literally" do not also take concubines they will never be able to explain!) A custom of enjoying more women than one wife continues, to this day, and surely will go on as long as our species.

I have had friends who maintained a single concubine in a tidy apartment known as "working late at the office." I have encountered some tycoons—and small businessmen!—who selected their female employees for beauty, grace and a special wisdom; i.e., the lasses they hired were first delicately informed that an occasional act of a concubinal nature would be included in the duty of typing, filing and so on. I even know one hardware manufacturer who considers the better-looking wives of his employees should, ideally, contribute to company morale by co-operating in a special way with their husband's chief. He does not *demand* such acquiescence but it is notable that the husbands of those girls who act as his helpmeets advance rapidly. Indeed, I was asked by one of the man's go-getters for advice on how to win his pretty spouse anew—for his boss. The lady had refused to assist her husband that much.

Classic concubinage rises from that same desire for somebody-else-for-a-change, even if Mrs. America has told herself (and most of her males) that this particular Eternal Verity, by God, better not be revealed unto her! Yet harems are disquieting —and I was put off by Akbar's, or, rather its looted wreck. (Such places in India have always been stripped of valuables by "invaders" and after the "invaders," if anything was left, by Tommy Atkins, the law-bringer.) That, also, disquiets.

But to have on hand, continuously, two or three thousand concubines is wasteful. Foolish. Even Casanova, according to my careful estimate, could have brought joy into the heart of a mere half thousand demoiselles approximately once a year in most cases. So Akbar's extra girls would be certain to pine. One is therefore drawn to the theory that a man with a thousand concubines, or thereabouts, was also a man made cuckold far above the average number of times. What mogul would be able, furthermore, to recall a girl's name and face, from one year (or so) to another? I could only assume the sustainers of such reams of enchantresses were compulsively driven toward making love exclusively with strangers, the queen, or the maharani, excepted. And that seems vaguely neurotic.

People, according to Freud, who lead unsatisfactory sex lives, will inevitably *be* unsatisfied—hence unsatisfactory *as people*. The great doctor was greatly lambasted for that notion. On my part, I always wonder why anybody imagines that an individual can decently "realize himself" (or herself) in the absence of *any* of those needs which, in living creatures, rise from biologic necessity.

It takes a house to make a house, so to speak. Windows alone, doors alone, or shingles in whatever elegant quantity, do not make a house. It must, in the same way, take "all" of a *person*, in suitable, adequate proportions, to make one complete. And I cannot see how anybody presumes a successful culture is conceivable if its mores, its morals or its laws forbid, overlimit or castigate as sin—on theological or even sane grounds—*any* drive or inner wish of its citizens that is natural and would harm no one physically (quite the contrary!). If—for example—a government were to ration water to that least degree required for survival, on religious grounds, the governed people would soon grow tired of the practice, particularly if they lived in a region that abounded in water of every type. Yet we Americans have as our ideal in sexuality, the rationing of its expression to that absolute minimum required for reproductive survival. We even add a biologically ridiculous corollary: the sanctioned marital relations must not involve those most natural acts of living beings which American law defines as crimes *against* Nature! Under such rationing, hardly one American in a million could (or does) achieve a completely satisfying expression of his or her true and total sexuality. Yet America abounds in erotic invitation. It clutters newsstands, and flutters on TV; it is the essence of movies and the principal means used to move goods by advertising. It lolls in person in bikinis on every beach. But to accept what America invites is sin; it makes spouses and relations mad; and it is against the law, besides.

Hence we are like the people I imagined who live in the

midst of lakes, rivers and springs but must confine water-use to that limit absolutely required for mere survival. All such biologically preposterous customs surely guarantee cultural disaster if the rules are enforced. Neither individuals nor societies can long endure a pretense of feigning what is *not* and of refraining from expressing what they are.

The problem has long fascinated me. To consider that aspect of our nature—as we do—intended only for licensed, limited breeding exercises is not the solution. The opposite extreme for males—the harem—seemed as stupid. What is called "permissiveness" by our Behaviorists, and refers to sex acts, does not—alone anyhow—produce the complete life either. For multitudes of Orientals and Asiatics obviously led full, gratifying "sex lives" and felt no induced shame or guilt. The same people, however, usually lived in shanties, lacked a sufficient diet, suffered hugely from disease and went without so many other ingredients postulated even by me for whole human beings, that I could not gauge even the putative benefit of their less-bigoted behavior in this one area.

Yet I could not, like the missionaries, connect all "backwardness" with sexual forwardness, permissiveness, reluctance to wear opaque garments in a hot country, and so on. For, as I said, I know Americans who are loaded with earthly possessions—and yet who outfornicate any Hindu. However, I can never equate in my mind (as our *courts* do) assault-and-robbery with, say, the affectionate impregnation of a willing, even demanding, but slightly minor girl. They are not rationally to be thought of under the same heading: crime.

I suspect the world needs, more than any other, a UN commission to find out how we *ought* to behave, sexually, in order to be *ourselves*. Certainly all past and present oafs, Episcopal, Shinto, Catholic, Hindu, Baal-worshiper, Gnostic or Marxist, have no solution worth a continued try. The UN Commission to find and ordain appropriate sex morals would attract real interest in the important parent body; it would wrangle for decades; and if it solved what, I suspect, nobody has yet even questioned

rightly, enforcement would take centuries. And that is a generous scale of all our folly here—past no more than present.

Now, a word about the part of the Red Fort that was *not*
harem:

The structure had just been used for a public reception of
India's most-loved Britons: Lord and Lady Mountbatten. So the
antique premises were blemished by signs and infinite strings
of Christmas-tree lights. The Government of India evidently
possesses more such lights and more such outdoor wiring than all
other governments put together. I have nothing against Louis
Mountbatten or his wife; but I could not help reflecting, as their
welcome blackened the press and blocked the streets, that no
American could evoke such enthusiasm anywhere outside USA
—and even Khrushchev got a thousandfold better hand than
our people do, in India.

The afternoon was waning and we were deliberating where
to go next when I noticed Dan and Singh in further discussion.

After long debate in their language, Dan turned to Ricky
and me. "You've seen all the main *tourist* temples," he said nervously, "but would you like to see a *real* one?"

He feared his invitation would be refused! It was plain, too,
that he was not in the habit of inviting customers to what, he
added, was his and also Singh's Sikh temple.

Of course, we went.

The temple stood between big buildings on a street brimmed
to the gutters with motor traffic and pushcarts. It reminded me of
Manhattan's Lower East Side. The temple steps were marble, very
wet and very dirty. People intending to enter were washing
themselves—face, hands and feet—at a fire hydrant. We were not
told to wash—but Dan asked Ricky if she had something to use
as a head shawl. She had. He was relieved, for the gay, easy-going
Dan had become serious and somewhat apprehensive. Singh was
also nervous.

We entered the temple. Inside, was a great, dim chamber
where hundreds knelt, where people slept, where whole families
sat quietly—some of them eating. Its walls and pillars were white

marble. They bore Vedantic texts engraved in large, gold letters. Two old men with yard-long beards were conducting a service in a portion of the dim tremendousness. One read a passage which was then responsively repeated by the listeners; after that, the other elaborated on its meaning.

Ricky and I were at once noticed by the multitude. And the people were plainly angered by our intrusion. A man, who had been prostrate beside me, rose. His intent was to stalk from the temple. But as he approached, he caught my eye, and I smiled at him in the way I felt: apologetic but interested, embarrassed, and certainly not furious, as he was. His pace slowed. He seemed to measure me. Then he bowed a little, looked directly in my eyes again, smiled slightly—and went back to his prostrate meditation.

A priest with a longer and whiter beard than the beards of the murmurous priests sat cross-legged at the head of the altar. Behind him was a glass-and-gold case full of garlands and images. He sat so still I first took him for an effigy. Above the congregation, wooden-bladed electric fans turned slowly: the sort that used to revolve above the wire-backed chairs and wire-legged tables in ice cream parlors. The fan blades were white enameled; on each, in black, was a Vedantic text. I suppose the turning, like the turning of Mongolian prayer wheels, was presumed to say a prayer with each revolution. But who could laugh—unless he also was convulsed by every sprinkled drop of every Christian baptism?

There was nothing absurd about the mood of the people. Like Buddhists, they used the temple as a family gathering place, but, unlike some Buddhist gatherings, this one was immensely solemn, even to people eating what we would call a picnic lunch. Ricky, Dan, Singh and I stood apart from the worshipers and were quiet.

By and by, indignant attention diminished. I saw the head priest give a sign of recognition to our guide. Dan then began to whisper the meanings of the symbols; and he translated some of the texts engraved in the white pillars that lofted up to dim nothing. What he explained was not unfamiliar to us, but, rather, much too simplified. So I told him a little about certain other temple symbols and Vedantic verses—whispering the old philosophy and discussing various Hindu deviations.

His astonishment at what I read long ago was equal to mine at the sudden awe in our playboy guide. After some further talk, he went over to the high priest and spoke softly. Then he hurried into an alcove. A dusty pamphlet was in his hand when he reappeared. It gave an account, in English, of the Sikh Guru for whom the temple had been founded—a man of incredible bravery subjected by the Moslems to tortures I do not want to think about, even now.

Dan and I—with Singh listening—continued to talk about the beliefs of Hindus. Then, again, he left us again to confer with various people. There was nothing frivolous about the guide's Faith! No one could have feigned the reverence he displayed here. He must have spread word through the congregation that Ricky and I were no mere curiosity-assuagers, but people who respected the temple's ethos, understood its principles, knew of its symbology. For within a few minutes, faces that had greeted us with anger turned to us again, serene and warm.

"*They* want you," Dan said after a while, "to be welcome. Singh and I welcome you to our temple, also. You are to be welcome here *forever*."

And I found myself knowing that we would be welcome there "forever."

When, finally, we moved to leave, I reached in for my bill clip: near the exit was a glass-faced recess in which were heaped coins and a few bills, illuminated by an indirect lamp or a candle. Beside that offering-box a guardian Sikh had stood, still and straight as the sentries at Buckingham, all the time we were there.

Dan saw my gesture. Gently, he caught my arm. "It is not necessary. The other temples, yes. Here, you are guests. Besides, your understanding is a great honor. The priest is in a heightened state, owing to the visit of both of you and to what you told me."

I protested. "From temple offerings you Sikhs feed and

clothe and instruct your poor. You probably donate some regular part of all you earn, and so does Singh. And here, we, too, have had a 'heightened experience.' I have seen people who hated me for what they thought I was doing, change their looks to affection merely because they know we respect the heart of their great ethical system. We have been moved here by that—by their way, in space and time and God, toward us. And the belief of our people, we also know, owes its origin to yours."

That quotation is not verbatim, but I spoke as eloquently as I could. For I *was* moved: it is the thing that always moves me most: the love that empathy elicits from humanity, the truth in that, and the freedom.

Dan took his hand away.

I stripped some rupee notes from my bill clip and started toward the glass-and-gold receptacle. But the oldest priest had turned. He made a gesture, as if to stop me. Dan whispered rapidly, in Hindi, and the patriarch smiled, turning away, after a moment.

So I dropped in my bills.

The Sikh guard instantly prostrated himself, brow to stone floor, and lay still.

Then the high priest stepped down and approached Ricky, his arms flower draped. Ricky bent her head. Then it was my turn. The whole congregation was watching in utter silence.

Next the priest beckoned Dan.

"No," Dan whispered, in English! "I only *guided* them here."

"Son," the priest answered, "it was a fine deed."

"But I do not merit the—" he went into Hindi.

I could guess the aged man's response: "Today, you do."

So the pleasure-loving, lazy big kid bowed, with tears in his eyes, to be garlanded. After him, our lowly driver, Singh, the Lion, trembling like a leaf.

We went out, festooned with flowers.

People halted us on the temple steps. I believe that word of our visit had spread outdoors. For old women with cloths and pans of water made us wait till they finished a hurried labor: the temple steps had been scrubbed snow white and now were dried. I felt as if I'd walked into the Old Testament—and found favor. We bowed to the people and they made namaskers. When we got into the car again, the whole street watched our garlanded departure—silently, affectionately, and everyone seemed a little surprised, pleasantly.

I didn't look at Ricky for a long time.

I didn't dare to.

10
the land of Canaan

India is a long way from Miami, Florida. Karachi is a long way, too, and even Beirut is quite a piece, but when the Air France plane curved over the sea I felt a change. To me, it was as if we had come suddenly quite near home, and though the sensation was lost later, that first sight of the Mediterranean established a connection. I knew the rest of the way home—though southern France was the nearest I'd been to Asia Minor, save for one glimpse from Russia.

As Ricky and I had traced our trip in the months of its planning, poring over globes and maps, I'd repeatedly put a finger-of-the-mind on Beirut and told myself: *When you get there, you'll have made it.* The great Pacific would be crossed; Japan, the Orient, Asia behind us—all the unknown places. And here was Lebanon.

The dawn-pasty but grinning faces of Betty and Doc Foster stood out in the crowd at the airport. They emphasized my illusion: *People* from home, old friends. Connection became complete, for a little while.

We hugged each other. Doc helped me swing suitcases into his station wagon. Betty, gay and pretty as ever, launched into an immediate, determined exposition of why we should not use our hotel reservations and be their guests, instead. A son and daughter were with them, taking a year out from American universities to attend the famed University of Beirut; so the apartment was commodious.

We hadn't intended to oppose any such proffered hospitality. Twenty thousand miles, even of the best hotels available, gives a good sound to "guest room." The intimation of a friendly veranda and a living room where strangers would not be sitting, of a kitchen one could enter to make noninstant coffee, or fry an egg—who'd resist much?

The car hurried, paused for a spectacular view of sea and mountain and moved into the city. Pastel stucco walls, tile roofs, a sun-faded sign: "Vins Huilles Savons," and a vista of the worn-out, lived-in hills. A quarter-century vanished for me—and all the miles: I was, once more, a young man (with a published novel) who dwelt in Bandol, in Var, in France, on the Mediterranean. Because nobody could write anything "important" in the Twenties, in Brooklyn or Montclair, New Jersey—nobody young, anyhow—nobody modern.

We stood in the Fosters' living room looking across French rooftops of an Arab city, and across a harbor at mountains beyond it—drinking genuine American coffee, fresh made by Betty.

"We're glad you two guys are here for a special reason," she said.

And Doc explained. "My boss—Rex Johnson—is due tomorrow. With his wife, Margaret. So——"

"Doc has been worried." Betty took over his worry. "We don't know the Rex Johnsons, socially. Also—we have what you call problems, here in the Near East. Like Arab refugees from Israel. Doc hopes Rex will be willing to scout the situation. After all, we've been on this UN job nearly our year! Doc has definite opinions on problems here—not to say, fears. Doc loves his boss; but he isn't sure how the boss will take to Lebanon. With you two around, it'll help. You *do* know Rex, Phil, don't you?"

I knew Rex Johnson, a little. I'd known him for twenty years. Once in a while I'd done a piece for one of the magazines published by his corporation. A short, solid man with a reputation for being "tough"—a word that can have two connota-

tions when it refers to a big businessman: "ruthless" or "coura-
geous." I didn't know which applied to Johnson; I knew only
that he was shrewd and well educated—Harvard, I thought—and
resourceful.

I remembered the last time I'd seen him, too. . . .

Nineteen fifty, maybe, or 'fifty one. Washington had decided
people in publishing, and radio, didn't properly understand the
implications of the Atomic Age. I'd been tagged to brief some
magazine editors and publishers on the topic. And Rex was one.

I completed my nuclear spiel by walking to the window of
his office and indicating, from forty storeys up, just where in the
Manhattanscape the rim of "total destruction" of a twenty kilo-
toner would be, if Nationwide's skyscraper were Ground Zero. It
was a fairly effective way of showing—quasi-officially—the new
order of reality in the world, of showing it at a time when men
like Seversky (who should have known better) had convinced
some publishers and some editors (and thereby far too many
common people) that the new Age wasn't really "different."

That effort of mine got to Rex. He'd heard me out stonily,
till then. But after I showed him from his own office what the
littlest A-bomb would do to his city, Rex strode to the bleached
mahogany plateau that was his desk and sat down hard. He looked
a long time at the city, himself the center of a great crater, di-
sheveled edifices all around, and a fire storm roaring. His face
slowly turned dark red. Not pale with apprehension but crimson
—with, perhaps, rage at what an enemy could do, or, possibly,
humiliation at his prior lack of understanding. He looked that
long, long time and said, "Yes, Phil, you're right. The Magazines
we publish ought to take a new tack on this thing. They will."

And they did. . . .

While I was remembering, Ricky said suddenly to Doc,
"You mean we've got *another* refugee tour to go through? I
didn't realize there were any here."

"That," Doc answered, "is the point. That's why *I'm* here,
in a way. Starting about eight years ago, the Israelis forced nearly
a million Arabs out of Palestine."

"How?"

"Intimidation. Attack in some cases. Those people have been refugees ever since—in Egypt, Jordan, Syria, here. And I want *Rex* to see them. Talk to them. You, too! But it may be hard to get Rex on such a trip. I can't picture him in messy places. Will you help me persuade him? Will you both go along?"

We sat on their porch a while and then went to our room to unpack.

"I'm sorry," Ricky said.

"Sorry?"

"More refugees. Can you take it?"

"Sure. They can't be worse than the ones in Hong Kong."

"Betty said it was pretty awful."

"I wonder if Rex can take it? After all, he's a city boy. Used to the best. Doc's always been fifty-one per cent saint. But Rex may be hard to convert. I just don't know."

Ricky sighed. "I felt—oh—let down, a little. I thought we could be sort of carefree for a few days here. Go see Damascus, and Baalbek, and Byblos——"

"We will."

"But you're so tired!"

She didn't say *she* was. She said I was.

Betty and Ricky stayed in the car.

Rex and I were conducted along mud wallows and cobbles, "streets," that might just have emerged from a flood. Footpaths, really. The car couldn't pass through them.

Doc and the UN official—a refugee Arab—led the way past "houses" where they'd lived for eight years: men and women, teen-agers, little kids, who walked along in our wake, silently, watching us look at them, at their "houses." Hovels with dirt floors and walls made of anything available—much like those of the Chinese fugitives from Communism in the streets of Hong Kong. But this village was outside Beirut. Not even the walls of somebody else's real house cut the wind, or gave an illusion of

shelter and the fact of somebody else's security. This was a hobo
jungle on a city dump. And the people wore rags hoboes would
discard.

"We inspected" the UN dining facilities, which were the
meagerest imaginable. A meal a day there, basic, measured, mo-
notonous. Added calories doled to the old, the ill and the very
young; less to the able-bodied. This is the science of dietitians: to
keep millions as close to starving as strong bodies will bear—for
economy's sake, the UN's till. There were no fat refugees, no
plump ones and no happy ones. Israel, and the United Nations,
too, had promised to compensate them for lost homes, property,
farms, groves and places of business. But they had had no com-
pensation; just this subsistence at a level of hardship that would
be intolerable to most Western people.

I stood in my slopped shoes shaking with hate of myself—
and of you, yes *you*. For who do we think we are that claim to
have brains, talk of our bleeding hearts and relate ourselves even
to God? We *men*, that let men live like this? You answer, not to
me, damn you! And not your infamous God. Let me hear you answer *yourself*, once.

Yes, Rex and I tramped in the muck, the filth and stench.
Finally, we were led into the "headquarters" where an old, old
man in missionary-barrel pants and a fez had us seated in kitchen
chairs—with the grace of an emir receiving kings. He was mayor
of this Slimeville.

The room had a wooden floor, bare walls and no heat. That
day, though sunny, was cold: about fifty degrees. Men hastened
into the room, bringing boxes to sit on, old chairs, chair bottoms
—or nothing: other old men, middle-aged men and young, filing
in silently until there were a hundred Arabs, or so. Rex and I
hadn't expected this "audience," hadn't been told what to expect; we exchanged glances that said so. Doc sat frowning, ab-
stracted, as if he knew what was coming and had no intention of
telling us, or perhaps was not sure and trying, in consequence, to
conceal anxiety.

The room was packed to the door, with more men outside,

rising on tiptoe to look. Thin, totally silent men who reeked of dirt and something else, which frightened. *Hate*.

The village headman pulled open a drawer in the bare table behind which he sat and produced obviously precious cigarettes, with obvious pride. He offered them, ceremoniously. Rex took one and I did. An Arab of about thirty-five in the front row—a good-looking man—struck a match for us.

Then coffee came.

I thought Rex flinched a little and I felt a squirminess now familiar: this wasn't a place to touch food.

The cups were small and unmatched. The coffee would be thick and sweet, according to *The Seven Pillars of Wisdom*. Nobody said anything while the stuff was poured and passed to the headman, Doc, our UN guide, Rex and me. I knew (and I thought Rex knew) this was the Arab welcome. I picked up my cup and made a half-toasting gesture to the village mayor, who did the same, with no smile.

I sipped. My tongue touched a semisolid in the sweet-sticky brew—something chewy and odd-tasting, an insect, I was sure: cockroach, hard grub, weevil. I got it down—and encountered two more of the nasty larvae.

Rex blanched. I saw it. (Our hosts had no place or way, I reflected, to keep food free of infestation.)

I took a new grip on my gagging guts and gulped the rest. To refuse an Arab's coffee, I knew, would insult him.

Rex not only swigged his, maggots and all, but he beamed afterward as if it satisfied his deepest desire.

I assumed our guide from UN would now translate. These strange men in remnants of Arabian clothing that was mixed with castoffs of the Western world—these silent men with eyes as black as tar and hot as fire—they'd said nothing. Surely, they could not speak any language but Arabic.

So I was startled—Rex, also—when one of them began.

"Mr. Johnson and Mr. Wylie," he said, "we are here today, to ask *why* we are here. Why we have been here for eight years. We ask you why the nations of United Nations have not kept their obligation? *Or* Israel." His English was good; but the last word, he made sound obscene. And his voice was furiously accusative: I felt he was charging me, in person, with his years, his misery, his rags, and hunger, his terror, eviction and loss.

When he had put those questions in further detail, he stood waiting.

Doc was watching Rex, and Rex was looking at the Arab with candid perplexity. I knew what Rex was thinking. I *said* it, bluntly:

"For one thing, until the other day, I didn't know there were any Arabs still living in exile because they'd been driven out of their homes by the Israelis. I knew there had been trouble, inside Palestine, years back, and some Arabs had fled. But I assumed they were all re-established in Egypt—or Syria—Jordan—or here in Lebanon. I didn't know there were almost a million of you, still in camps, after eight years."

The man was about to answer, but someone behind him took up the matter—also in excellent English:

"Of *course*, you did not know. And why do you Americans not know the truth about us? The mere *fact* of our existence— if you can call this starved hogpen existence? *Why not?* It is simple. Your American press—your whole country—is under the thumb of Zion. Jew-controlled! You cannot, you dare not print a word about us. Dare not murmur a word on your radio. Show a picture of us on your TV. You're Jew-cowed!"

"That," I said, "is hooie."

"Then—why don't you know?"

I looked at Rex, whose face was still baffled. "Why don't I know?" I asked him.

Another Arab shouted, "Yes, Mr. Johnson. Mister Big Publishing Man. *Why?*"

Rex fixed his steady blue eyes on the tight-packed mob; it leaned toward us, an arm-length away. Rex, with a quizzical, half-apologetic smile. "I'm like Mr. Wylie. I didn't realize your problem had gone unsolved. But I can assure you this idea that Jews control the American press is ridiculous."

"Prove it," some one muttered. "When you return, publish our story!"

"I daresay Mr. Wylie might write it, and I'm sure we will publish it."

"Bah!" somebody called. "The Jews will forbid it."

"Mr. Wylie," Rex went on imperturbably, "is among the most outspoken of American authors. I can assure you that nobody in America—not Jews—not *anybody*—ever stopped or *could* or *would* stop Mr. Wylie from writing and publishing his opinions, however unconventional. Let alone *facts* known to him. And Nationwide—that's my company—has published Mr. Wylie's opinions for—how long, Phil?"

The first speaker interrupted eagerly. "You would take a chance? Write about us? In the teeth of Zion?"

"*Look*," I broke in, "Americans are self-satisfied, like all successful people. They don't know about you simply because they're too busy with themselves to study all the injustice and wretchedness in the world today. As for Jews, in America I've been known all my life as a man who detests race prejudice. But that includes anti-Semitism. I think I can say that no living American author has attacked anti-Semitism and anti-Semites harder than I. I am a friend of all Jews in that way—as I am of all *people*, the same way—as well as a close, personal friend of several Jews!"

The youngish, good-looking man sneered, "Ah! Then *that's* it. Friend of Jews!" He spat on the floor at my feet.

I dislike people spitting on, at, or around me. But I kept my temper. "I, myself, always thought the Zionist idea was wrong and always said so. I think it's wrong for any people to try to re-create a nation that has been scattered, nonexistent, for more than a millennium. I think all such nationalism is crazy. I think people should try to come together—not to get farther apart, in little hothead nations. I thought it was wrong to try to build an 'Israel,' in a land that had been Arab so long. I thought it was a mistake to try to create a modern, mechanized culture, in a desert. I felt sad and bitter about the homeless remnants of Jewish people left by Hitler—and I detested Nazism—but I did not believe that it made sense to carve out a hunk of Palestine and call it a homeland, to maintain it forcibly and artificially, and to resettle Jewish refugees there. I thought the nations of the world should open their doors to those refugees. And I *said* all that, in print, in America."

"In the American press?"

"Yes. Often. And in books."

There was a pause, now, while the gist was murmurously translated for some of the crowd who did not understand English.

Finally, the man who had spat spoke again, with the utmost belligerence: "What are you going to do for us now, then? When will you get our homes back for us? This, you *must* do."

"Why 'must' we?" I asked.

That question was loudly translated. The room seemed to swell, with a rage the sleazy walls could hardly hold.

Another Arab said in a menacing tone, "If you do not act soon, you treacherous, lying white people, we have our answer! *Russia* will give the Arabs arms. Then Arabs will hurl the Israelis into the sea."

When a murderous murmur died away, I said, "Okay. You're Moslems. I've been all over Russia. I know what happens to your belief, your mosques, your Mohammed, your Koran in Communist countries. If you accept Red arms, you'll become Red slaves. Your religion will be a thing for two hundred million Slavs, and six hundred million Chinese, to spit on. So—go ahead! *Take* Russian arms—drive the Israelis into the sea—and commit suicide. Do you really imagine you can scare *Americans* by shaking Russia at them?"

That further enraged them, of course.

It occurred to me then that there might be a limit to their self-restraint. I could see our UN guide grow pale. The mayor was tugging his beard and staring at his tabletop, panting a little, mouth awry. But I was angry, also. I went on. "Tell me this, you men: Why do you just sit here for eight long years, doing nothing, taking a dole, living like pigs? Why not do something, *yourselves*, for your families?"

Someone roared, "We sit here till we get our homes back."
"Suppose you *never* do?" I said. . . .

A few weeks later, at dinner one night in Rome, Rex said he
thought, when I put that question that flatly, we were going to
be attacked. He said he was pretty sure the idea was there—and
violence mere seconds away. . . .

I knew they were furious—I meant them to be—and I kept
on talking. "My ancestors were driven from *their* homes by religious persecution, by killing and massacre. *They* had to go
thousands of miles, across the Atlantic ocean, to get away. They
built log cabins in the wilderness. And they *never got back home*.
They couldn't go back. What they helped start is, today, the
United States of America. So—when I ask you what you'll do, if
you never get your lands and homes, I am not just tormenting
you. I am an American, whose ancestors suffered more grievously
than you are suffering, for the same reasons; and who could not
regain home or their rights in a century of bloodshed. In those
days, there wasn't a UN wet nurse. So my people went to work
and helped create the most powerful nation in human history."

That was translated around—and the violence ebbed from
them. They thought of America as primarily responsible for their
woes because America has the most money and the most influence. They had never thought of the American people as rising
from, and above, circumstances similar to their own. . . .

In Rome, that subsequent night, Rex expressed not just his
relief, but some admiration, for the way I'd "dive-bombed them"
and then figured how to "pull out alive." But I'm a writer; and
maybe I think in forms, for I wouldn't have taunted them without a plan. The point about our bold American sires had occurred to me before I asked, "What if you never got home?"

That day, no longer angry since I had put across my point, I
went on a bit: "If I were you refugee guys, I would write off the
injustice, get off my butt and go out in this part of the world—
your Arab part—and try to make it into something more than a
backward, beat-up camel pasture. My own ancestors did exactly
that. And in your place, I think I could, and I think I would.
I'd try to outcivilize and outproduce Israel, not to wreck it. For

if you managed, you'd be home, all right—not squatting in a dump like this, which you've made into a shambles, yourselves."

That was something they didn't want to hear because it emphasized an obvious fact: vengeance was their present motive for living. Their very acceptance of squalor stoked that vengeance even while it degraded them.

True, there were not enough jobs, not enough funds, not enough opportunities in the Arab world for the swift assimilation of all these refugees. But myriads *had* been assimilated. And many of the million still in camps were not even trying to improve their conditions. They tried instead to compensate for their flaccid bellies by swelling their hearts with hate. It was plain. And there was not much else to say to them.

When that "meeting" broke up, we went to see the wretched living quarters of individuals in the crowd.

Afterward, we visited two more refugee villages, one occupied by Bedouins and one by Roman Catholic Arab converts. The first, where I all but stirred up an international incident, was by far the filthiest and most impoverished. The third one, the Christian village, by comparison, was like a poor suburb. The Christian Arabs, moreover, were at work—some taking part in the Lebanese culture, others schooling themselves to live in the world beyond. They had almost abandoned hope of repatriation, if not bitterness about their exile.

Two more cantonments. And two times more we drank the coffee.

I remember Rex's whispered, "Oh . . . no!" when the third serving was pressed upon us. But he drank it.

We also sampled their bread at a community bakery; we looked into pitifully ill-equipped schools, woodworking shops, and dressmaking rooms—where women patched over patches, or embroidered to earn a little money.

Thousands of children had been born in the scrofulous, penned-up environment. And I noticed in the first two camps that there was not a toy. The kids used stones for marbles, and billets of wood for balls.

But I found most startling, not the fact of so many refugees about whom I'd known nothing, but an even greater ignorance on my part:

These Arabs—even the Bedouins—were not, as I'd presumed, barbarians in burnouses with whom only a Lawrence could communicate. They had been farmers and grovers, tailors, barbers, doctors and priests—not in a few cases, but in many. And many spoke English, French, German, Italian or Greek.

I'd seen a few Iraquis in the elevators of the Westbury Hotel, where we stay in New York—part of the entourage of Ibn Saud, I believe, men in those desert togas, gold bordered, with kepilike headgear, and women with face veils—though not the peepholed hoods of Moslem women in India. But here were Arabs who, given less tattered clothing, wouldn't be looked at twice, on an American street and even as they were would not be exceptionable in East Side Manhattan! Men who could translate for certain East Siders. Bedouins who showed us the pathetic little room in their village called the "library." But in that library, a dog-eared file of "Life" magazine. And here were Christian Arabs with confident plans of attending Harvard!

When that long, weary day of rage, grief—and reluctant amity—at last was done, when the car started back toward Beirut, Betty and Ricky compared notes with Rex and me. They had made separate visits and held separate conversations, part of the time.

We agreed that the refugee situation was shameful, agreed that it was a real and justified source of Arab rage against the West, and, of course, against the Jews of Israel.

"But," Ricky said, "not all these refugees were thrown out by Israelis. Quite a few were promised by their own Arab states that if they'd migrate from Palestine for a while they would eventually be returned or given equivalent lands and homes. The Arab states welched on those promises. So a lot of refugees live in these camps because their own people betrayed them."

Doc had said almost nothing all day, letting Rex and me and the Arabs and their violence and verminous near-starvation talk. Now he spoke quietly. "Some of the people you saw, some of the worst-housed and worst-fed, are actually better off here than they ever were in Palestine. Not a great many—but some. And most of them, we think, if they did get a chance to go back wouldn't take it. But they'd leave the refugee camps. They'd have won their point. They'd settle in the Arab countries, in that case. Hardly one in a hundred families would actually go back, we feel. They want *moral* justice. And they want restitution for what was taken from them—which they've been promised and never received. But they don't actually yearn for the home they demand. The Israelis claim they could not reassimilate all of them, which is true. But they'd never have to."

He talked on as we entered Beirut, spelling out the dangers of this dismal status quo:

The near-million refugees would make an appallingly effective "case" for an anti-Semite. One could easily imagine an American bigot, who'd spent such a day as ours, writing articles concerning these Arabs and their treatment by Zion which would *seem* to justify the unfounded anti-Semitic fungus that even now infests some American minds—mean minds, moronic or mad.

"Why hasn't it happened?" I asked Doc.

"Just because no articulate anti-Semite has happened to come through here yet."

"Of course," I said, "the great majority of Jews in America have no interest in the Zionist movement. A lot of them may contribute, out of sentiment. But I bet most American Jews don't know the Israelis have let this mess fester for eight years—any more than I did."

"Still," Doc nodded, "the knowledge *could* be used to stir up a tumult of anti-Semitism. Yet, if the Israelis would make even the gesture of starting to keep their promises—if they'd just begin to pay a few of these refugees for actual losses suffered—or start screening a few and taking some back—the volcano would simmer out. All the hate. The determination of these poor dopes to hang onto nothing in the hope of getting, not what they lost, but vengeance. Which they call justice. And I guess, for many, it *is*, too."

"Why doesn't Israel do that then?" Rex asked. "How can

Ben-Gurion, and those people, let such an incubator of potential anti-Semitism breed away, here?"

"Go down to Israel and ask 'em. They're absolutely adamant about it. *They* hate Arabs as Arabs hate *them*. They're 'way beyond even considering promises, or justice! Go ask."

"I think I will," Rex said quietly.

And he did—a few days later. . . .

Furthermore, when Rex came back to the States, various magazines in the Nationwide group published the facts about the million Arab refugees, with pictures: the very truths the Arabs claimed would never appear in the American press, owing to "Jewish control."

I hope Rex saw to it that those various articles and features got back to the villages in Lebanon—and all other refugee villages—to scotch the deeply believed notion that America's press is censored by, or slanted in favor of, Jews. I wish Rex, or somebody, could find as good a means to halt the united idiots of earth from their paranoid talk of a "secret Jewish conspiracy," too. It is as nonexistent as Atlantis, but as credulously believed in, by some Americans, as little men from Mars.

The existence of so many refugees, for so many years, in the Arab states has also given the Communists a real and mighty instrument against us all.

Because of those refugees, UN—which is regarded by Arabs as a "Western" agency—is not trusted. To all Araby that means the United States is not to be trusted, either. No American commitment, in business or diplomacy, concerning petroleum or anything else, seems reliable to them.

A boil, a cancer, a purulent sore, called "refugees," persists in everyday Arabian life; and a dishonorable USA is held chiefly to blame. That is a point our industrialists should brood on.

Russia "also" may lie. Russia "also" may use "propaganda." Russia is powerful and a tyranny. But most Arabs are accustomed to tyrants—and nothing else! So the choice between the Free West and Communism, to Arabs, seems a choice among evils. And that side which finally gives the best evidence of ending what the Arab world feels to be (and what is, to a great and

tragic degree) the injustice that accompanied the establishment of a Palestine homeland for Jews, will be the side the Arabs
may join, if taking sides becomes unavoidable.

The economic fate of Britain hangs on Middle East oil. It
is no more secure than a kite sent up where a tornado may pass.

And my argument that Moslems would "commit suicide" if
they accept Soviet aid was weak. They have heard something, no
doubt, of Red atheism, and of the use of mosques behind the iron
curtain for warehouses or for exhibits ridiculing the Prophet.
They have never experienced those things; meantime, Soviet
agents perennially assure them such matters will change. But
Islam has had much experience of the hatred borne for its faith
by Jews, and by Christians; also: a thousand years and more
of bloody experience. So if they must choose—well . . .

How would *you* choose?

How *do* you choose? You choose, always, (in part) because
of some old book, some Talmud or Koran.

Old books preserve the universal legends, the archetypes; but
the universal meaning is discarded. Every Saint and Prophet,
Savior and Philosopher was "miraculously conceived" or ges-
tated, performed "miracles" himself, handed down the "Word"
and was martyred. The Old Books say so. Actual efforts of such
good men, attempts to express life's meaning, man's need for
humility and his affinity with Nature, are found in each Old
Book. But the "Thousand-faced Hero" has a single name in each
particular Old Book; so he, and he alone, becomes the Special
Godhead of a Tribe.

Thenceforward, the constantly more distorted "record" of
his doing becomes altered in subsidiary Old Books, often to the
opposite of his intent. Some simple, good, wise man, who no
doubt was once alive, perceived and taught certain human truths.
Made by Old Books a specialized God, his one act then became
the protection of *his* faithful, the establishment of a Paradise for
them—and the punishment of dissenters. The ancient men
spoke to all men. But the addicts of Old Books determine, ever
after, who is faithful and who, doomed. Moses, Mohammed, Buddha, Jesus—it does not matter whose name is used: each was

Every-man-Incarnate and Man at his Best. But each has become God to somebody, or Quasi God. And then each serves to renew human vanity, in some new, experimental, changing style. Old Books are the recipes, and not for eternal salvation but for perpetual regression, not for humbleness but ruthless pride, not for a willing spirit and open mind but for harsh absolutes called "Law" and "Truth." So each gospel is recast and often gives the lie to every syllable of every man who ever inspired one!

Because "Israelites" marched to the "Promised Land" a thousand and a thousand and a thousand years ago, Old Book readers (no more "Israelites" today than the old Tribes were motorists) march back to that same Land to *make* Jehovah keep a "promise" stated in the Old Book's arrogant legend, one no more relevant, no more real nowadays, than a land grant from Genghis Khan, a title from Attila, or a deed from Nebuchadnezzar.

What folly founded on folly.

For all that *all* the Saviors said was this: The meek shall inherit the earth; truth will make you free; love one another. But every Old Book *concerning* Saviors has set forth a Faith that appeals to pride and brings Holy War.

How long will these overweening Believers continue to turn themselves into beasts violating what their saint or savior said, to gain the Illusion they are God? When will they heed what was said, and be human *Men?*

Ricky and Margaret and Rex went to Byblos where, in the space of a few score acres, layered like a cake lies all civilized History. First, signs of some nameless, prehistoric people; next, shipways where the Phoenicians built the fleets that carried the commerce of the Ancient World—fleets that founded Carthage and mined tin around Britain; then, evidence of conquerors: Persians and Babylonians, Hittites and Assyrians; next, Pompey's Graeco-Roman "new order" and its theaters and temples; then the beet-shaped domes and broken-arched portals of Islam; and after that, a fortress-castle of the Crusaders.

God knows what will follow, on that slag heap of True Belief, embattled-without-Mercy-or-Humility, all the time and way from Moloch to Marx!

For two signs abound there still: of Belief, and of Battle.

Some days later, at a luncheon given by Ambassador and Mrs. Donald Heath, we listened to a very skillful exposition of the tangled politics of the Middle East. We met Charles Malik, there, and he left his own dinner party one night to spend some hours with us. But first. . . .

The fascinating foods were consumed and the more fascinating talk was interrupted. Ladies and the gentlemen separated for liqueurs, coffee, cigars, cigarettes—and for what we call Comfort in what we know as Rest Rooms, a matter regarded as both delicate and crude if ever its intent is revealed to members of what we refer to as the Opposite Sex.

The Ambassador and I had happened to move apart from the other guests. We sipped a liqueur together, and discussed one or two matters left incompleted at the table.

"You seem to know a great deal," he said presently, "about the philosophy and psychology of the Soviets. And about Russia, itself. How did you learn?"

"First I read," I answered. "And I listened to several friends who went there—so-called liberal intellectuals, mostly. That was in the early Thirties. Finally, I decided I had to see for myself. Eyewitness accounts were very contradictory. I was sure some were prejudiced—or 'loaded'—and others, uninformed. I took along my kid brother, Ted Wylie—half-brother, actually—one summer. It was the only year that they allowed tourists to go wherever they chose. Ted and I soon jumped the rails of a 'planned tour.' We bought our own tickets—air, rail, water, bus. Went where we pleased and that meant to a lot of places journalists didn't bother to inspect and most liberal-intellectuals never heard of. We ploughed through Russia, from Leningrad to Baku and came out from Shepetovki.

"In Tiflis, we let it be known that what we'd seen was appalling to us, that we were itching to get home to tell the world.

After that—the GPU tagged us everywhere. Once, we were in a bus accident that we thought might have been rigged. We became the only passengers aboard, as people got off at various stops. The bus skidded over a cliff but Ted and I jumped even faster than the driver. However, we got to Warsaw, finally."

I thought I might be boring the Ambassador. He had twenty other guests, too. But as I'd talked, a strange, tense look came in his eyes. "And then?" Mr. Heath asked.

"I came down with some never-diagnosed combination of diseases, in Poland. One was probably cholera. My kid brother didn't catch any of them. But early one morning when I was presumably a lost citizen, Ted went to his room after a dinner and a long evening with some of our embassy people. I'd made him go out. He'd sat five nights and days with me. I had a nurse, by then. And a few minutes after he entered his hotel room, adjacent to mine, he was found dead on the pavement, five storeys below." I thought back a moment:

"Our consul and our Embassy thought it was the work of Soviet agents. We had seen too much—and we were writers. They came over at once. They were swell to me. Though they did ask a lot of questions, of a man supposed by the Polish doctors to be on the way out, right behind Ted. There never was any proof Ted was murdered. After that—after a year spent in recovery, I was partly paralyzed for months—I really studied Communism. I had a personal motive, besides my original, intellectual reasons, and humane reasons."

Ambassador Heath had been waiting for me to finish. "I remember that," he said.

"Remember! *You* remember. . . !"

"I'd been Ambassador to Poland, shortly before 1936. Had another post in Central Europe then. But all the American Embassies in Central Europe were indignant about it: two young Americans came out of Russia with a lot of information. One got sick, was apparently dying of some unknown disease. The other—was killed. The Ambassador in Poland wired me for advice."

I was stupefied. And there was no adequate way to make Ambassador Heath realize how much this meant to me. I tried my best:

"I've often told the story. Even written it. But most people thought, in 1936, and afterward, that I'd exaggerated my sickness, and my brother was either drunk and fell from the window, or committed suicide!"

"*We* didn't think so," the Ambassador answered grimly. "I'd forgotten your names, you understand. I've forgotten some of the details, too—but . . ."

I will never forget the details he had lost to view in the twenty intervening years of his hard, complex duty.

We talked urgently, then. For I never forget at all . . . !

Never forget the massive misery of Sovietland. The degradation of humanity. The evidence of violence and terror and torture. Or my growing rage, and Ted's. . . .

Never forget the night in Tiflis when, amidst a score of tourists and Russians, we were asked "what we thought of the USSR." Ted and I let loose. Documented tirade. . . .

I won't forget how the GPU men followed us afterward, or how we mocked them (since they pretended not to understand English). We'd describe them within their hearing, using the most insulting terms we could imagine—to watch their color rise. Or fade. But they went on, in relays, tagging us and listening to us, and pretending, *still*, they didn't know a word of English.

I won't forget the night in Odessa. We were ready to take our last train-ride in Russia—to Poland. And God, how happy to be leaving! A bottle of Scotch was offered for sale by the hotel barkeep. We'd drunk little: the beer was bad, the vodka worse. So we bought the Johnnie Walker and split it with two Americans.

The next morning, we woke in a car of a train occupied by Red Army soldiers only. We had hangover thirsts, but there wasn't a drop of water on the train. Our car was shoved on a siding. The troops marched away. Ted and I sat alone, all day, in the heat of some uncultivated, uninhabited part of the Ukraine. We were still too stupid to be scared. Just *thirsty*. When, at last, a train picked up our car we appealed with parched mouths for "voda." The trainman brought us water, a carafe of it. The stuff looked brownish, tasted odd, but we drank it all.

Five days later, in Warsaw, I fell hideously ill. From that water? If so, Ted was immune to the bacteria it had contained. But such immunity is not rare.

I remember the fever, the puking, the odd diarrhea, the crawling on hands and knees to the toilet, Ted helping. I remember the big purple blotches that came out on me, the onset of paralysis, the pain. I remember that, often, I could *not* remember.

Some days after that, I was continually conscious again— and agonized. The Polish specialist finally told me one afternoon (in voluble, solemn French) I would be dead in a few more days.

My brother Ted entered his room late that hot night, opened French windows that gave on a narrow balcony, and plunged into the street. Pushed out, our people in Warsaw thought, by an agent hidden in his closet: a familiar Soviet gambit. Liquidate your enemy in a country outside Russia; leave no proof of murder; escape while he falls. The old open-window trick.

I sent Ted's body to Gdynia—Warsaw was Catholic, then, and had no crematory. And I sent Ted's ashes home.

For a month after that, I lay paralyzed in one arm and one leg, my fever abating slowly as ankylosis and atrophy progressed. I was often in near delirium owing to chronic agony—and grief. A guard was set at my door to prevent any further acts of "agents."

I remember! Who wouldn't?

I was moved to Paris by stretcher and wagon-lit. A French physician named Fernand Layani started my long healing. . . .

In more months, I returned to Manhattan and continued hospitalization. But little by little, the use of my joints was brought back. The debilities that followed cholera (if it was that) and plague (if it was that, also, as some doctors thought) diminished.

I went to work in Hollywood, finally. We needed money. But the heart was out of me. Ted was dead. Murdered. He certainly had not killed himself and he was known not to have been drunk.

My family was crushed by the tragedy. Loss of the brightest son, the football star and track champion, the most gifted writer, the most vehement and imaginative, the young Wylie who —at twenty-three—had published his own first novel, ghostwritten a great arctic book, gone abroad the first time to see the Soviet Terror close to. And he had seen it. All.

For twenty years, I carried the recollection of that Red hegira, the memory of humanity-in-horror, and my private sorrow —the unprovable murder of a young brother, along with my own remembered agony and near death.

I had become *afraid* to travel and stayed afraid for twenty years. Bermuda, perhaps. Havana. No farther! I could sweat, wide-awake a whole night, just imagining being in Europe. The phobia consumed me. *Stay home. Be safe.* It is one of the reasons for my interest in psychological theory, one reason for prolonged analysis. And it was *the* reason Ricky always wistfully said to travelers, "I've never been anywhere."

I wouldn't take Ricky anywhere. Not "anywhere" far from USA. My private horror would dig in, resisting, panting, shaking, perspiring—if we even *idly* considered going to Paris "someday." I was sick with it.

. . But now I stood, most of the planet behind me, freed of fear. Across the room, in the lovely dress she'd bought for "occasions," was Ricky, who had never been "anywhere," because of my fear. Ricky smiling, talking eagerly and eagerly listening—in the midst of some of the most informed and urgent lovers-of-liberty on this earth. In *Beirut,* in *Lebanon*—which used to be part of the Land of Canaan and is far, far from Miami.

Before me stood an ambassador who gravely drained his liqueur glass.

"They play rough, the Soviets. And they play exactly in that fashion you know all about!"

"I'm glad you recall," I said again.

"Did you write about Russia?"

"Certainly. Beginning in 1937, when I could move my right arm again. And ever since. The *Daily Worker* somehow assumed

Admiral Wiley was my father in those days and they used to review what I wrote about Russia with the same opening phrase:
'Philip Wiley, the snot-nosed son of Admiral Wiley . . .' "

He grinned briefly. "I *do* remember," he said then and almost to himself: "We couldn't do *anything*. It was always that
way: no evidence. Just somebody who'd learned too much about
the Soviets and mysteriously became the victim of an odd, fatal
disease. Or an accident. Became *dead*. We would be furious at
the Embassies—and impotent."

His penetrating eyes flashed, and his grim-shut jaw grated
audibly. "You sure learned Communism the hard way."

Before he returned to his other guests, he added, "But you
sure did *learn* it. I wish all Americans understood it as well because, then, the danger *they'll* have to learn it, *the hard way*,
would not exist." For an instant, he looked out through a great
window of the Embassy drawing room, looked out at the walls of
Beirut, brown-gold in the sunny, cool afternoon. His expression
was that of a man seeing legions of foes storming outer walls. A
man who had foreseen the attack, a long time; and one who'd
given ten thousand warnings. Ten thousand alarms unheeded by
his now-beleagured countrymen. He shrugged, turned, stopped
and said over his shoulder, "I enjoy seeing an American like you,
once in a while—somebody from home who realizes what we face
here. And everywhere. And I'm sorry about your brother. But in
1936 we didn't know quite enough to warn crazy young Americans like you that the more Russia you saw, the less talking you
should do—till you got well away. *Baiting* Ogpu men. Good
Lord!"

We shook hands hard, when Ricky and I departed.

He said, "Keep writing!"

I said, "Keep watching!"

At Doc and Betty's, over late afternoon coffee, I told them
about the Ambassador's recollection of the Russian journey that
had ended in tragedy. "So I have a witness, after all," I said. "He
remembered what officialdom knew, and surmised. It was the
Embassy's idea I'd been dosed with germs after that thirsty all-

day stall in Ukrania. That the whiskey, the waterless train, was planned. And that Ted was assassinated. It didn't even occur to me until our Consul in Warsaw—Bevan, I think his name was— got the tale of our Russian travels from me by asking questions. I was almost too sick—and sad—to try to answer."

"What in God's name," Doc asked, "made you and Ted tell those muzhiks what you thought of their country?"

"It just didn't enter our heads we couldn't say what we pleased. Even after they put the GPU on our tail, and after that bus skidded over that cliff, Ted and I were placid. We assumed the plain-clothes act was routine, the skid was just more bum Russian driving. We never dreamed we were on a bump-off list. It took our officials, in Poland, to put those features together."

I remembered:

"We were *mad*. We'd seen too much brutality to bear! We'd had a few vodkas, besides. But it was 1936. I mean, we both still believed cloak-and-dagger stuff only happened in E. Phillips Oppenheim. So we shot off our mouths in Tiflis! Being older than Ted, I've always felt responsi——"

"Skip that one!" Doc snapped. "It's the one that never helps, just harms *you*."

The Fosters gave a cocktail party just before the Rex Johnsons and Ricky and I departed for Istanbul. It was a large and lively party. I suppose the people were as "cosmopolitan" as any guests among which ever we were numbered. Almost all of them spoke some English; but I was glad my French remained voluble and that I knew some German. More languages would have helped, too. The Foster apartment was like a penthouse with broad porches above the light-splashed city; it faced mountains across the harbor which turned third-by-third to ghosts, with twilight—a wondrous place for any party.

That night was the one Dr. Charles Malik chose for his talk with Rex and me, leaving his own dinner guests; it was the only remaining chance for the three of us to be together.

In remembering the evening now, I hesitate to set down my impressions of Malik. This man is often called the "foremost spokesman for the Middle East," often introduced after a sotto voce aside: "the great *Christian* Arab, you know." I hesitate, for fear you will begin to believe I made my journey with a bias *toward* men and women of other races. I have, to be sure, shown that I admired a great many. But I have not told (this is not the place to discuss) the many, many times that number of my own countrymen whom I know better, and admire as much, or much more—let alone the Americans I admire whom I have never had the chance to meet. . . .

Charles Malik is a husky man, a gray man, who wore a gray suit that night. He has a large, shagged, gray head; he smiles often and speaks softly. In repose, and only then, deep seams in his countenance tell how his character was made: of uncountable disappointments transcended each in turn by his hope.

Diplomacy, charm, courtesy, conversational brilliance— they are common attributes. Worldliness (or sophistication) is mandatory in the "international set." But is courage? Wisdom? Kindness? Patience? Erudition? He was—once—a mathematics teacher, a physics instructor and a professor of philosophy. He earned his Ph.D. at Harvard. He has been Lebanese delegate to the United Nations and now heads the American University of Beirut—among other things. He embodied once again my meaning of "man" in man's best shape. Malik also came as envoy from Lebanon, to America—which had sent the remembering Donald Heath to Beirut, Cooper to India, and other fine men elsewhere, but which also exports on sundry errands of importance, rich nitwits—and a veritable rabble of opinionated ignoramuses with whom no Malik (no Lampur, Lall, Wong or Ishishi) should be asked to pass the time of day.

I admire people—not races. I am ashamed of the inept "opposite numbers" we Americans too often pick as representatives of or agents for a land that has an abundance of its own "Maliks."

He cheerfully made the rounds of the by-now exuberant stay-lates, the people who either dine customarily on canapés and liquid carbohydrate or, like Russians, take dinner after midnight. Then he found a reasonably quiet corner. helped assemble chairs and sat down tiredly with Rex and me. A coming-and-going bevy of kibitzers attended, too: envoys from other lands, students from the University, UN people, and those unidentified pretty women who, if they are wives of guests, do not give away the fact and are not betrayed by husbands—perhaps because, however much they love their wives, such husbands retain and exercise at cocktail parties their premarital fondness for all pretty women. It is not the uncommon, but the increasingly usual, way of married behavior, in USA, at such affairs.

Dr. Malik and Rex began to talk.

I had thought the Arab—who deserves his adjectives—wanted to discuss world problems only with Rex—who exerts presidential influence in a corporation that produces many of the magazines and books most influential in America. I thought I was invited to sit with them out of courtesy. But as the talk continued I realized there was something Dr. Malik wanted from me; and I knew what it was. The fact depressed me:

At lunch, at the Embassy, I'd sat beside Mrs. Malik. She has as much charm and poise as her husband, his empathy, and a comparable knowledge of and anxiety about world relationships. That day I talked to her, and talked well—perhaps because she did apprehend swiftly, perhaps because she asked the right, incentive question every time I paused, but more likely because she was excited by my résumé of the adventures and ideas you have read here, and my conclusion exhilarated her: my conviction that the American people could and would rise in time to meet the dreadful world occasion they have not yet even descried.

It was what Ricky calls "one of your monologues." Now and then, they turn out as well as the one Mrs. Malik solicited. Or elicited. She had told her husband. Now, I could see, when his eyes occasionally rested on me, a light rise in them: he wanted to hear it at firsthand—*my* hope, *my* American hope, said in a language new to his wife.

But that sort of expression is extemporaneous with me. I cannot recapitulate it by an effort of will. Its efficacy depends on shades of feeling. And to have sharp gradations of useful emotion, one must have energy to light up the brain, force from it precise phrases, imagine, paint, sing—and also perceive where the listener falters, even before the listener is aware of puzzlement, so as to recast appropriately before going on: that and more! But I cannot do it by determination. I cannot even write by "will," exactly, but only from a natural *feeling* that produces relevant thought, or, in a more professional (but less natural) fashion, by willing the *feeling,* first.

That night I was exhausted. Packing lay ahead, before sleep and an early plane departure. The cocktails I'd had earlier had worn off and left me fretful, vaguely disquiet, reluctant to commune with anybody. And now I was to be asked for a hard, emotional effort that would require the exploitation of my feeling and still fall short.

Reason is not the problem. It *never* is. For thought, I am certain, if thought means a logical process that ends in some new, more true formulation—i.e., if it means "creative thought" —is something most people never experience. I've said the human race is lucky if it has five minutes of thought in its collective heads per century. Parsimonious that may be, but Einstein's basic insight occurred in a flash. All that Freud developed rose from two or three insights of feeling—as sudden as unexpected. Taking the knowledge and thoughts of others, and reconstruing them in merely "creative" words, is fired off—as I believe every stroke of creative genius to be—by some sort of precursory spark of *feeling.* Einstein's feeling was for a particular, obscure geometry when he "felt" his way into the Michelson-Morley quandary. *After* the feeling came the thought we call Relativity. Freud had a "feeling" about human sexuality before Dora supplied material that turned it into thought.

So we all *feel first.* And so, the actual composition of all that almost all of us believe to be thinking and even "creative thinking," as well as the process we consider to be logic, is but an expression of values, rearranged with symbols, or, more commonly, mere rationalization of old premises, laws, concepts, worths and nonworths. A billion lives are talked away with never one thought expressed, even entertained!

The process of "feeling" is the mind's method of evaluation; it can, but need not, lead to the inner expression we call "thought" that is so rarely anything more than permutations and combinations of old thought, old error, *junk*. Someday, I'm sure, the neurologists will find that out and quit arguing about the reality (or absurdity) of libido—or of Jung's "anima" and his "four functions of the mind," of which he says "feeling" is an invariable component.

That night exemplifies the thesis. I did not want to "think" aloud, talk, or try to force my *feelings* to the pitch they had attained on a different day. I was *cross*. Sullen. Irritable. Admiration of Malik and Rex could not stir me to philosophize and psychologize (on a level that I *feel* is warranted by the American nature). Even patriotism could not. So, when my turn came, I believed I merely heckled the old man (I was shocked, later, to find *I'm* four years older!). I felt I was trivial and disputatious. When he'd gone, bowed with Atlas's burden, when we were at last undressing in our room, I told my wife I'd surely given Dr. Malik the impression I was a pesty poop, a contentious twerp, not worth crossing a Beirut street to chin with.

She wasn't especially sympathetic. She knows I can, and often do, give, as if it were all, a part of me that nefariously reveals itself on inopportune occasions. She is resigned to it. For she also knows I cannot even copy one sentence of my own, moments after writing it; my "feeling" will already have changed and I will therefore change the words!

But it turned out I'd somewhat underrated my mood and its effect, anyhow. . . .

The first significant remark directed at me by Dr. Malik not only demanded a mental effort I did not want to make but contained a query I felt he could answer better than I—one with a derogatory implication, too! "Mr. Wylie," he said gravely, "there's one thing I forever struggle vainly to ascertain: the basic policy of the West. What is it?"

I thought of India's dilemma over the same question—and of Lampur. The "policy" was Dulles; and Dulles (Lampur implied) had no policy; just his Presbyterian convictions and the big, convinced ego they had inflated—which added up to what Lampur described as being "sincere," when the word meant blind, ignorant and willful.

But Charles Malik, asking about the "West," meant not just USA but Europe. That further irked me.

"What do you mean," I answered, almost rudely, "by the West? You're talking, after all, to an American."

He said words about something his wife had told him— words I didn't catch because I am deaf and because at that moment a voice in the background lofted into song: "Hi! Hi! Jerusalem! The harlot of Jerusalem!" The voice was hushed and I heard what followed. "I mean, of course, *The West*: the nations led by your own."

"Then," I answered, "the word 'policy' is wrong. You've lived in America. You surely realize that the American people do not for a moment consider themselves part of Europe, leaders of any Occidental Co-Prosperity Sphere?"

He grinned feebly.

I went on: "We think—the very great majority of us—that Europe is a distant group of unintelligent, quite backward, mercenary, dependent nations whose people are not even poor relations, but parasites, or, at best, remoras."

"I beg your pardon?"

"It's a fish with a sucking disk on its noodle. It clamps onto bigger fishes, rides free and, when the big fish makes a kill, casts off and free-loads."

"Oh! Yes. *Remora*. Good! The so-called isolationist viewpoint of some Americans, I know. But——"

"——but I don't mean isolationists. I refer to the *national* American subconscious, the shape of American instinct, in this Year of Grace. To almost every living American, Dr. Malik, 'The West,' unless first *differently* defined, means the American West, where young men were once abjured to go."

Rex, I thought, tried to mend my poor manners. "Mr. Wylie is just trying to explain that if you say 'The West' to the average New Englander, or New Yorker, he thinks of Ohio, say. To an Ohioan, the phrase means—maybe—Nebraska. In Nebraska, 'The West' is Wyoming. And so on, right through California, where there isn't any 'wester West.' To Californians, The West means California and adjacent states."

Dr. Malik moved his large body, uncomfortably. "I fear you both still do not get my meaning. Of course, I understand the local use of the term. But I keep trying to perceive how the relationships of the Western powers are meshed to create a policy."

"But we *do* get your point—perfectly," I replied. "You fail to get ours. *Mine*. I'll take the responsibility for it. The policies of USA, in the long run and such as they are, represent a consensus of the American will, slightly sifted through the colander of politics, and occasionally given a new direction by some Wilson or Roosevelt—a direction invariably turned *back again* if it fails to coincide with America's collective will, or wants, wishes—or whatever."

He was frowning. "I still fail . . . ?"

"What I mean is this: Americans do not, and perhaps will not for a long time, consider for one instant that they have *mandatory policy ties* with Europe, Canada, Latin America or any other country! We think of ourselves as Americans—exclusively: a self-determined nation with no necessary foreign ties, duties, imperatives, unshatterable alliances, and so on."

"But . . . !"

"There *is* no but, Doctor. Believe me. We may feel that we ought to do something *for*—or *about*—Europe. Or a European nation. Or any other. We do feel that we go over and win wars they stupidly got into—win for the right side. We lend and give Europe money. We play along with them, suffer for, or fight for them, when it suits us. Some Americans know Europe depends utterly on us, now. Of those, most think of that dependency wholly in economic and military terms. For instance, a few of us realize that if the tin and rubber in Malaya fall to the Red Chinese, or if the oil, here in Arabia, is Sovietized, it'll wreck the thin British economy and put sixty-odd million Britishers—along with the French—on an American dole. *Some* Americans are aware of *that* sort of dependency. Some know only a hydrogen-muscled, big-area nation can even challenge the Reds with effective bluff. *Most* Americans aren't aware of the sober truth of the Atomic Age or of what all-out war means. Of those, however, who know Europe exists, all will freely moralize about what England, France, West Germany, Pakistan or *anybody* 'ought' to do, in a given situation. We Americans currently don't yet know, or refuse to face, all realities inimical to our self-sufficient dream. That's a kind of ignorant but well-wishing vanity. Mr. Dulles—who definitely *does* know Europe exists—often is just such a moralizer. Intellectually, we Americans have *no* policy shared with 'The West' because we don't think about ourselves as a part of it—in the way you do, and everybody in Asia does."

Dr. Malik turned and spoke to Rex, who was smiling—embarrassedly, I thought. "Surely a hundred and seventy-five million people, the world's most extensively educated, cannot take so provincial a view!"

"I think," Rex replied, "Phil has it about right. Of course, when the chips are down . . ." He stopped, and his smile diminished.

"That's different," I went on. "American policy is not describable and it can't be written out. It cannot be shared in its present form. But it isn't *exactly* the slaphappy opportunism it usually seems. For, when our policy requires *acts*, Americans do act. They act, however, not from prior written policy but from an assorted set of deeply unconscious instincts, traditions, ideals, hunches——"

"Generous," Dr. Malik nodded. "Brave. Not self-seeking in any colonial sense, but, rather, vastly the contrary . . . !"

"Wonderful people," I agreed, "in action. But as for policy—children. Maybe we don't need it so long as we have the instincts of free, self-determined men."

Dr. Malik was disturbed. "I agree, you are capable of splendid acts. History has no parallel for your generosity to others, or your fury when, as Mr. Johnson says, 'the chips are down.' But it will be perhaps too late to act when America finally sees the *Communist* chips have already been put down! How can America—if she shares no policy with what I call The West—be led to act, in time, if she sees no chips down? No war going on? No definitive crisis? Just penetration, the forward-moving curtain, subjugation, violence?"

"We started, once," I answered. "Korea."

The Arab spoke rapidly. "Ah, but there *was* a chip down: North Korea invaded by Communist-trained, Chinese-led Red Troops! Certainly, then, President Truman acted. But it would seem Mr. Truman changed your American policy-by-instinct. As you put it. The American people reversed his effort and walked away from Korea without victory. I would say, if you play bridge, they reneged."

"I play bridge. And America reneged on a fight—for the first time in her history." I tried to explain in some other way: "We are so much America, so much alone, and we feel so self-centered and remote, that what I call the collective instinct failed to carry through in Korea. You see, our attitude toward Russia—though ambivalent—finally gave us a dominating urge to pull out of Korea, not to win."

"Ambivalent?"

"Again—*unconscious*. We Americans, most of us, consciously assume that we can lick the Soviets and Red Chinese, if we must. We were brought up to believe we could lick anybody —or everybody put together. But *unconsciously* it's different. A great many, if not most, plain, ordinary Americans assume, without realizing it, that any next all-out war will simply destroy America—and probably everybody else."

"Why do you think they believe *that*, even 'unconsciously'?"

"Because I'm quite sure that Americans have faced such unpreparedness, at the start of the two World Wars, that if they had an instinctual feeling they *could* survive a Third, they'd prepare themselves. Civil Defense, I mean. But they don't and won't. Why? Because they 'know'—in a region beyond knowledge—it's ridiculous to try. Hopeless. If 'there is no defense,' there's no civil defense."

He turned bewilderedly to Rex, who shrugged. "Phil writes —*and* talks—from a psychological viewpoint. That's his personal explanation. But I don't think it should be underestimated, Dr.

Malik. Phil's been attached to the Federal Civil Defense Administration, as an expert consultant, under Truman and Eisenhower. He has a very high clearance in this whole atomic show. And the simple facts are that atomic weapons do exist, Russia has plenty, and we in the United States don't make even a pretense of getting our cities ready for H-bombs. It doesn't seem possible to *get* them ready—to me."

After a moment of reflection, the Arab leader went back to the original topic. "And, Mr. Wylie, you believe that Americans feel free to act, in your words, 'on their own,' without regard to the *other* Western powers?"

"Without regard to anybody! We will act with, for or against England, or France or Ecuador—as Americans. We'll act from what *I* feel to be instinct. But how do you make Americans, right now, realize that, once again, the chips are down, and their fate is at stake? How do you arouse their really wonderful instincts and start USA working out *effective* countermeasures against the Red religion? That's something *else*."

The talk went on in that vein for some time. And when Dr. Malik went home I felt chagrined. He had wanted a blazing but documented description of what instinct, once awakened, would lead free men to do about the enslaving slave people. And I'd just shot off an empty mouth.

Months later, in New York, I showed Doc Foster all that I've written about the Middle East except the foregoing. Doc read it with assent—excepting for a disclaimer concerning the way I have here characterized him and his wife. "But why," he asked, as he finished, "did you leave out that terrific insight you gave Charles Malik, at our party?"

"Insight! All I did was argue with the guy! I was too bushed to do more than bicker."

Doc's reaction astonished me. "Man, don't you know Malik has been quoting you—and explaining what you explained to him—all up and down the Arab world ever since that night? You *really* showed the guy something he hadn't understood. He thinks you're one bright American! W*rite it*."

"I can't remember saying anything worth putting in a book."

He gave me the dazed smirk people wear when bright things are said by lunatics. "Don't you remember telling Malik about how Americans think 'The West' means the Western United States, that Americans don't consider themselves as part of the European 'West'?"

"Oh. That. Sure. But he must have already realized! He was at the UN in Manhattan for a while—went to Harvard."

"Look, Phil. Charles Malik came to me later and told me what you said. He was tremendously excited. He felt you'd finally made America and America's idealistic acts comprehensible to him. As a matter of fact, till Malik recited your argument, I, myself, hadn't thought of it. But that's how we *do* feel about 'The West.' By God, that's how *I* feel."

I said, "Sure."

"You moron! You idiot! Look what just happened. England and France went after Nasser and Egypt. And the United States *stopped 'em. That*'s something you made Malik able to understand. You said Americans acted on instinct. You said, in effect, that we're a 'new world' and *actually* self-determined. You said West meant the United States to Americans—not Europe. Don't you even remember?"

"It was obvious."

"Obvious, in a pig's eye! I just told you—*I* never realized consciously, myself, how we feel. Don't you realize that this very day, after what you taught him, Malik is perhaps the only big shot in the Near East who can say, 'I've been telling you for months Americans consider themselves independent of "The West"! Now you can see that they are.' He discovered that freedom does something to human instinct. Something American— and *swell. Put it in the book.*"

So I put it in. . . .

Rex and Margaret have a teen-age son, Jimmie; he flew from a New England prep school to Beirut to spend the spring holidays with his parents. A dandy kid. Ricky and I wanted to see

Damascus and Baalbek: the latter, most; so, with Margaret and Jimmie, we drove there.

Heliopolis, the Greeks called it, and the ruins are the planet's most mammoth. In fact, we'd been told it so dwarfed the Acropolis that a visit to the Parthenon, afterward, would be a waste of time. That is not true, of course. The Parthenon is something *else*. But—Baalbek!

We walked along walls made of blocks of rock bigger than houses. We clambered in a vast, ornate temple that could be used today, with a new roof. We stood beside the greatest columns ever raised by man. Trod on the greatest stones ever quarried. And strange, strong sensations made us quiet.

Baalbek is staggering! But I tried to chase down the reason— or reasons—for my creepy awe in the place. I found this one, for what it's worth to others:

Baalbek is the greatest symbol of God on our planet; maybe I should say, of godliness.

Baalbek was begun, no one knows when or by whom. It once marked the geographical center of the Roman Empire. Before that, it lay on a crossways of the trade routes of ancient peoples of the Tigris, the Euphrates and the Mediterranean. It was near the middle of all the earliest civilizations.

A gigantic green valley surrounds it, one that could feed the million slaves, and domicile the artisans, who raised up the hugest blockwork and the most prodigious columns and the heaviest one-piece stairways that men ever carved—in God's name or for any purpose.

Staircases were carved there in single stones bigger than my living room. Colossal walls contain a solitary structural stone eleven feet high, fourteen feet thick and sixty-two feet long!

Walls in that scale enclose a handmade plateau, topped by the titan temples and the arcades of pillars, in matching dimensions. Under that Brobdignagian dais are deep-hewn, broad streets and cavernous cisterns and stalls for regimental steeds and caves for storing food and mighty, connecting tunnels.

They worshiped primordial Gods here, first—unknown gods; then Istar (or Astarte) and Milk (whom Ezekiel called Moloch) and Baal—who was many Gods and many kings. Thoth and Isis reigned on the coast for a time but not inland, probably. The Graeco-Roman gods and goddesses followed. Afterward, Christ— and then the Prophet, Mohammed.

But no man really knows how many gods were reverently enjoyed here—or feared. How many million times what Vestal Virgin here lay, with whom in honor of what gods, no one knows; or how many babies were disemboweled (or burned alive) to stave off what threats of Nature or what hordes of what infidels —or to make the devout more fertile, or more secure, or holier.

Myriads, myriads! People, as leaves in a forest.

Some latter-day ceremony could be envisaged here. Say, a parade devoted to the new tyrant deity: Anti-God; or to St. Mary. I could see, as if it were Red Square, these brown stones re-painted red and maids from Moscow, Murmansk and Minsk do-ing physical culture routines and throwing showers of javelins as they marched. They would follow, of course, Red Army Units, drilled till their very whiskers varied less than a micromillimeter. Baalbek would be ideal; it is the seat of collective pomp and the center of serfdom-through-doctrine—ultramodern or older than Adam.

But I could *not* see that Baalbek would be of symbolic worth in any celebration of Liberty. The entire, tipped-over tremendousness spelled just one fact: man's enslavement to man through Belief. Here, in stone, was solemnized each suc-cessive "Truth" that, in its day, was everybody else's "Lie" and hence everybody else's "Devil." Here, stone said the awesome faith: *To my God, Who, because He is mine, is your Satan, and your doom, forever!*

Human goodness is thus transmuted into evil. The capacity for love, that starts each man seeking truth to gain freedom, is thus metamorphosed to hatred. Baalbek is the whole lesson of Belief and the clearest of all proofs of that truth-above-old-truths:

Man's faith, stripped of man's noble nerve to doubt, be-comes his Vanity, and so his Doom, for that it dooms Others.

What use could free men make of Baalbek?

Bring every Old Book here and burn them all!

Begin a new Monument here to *Love in the people*, not *in stones* that turn love itself into stone. Into stone altars, where the flame is not for warmth, but a means for torture of dissenters! Into stone altars competitively built, gods-versus-gods, at last to Baalbek specification so any eye can see how humility is crushed, and love, by the monolithic arrogance of monotheism, polytheism, theism, atheism, *all* One Gods of Pride and Certainty.

People are their only monument. And only the *living*.

When will they know *that*?

When will men cease trying to become some God that they are not and, so, turning themselves back into animals which—also—men are not?

When will our endeavor to be men have its true temples placed properly: within living men?

More ages, ages . . . ?

Baalbek is God-the-Vanity, God-the-Human-Evasion, God-the-Lie. It is the great five-thousand-year-old Error-God of us all. Every God-name of that first God-Blunder is graven on its chiseled facets, or implied by them—from Ra to Manitou to Mary Baker Eddy!

And Baalbek, today, expectantly awaits the coming of the next Outer Barbarians. Its platform is still sound. Its stones are still there for new sacrifices to the New Faith. Even now, conquering hordes approach the immemorial ruin—worshipers of the God they call No-God, or call Earthly Father Lenin. Can men called Christians let such murderers make conquest of the axis of Belief by alien words, and owing to their default in Christ's actual teaching: truth; and owing to the spiritual enervation caused by producing so many electric dishwashers?

Shudder after shudder wracked me as I stood on the square lumps of idolatry, that dazzling day. Stood on the waiting stones used so long by men to deny their deities are Onegod: Process! I could feel the terrible confidence of these habituated slabs. This is for certain the most horrible place on earth: Baalbek.

But, finally, my shiver itself froze and I was calm.

Near the head of the slave-sustaining valley, a snow-covered mass shimmered against the turquoise roof of midday: Mt. Hermon. Just beyond, in another vale, lay the Sea of Galilee, where the One Reality of God (here denied in geologic cubes) was twice stated. Let me repeat:

"Ye shall know the truth, and the truth shall make you free." Being interpreted, that also means: "Love one another."

Hear that, you mere *worshipers!* And *rejoice!*

Soon after that journey to Baalbek we said good-bye to the Fosters and took another plane—this time Dutch—for Istanbul. While we were eating a good Dutch breakfast (and flying over beleaguered Cyprus), I began talking to Ricky about Rex, who sat with Margaret and Jimmie, some seats away.

Most of his "toughness," I said, was the kind that represents courage. More novels, I went on, should be written about such men: men who headed great corporations, who had great wealth, but were not Babbits, pirates, "self-made boors"—not the villains monotonously pilloried by American authors.

Like Rex, some men are born to power. Others had put themselves through college and worked their way to the top. Many such are as perceptive, as sensitive, and as articulate as the writers who scorn business and denigrate men in business. But there are many, with wives as gracious and appealing as Margaret, and kids as full of beans and brains as Jimmie, who are, also, artists. I know a corporation head who is among the world's finest cellists. I know a dozen millionaires who are more nearly scientists than bankmen. I mentioned a rich merchant who——

Ricky broke in to agree with me. To agree, till I said, "Look at the way Rex stood up to those Arabs! Shoulder to shoulder with me, on the straight, hard grounds of freedom. I know he never did a filth-wade like that refugee tour: he said so. But he helped me bait them, which was necessary. He didn't bat an eye."

"Aren't you getting yourself, and Rex, on a phoney bandwagon? After all, the refugees *live* there. We could look—and go home and wash!"

"That isn't the point. In the liberal-intellectual view, Rex Johnson would only peer from a limousine window at such a place—if that! No big businessman would spend the weeks Rex has, doing what he and his wife have done to learn the truth. To learn it on the scene. But writers are *supposed* to scout hellholes. I'm trying to talk about men like Rex from the American literary standpoint. Does Faulkner or Ernest or Buck—or did Red Lewis —ever portray one American businessman with the will and the plain guts to—Well, even to go on calmly drinking cup after cup of coffee that's full of dead roaches or maggots or some damned larvae!"

"*Roaches? Maggots?*" Ricky seemed startled. "You mean those little lumps in the village coffee?"

"You and Margaret choked on a few?"

"Certainly! Those weren't *bugs*. They were coriander seeds."

I looked at Cyprus for a while. . . .

Still. If you think they're bugs, it amounts to the same thing. . . .

11
homeward and bound

The traveler should certainly read Herbert Muller's *The Uses of the Past*, before looking into the mosques and bazaars of Istanbul. Muller disagrees with Toynbee, and points out errors and misconstructions in the work of that great historian, though I doubt Muller has discredited the broad thesis of Toynbee. However, he has made a different and brilliant contribution to the art of looking backward—and another to the technique of studying old skylines that only here and there mention time-present, with an Istanbul-Hilton Hotel. Take Muller to Turkey—and Kleenex, nail polish, shaving lotion.

We queued up at the airport for customs. Rex Johnson was paged. A lean young American (one of Nationwide's correspondents, I assumed) began to talk with Rex. I was surprised when we were paged next—and the young man introduced himself as head of USIS in Istanbul. His name was Evans Bailey. "Would you like," he asked, "to take a boat trip up the Bosporus, to the Black Sea, tomorrow morning?"

It was one thing we'd hoped to do. . . .

Amidst stage-sets for *Arabian Nights*, stands the Istanbul-Hilton Hotel: glassy façades, free-form terraces and curved staircases such as gift-wrap Miami Beach. Inside, night clubs, bars and restaurants—all "the most." The view from our room of the

Bosporus was as dramatic as Conrad's castle in Constantinople. And the room seemed to be—until we found doors that wouldn't work, lights with burned-out bulbs that we managed to have replaced only with great difficulty and dirty towels hung by previous guests all about our unwashed bathroom.

That first afternoon, we tried to bring order in our always hastily packed luggage. All across India, day and night, we'd been occupied. In Lebanon, we'd hardly slept—there was so much to see and do and say and hear. So we sorted, folded, laundered, housekept and rested. . . .

The next day, with Evans and his wife, a Navy Commander and his wife, the Johnsons, and a Turkish skipper, we assembled at the dock to board a small boat. It was bitter cold and a strong wind blew, and the sun was a pale, lemon disappointment. To the humiliation of our Navy officer, the one-man "crew" did not show up—and, unfortunately, he had the cabin keys. It was necessary, therefore, to send for tools and break into the cabin. Meantime, we passengers became thoroughly chilled before we embarked on what was to be a constantly-more-chilling voyage of many hours.

We saw the Bosporus.

That is, I did. So did Ricky. And Rex. Our hosts, however, had made provision against the anticipated discomfort: two gallon Thermoses of mixed sidecars, and several quarts of scotch. Some of our party stayed below, accumulating internal warmth (or the illusion of it) and saw nothing of the scenery, of Europe on one bank, and on the other, Asia Minor.

When the strait opened into the Black Sea I asked for a chance to spit in Communist water. The Commander and I had sat in the open stern cockpit, much of the way, and I'd told him about my Soviet hegira. So he gave the Turkish skipper orders and we went out a ways.

It was not drink that inspired the childish ceremony—for I hadn't taken any—but partly an inward exuberance over the fact that, after twenty years, I'd overcome my travel dread that had its origin hereabouts—and partly, I felt Ted would have enjoyed having me spit in that Red-dominated Black Sea. Among his last days were five we steamed there, on a Soviet boat that also carried a deckload of three thousand unsheltered, pest-ridden, hungry, toiletless, vomiting, bedless citizens of the proud CCCP who, if they complained of rain or cold or feces in their faces, were manhandled by Red soldiers, on board just to do that. It was part of my long remembering—Ted's short one—and I spit, as a wreath for him.

We went ashore for lunch at the Black Sea end of the Bosporus. The restaurant was warm, the sea food excellent. But we dived into the frigid air again—all too soon. I had helped land the boat and now helped to cast her off, handling the wet lines with numb fingers—yet glad of my long experience as a deep-sea fisherman. For our Turkish skipper was evidently above touching mooring lines, and our Navy compatriot seemed oddly clumsy in the matter. Possibly a big ship man, used to hawser and cable.

It was evening when we finished the tour, scouting the harbor and the Golden Horn. A fabulous and hard day—but harder for those of our party who had put up a gallant fight against the weather, with sidecar volleys and Scotch broadsides! We took warm tubs but neither Ricky nor I could get the feel of coldness out of our bones.

It grew colder, the following day.

The publisher of a Turkish newspaper gave Ricky and me a luncheon. Then his wife took us for a long inspection of museums. We saw the government's collection of Chinese porcelains and of gold and silver plate, presumably the world's best. Our hostess also arranged to have the harem especially opened for us. So we trekked more miles past still-brilliant tiled walls and faded tapestries and rugs, looking at beds where one sultan after another made evening rounds of beauties for whom the farthest reaches of Islam were scoured by discerning agents.

The way by which those sultans entered the harem led through the grandest apartment of all—one which not only guarded the girls' quarters but overlooked their private places of entertainment. That strategic apartment was occupied by the rulers' mothers! So—even in this place, which some Western men regard as the robust male's paradise, mom stood supreme. *She ran the harem.* One therefore must face the result: on many a night, a sultan bent on a date with Scheherazade, got sidetracked by his adamantine mom to the couch of Maude or Liz—plainer girls, for whom her son had no appetite, but girls whose buttery ploys had won mom's nod.

Everywhere it was ice cold. Indoors the cold seemed more penetrating than out. Two or three times I left the ladies to their enchantment with goldwork and porcelain, and stood against a wall where weak sunshine fell, beating myself with my arms, trying to get warmth into my stiff muscles. . . .

That night Ricky was sick. She slept badly and stayed in bed the next morning. We took her temperature: 102°. I got in touch with Evans Bailey who summoned a doctor.

She had a cold, the doctor said.

No wonder!

Disappointedly, I went on alone with our program.

I visited the American-sponsored home for girls. I talked with the head of a men's college. I walked with awe through St. Sofia, the Blue Mosque, and other mosques. In the great bazaar, I bought some "genuine" Turkish daggers, as souvenirs for dead Bob Lindner's two sons.

And that afternoon I had guests for tea: a Turkish business-man, Mr. Itaff, his gorgeous wife, and his nephew—a scientist trained at M.I.T., and brought along as interpreter. Mr. Itaff had been appointed, through our Consul, as "Istanbul representative" of the International Game Fish Association. And I'm one of its Governors. Tea, therefore, was for the official end of more sports-manlike sports fishing everywhere.

I have rarely met people with more charm than Mr. and Mrs. Itaff; and we didn't need an interpreter, as all of us spoke French.

It was pleasant, but odd, to sit in the foyer of a hotel with a plushily familiar South Florida atmosphere—eating cakes, drink-ing coffee, listening to a tea-dance orchestra play American mu-sic—while talking about deep-sea fishing in French to three Turks.

Big tuna and broadbill swordfish can be taken in the Sea of Marmora! But prospects of establishing a sports fishing club in Turkey were not good, I found. Mr. Itaff and his nephew appeared to be the only Turks who'd managed to import a suitable rod and reel. They'd had only one adequate line for the gear at that—and lost it on a big fish. So they'd been obliged to return to their prior but not official angling method: harpooning. I offered to send some new line, upon my return home—and discovered that it would be too difficult to get it into Turkey. The duties—like the prices—were fantastically high. And such luxury items were more or less proscribed.

Ricky appeared—fever and all. It was not very sensible; but I never heard her regret her act. She hated to miss anything, anybody "new." We were soon to miss a good deal.

I could hardly bear, that night, to consider going to one more place or looking at one more sight. But Evans Bailey had been kind to us—taking us for that tour, supplying cars, guides, introductions, and, when Ricky fell ill, sending to her all the paper-back mysteries he could lay hands on, several packages of American cigarettes, a box of Kleenex *and* an able doctor. I could not refuse his urgent invitations to visit the United States Information Center, of which he had charge. And I went after dark, colder and tireder than ever.

Ricky was back in bed, and worse. . . .

A visual display of forestry conservation was being carpentered noisily in the lobby of the Information building. Upstairs, an exhibit of abstract painting by Turks had attracted several dozen interested citizens. In the library, stood a framed wallboard on both sides of which were exhibits of my writing!

That was what Evans had wanted me to see.

He introduced me to the Turkish girls who had assembled the collection from files of magazines. There were "pieces" I had forgotten I'd written—a "letter to the editor" of the then "Saturday Review of Literature" defending Carl Jung against unjustified charges of Fascism, another "letter" attacking a smug essay on education, several articles about the atomic bomb written eight or nine years before—and other articles in the "Saturday Evening Post," "Cosmopolitan," "Redbook." And one book—a light love story, a magazine serial later published between hard covers. The proud and pretty librarians brought pen and ink and had me autograph that book: they'd been excited to know that a live American author whose works were familiar to them was in the city. Their pleasure at my visit was inordinate. So was my amazement.

While I signed the book, Evans said, "Unfortunately, most of your books—being critical, at least in part—are taboo for our use."

A good many of my books are unofficially taboo for the shelves of some libraries, at home. One of them, in fact, is monotonously smuggled out of libraries and destroyed by pious, parochial do-gooders.

Half a dozen of my efforts are on the Catholic blacklist, though I think people truly deserving of freedom would blacklist one sort of publication only: blacklists.

I said that.

Evans nodded. "In the Overseas Information Services it's hard to get *any* books that are critical of America." I did not ask why. I already knew. Our information policy abroad is as disastrous as many other policies.

A committee appointed by Congress selects the material used: novels and non-fiction are on the booster side. Once, that didn't hold true. But certain McCarthy appointees went through America's libraries abroad, and labeled "Communist" those books that expressed opinions contrary to their biases.

Five thousand people a month come into our Istanbul center to read American books and periodicals. Many are exclusively interested in technical information. A wing of the library is devoted to such books. But ever since the general reading files were censored, the Turks—like other nationals all over the world—have concluded that USA is *not* a free country with a free press, but a nation with a censorship like Russia's.

The use of censorship in that, or any comparable fashion, is tyranny. Its intent is a sort of brainwash. So, to impartial outsiders—like Turks, Asians, Europeans—the committee appointed by America's Congress to "watch" material sent to our foreign Information Centers acts exactly like any Communist committee. The McCarthy style of mind is incapable of seeing that fact, for, if it saw, it would also see its attack on Communism misses its aim, but savagely damages the ramparts of USA.

I said to Evans, "There are, however, some articles critical of us, in these magazines."

He shrugged. "And in Russian periodicals, too. Soviet 'self-criticism,' government permitted and government sponsored! But we are dealing, in US Information, and dealing with the literate upper crust of every country." And I knew what he meant by that, also.

The people in that group in every nation form public opinion, in the end. They know that things in America are not so harmonious and perfect and paradisal as our censored libraries try to make them seem. But so long as Congress has books selected by fundamentalist aunts in Arkansas, by DAR "experts" on Americanism (ladies for whom, if they'd foreseen their heirs, not one Revolutionary ancestor would have cocked a musket) or other such mindless bigots, countless foreigners will make the logical-seeming deduction that America no more has a "free press" than it has a window at every bank where you can get free money.

The "information" that a censored USIS is actually giving the world is that, insofar as liberty is concerned, there's no choice between Democracy and Communism. Both lie. And how can a foreigner tell that the Soviet lies systematically, purposefully and cleverly for its own ends, while America "lies" merely from hysteria?

"There is a difference," I said to Evans. "Our press is free at home."

He sighed. "Censorship is censorship—internal or external. The Commies are forever putting their best foot forward—that's their game and everybody knows it. Now, we're playing the same game. Yet the only game we could usefully play in the world would be the good old game of freedom. Phil, we're losing the

people who could be on our side, who want to be and long to be
—because our side *isn't* the side of complete liberty, any more!
After the war, the United States was the hope of the world. With
the atomic bomb, the world *had* to have hope. But now . . ."

I went back into the cold night. Men like Evans Bailey—all
over the earth—were fighting for their country and their country
was holding their arms! Brave Americans, disarmed by American
fools and professional cowards. I thought—once more—of my theory that a convinced believer cannot oppose another convinced
believer adequately, and for liberty's sake, because his faith
makes him blind to his opponent's parallel authoritarianism.

It always happens. . . .

It is a price of progress, this false faith.

For whenever man makes a great, new forward step in
learning, his duties and responsibilities increase by that much.
But men are loath to take up an increment of duty or responsibility. They prefer to exploit new learning, and only for such increment as it may furnish in comfort, luxury, a higher living
standard. But they know deep within themselves that their exploitation is irresponsible. So they grow guilty, and guilt is a constant, eroding river of anxiety. Anxious, they take the last wrong
step. To quench their worry they turn *back* to the "old faiths"
that soothed them before the new learning brought their gains,
the responsibilities they evaded—and the guilt for that. They
pretend that the new learning offers *only* physical benefits for
them, and does not demand the new duty, the new responsibility
of *rethinking everything;* of *changing themselves.* The prior
faiths are always there: obsolete, now, but ready to shore up
nervousness for all who will blind themselves. And that is easy:
one becomes blind by ceasing to look ahead honestly. Then one
sees only that which lies behind—and is no longer the whole
truth.

What men need is a faith equivalent to, and congruent
with, the latest knowledge. When men reaffirm outworn dogma
to evade new learning and self-change, they destroy themselves.
For their "undoubting faith" has become a rejection of reality.

Baalbek is a monument to the phenomenon.

Half a score of "old gods" flourished and were worshiped there, turned obsolete in the light of new learning, and foundered, serially, drowning their back-grasping devotees.

Today we Americans are offering mankind not freedom but a worn-out "moral authority." At home, we are manifesting a mighty resurgence of old-time religion. We are closing in on liberty to protect an old order of belief which, truly, no longer exists. We do so because we are afraid.

And whom we fear is . . . *ourselves*.

God knows, we should, who grab yesterday's gods to hide from today's truths!

My cab had stopped. Tiredly, I opened my eyes.

Ricky was reading in bed—and her fever had risen. She wouldn't eat.

The doctor came again, shot penicillin into her and told her she could travel in the morning if her fever diminished.

I was very worried. But I made arrangements.

In the morning, miserable but gallant, Ricky reported her fever had all but disappeared.

I'd packed the night before.

We took a slow bus through occasional swirls of snow to the airport. On the way, the bus ran out of gas and we waited a cold half hour while the driver strolled back along frozen earth to a pump.

We'd long looked forward to the flight, hoping to be able to see the Aegean below, and interested in what would be our first trip on a turboprop plane. But the view was occluded.

Soon after we took off a series of violent chills shook me. They lasted all the way to the airport at Piraeus and I forgot to notice the turboprops. We waited an hour in an open car, where a foolish Greek girl made us sit although it was evident the vehicle would not accommodate its passengers and their luggage. After that hour, we were transferred to an adequate bus.

We could see, on the road into Athens, the Parthenon above the city. The windows at the BOAC office were smashed: the Athenians had rioted, over Cyprus, the day before.

The hotel was quiet. Ricky tried to bolster herself for luncheon, with two cocktails; she managed to sit in the dining room and make a pretense of eating. But her fever was high again, and she went to bed—in a rather small, dingy room which gave us a view of a bleak, interior court.

I went out to buy, if possible, some magazines, cigarettes, and a few items needed for Ricky's comfort. I found magazines in kiosks—and I got the cigarettes—but the drugstores were closed all afternoon. It is, apparently, a Greek custom not to do business in the afternoon.

When I returned, I took my temperature. It was 103°.

We had flu, in Athens. . . .

The hotel people—desk clerks, valets de chambre, femmes de chambre and waiters—did what they could.

I asked for a doctor.

John Adamopolis, M.D., attended us.

Every six hours, day and night, he telephoned, and then appeared: a chunky, brown-eyed man with a soft voice and an affectionate manner. He called us both "dear." He had us turn on our backs and shot us with aureomycin and streptomycin. He said we would be all right if it did not turn out to be infectious hepatitis. In that case, of course, we'd spend some months in a Greek hospital. . . .

He told endless stories of the years of horror in Athens. "I've seen," he would say gently, "people die of starvation right on the sidewalk in front of this hotel. That was when the Germans occupied Greece. And during the *revolution* . . . !"

On and on went the mordant but fascinating stories. And when he felt he had to leave, he would say, as if to reassure us that our affliction should be borne with grace, "Life is nothing!" His hand would wave. "Nothing . . . nothing . . . !"

Then he'd go—and Ricky would giggle.

"What a bedside manner! But he's really trying to be charming—and kind. He's just *philosophical*."

"If I were well," I'd reply, "I'd be crazy about the guy. But why doesn't he give us something for this God-awful aching?"

It was severe.

Nights began to pass without sleep, days without food.

I had the 1917 flu. I've had dengue, or "breakbone" fever. And I had whatever I had—in Poland. Only that last complex of diseases made me ache more than this sickness . . . whatever it was.

And now, as the grinding days dragged by, I suffered a formidable upsurge of the old fear: Suppose we were getting hepatitis? There'd been 200,000 cases in New Delhi—and epidemics of more serious strains, elsewhere, to which we could have been exposed. Suppose we were hospitalized for months in this city where we knew nobody? Suppose it would be *Poland again?* Suppose one of us *died* here? I took a brother to Russia and lost a brother . . . !

No need to go further into that state of my mind.

Dr. Adamopolis flatly, though very courteously, refused to prescribe for the wracking joint-pains. Once, in fact, when he caught Ricky taking two aspirin tablets he vehemently ordered her to confine herself to one a day. I suppose he had grown so used to suffering during his piteous career in Athens—and to drug shortage!—that he felt any painkiller should be reserved for people in extremis.

I had, however, a considerable experience of Polish doctors with the same, to me incredible, unwillingness to prescribe any palliative for "mere pain."

So we endured the red-hot surges for several days.

In our kit, as an ultimate emergency drug in the event, say, of shattered survival after a crack-up of a plane in some wilderness, we had a supply of Demerol in a rubber-capped, sterile bottle, as well as a hypodermic syringe and the means wherewith to sterilize it. Every day and every night I thought of that equipment. But I refused to suggest it, refused to break it out and end our misery, temporarily. I wanted to save it against the possibility of more terrible pain; but even more, I wanted to win my argument with Adamopolis and get him to prescribe the clearly indicated remedy—codeine.

I never did.

After five days and nights of fever, after canceling our booking to Rome and our hard-to-get hotel reservation (it would be Easter), I became angry.

We'd lost about twenty pounds apiece before reaching Istanbul. Now we were skeletons. Our fever stayed up and our aching persisted. When, on a Saturday morning, Dr. Adamopolis made his courteous and habitual phone call to announce his impending arrival, I decided to fire him.

I hated to do it. I was fond of him, by then. Few doctors have seen more human suffering, disease, calamity, terror, violence and pain. But few gentler people live.

Ricky is a doctor's daughter and, as I've said, a reluctant taker of medicine. But now, she was even more indignant at John Adamopolis than I. His antibiotic therapy had been the best possible treatment. But we wanted "out" from our pain.

I made one last effort. I reminded J. Adamopolis that he'd once taken courses in an American hospital in Boston—that *we* were Americans—that we needed American treatment: codeine. Dr. Adamopolis was sweet, firm—and negative. So I told him we'd get another physician.

Shaking, weak, I asked the operator to ring our Embassy. It was closed.

Try the Consulate.

The operator tried.

By and by, a call came back:

It was from a woman whose name, I believe, was Mrs. Willing, the wife of some member of our diplomatic staff in Athens. She was pleasant and fluttery-sounding, and also, it proved, a fan for my books. She was "utterly desolated" to hear that my wife and I had been lying, sick, in Athens. I told her we wanted a doctor who would prescribe codeine and Empirin for our flu. She promised to do what she could.

Half an hour later, a businesslike Navy lieutenant phoned. He said he was not supposed to treat tourists. However, he asked our symptoms and I described them. He marched into our room within another hour, holding two large bottles in his hand: "Here's codeine-and-Empirin," he said, "and here's plain codeine! *Now*. Let me examine you."

Young and brisk and fresh from Pittsburgh Medical. We'd be all right, he said, if we weren't getting hepatitis. "Call me again, if you notice such-and-such symptoms."

He went.

Codeine soon quenched the fiery aching. Our "moral victory" over the ultraconservative Greek—if that is what he was—helped.

But Mrs. Willing, by a means that would certainly have distressed her intensely, became the true agent of our convalescence!

Not long after the Navy doctor had gone, the valet de chambre brought in a huge paper bag. Pinned to it was a note from the kindly Mrs. Willing: "I have had experience all over the world," she wrote, "with these enteric troubles." I read aloud that far, and looked at Ricky, who explained:

"She thought you said 'flu' as a euphemism." (Ricky could grin—already!) "She thought you didn't want to tell her we had what most tourists have: trots."

"Oh." I read on. The exact wording of the note escapes me —since it was destroyed, along with our benefactress' name and address. But she had sent us a remedy—tried and tested in consular spots the world over, I don't doubt. A remedy for *enteritis*. Scraped banana and powdered milk, mixed in a Waring Blendor, with melba toast on the side. Eating the concoction, her note promised, would not only soothe our intestinal pangs but exert a truly remedial effect. Maybe it would have—if our distress had been visceral.

I lifted up, so Ricky could see, a two-quart glass jar filled with the brownish, pasty substance—and I dropped it back into the paper bag, with a shudder. We hadn't been able to eat even the occasional plate of soup or baked potato we'd ordered—for five days. The gooey mass of banana and powdered milk was as far beyond our capability as it was outside our need. I pushed the big sack back on the bureau and crept into bed.

Our fever was lower that night. We spent Easter Sunday in bed, and not—as we'd intended—in Rome. The following morning, while Ricky was reading a newspaper in supine comfort and I was sitting on the edge of my bed trying to muster the strength to take a bath, Mrs. Willing's enteritis cure exploded. It blew up with a wall-shaking, window-rattling boom. Glass shards ricocheted from our walls. The screw top of the jar, ringed with saw-toothed glass, thudded into the bedcovers at my side. Ricky was spared extensive laceration—though her bed was nearer the blast—by a thick spread that had been folded over its foot and a silk kimono, bought in Tokyo, that lay across the spread. Into that barrier slashed a double handful of fragmented glass at hand-grenade velocity. If we had happened to be standing near, or over the glass-jar-bomb, we'd have been ripped to pieces.

With the glass, two quarts of the brown sludge were distributed on wall and floor, ceiling, mirrors, beds, tables, chairs, bureautops and in open suitcases. It seemed as if bushels of the stuff had been hurled about: so many things were so thickly porridged. A *whoom!*—and the place was a shambles, glinting and oozing.

With the explosion, Ricky almost fainted. She could not see or guess what had happened. Her heart stopped. She said nothing because she had lost the power to speak. But I'd been facing the source of the thunderous noise and saw what had happened. Since, by incredible good luck, not even the smallest bit of glass struck me (though I was liberally banana-pocked), I was not so shocked as she. In fact, with what I have always considered great presence of mind and irony, I broke the echoing silence that followed the catastrophe.

"*Fabulous*," I said. I turned to her. "Are you hurt?"

Ricky rallied. She wasn't hurt; just frightened half to death.

People were running toward the room by then.

It took three hours and many persons to remove even the gross traces of the blast which, the kindhearted Greeks told us, sounded in the hall like a wartime bomb coming through a window.

Ricky collected herself. She took the splattered kimono into the bathroom to wash it as best she could. I remained on the bed, attentively viewing the mop-up activities of the appalled hotel crew. Presently, I felt an impulse to chuckle. Soon, I heard an independent giggle coming from the bathroom. Ricky had blamed herself for not following her housewifely impulse to rid ourselves immediately of the gift remedy: Ricky is neat, and careful. But now, she laughed.

In seconds, we were both rocking with laughter.

The Greeks had been busy with mops, brooms, pails, rags, shovels and scraping tools. They stopped work. They studied us. Then they, too, began to chortle. Soon, laughter ran through the hotel.

Minor officials came to stare—and hoot and roar over the spectacular ruin, the awesome debris. Everybody explained to everybody else that we were victims of a record instance of fermentation in a singularly strong container. Nobody was mad. Our wrecking crew increased in size, by the minute—and in hilarity. Battered, tattered, smeared items of furniture, sundry fixtures, bed linen and blankets, drapery and table doilies, all were replaced. By midafternoon, we were spick and span again—save for wall stains, and the fact that my suitcase had received the biggest charge of banana-cum-glass. Eventually I got out the shards; but I kept finding thin, desiccated "wafers" in jacket pockets and clean underpants, after I'd reached Manhattan.

Somehow, that blast and the laughter was a better cure even than the pain-relieving drugs or the antibiotics. Quite likely, too, the savage strain of influenza virus had about run its course. At any rate, on the next day, we had our first meal in the dining room in a week. On the day after that, feeble and shaky, we covered as much as Athens as we could—and, stopping often for breath, we climbed up on the Acropolis and lived, for a couple of intoxicated hours, that dream of all earnest kids who ever studied Ancient History.

And the next day, we said good-bye to Dr. Adamopolis. For, after I had "fired" him, with an unaltered good temper he asked if he could visit us as a "friend." And he did! He picked wildflowers and brought them in bunches for Ricky. And he sat with us, telling us of his life, of Greece in its long agony, of heroism and cruelty and all the other ingredients of the vilest sorts of war.

He also told us, in such a way that we could never mistake

its truth, that all the rest of our lives, when we came to Athens, we would have a friend there. I watched him leave the hotel lobby and go down the street—a small, quiet, infinitely affectionate man and a good medical doctor, for all I'd rejected him; and brave as his own Greek Heroes: a saint, who did not have the faintest idea he'd been invisibly canonized and made blessed.

In the very brief time we spent in Rome, we nevertheless saw St. Peter's. Indeed, since the Easter weather had been bad, the Pope held an extra audience for belated pilgrims, and we saw him, too.

Ricky and I had been told he would merely wave from a balcony and bless whatever the crowd tendered. But he did not show up. So we went into the great cathedral, carrying rosaries we'd bought to have blessed for friends, rosaries—still as blessingless as any beads. Somebody was talking, as we entered; and upwards of ten thousand persons were standing in the gigantic place, listening. I asked a Swiss Guard who the speaker was, and after tried French and then German, my question had dazed the man. "The Pope!" he whispered.

Ricky and I, pushing in, among and around the multitudes, had our rosaries blessed by His Holiness, who seemed an intelligent, pleasant old man. And a linguist of remarkable ability, too! He greeted his great audience in six languages, of which I knew four well enough to appreciate how measurelessly better the Pope knew all *but* English. That fascinated me. So did the barbarous magnificence of St. Peter's. And I was delighted to have the rosaries blessed six times instead of a mere one!

It may seem strange to come to the end of this account of our travels, and find one American man (one so sure his cultural versions of what his fellow citizens call Christianity are mistaken) standing in St. Peter's, holding out rosaries.

But we both did. We moved as close as we could, without being rude, to that big dais which is, I suppose, the papal throne: a thing like a fourposter bed built for a man twenty feet tall, gold inlaid, scarlet enameled, draped with precious fabrics—sufficiently rich and imposing for the most avid pre-Christian emperor, for any Pharaoh, any Sultan, any lord in history but one: Jesus. We spent an hour watching the Pope from a distance of only a few yards.

The rosaries we held had been bought when we learned they would be blessed, in the expected balcony appearance—and that the papal benediction would stick even though the beads were held by nonbelievers.

But if this portrait of the Wylies does seem incongruent to you, I have failed in my purpose here.

Ricky and I have many dear friends who are Roman Catholics. One man I cherished, and believed among the finest Americans I'd ever known, was Catholic, and is gone, now: Brian Mac-Mahon. I thought of him in that vasty temple. And I thought of other loved Catholics who would never go to Rome and never see their Pope because they are too poor. To them, the multiply blessed rosaries would be (and are!) treasures beyond price.

For neither of us deplores the believing individual. Both of us know that every set of dogmas has risen from a real process and represents it, in some degree. We are aware that persons have used *all* those old, inner languages, and dialects in their proposed fashion: making themselves neither masters of love, nor its servants, but love's embodiment, thereby, as St. Paul said, revealing the nature of their beliefs by their acts. Ricky and I never attack people for their faith. We never discuss religion with people—unless they invite discussion. We are eager to find and respect elements in any faith that lead to noble acts, and to wisdom.

My continual protest of all faiths is something written, that no one is obliged to read.

For all I oppose in any of the believers is that *act*—in whatever form—which purposes to deny or restrict my right to believe as I see fit, and my right to act accordingly, so long as that behavior interferes with the freedom and the dignity and the open opportunity for the mind, or the soul, of *no other human being*.

We are, I think, tolerant, and I hope, above all else, loving.

12
conclusion

The wheels of one more plane touched down. One more stewardess waited till one more door opened. Fresh air came through the arch-shaped opening—fragrant and spicy, with a subtle redolence of mold: the near-May air of Miami.

"Smells like Bangkok," Ricky said. . . .

Our maid had left for the day so the house was silent; and the yard boy was not working that afternoon: the only sound in the garden was made by birds. Sunlight brass-plated our palmettoes and ruled them with shadows of straight pines.

Ricky started coffee.

I drove to the vet's and brought home our cocker spaniel, Popcorn. . . .

It was all behind us now. Nice, where Ricky had relapsed; Paris, where we'd regained health—Fontainebleau, Versailles, Chartres; the frozen seas of Newfoundland; Manhattan—family and friends; bereaved Baltimore.

The world behind us!

In a desultory way, I opened mail that cascaded from heaps on the furniture in Ricky's office. I also opened a cryptic carton. It contained two rattan dragons, featherlight and absurd.

Nowadays we often deck their serpentine backs with hibiscus blossoms. . . .

When we were leaving Hong Kong a stranger rushed up, handed us a brief case, asked us to "mind" it—and disappeared. Our plane was announced presently. We loitered—but finally I had to turn over the portfolio to an air-line official.

After the plane took off, the stranger reappeared and told us gratefully that he and his brief case had been reunited by the official and put aboard while the plane was held. His name was Edgar Moser and he made frequent trips to the Far East in search of objects that would attract attention to store fronts. He had a window-display business.

He asked what we'd bought in Hong Kong and we made the common small talk of tourists in the area; it concerns the excellent tailoring, fine materials, and the startling cheapness of clothing in the Free Port. By and by, I added idly that I wished I'd also bought a "wicker" dragon I'd seen in a Kowloon shop window.

"Very amusing!" Mr. Moser agreed. "I saw it, too! Know the fellow who owns the store, a Chinese friend. I have hundreds of close friends in the Orient, India, the Near East . . . fine men."

We traded addresses and I had forgotten that Moser promised me a dragon until I opened that carton that day and saw the rattan fantasies, smelled again the sweet water, the joss, the spices.

A gift of dragons!

We encountered many "Edgar Mosers" in many places—ordinary men perhaps. Some hadn't finished high school and were ignorant, maybe—naïve, too—in the crafts of state. But they had Mr. Moser's "hundreds of close friends" in unlikely ports and thought them all "fine men." They visited the homes of customers, played all day with the kids, ate the food of their hosts and often spoke the languages: buyers and sellers—bighearted, loving and loved.

They go in annual thousands on their long, lonely rounds and come home a little alien. They can't explain to Wake Forest or Queens neighbors what they feel about a garage owner in Java, a storekeeper in Ceylon or the kids of a Chinese wholesale liquor dealer in Saigon. Most of Wake Forest wouldn't listen or care right now; and Queens might even take umbrage.

Yet our State Department has few peers among the professional emissaries. For these Eds and Harrys and Bills *are* America. Whoever in a far land comes to know them will know more of America than all our journals, movies and information centers tell. Each such person—man, wife, growing youngster— will learn what "being an American" means from living acts of one who might be unable to say in English (let alone Siamese or Urdu) what he is. He does *better* than all saying. Incorporate in the man is his experience of American being: he feels what he never tries to say . . . and needs not.

These, also, are innocent ambassadors. Use-of-force and pride-in-power are foreign to them. They understand the appeal of freedom to others, concede the right of self-determination and recognize that it includes the right to be wrong. (How long would America survive without that sacred franchise?)

But our American today is governed by yesterday's old-book faiths, by the old men who administer them and those prematurely aged young men grappling for the national helm who would steer by concentrating on the wake of our history!

Soldiers, statesmen, politicians. . . .

Today inexorably becomes tomorrow. New truth belies old faith. Data change; dogma must. The men who govern by yesterday's beliefs shall pass away.

What of the *beliefs*?

Shall we try to retain them by making a scapegoat of a single brave, determined man who but symbolized our common blindness? Was John Foster Dulles sole author of all dilemma? Roosevelt? Truman? Or was Eisenhower alone responsible, in that he constantly upheld his Secretary of State? Who upheld Eisenhower? Most of us—with ballots! And many with mawkish awe, besides, timidly delegating our common sense to him and withholding every demurrer, timidly.

When things go awry for America, the first person to *question* (and the last to fear!) is the President of the United States. But the *blame* forever falls on ourselves, the citizens. . . .

Beside the Potomac, soldiers strive, also, to retain the old faith. Nobly they have sacrificed their own freedom—the better to defend our general liberty, even to death. Urgently, they stock their arsenal. Earnestly, they project hydrogen fire-fights, develop new concepts of "graduated weapons pressure" and pore over their "Theory of Games." The megaton muscles are necessary to hold off our enemy. But more is needed that soldiers are ill equipped to furnish:

What if the "game" itself is different now—as I here assume? Where is the American counterassumption? What value rests in kiloton checkers, megaton trumps—if our adversary also plays and ceaselessly wins at *chess*? Plays and wins with pieces insidiously whittled from psychology and politics, anthropology, sciences unknown to our soldiers, and philosophy, also? Shall we forever muscle up for yesterday and keep our "godly" minds so mummified we cannot even engage in the battle of ideas now snatching tomorrow from us? What counter could we use?

Free men! Free men, alone, are the counters! And any American, every American, can exhibit usefulness by stepping forward! The very step, the act, is his salvo since, *slavery excepted, there is no substitute for individual responsibility.* How many Americans, then—Christians, Jews, freethinkers or plain pagans—are *free enough* to meet the future? Free enough, in that sublime part of a man my friend Ishishi called his "conscience," *to grant freedom to others?*

A sufficient number of us . . . I honestly believe!

For I, too, have my "religion" and my faith.

My faith is in you. My faith is you. Its only dogma is my belief that freedom for the human mind is man's one absolute and infinite dimension—whatever enclosed shapes the minds of men may accord freedom, at any given moment.

My "God" I here define in this fashion:

What some human beings have been and most should someday be, is in His Image.

I have other ways to characterize my "God"; but let that suffice, here.

I believe we Americans have most disclosed this faith. We are superior to no one—but with our better chance we have achieved a little more. So I conclude that we shall see how our central Belief is menaced now, and embark on the new mission of free men in time to save liberty by setting pleasure aside taking up our bravery.

For free men can alone know truth; and men concerned with truth alone can love.

These things, according to St. John, were clear to a man we call Jesus, long ago. And they have not changed. Nor we.

When enough Americans approach mankind in liberty and brotherhood, we will dispel the gospel of men-as-animals. We will restore men to humanity. And we will save liberty. Then our America will survive—an incident of mere American *being*, of our reassumption of our Liberty.

And hear this:

Everyone who goes forth in that fashion nowadays, or ever, will be welcome. For I have looked into a million brown, beseeching eyes, and in all I saw the light of liberty, here dim but there radiant. And all those eyes implored me to tell you.

index

FLORIDA STATE UNIVERSITY

3 1254 02024 2141

DATE DUE